Living through Divorce

The Guilford Family Therapy Series
Alan S. Gurman, *Editor*

FAMILY THERAPY AND FAMILY MEDICINE: TOWARD THE
   PRIMARY CARE OF FAMILIES
William J. Doherty and Macaran A. Baird

ETHNICITY AND FAMILY THERAPY
Monica McGoldrick, John K. Pearce, and Joseph Giordano, *Editors*

PATTERNS OF BRIEF FAMILY THERAPY: AN ECOSYSTEMIC
   APPROACH
Steve de Shazer

THE FAMILY THERAPY OF DRUG ABUSE AND ADDICTION
M. Duncan Stanton, Thomas C. Todd, and Associates

FROM PSYCHE TO SYSTEM: THE EVOLVING THERAPY OF
   CARL WHITAKER
John R. Neill and David P. Kniskern, *Editors*

NORMAL FAMILY PROCESSES
Froma Walsh, *Editor*

HELPING COUPLES CHANGE: A SOCIAL LEARNING
   APPROACH TO MARITAL THERAPY
Richard B. Stuart

Living through Divorce

Divorce

A Developmental Approach to Divorce Therapy

JOY K. RICE, PhD
DAVID G. RICE, PhD
University of Wisconsin, Madison

THE GUILFORD PRESS
New York   London

© 1986 The Guilford Press
A Division of Guilford Publications, Inc.
200 Park Avenue South, New York, N.Y. 10003

Library of Congress Cataloging in Publication Data

Rice, Joy K.
    Living through divorce

    (The Guilford family therapy series)
    Bibliography: p.
    Includes indexes.
    1. Divorce therapy.   I. Rice, David Gordon, 1938-
II. Title.   III. Series.
RC488.6.R53   1986   616.89156   85-27173
ISBN 0-89862-061-9

ACKNOWLEDGMENTS

We wish to acknowledge our deep appreciation to our family, friends, colleagues, and clients who so generously shared their ideas and support in the writing of this book. We also are grateful for the assistance of the editorial staff of The Guilford Press, and a special thanks goes to Alan Gurman for his careful reading of the manuscript and his many helpful suggestions.

PREFACE

As practicing marital therapists for many years, we have seen more and more couples choosing to divorce. In the early years of trying to help these couples, we were struck by the paucity of clinical literature on the subject. It was as though divorce was a reality no one wanted to address or study because divorce represented failure, not only to the clients, but to the marital therapist as well. The events of the last decade have significantly changed that picture. Not only is the divorce literature rapidly expanding, but we are witnessing a notable change in how we deal with divorce and our attitudes about it. Its very prevalence has forced both client and therapist to face its potential for good and bad as a life event of major magnitude.

In trying to assist our divorcing clients, we realized how important it was not only to help them gain the tools and skills to traverse the divorce experience successfully, but also to understand its meaning psychologically and to use the stress and conflict developmentally. From these many therapeutic encounters came the realization that divorce needed to be integrated theoretically in the individual, marital, and family life cycles. The conceptual model of divorce presented in this book explains its significance and ramifications in terms of both object and role loss. If a therapist thoroughly understands the processes of narcissistic injury and role disorientation accompanying divorce, he or she is in a better position to help the client accomplish the related therapeutic and developmental tasks: ego reparation and role restructuring.

Our many divorcing clients have helped us not only to understand divorce from a new perspective, but to be far more compassionate and less judgmental about it. The many case studies offered in this book represent composite portraits of these clients who have faced divorce in therapy and often used the experience to grow and change significantly. As a viable model of theory and practice begins to be articulated, divorce therapy is more likely to be accepted as a mode of treatment along with marital and family therapy. It is hoped that this book will offer a start in that direction.

Joy K. Rice, PhD
David G. Rice, PhD
Madison, Wisconsin

CONTENTS

SECTION III. THERAPEUTIC STRATEGIES FOR EGO REPARATION AND ROLE RESTRUCTURING

SECTION IV. DIVORCE AND THE FUTURE

Living through Divorce

Divorce: Social, Historical, and Therapeutic Perspectives

Chapter One

The Phenomenon of Divorce and Its Causes

Divorce has become a significant and predictable life event. In the past two decades the number of divorces has tripled. Over 1 million marriages now end yearly in the United States alone, and over three quarters of these marriages involve children (National Center for Health Statistics, 1984). The dissolution of these relationships affects an interpersonal system that includes many people besides the spouses involved. It is estimated that as many as 5 million people will be closely tied to the more than 1 million divorcing persons (Irving, 1981).

The divorce rate per 1000 population is usually regarded as a more reliable index than the gross number of divorces. It doubled in the 1960s and '70s, peaked in 1979 and 1981 at 5.3, and leveled off in the '80s, hovering between 5.2 and 5.0 per 1000 population (National Center for Health Statistics, 1984; Norton & Glick, 1979). Despite the apparent stabilizing of the divorce rate in the United States, two out of every five couples who reach their fifth anniversary will ultimately divorce, as will over a quarter of those couples reaching their tenth. The high percentage of divorce does not represent disillusionment with the institutions of marriage and family; four out of five people who divorce will remarry, most within 3 years of their divorce ("Changing USA Families," 1984; Glick, 1980; Weingarten, 1980).

If, as the statistics indicate, divorce and remarriage have become more frequent and predictable life events, then divorce, like first marriage, can be viewed in terms of a developmental process. We are rapidly approaching an era when half or more of the people living in our society will experience a coupling, a dissolution, and a recoupling, a cycle that may be repeated more than once, as it has been throughout history in many cultures across the world (Murdock, 1964). Divorce as a predictable life event has not yet

3

been integrated theoretically or therapeutically by many individuals in the helping professions. Nor has it been anticipated and mastered by the average person to the same degree that other high probability life events and transitions, such as schooling, marriage, birth of a child, first employment and change of employment, death of a parent, and retirement, have come to be expected.

Our culture increasingly accepts divorce, much as one accepts the possibility that anything one values in life may end. However, the valence attached to the process and event of marital dissolution is rarely positive. Only one culture in the world regards divorce as a positive event that enhances self-esteem, and that is the Crow Indians. In no contemporary society, primitive or industrialized, is divorce actually valued (Goode, 1962). The high value society places on family life and its function in producing and socializing new members of society may in part account for the universal disfavor associated with divorce. Another important factor is the increasing recognition, at least in most of western society, that the process of marital disruption is a stressful life event of the first magnitude. On a scale of stress accompanying positive and negative life events, divorce is judged as second only to the death of a spouse in terms of intensity and length of time necessary to achieve psychological resolution (Holmes & Masuda, 1974; Holmes & Rahe, 1967).

Divorce has become so common and the trauma associated with it so widely discussed that over 500 books and articles on the subject have been published since the early 1960s (Hunt & Hunt, 1977). Many of these books were written in a popular vein, designed to help individuals cope with the changes wrought by marital disruption (e.g., Gettleman & Markowitz, 1974; Johnson, 1977; Krantzler, 1974).

Although there is a paucity of research, the studies that have attempted to gather data on the frequency of therapy prior to, during, or subsequent to divorce generally report that a large number of individuals seek professional help (Bloom & Hodges, 1981; Briscoe & Smith, 1973; Brown & Manela, 1977; Chiriboga, Coho, Stein, & Roberts, 1979; Hunt, 1966). Remarried individuals are more likely than first-married to acknowledge getting help for problems at some point in their lives (Weingarten, 1980). Other research suggests that the divorced utilize mental health services more frequently than other marital status groups (Bachrach, 1975; Redick & Johnson, 1974; Taube, 1970). Abundant clinical evidence suggests, and postdivorce outcome research documents, that divorce is a stressful process. It is no wonder that help from the professional sector is commonly sought, increasingly from therapists as well as from clergy or the family physician.

Divorce therapy as a clinical subspecialty is a relatively new phenomenon. Outside of the proliferation of self-help books, there is little in the way of professional literature to aid the therapist seeking to become proficient in this growing field. The present book is dedicated to helping therapists by providing a theoretical context as well as a therapeutic orientation and specific interventions designed to help the divorcing client.

The available evidence suggests the possibility of both positive and negative consequences of marital disruption. As previously mentioned, divorce is, almost without exception, a highly stressful experience. However, divorce can also be an opportunity for personal and interpersonal growth and development through the enhancement of independence and autonomy (Brown, 1976; Singer, 1975). Contrary to popular folklore about individuals who are "divorce prone" or "two-time losers," the experience of divorce and remarriage may provide learning experiences that contribute to a happier, more realistic, and more egalitarian conception of marriage (Albrecht, 1979).

While divorce clearly can have positive and negative psychological consequences for adults, the effect on children is more equivocal. It probably is fair to say that divorce is likely to be an even more negative experience for children than for parents. Their dependency and immaturity enhance their vulnerability to loss, particularly when one parent is no longer available to them. While the experience of marital dissolution in the short run may have deleterious effects on children, the long-term consequences are unclear (Lamb, 1977; Nock, 1982). Clinical evidence drawn from the longitudinal study of individuals throughout adolescence and into adulthood suggests that painful and stress producing experiences can contribute to "sharpened awareness, more complex integrations, better skills in problem solving, clarified goals, and increasing stability" (MacFarlane, 1964, pp. 122-123).

One thing seems clear from our experience in dealing with families struggling with divorce. Generally the better the adults adjust to divorce, the better their children do. The less the lingering animosity and the more cooperative the parents, the more likely children can survive divorce unscarred (Nelson, 1981; Wallerstein & Kelly, 1975). A central emphasis in divorce therapy then is to defuse, ameliorate, and/or resolve the negative consequences of the transition from marriage to separation to divorce. An additional goal is to realize and enhance the potentially growth-producing aspects of the experience, both for the individual and for his or her significant others.

The causes as well as the consequences of divorce may also be viewed in positive or negative terms. Divorce has been seen and studied theoretically and empirically as an index of social disorganization (Burgess & Locke, 1953; Kirkpatrick, 1963; Winch, 1971), as both a precursor and an outcome of personal psychopathology (Blumenthal, 1967; Loeb, 1966), and, from a religious standpoint, as an index of moral deterioration. More neutral or positively toned explanations of divorce posit social-psychological models, such as exchange theory (Levinger, 1976; Scanzoni, 1979) or conflict resolution, (Scanzoni, 1965; Sprey, 1969). From a sociological perspective, divorce can be viewed as a social safety valve, a necessary and functional alternative for untenable relationships.

The theoretical perspective a therapist holds, and the personal values he or she attaches to marital dissolution will color the treatment process. The theoretical perspective of the present authors neither views divorce as pathological from a macro or micro level, nor minimizes its stressful effects while glorifying its potential for growth and change. An understanding of cultural as well as developmental and social psychological factors can help therapists approach divorce in more value-free terms, thus responding in a less chauvinistic and ethnocentric manner. One can then provide an accepting, nonjudgmental milieu for the divorcing client.

This chapter attempts to analyze the antecedents and consequences of marital dissolution from such a framework. The economic, sociological, and social psychological variables related to the prevalence of western divorce are reviewed in both historical and contemporary contexts. It is also important to analyze the complex interaction of divorce trends, as well as to place them in a cross-cultural context. Such an analysis can provide a historical and cultural framework for understanding divorce not as a psychopathological manifestation in couples or in society, but as a predictable phenomenon and consequence of an advanced society that values individualism, immediacy, independence, and, to a lesser degree, introspection. Particularly in a culture that reinforces narcissistic feelings and behavior, divorce can be viewed both as a result of the failure to meet narcissistic needs and as a narcissistic trauma itself. The therapeutic approach presented in this book of helping people to deal with, experience successfully, and complete the divorce process and its aftermath is based on this general conception.

THE CAUSES OF DIVORCE

During the past decade, divorce as a solution to interpersonal and familial conflict has been discussed and analyzed as a social phenomenon with important consequences for society as well as for the individual. It has been convenient to categorize the possible causes of divorce into "private" and "public" factors. The former includes demographic variables such as age at first marriage, race, income, social class, and personality variables such as pre- or postmarital psychological dysfunction. Within the public sphere, one could include institutional influences and social trends, such as declining religious influences, industrialization, the secularization of marriage and divorce, and resulting legal changes (e.g., "no-fault" divorce).

The public and the private sectors, however, are intimately connected and one cannot truly separate them in order to analyze their manifestations and interaction. For example, when people are asked retrospectively to come up with the "cause" of their divorce, infidelity usually ranks first or close to first (Albrecht, 1979; Bentler & Newcomb, 1978; Bloom & Hodges, 1981). The individual reconstruction of extramarital sexuality as a self-reported "antecedent" of the marital dissolution, however, cannot be considered in isolation from the so-called "sexual revolution" in contemporary society, which has resulted in both a liberalizing effect on sexual experience and pleasure and the desanctification of sexuality within marriage. Nor can the liberalization of sexual attitudes be considered in isolation from the many various social trends previously mentioned.

Just as one cannot separate the public and private sectors of divorce, neither can one neatly subcategorize antecedents as primarily economic, social, or psychological. This type of breakdown has been utilized often in the past to achieve a convenient organization of the topic. For example, the women's movement, with its emphasis on achievement outside the home, has been cited frequently as a possible contributor to the higher divorce rate. The reasoning is that because more women feel freer about a work role outside the home and correspondingly do work outside the home, their economic independence makes it possible to consider a divorce and leave an unsatisfying marriage. Freed from the economic and social constraints of marriage, and the felt "burdens" of nurturance and service to others, it is believed women can then more easily and independently pursue self-development (Bernard, 1971). Yet, interestingly enough, a greater percentage of divorced women than married women work outside the home (approximately 75% of divorced women and 55% of married women). Perhaps working status is not necessarily predictive of a later divorce, but divorce is predictive of a later working status.

The supposed correlation between working wives and marital instability was an easy, but faulty, assumption to make as the growing incidence of marital dissolution roughly paralleled the marked increase in women entering the labor market. More recent data, analyzing historical cohorts, indicate that the increase in the number of wives who are working outside the home apparently has little or no bearing on the fact that more marriages today are ending in divorce. The trend seems to be actually in the other direction. Based on U.S. Census figures for 1950, 1960, and 1970, by the latter date working women in their late teens and early 20s actually had a larger proportion of their first marriages intact than did their counterparts outside the work force (Carlson, 1976). The pattern holds across age categories, occupational groups, and number of children in the family. In each case, the sharpest recent increases in marital dissolution occurred among women who were not employed outside the home.

As work ceases to be seen as culturally "deviant" behavior for women, employment loses its value in the prediction of intact or divorced marital status. To understand this phenomenon, it is necessary to consider carefully the interaction between sociological, attitudinal, and economic variables. In the shift from employment being less correlated with marital instability and more positively related to stability lies what the economists call an enhancement effect (Cherlin, 1979). Income, rather than employment per se, appears to be the important variable. A wife's second income also contributes to the family's total income and a higher total income generally lowers a couple's chances for divorce and separation. The enhancement effect from the wife's income and its positive contribution to marital stability may also be accompanied by a shift in the balance of power in the relationship accruing to a woman via her earning capacity and income. Such a shift gives her the choice to *stay* as well as to leave.

Although women who make higher incomes may be in a better position to consider separation or divorce, both men and women, but especially women, lose out economically after divorce. The higher the prior joint income, the greater the shift (Kohen, Brown, & Feldberg, 1979). Financial problems are listed as the number one problem of the remarried (Albrecht, 1979). A family often needs two incomes to survive marginally, let alone comfortably, in today's society. The halving of that income via divorce especially penalizes the woman. As a general rule she can anticipate earning only 60% of the wages of her ex-spouse, despite her occupational level, and in the majority of cases, can anticipate being the custodian of her children's economic welfare. Nor does a woman today usually have the benefit of alimony or, as it is euphemistically called, "maintenance."

Economic variables thus can still lock women into marriage, primarily because of traditional social and cultural attitudes associated with institutions such as marriage and the labor market (Feldberg & Kohen, 1976; Herman, 1977). Similarly, while a high income and good employment may better afford a woman the choice to divorce or, conversely, act as a inducement to stay in the marriage, her own *attitude* about working may prove, in the final analysis, the most important variable. Cherlin (1979) found that women who reported that they approved of married women working outside the home were more likely to separate or divorce during the subsequent 4 years, independent of their actual or expected wage, their husband's wage, his employment stability, and the amount of their savings.

Bearing in mind then the many problems in examining cause and effect relationships, other hypotheses concerning the antecedents of divorce are briefly discussed in the following sections.

SOCIOLOGICAL CONCEPTIONS

From a sociological perspective, an understanding of the high incidence of divorce in contemporary western society would include references to religious, cultural, social, legal, and economic factors. Certain factors appear repeatedly in the divorce literature and will be briefly discussed here: (1) the industrialization of society; (2) the liberalization of laws permitting marital dissolution; (3) changing cultural values; (4) the growing social and economic freedom for women; and (5) demographic trends such as the greater acceptance of childless families. All have been cited as contributing to more ready acceptance and utilization of divorce as a solution to interpersonal discord.

Taken in isolation, it is easy to see why social scientists in the past have attempted to correlate obvious changes and deviations in the social order with an observed "disintegration" in the familial structure, as manifested in the rising divorce rate in the United States. Yet one must be cautious in interpreting such phenomena. For example, the industrialization and urbanization of a society as factors in the increase of divorce have long been accepted as a truism. A very interesting exception to the industrialization/divorce hypothesis is the case of Japan, where divorce rates actually decreased gradually and steadily from 3.39 per 1000 population in 1883 to only .79 in 1957. Kawashima and Steiner (1960) speculate that the real reason for the decline was the change from building the stability of the family formerly around patriarchal lineage to constructing the family around an individual husband–wife dyad. As the ties of patriarchy weakened, the importance of the conjugal tie between husband and wife increased. Divorces decreased in number as the tradition that had sustained a high divorce rate weakened. Some social changes then may actually *reduce* the rates of occurrence of phenomena classically labeled as social disorganization, such as divorce and separation (Goode, 1962). The effects of such social changes are further complicated by the interaction with other variables such as income, race, and social class.

The Law and Social Attitudes

In most contemporary divorce books, reference is made to how changes in our divorce laws affecting the period of residence, length of separation, acceleration in timing, and the neutralization of grounds for divorce (from adultery, abuse, desertion, and the like, to "no fault") have created conditions for easy divorce and thus an increase in the rate of marital dissolution. Historically, however, there have always been some religious, social, or legal means to obtain a divorce, except they were usually available only to the upper classes and the wealthy who could afford counsel and petition.

Few would argue that the social acceptance of voluntary separation or no-fault divorce is one of the more important changes in our society's conception of marriage. Thus partners psychologically do not promise each other a lifetime commitment. The relationship lasts only as long as either partner wants it to last and he or she may not have to prove anything to end it, not even incompatibility. The net effect of no-fault divorce is that divorce is reduced to a legal recognition that the marriage has broken down. Proof of the breakdown need be no more than a separation. Judges cannot deny a divorce primarily on social policy grounds, that is, in terms of who might benefit or not: husband, family, community, children, or society.

Therapists would agree that the more important part of the divorce process is psychological rather than legal; yet some authors state that divorce is a legal rather than a psychological concept (Bernard, 1971). Historically, western law has specified four kinds of grounds that would permit divorce: adultery, mental cruelty, desertion, and nonconsummation. The permissible grounds for divorce also reflect our conception of what marriage is and what is not acceptable within a marital bond.

Infidelity has generally had universal acceptance as grounds for divorce, yet even that basis for dissolution is changing. Two decades ago, less than 2% of divorces were granted on the legal grounds of adultery and even fewer divorces are so decreed today. Similarly, in the case of physical or mental abuse, 20 years ago half of all divorce suits were based on grounds of mental cruelty. The use of mental cruelty as grounds has declined as we opt for the more private, nondescript "no fault."

Mental cruelty is harder to define than physical cruelty and has come to be termed "incompatibility." As our standards for emotional involvement in marriage increase, the possibility for feeling interpersonal incompatibility also increases. Our new definitions of "mental cruelty" or "incompatibility" now include withdrawal of affection, emotional distance, unkind words, the lack of psychological support, and the inability to share feelings. Individuals expect marriage to meet emotional and companionship needs and increasingly more is asked of the marital bond in the interpersonal realm. The new conception is that of "companionate" marriage (Burgess & Locke, 1953) rather than legal, economic, or social union. People are now bound to each other by ties of love, companionship, and personal duty, rather than, as previously, by legal, religious, and/or economic forces. Many would argue that psychological bonds are fragile and more difficult to maintain, accounting in part for our rising divorce rates. People become frustrated and disillusioned with the inability of their marital partner to satisfy their high expectations of emotional and sexual fulfillment, continuing romantic love, self-realization, and self-aggrandizement.

Cultural Values

Other writers have speculated that the alienation in interpersonal interaction in our society leads people prematurely and perhaps inappropriately to turn to marriage and the bond it offers as a way of counteracting the meaninglessness and estrangement they feel in the culture (Singer, 1975). The values of our contemporary culture, in terms of the strong emphases on self-realization, individualism, and narcissism also potentially reinforce a sense of personal alienation and contribute to unrealistic expectations of what an intimate relationship can provide (Weiss, 1975). We are living in a narcissistic age, where immediate gratification is valued often over long-term investment. Individual reward is preferred frequently over the group "good." Adaptability, mobility, and replacement are praised over perseverence and loyalty.

These cultural values are bound to be reflected in our conception of what marriage is all about and the possible parameters for ending it. The expectation that marriage will provide narcissistic enhancement creates many pressures for its eventual dissolution. The assumption that one is *owed* emotional fulfillment and self-realization through marriage and personal happiness from the marital partner is at heart a narcissistic conception. In ancient allegory the "other" is seen as a mirror of reflection, and the reflection must be positive and self-enhancing. Personal growth is expected to be provided for and nurtured by one's partner, instead of promulgated through one's own efforts and in interaction with one's partner.

Tied in with the narcissistic expectation of self-realization in marriage is the whole notion of romantic love in western culture. The love felt so necessary to marriage is a legacy of the early French Renaissance and the chivalric tradition. To get married in this tradition there must be a spiritual bond, euphoric feelings, fidelity, and some novelty and excitement (Gardner, 1974). Such a composite of reactions is not likely to be sustained in the face of one's own and one's spouse's human frailties, imperfections, and the eventual mundane necessities of day-to-day existence. In response to inevitable disillusionment, one replaces and moves on, because present-day society also reinforces consumption, that is, the belief that it is preferable to replace an object, even a loved one, with a new, potentially more exciting and novel one. It is also felt to be better to keep moving up the yardstick of life and love, than to stay in one place. Finally, aspects of culture emphasize that it is better to gratify oneself than to please others.

A caveat is in order here. All these cultural values that influence one's sense of what to expect in marriage and the right to dissolve it are neither inherently positive or negative in valence. The value system that stresses change and mobility can be praised for its contribution to individual and societal growth and improvement, just as it can be criticized as wasteful or impulsive. Valuing individual conscience and gratification can be seen as enhancing autonomy and freedom, just as it can be perceived as selfish and insular. These value-laden perspectives will also color the therapist's perspectives on divorce and divorce therapy. Thus, "divorce can herald freedom, independence, growth toward self-actualization" praises Singer (1975). In contrast, Fisher, in answering the question "why do they divorce?" comments, "Indeed, in their drive for autonomy, marriage, children, and husband seem to be considered inconsequential if not forgotten by some women. Such words as 'devotion,' 'commitment' and 'responsibility' appear to have left the language" (1974, p. 7).

Gender Differences

The expectation of differential growth in marriage has led some sociologists to the conclusion that marriage may be good for men, but not so good for women. Bernard (1972) is one proponent of this view. She cites studies that repeatedly indicate more wives than husbands report marital frustration and dissatisfaction, consider their marriages unhappy, regret their marriages, and/or have considered separation or divorce. In contrast, notes Bernard, the superiority of married men over never-married men is impressive on almost every index of adjustment, be it demographic, psychological, or social. Bernard's data, however, have been criticized on conceptual and methodological grounds.

It is overgeneralizing and overly simplistic to say categorically that marriage per se has been a "bad" thing for women and a "good" thing for men. It is probably more accurate to say that overall men have stood to benefit more from traditional marriage than have women. A married state not only appears to enhance a man's health, but is good for him economically, as it provides him with a person to fulfill maintenance needs, while freeing him to work productively. "What I need is a good wife," is the lament of most women who work, precisely labeling the lack of this provision in marriage for many women. Traditionally, men also gain an emotional caretaker when they marry. The conventional role for a woman expects that she will develop sensitive antennae to the mood fluctuations and emotional needs of her spouse and family. Given these expectations, it is not surprising that most often it is the woman who initiates marital therapy. It is a woman's job to sense psychological fluctuations in the relationship, to maintain the equilibrium, to complain, and to take action when the situation becomes problematic.

As we ask increasingly of marriage that it provide an emotional bond and personal fulfillment, women have come to expect that they will not have to bear this burden single-handedly. A very common complaint of wives in marital therapy is that their husbands don't know how to express feelings, that they don't share their deepest emotions, and that they are inept in the expressive dimension. Indeed, men are socialized into American culture in ways that traditionally have led them to feel reinforced precisely for not demonstrating feelings, but instead for suppressing them. Men are not trained from the crib to the rocking chair in introspection and the communication of that analysis, much less in making small talk that ultimately can lead to deeper levels of intimacy. While both men and women today are demanding emotional fulfillment in marriage, men may have the greater handicap in this regard. In the meantime, more women feel they cannot wait while men catch up.

The gender gap is historical and cultural and likely will not be closed in one or two generations. In the meantime, there will be more divorce, and perhaps more frustrated women reluctantly seeking divorce. More women than men do indeed initiate divorce (Zeiss, Zeiss, & Johnson, 1980). Even taking into account the chivalrous tradition in which men are "supposed to graciously allow" women the final and public decision to leave, many studies corroborate that it is indeed the woman who more frequently decides when to end a relationship, marital or nonmarital (Bloom & Hodges, 1981; Hill, Rubin, & Peplau, 1976; Norton & Glick, 1979).

The ability of women openly to initiate a legal divorce is a largely contemporary phenomenon. Until the 19th century, desertion was usually the only option open to a woman who was dissatisfied with her marriage. In 18th-century colonial America, in the overwhelming majority of cases it was the woman who left, and not the man, who then announced desertion in the local newspaper. "This picture of female discontent in the home is certainly at variance with the contented picture of usual early American women. Indeed, such behavior on the part of women suggests an assertiveness that has not been recognized and possibly has been underestimated" (Lantz, 1976, p. 16).

Women historically have gained a measure of protection, status, and security through marriage, but paid a high price in terms of personal freedom and psychological health. Bargaining power in the marital relationship appears to have increased for the wife during the 20th century, with the "owner-property" arrangement in marriage being replaced by a "head-complement" consensus arrangement. In the latter relationship, the husband bargains for his desires, which are supposed to be reasonable and fit in with a wife's desires (Scanzoni, 1979). The wife, correspondingly, has at her disposal a potent source of power, in the form of her "love" and the expressive rewards her husband wants. In return, she stands to gain both economic and expressive rewards from her husband.

When a woman enters the labor market, another shift in the balance of power occurs in the relationship. In social-psychological terms, she must balance the internal expressive and economic rewards of the marriage with the external rewards, namely her occupational resources and gains (Levinger, 1965). As women gain more power outside of the marital relationship, they gain more power within it, and they become tougher bargainers and negotiators. In this kind of an analysis, divorce represents basically a change in the balance of power in the relationship and particularly the power of the reward system within and outside of the marriage.

One problem with a cost-benefit or exchange theory approach to marriage and divorce is its linearity. One can, for example, conveniently line up the material and emotional rewards of staying married on one side of the ledger (e.g., higher income, home ownership, social status, companionship, and sex) and the costs and barriers to leaving on the other (e.g., loss of children, lowering of income, social isolation, and loneliness) and discuss them as though they were unidimensional or additive. Even a more sophisticated analysis, accounting for other variables such as age, education, or occupation, does not take into account the marked effects of subcultural norms and differences in values. As Levinger (1979) notes, this type of analysis spotlights the dyad, but does not intend that the pair be seen as a closed system.

Demographic Variables

In analyzing the "causes" of divorce, pregnancy before marriage has probably been one of the most consistent factors correlated with the probability of divorce in the United States. Historically, investigators have concluded that an increase in family formation under such circumstances tends to increase the divorce rate (Christensen, 1960, 1963; Coombs & Zumeta, 1970; Davis, 1972; Furstenberg, 1976; Sauber & Carrigan, 1970). Explanations for this association have included assumptions that individuals entering into such unions are less capable of or committed to marriage, that the process of preparation for married life is cut short, and that marriage often begins without the benefit of accumulated savings.

Age before marriage is a related and also frequently discussed correlate of marital dissolution in the United States. Findings of different studies on the topic are quite consistent (Glenn & Supancic, 1984). The divorce rate is much higher for people who marry very young than for those who marry at or near age 20. Additional increments of age are associated with small, diminishing decreases in marital dissolution up to age 23 for women and 26 for men.

Some data indicate that marital instability in our society may also be related to childlessness and to the gender of the children (Spanier & Glick, 1981). The likelihood of marital disruption seems to be greatest for women with no children. A comparison of ratios of women separated or divorced with women married once and living with their husband reveals a relationship between the number of children and the propensity to divorce. The greater the number of children, the less the likelihood of divorce. Further, women who have at least one son are most likely to remain in their first marriage. Marital disruption is also somewhat more likely if all the children are girls.

Explaining the Spanier and Glick findings is another matter. One might speculate on the remnants of patriarchy and chauvinism still present in our society or focus on the reluctance of mothers to divorce in anticipation of raising sons alone with no male to model gender role behaviors or to help with childrearing (Hetherington, Cox, & Cox, 1979). These data relating childlessness to divorce seem to fly in the face of speculations that a decrease in the birthrate and a delay of marriage and marital age would decrease divorce by promoting longer courtship experience, greater maturity, and emotional and economic readiness for marriage. Spanier and Glick (1981) report on a sample of women under 30 years of age at first marriage who were married between 1950 and 1970. The values of this cohort of individuals may be different from those of the upcoming generations, who may value childlessness, and not see children, male or female, in a particularly positive light.

Several other demographic variables are mentioned frequently in the sociological literature related to the likelihood of divorce. The higher the income, education, or social class, the lower the probability of marital dissolution in our society (Kitson & Raschke, 1981). Low religiosity as well as race are also cited, with blacks having higher divorce rates than whites (Glenn & Supancic, 1984); however, the difference is probably confounded by income. When income, home ownership, and difference in family size, all variables highly correlated with race, are controlled, black families have been shown to experience separation or divorce less often than whites (Hampton, 1975). Of all these factors, income may have one of the most potent but least understood effects, as it seems to be a fairly powerful intervening variable for a number of other variables like education, early marriage, and pregnancy. As the incidence of divorce increases, the importance of socioeconomic factors probably decreases for predicting marital dissolution. Divorce is clearly and increasingly cutting across all socioeconomic, religious, and racial categories (Norton & Glick, 1979).

Finally, having been divorced before is cited as a variable itself in predicting future divorce. The hypothesis has been called the "intergenerational transmission of marital instability." In simpler terms, divorce breeds divorce (Kulka & Weingarten, 1979). In a domino effect, the personality problems and characteristics of divorced parents are hypothesized to produce similar problems in their children, leading to further marital instability. Children of divorce are more likely to marry at younger ages, be pregnant at marriage, and marry husbands with lower status occupations, all conditions favorable to further divorce (Mueller & Pope, 1977). The role modeling effects posited in the "divorce begets more divorce" theory suggest that there are certain personal behaviors, attitudes, or even traits associated with marital dissolution that might be learned and passed down from generation to generation.

PERSONALITY VARIABLES

Another body of literature turns not to societal variables to explain divorce, but to the individual and his or her own predisposition, personality, or personal mental instability. When one asks a couple why they decided to divorce, a "laundry list" of causes and reasons is often presented, such as physical or verbal abuse, drinking, lack of love, or financial problems. Individuals who have been in therapy are more likely to cite more "neutral" causes, for example, growing apart or personal incompatibility. These formulations have been labeled as "accounts" by Weiss (1975). They represent the self-perceived, reconstructed history of the marital breakdown, tend to be highly individual, and are likely to focus on a few dramatic events, a last straw, or dysfunctional behaviors that seemed to characterize the marriage. The reasons or causes listed in these accounts are likely to be seen by mental health professionals more as symptoms of the breakdown than the actual cause of the divorce, much in the way alcohol abuse is seen as symptomatic of underlying personality disturbance or extramarital promiscuity as symptomatic of immature psychosexual development.

The intrapsychic approach to analyzing divorce and its rising incidence in our society assumes a kind of divorce prone personality. In this model, a person through role modeling, inadequate parenting, emotional deprivation, or other problematic antecedents ends up with a psychological disability that predisposes him or her to divorce or at least makes it improbable that a given individual can effect a successful long-term coupling. There are certainly some people who divorce who do have a clear-cut psychiatric syndrome as a contributant (Briscoe & Smith, 1973, 1974; Rushing, 1979). However, it is hard to believe that the nearly one-half of all Americans who will at some point in their lives experience marital dissolution, are suffering from a mental disorder sufficiently disabling to interfere seriously with successful interpersonal intimacy and commitment.

The approach of looking for individual or dyadic personality traits to explain marital stability and dissolution dates back almost half a century (Burgess & Cottrell, 1939). Concepts such as homogamy and heterogamy were introduced in order to explain why similarities or differences in the two individuals' personality could contribute to marital instability.

The concept of marital aptitude and attempts to operationalize the overall contribution of personality to marital outcome were studied as far back as 1949 (Terman & Wallin, 1949). Having so-called "successful marital aptitude" also implies that its lack can lead to unsuccessful marriage. Indeed, Bergler (1948) insisted that "divorce won't help." In this view, divorce and remarriage would only mean the replay of the old marriage, and the only cure was felt to be psychoanalysis. Similarly, Terman and Wallin noted that it was impossible for only one partner to be normal; neurotics would seek as partners other neurotics with whom to play out their own neuroses.

There are still some family and marital therapists who take the position that "divorce won't help" and feel that psychologically one always remains married to the original spouse (Keith & Whitaker, 1977). Most helping professionals today take a more benign and optimistic view of divorce, admitting that while individual or systems pathology can certainly contribute to marital dissolution, the psychological causes are usually not unilateral nor do they act in isolation from situational factors, societal trends, and subcultural mores. What is "neurotic" in one situation may thus be functional in another.

If marital dissolution is studied cross-sectionally, rather than longitudinally, one really does not know whether personality patterns are the cause or consequence of marital failure. The effects of background or demographic characteristics can be studied cross-sectionally as they are usually not subject to change by the passing of time. This is not necessarily true of personality traits. Unfortunately, very few longitudinal studies exist. There is some compelling support, however, for the homogamy hypothesis. In a 4-year longitudinal follow-up of a group of 77 couples, personality traits were measured at the beginning of the marriage. Correlational similarity between marital partners was substantially higher for couples who remained together than for couples who decided to end their marriage after 4 years (Bentler & Newcomb, 1978). The same pattern was found for background or demographic variables, but personality traits had a much greater longitudinal predictive effect than these other variables.

A more promising approach to understanding psychological predispositions to divorce is offered by a developmental perspective. This approach emphasizes the interaction of individual and interpersonal change, the problems and conflicts associated with such change, its working through and resolution, and the ultimate benefits that can accrue individually and interpersonally. From this viewpoint, divorce, like most life transitions, has the potential for much conflict as well as for ultimate growth. Of the many demographic variables that have been studied in analyzing correlates of divorce, age emerges as a critical predictive variable. Readiness, maturity, and in particular the premarital accumulation and actual experiencing of certain key life passages and conflicts are very important antecedents to successful coupling.

THE CONSEQUENCES OF DIVORCE

If divorce can lead to both conflict and growth, what are its consequences in our culture? A growing body of divorce outcome research is available to help therapists answer this question.

Studies that have investigated the consequences of divorce by correlating marital status with physical and mental health status variables paint a grim picture. On most indices of such adjustment, research has concluded that the divorced are less well adjusted than the married or the widowed. Across studies, divorced individuals, compared with married persons, are more likely to be diagnosed as having a mental disorder, alcoholism, nervous breakdown, or senility, and contribute disproportionately to psychiatric admission rates, completed suicides, motor vehicle accidents, and higher death rates due to physical disease. The relationship between marital disruption and psychopathology also appears to be stronger for males than for females (Bloom, Asher, & White, 1978).

Interpretation of these findings are by no means unequivocal. One could argue once again in terms of a divorce prone personality, that is, that the parties were disturbed *before* the divorce so they could not function adequately in marriage. Conversely, one might interpret the data to mean that the stressful events associated with divorce produce the frequently reported health and role inadequacies. As was noted in the prior discussion on personality variables that correlate with divorce, cause and effect relationships are difficult to untangle in cross-sectional and retrospective data. Whether or not divorce precipitates postmarital disability or whether premarital disability acts to increase the probability of divorce is an important matter to those who provide psychotherapeutic help to both the married and the divorced. How this question is answered can strongly influence a therapist's perspective in treating divorce from a pathogenic, a developmental, or a learned behavior perspective.

Several explanations have been put forth to explain the association between marital status and psychological outcomes (Bachrach, 1975; Bloom, 1977). Selectivity theory points out that psychopathology is the cause rather than the effect of divorce or separation. Psychological disorder may have preceded or occurred during the marriage and acted as a selection factor for divorce.

A second view, based on role theory, leads to a protective marriage hypothesis. Roles played by people in marriage are generally the most approved and rewarded in society and therefore lead to the least risk in terms of health and well-being. The life-style associated with marriage could thus be a protective agent from psychopathology.

A final line of reasoning derives from stress theory, which would see the change in marital status itself as the direct precipitator or stressor of mental disorder. Little research has been done to test these competing hypotheses or to analyze their complex interaction (Goetting, 1981; Kraus, 1979). Marital dissolution and the presence of psychological distress or disorder are obviously interactive and each one has the potential to influence the other.

Part of the reason for the paucity of research is the very real methodological and conceptual problems in this area. Many of the studies have employed patient populations. There are limitations in generalizing from a psychiatric to a normal population. Furthermore, since most of the divorced remarry, and do so within a few years after divorce, many samples of divorced subjects are heavily biased in favor of the select individuals who will remarry late or never remarry. Comparing divorced people only to married people and not also to single people is also questionable. The observed psychological differences between groups could be accounted for not by the divorce, but by the experience of being single in our society (Kraus, 1979).

Cultural expectations also intervene. For example, society may expect and permit a divorced individual to report distress more readily than a married one, who is "supposed" to be happy. Such cultural biases influence psychiatric raters as well as therapists. Both researchers and therapists may sometimes misinterpret the short-term acute psychological distress associated with marital disruption as indicative of severe underlying psychopathology instead of representing a situational and temporary state of personality disorganization. Evidence indicates that, in 6 months to 1 year after divorce, the majority of divorced people are indistinguishable from their married counterparts on a variety of indices of adjustment and reported well-being (Albrecht, 1979; Weingarten, 1980). Within 6 months of divorce, significant increases on measures of mental health and self-esteem are reported in the literature (Gray, 1978).

Early investigators in the field of divorce therapy indicated that a period of 3 to 4 years was required for stabilization (Weiss, 1975). More recent studies suggest that few overt negative emotions, such as depression, anxiety, and hostility, appear after 6 to 12 months postdivorce. Such results support the idea of an adjustment process with temporal and transitory characteristics (Hackney & Ribordy, 1980). One might speculate that, as the incidence of divorce increases in our culture and divorce is increasingly accepted as more normative and nondeviant behavior, the length of time required for personal readjustment may correspondingly decrease.

The above evidence suggests that it may be inappropriate to emphasize severe pre- or postmarital disability as the norm in divorce. Nearly half of those who marry in the United States now go on to divorce and most will remarry and/or go on to develop another life that is generally satisfying and functional (Bohannan, 1971a; Brown, 1976; Chiriboga et al., 1979; Weingarten, 1980; Weiss, 1975).

The adverse effects sometimes associated with divorce may actually result from marital and family discord that preceded the divorce. Divorce may act to relieve rather than to precipitate stress in the long run and to neutralize the debilitating effects of prior marital discord. It may be the psychologically healthier individuals in unsatisfactory marriages with high discord who are able to make the break from their spouse. When race, sex, and age are controlled, unhappily married people are found to be less psychologically healthy than divorced or happily married individuals. Furthermore, divorced persons who go on to a happy remarriage report fewer mental or physical illness symptoms than do unhappily married individuals who never divorced (Renne, 1971). The greater the lingering attachment to the former spouse, the higher the reported distress associated with divorce (Brown, Felton, Whiteman, & Manela, 1982; Hynes, 1979; Marroni, 1977).

There are several implications for the above findings for therapists. These include (1) the advisability of careful diagnosis in postdivorce therapy; (2) the careful assessment of the contributants to stress, including societal and cultural factors, as well as individual and circumstantial ones; and (3) the adoption of a treatment plan that includes elements of crisis intervention as well as psychological insight. A therapist must have a keen appreciation of the actual social and economic changes, both positive and negative, that accompany divorce and how they act and interact to produce not only transitional stress but also possible long-term benefits for the divorcing individual.

Being single again or becoming a single parent means a change in role status and the necessity of redefinition, which can lead to more autonomy or to anomie. Similarly, studies have shown that income and economic status may produce marked anxiety and pessimism as well as increased feelings of personal control and power over the external exigencies in one's life (Kohen et al., 1979). The loss of old married friends and the family of the ex-spouse can lead to social isolation and loneliness. In contrast other empirical evidence notes the development of greater independence, new friends and intimates, and a blended, enriched family after divorce (Nock, 1982). Given these differing potentialities, what are some of the mitigating factors that influence successful adjustment to divorce?

ADJUSTMENT TO DIVORCE

It was noted previously that investigators of marital instability and dissolution have turned to philosophical, economic, and sociocultural explanations of the etiology of divorce. Another body of research has explored the consequences of divorce, both for the individual and for society. Other factors can influence one's ultimate adjustment to divorce. Some of these are modifiable by the individual, but others are more fixed, inherent factors like age, the presence of children, or the characteristics of society, for example, the attitude and mores regarding divorce. A therapist equipped with a sound understanding of the range of forces affecting a divorcing person is in a better position to assess the client's potential for adjustment and is more able perhaps to effect that outcome.

Some of the factors that appear to make a difference in how well people adjust to divorce are age, gender, ethnicity, the number, age, and sex of one's children, the length and type of separation and who initiated it, the length of the marriage, one's social supports, the quality of the relationship with the ex-spouse, personality factors such as ego-strength and assertiveness, one's socioeconomic status and income, remarriage, psychological resources such as psychotherapy, and finally how the culture one lives in views divorce.

It stands to reason that the longer one is in something, the harder it is to get out. Most of the data seem to support such an expectation in regard to age, length of marriage, and adjustment to divorce. While the evidence is mixed, the ending of a longer marriage may lead to more traumatic effects and more difficult adjustments (Blair, 1970; Goode, 1956; Pais, 1978). Other studies, however, report either no effects of duration of marriage on subsequent adjustment to divorce or positive outcomes (Granvold, Pedler & Schellie, 1979; Raschke, 1974). The data on age and adjustment are less equivocal. The older the person, the more difficult postdivorce adjustment appears to be, particularly for women (Blair, 1970; Chiriboga, Roberts, & Stein, 1978; Goode, 1956; Marroni, 1977; Pais, 1978). A lowered sense of "marketability" for remarriage or lowered self-esteem and insecurity about reentering the single scene could account for these findings.

The length of separation, like the length of marriage, probably has an effect on adjustment to divorce. Clinical experience suggests that the longer the time elapsed since physical separation, the lower the distress and the fewer the adjustment problems (Chester, 1971; Chiriboga & Cutler, 1977). Hetherington, Cox, and Cox (1976) report increased distress for both men and women during the 2 years after divorce, followed by a subsequent reduction in felt distress. Length of separation may have an ameliorative effect on adjustment by providing a longer recovery period (the passage of time is one of the greatest healers). Clinical observation, however, suggests that too many "on and off" separations can have a deleterious effect on overall adjustment, prolonging eventual adaptation and resolution.

How the relationship breaks up and who initiates the decision to leave also appear to be factors related to adjustment. Some research on premarital relationships indicates that both men and women feel less depressed, less lonely, freer, and more guilty when they initiated the break-up of a premarital relationship (Hill et al., 1976). While there is certainly more at stake in ending a marriage than a romance, clinical experience usually indicates that the person who makes the decision and has control of it experiences somewhat less distress than the person who perceives little control or is the recipient of someone else's decision (Brown et al., 1982; Davis, 1977; Goode, 1956). Such differences in outlook tend to diminish over time as both the "leaver" and the "left" share the experience of being divorced, particularly the pain of dislocation and loneliness (Morris & Prescott, 1975). Both individuals experience the distress of divorce, but the nature of their dysphoric feelings may differ. While the initiator may feel more guilt, the party who is left may feel hurt and abandoned.

Evidence for the type of divorce complaint and its effect on subsequent adjustment is mixed. Some people have found that alcoholism or marital infidelity makes for more difficult adjustment to a divorce (Weiss, 1976). Others believe there is little relationship between reported precipitating causes and subsequent adjustment difficulties (Raschke, 1974).

As noted previously, more women than men initiate divorce. If being the initiator and thus feeling some control portends well for later better adjustment, do women have an easier time adjusting to divorce than men? Many people believe that is the case (Chiriboga et al., 1978; Gove, 1973; Johnson, 1977). The explanation for their better overall adjustment may be attributed to women having learned skills necessary for autonomous living, both emotionally and domestically. In addition, women usually have more social supports for adjustment and are more likely to seek them out. They may be socialized both to admit to distress and to seek professional help more often than men. Finally, women may lose less of their immediate current emotional–social network in a divorce; they are more likely to remain in the home with children and other familiar surroundings.

Women may be better equipped through their expressive socialization to adjust emotionally to divorce, but they report themselves to be more distressed by divorce than do men (Brown & Fox, 1978; Johnson, 1977). The difference may be influenced by women's lower economic resources and the felt burden of having custody of children. Gender-linked early socialization patterns probably also contribute to reporting distress. Being more able to acknowledge stress because of socialization and social approval may directly influence women's *initial* better adjustment to divorce. Admission of distress is the first step in dealing with a problem. Such expression can lead to catharsis as well as to the more active seeking out of resources, solutions, and supports. Thus, one would expect a positive correlation between the degree to which a person is able to express his or her feelings of discomfort and the degree of adjustment to marital dissolution. To date no one has tested this hypothesis, yet it bears directly on a therapeutic model for divorce therapy.

There is some evidence from other fields of a positive relationship between being able to express distress and outcome. Some interesting studies on treating cancer patients by means of guided imagery coupled with psychotherapy report such an observed relationship (Simonton, 1982). Often the complaining patient who gives health professionals the most trouble improves, while the model patient who stoically accepts his or her pain may experience a fatal recurrence of carcinoma.

In summary, it is very difficult to separate out the effects of gender alone on adjustment to divorce. The whole context of a given individual's circumstances must be considered. For example, irrespective of gender, a high income and/or the establishment of a strong social life independent of the marriage may ease the postdivorce adjustment. The presence of one set of resources may balance the lack of another.

How Personality Affects Adjustment

From the viewpoint of crisis theory, divorce represents a temporary state of conflict and distress whose outcome can be directly influenced by the presence of a number of contributing resources: personality, interpersonal or social, familial, economic, societal, and legal (Kraus, 1979).

Research findings indicate that the enduring personal characteristics of individuals are as important in adjustment to divorce, and possibly more so, than variables such as age, gender, and length of time divorced. People who seem to make the best adjustment to divorce score significantly higher than individuals who adjust less well on measures of dominance, assertiveness, self-assurance, intelligence, creativity/imagination, social boldness, liberalism, self-sufficiency, ego-strength, and tranquility (Thomas, 1982). "Better adjusted" people are judged on the 16PF psychological test to be less apprehensive, less tense, more happy-go-lucky, more emotionally stable, and more venturesome than "poorer adjusted" groups (Heritage & Daniels, 1974).

Other psychological characteristics significantly correlated with postdivorce adjustment are gender role attitudes and dogmatism. In reviewing several studies, Kitson and Raschke (1981) found that non-traditional and/or egalitarian gender role attitudes in divorced women were related to greater personal growth, less distress, and better adjustment. As is true in much of the research on the divorced, unfortunately, males were not studied.

Higher tolerance for change, lower dogmatism, and internal, as opposed to external, locus of control have all been associated with better adjustment (Kitson & Raschke, 1981). People who are likely to make a better adjustment to divorce appear to be more relaxed, confident, self-reliant, tolerant, and flexible. The stress of the process of divorce may temporarily mask these underlying qualities. Over time one would expect them to reemerge as important psychological resources for the person going through a crisis, such as that occasioned by divorce.

What Is Adjustment?

There are several problems that arise in interpreting the results of studies on postdivorce adjustment. Most samples only test their participants after the divorce. How does one know that these personality traits, while presumed to be enduring, were not influenced by the divorce itself? It is still unusual to think of divorce as positively affecting outlook and personality, or as adding to and improving personal development. Secondly, across studies different criteria and measures have been used to define adjustment. Adjustment per se would be viewed by most therapists as a multifaceted concept incorporating attitudinal and behavioral dimensions that cut across personality, work, family, and relationships. Yet, in most studies divorced people and their children usually are rated dichotomously as adjusted or not adjusted, depending on their score on paper and pencil indices of personality traits. Many instruments and methodologies have been used to measure emotional adjustment following divorce: the Q-sort (Heritage & Daniels, 1974), the Affect Balance Scale (Bradburn, 1969; Nelson, 1981), structured interviews assessing positive and negative emotions (Chiriboga et al., 1978), and the Self-Appraisal Inventory for Children (Nelson, 1981). Adjustment has been measured behaviorally using the Social Adjustment Scale, the Behavior Problem Checklists (Nelson 1981), and the Blair Divorce Adjustment Inventory (Thomas, 1982). The reliability, validity, broadness of use, and standardization on various normative populations of these measures varies widely.

An additional caveat is in order for therapists evaluating data that purport to correlate personality variables with postdivorce adjustment. If you define adjustment as the absence of negative emotions, and you categorize adjusted people as those who do not report such feelings, the resulting sample of people may be biased. Individuals who are loath to admit anger, unhappiness, guilt, frustrations, and other negative emotion, are more likely to answer with socially desirable responses.

Timing is also important. The report of such feelings will be quite different depending on the temporal proximity of the divorce to the questioning. This interval varies widely among studies, making generalization difficult.

Interpersonal as well as personal resources also affect one's adjustment to divorce. High levels of social support provided through friends and family, organizational participation, and public agencies seem to be related to lower reported distress (Hynes, 1979; Pearlin & Johnson, 1977). Similarly, higher social participation, dating activity, and sexual activity have been related to lower trauma and better adjustment (Goode, 1956; Hetherington, Cox, & Cox, 1976; Hunt & Hunt, 1977; Spanier & Casto, 1979; Weiss, 1975).

Maintaining old and initiating new social supports is not always easy or feasible for the divorced person. Society is organized primarily around couples and two-parent families. The married often exclude or ignore their divorced contemporaries. The loss of old friendships has been referred to as "community divorce" (Bohannan, 1971b). A pattern of reduced social contacts immediately following divorce and an increase in social involvement over the following 2 years is reported in several studies (Hetherington *et al.*, 1977; Raschke, 1977). The presence of children can also affect the social support network (Bloom & Hodges, 1981; Hetherington *et al.*, 1977; Spanier & Casto, 1979). Being the custodial parent may mean receiving more sympathy and help from friends. On the other hand, the custodial parent may feel locked into a child's world. Even if the parent has adult contacts, for example, by virtue of employment, there is often little time and energy left for a social life after the demands of single parenting and outside work.

Children and Adjustment

By 1990, it is expected that a third of the children in this country will experience parental divorce before they are 18 years old; however, the body of literature on children and divorce is a confusing one. Kanoy and Cunningham (1984) recently reviewed this research and concluded that both conceptual and methodological issues accounted for some of the discrepant conclusions and results concerning the effects of divorce on children. Children are certainly affected by divorce and there is a widespread cultural belief that divorce is usually, if not always, harmful to children. Many people believe that it is better to maintain the facade of a marriage, at least until the children are grown, despite the realization by both parents that their marriage is unsalvageable.

This point of view is also reflected in a large body of literature from the 1970s that attempted to show the deleterious effects of "father absence" on the psychosexual, emotional, and behavioral development of children (Lamb, 1977). Father absence may have been the result of death, neglect, or desertion, as well as divorce. Unfortunately, however, this body of research often does not differentiate between family dissolution due to the death of or abandonment by a parent and dissolution due to divorce. Nor have there been any comprehensive studies comparing the adjustment of children in mother-absent families with children in intact families. Reviews of the massive research on father absence can be found in Biller (1971a, 1974, 1976), Hetherington and Deur (1971), and Lamb (1976). The implications of this research on father absence largely have influenced the more recent work on the effects of divorce on children. Lamb (1977, p. 465) summarizes these implications as follows:

1. The absence of a male adult whose role sons can learn to perform through imitation and daughters can learn to complement through interaction.
2. The absence of a major socializing agent or disciplinary figure.
3. The loss of family income. The decline in income results because of both the withdrawal of a major breadwinner and the cost of maintaining two households rather than one, and usually entails substantial social stress or reorganization.
4. The loss of emotional support for the wife/mother. This combines with the loss of economic security (point 3) to depress the socioeconomic condition of the family and threaten its stability.
5. Social isolation, engendered not only by disapproval of divorce but also by the social exclusion inevitable in a social system in which families and couples are often treated as elemental units.

Other investigators have challenged the presumption of the deleterious impact of father absence on children. Some argue that the negative effects of father absence can be accounted for largely by the poverty stricken economic conditions in which many father-absent families live (Bane, 1979; Herzog & Sudia, 1970, 1973; Rutter & Madge, 1976). Still others purport that the mother's response to divorce and her adjustment to the new social and economic demands substantially influence and modulate the impact of the father's departure in the divorce (Biller, 1970, 1971b; Biller & Bahm, 1971; Lamb, 1976). Lamb (1977) also makes the cogent point that a father may be nominally present in an intact marriage, but psychologically absent. The bulk of the psychological damage may have occurred prior to the divorce. Inaccessible fathers are not psychologically helpful fathers. Interestingly, many fathers seem to become more involved with their children after a divorce.

The current thinking and research on divorce indicates that marital tension and family discord prior to separation/divorce may be more strongly related to children's adjustment than father loss per se or diminished contact with one or both parents following marital dissolution (Hetherington *et al.,* 1979; Hodges, Wechsler, & Ballantine, 1979;

Jacobson, 1978; Rutter, 1971). Dysfunctional behaviors such as lowered self-concept, poorer school achievement, impaired social or moral development, and antisocial behavior are even more likely to be found in unhappy but intact homes, where the amount of interpersonal conflict is high, than in divorced homes (Goetting, 1981; Nelson, 1981; Raschke & Raschke, 1979; Zill, 1978). Even a good relationship between a child and one or both parents can fail to mitigate the ill effects of a poor marriage; 40% of the children in situations of this kind showed signs of antisocial behavior (Rutter, 1971). An unhappy married couple with children who have a poor relationship with both parents leads to double jeopardy: 90% of these children had antisocial behavioral problems (Rutter, 1971).

Thus, the emotional climate of the home emerges as a critical factor in the adjustment and well-being of children after divorce. It is as important, if not more so, than the type of family structure. The effects of divorce on children may be as much due to the marital discord that preceded the divorce as to the trauma associated with the loss of the family structure. Divorce, then, may also serve to relieve stress and to neutralize the debilitating effects of marital discord on children (Goetting, 1981).

Relationships between the ex-spouses and the parents and children after a divorce also appear to be important moderator variables of children's adjustment to divorce. Prolonged and continued tension between the divorced parents has been found to hinder the positive well-being of the children (Hess & Camara, 1979; Jacobson, 1978; Kelly & Wallerstein, 1976). The more amicable the settlement between the parents, the happier the mother/father was upon separation, the shorter the separation, and the longer the passage of time, the better the positive emotional adjustment of the child (Hetherington, Cox, & Cox, 1977; Nelson, 1981).

An important developmental factor also emerges in this research that is related to the age of the child at divorce. Wallerstein and Kelly (1980) suggest that as children get older, especially past 8 or 9, their perceptions of divorce become increasingly mature, complex, and reality oriented. By fourth and sixth grades children felt they had little to do with their parents' divorce and did not blame themselves. In another study children from divorced homes less frequently attributed the cause of divorce to the child than did children from intact homes. The former children were also more likely to perceive fewer enduring emotional and behavioral problems for children after divorce. Whether this is due to the more realistic experiences of the children who have actually experienced divorce or the adaptive use of denial to numb possible painful affects is unclear (Kalter & Plunkett, 1984).

In several studies children have been asked directly via questionnaires or interviews what they think of their parents' divorce or their reactions to it (Kurdek & Siesky, 1980; Reinhard, 1977; Rosen, 1977). The children in these research projects ranged in age from 5 to 28 years old. They generally felt that their development was *enhanced* in several ways by the divorce. They reported few negative effects. The positive effects of increased responsibility, maturity, and interpersonal sensitivity were some of the major perceived personal benefits to them of their parents' divorce. Kurdek and Siesky's (1980) comment characterizes the result of these studies: "Clearly, children's own perceptions tend to modify the crisis flavored tone of literature regarding the effects of divorce on children" (p. 341).

As was previously noted, children's and parents' adjustment to divorce is interactive. Children who are disturbed by parental separation may also be a source of stress for their parents. Children's behaviors, especially those of boys, can cause emotional responses in mothers, such as anxiety, feelings of helplessness, incompetence, and depression (Hetherington *et al.*, 1976, 1977). The multiple demands of very young, dependent children may be especially stressful to a divorcing parent (Longfellow, 1979). An interaction effect occurs between parent and child, as each is capable of causing or modifying stress or adjustment for the other. The better the parent's adjustment, the more likely that the child will be adjusted and the better the adjustment of the child, the happier the parent. Finally, the older the child, the less his or her adjustment will depend on the level of adjustment of the parent (Lamb, 1977; Longfellow, 1979).

The emotional strains associated with the presence of children in divorce have been noted frequently. Less attention has been given to the assistance and support that children may offer to the custodial parent in reducing stress and promoting adjustment. Responsibility for children may help keep a parent going, in that it provides a context and a meaningful purpose in the midst of a struggle to survive a crisis. Children may also act as supportive agents themselves, much as would an adult friend. Their laughter and daily foibles may be the leavening agent welcomed after a humorless encounter with a lawyer or ex-spouse. Their ever-changing behavior provides a reminder that life and further development goes on.

In summary, continued conflict between the parents following a divorce clearly hinders the positive adjustment of children, as does a poor relationship with the custodial parent. A most important related factor in the adjustment of the custodial parent, as well as the child, is the quality of the relationship between the ex-spouses. Evidence suggests that children do best when a final dissolution follows a relatively short separation, compared to multiple, long, and/or protracted separations. These results all suggest that it is important for therapists to help limit and mitigate the effects of further damage in a conflict-ridden home with an unsalvable marital situation by discouraging the fictional picture of marriage for the sake of the children, encouraging a clean break, and promoting civil relationships between the ex-spouses after divorce. The results also suggest that by helping the parents successfully adjust to divorce, therapists can also aid the future adjustment of the children.

Economic and Educational Resources

The review presented above indicates how limited the concept of parent absence per se has been to the understanding of the effects of divorce on a child's adjustment. The absence of the father may have its most direct impact not on the child, but on other factors, especially the economic and social position of the family and, in particular, the economic situation of the single mother. Nine out of ten children of divorce live with their mothers ("Changing USA Families," 1984). More than 50% of children in female-headed families are in families with incomes below the poverty level, compared with less than 10% of children in male-headed (mostly husband-wife) families (U.S. Bureau of the Census, 1977). Women with children, but without husbands, find themselves in desperate economic straits for a variety of reasons. Among these are the greater prevalence of divorce and death among poor families; low and irregular levels of alimony, child support, and public assistance; and the presence of fewer adult wage earners. While the labor force participation rates of female family heads are high, unemployment rates are also high. Female single parents who work are often subject to the effects of wage discrimination, occupational segregation in low paying clerical and service jobs, and the lack of opportunities and resources for training.

The presence of economic resources, particularly in terms of income, seems to be related directly to adjustment. A review of the literature suggests that, across studies, the more economically independent one is and the higher the actual amount of income, the better the adjustment and the lower the reported distress (Kitson & Raschke, 1981). This relationship holds true particularly for women. Income, whether the actual amount, the source, anticipated amount, or stability of income, all appear to be positively related to adjustment, both to the custodial parent and child and to the noncustodial parent. In one drastic example, it was found that all maladjusted children in a small sample of divorced families came from families who reported a 50% drop in income immediately following parental separation (Desimone-Luis, O'Mahoney, & Hunt, 1979). Such economic consequences also may make it necessary for the divorced mother to return to work or to school in order to retrain and obtain further education (Rice, 1978). This economic necessity again may have consequences for the children who "lose" still another parent when the mother is now less available to the children (Hetherington et al., 1976).

In contrast to income, level of education appears to have little effect on the amount of felt distress or level of psychological adjustment associated with divorce (Chiriboga *et al.*, 1979; Kitson & Raschke, 1981). Level of education does appear to be correlated inversely with the incidence of divorce. Men and women with college degrees have especially high levels of marital stability; men and women with less than high school education have especially low levels of marital stability (Spanier & Glick, 1981). The only exception to this pattern is that women with graduate school training have a very high marital disruption rate, compared with women with 4 years of college. The effect is even greater for those women with 6 or more years of college than for those with 5. Men with 6 or more years of college also demonstrate an increase in the probability of marital dissolution, but the increment is slight (Houseknecht & Spanier, 1980).

For women, the effect of education on divorce persists even when race, earnings, and occupation are held constant. This implies that education per se has an impact on marital dissolution other than through income and occupation. These results are compatible with the fact that education is one of the most important variables for predicting women's attitudes about sex roles and the women's movement (Mason, Czajka, & Arber, 1976; Rice & Anderson, 1982). They also fit with the previously mentioned fact that women who approve of married women working outside the home are more likely to separate and divorce, regardless of their actual or expected earnings (Cherlin, 1979). Having higher education may also be related to less stress and to an easier role transition from married to divorced (Everly, 1978). There are other women who experience difficulties with adjustment during a separation, withdraw their divorce petitions, and go back to school or obtain a job before they file again. Educational and vocational preparations for divorce need to be addressed carefully by professionals in the field of divorce therapy.

Access to Psychotherapy

The personal, social, educational, occupational, and economic resources one brings to a crisis, such as a divorce, may also be influenced by another resource, namely access to counseling and psychotherapy. Often people who either are considering divorce or experiencing it seek some kind of professional help. Few studies to date have explored how individuals differ in adjustment as a result of whether or not they received such assistance (Briscoe & Smith, 1973; Brown & Manela, 1977; Chiriboga *et al.*, 1979).

In a recent review of the literature, 22 studies of divorce treatment were examined substantively and methodologically (Sprenkle & Storm, 1983). Although all these studies incorporated some components of divorce therapy, none of them investigated what is probably the most widely practiced form of divorce therapy today, that is, helping couples and individuals work through the emotional trauma of divorce. Included in the Sprenkle and Storm review were studies on mediation counseling, consumer evaluation studies, divorce education groups, separation techniques, and marital therapy with divorce as an unintended outcome.

Various outcome variables were used to evaluate the results of these interventions. The divorce mediation studies appear to be the best controlled and report the following specific outcomes: (1) a high rate of pretrial stipulations or agreements; (2) a significantly higher rate of satisfaction with mediated agreements than with those imposed by the courts; (3) a significant decrease in the amount of litigation following court orders; (4) an increase in joint custody arrangements; and (5) a decrease in public expenses (court costs, etc.). However, this specific form of structured intervention is most successful within a fairly limited range of cases. The best candidates for mediation are couples who come for treatment early in the divorce process, with few and uncomplicated issues, adequate finances, low to moderate conflict, desire for cooperation, ability to negotiate for themselves, mutual acceptance of emotional divorce, and no complications by adversarial lawyers or trouble-making third parties (Sprenkle & Storm, 1983). Clearly these ideal circumstances fit only a small minority of the couples who find themselves in the middle of a divorce process.

Other studies use measures of rated helpfulness of the type of intervention or general client satisfaction measures and report fairly high success levels. Unfortunately they do not report baseline data or use control groups, making it difficult to interpret the meaning of such results. The gross "helpfulness" percentages are consistent with the general improvement percentages reported for uncontrolled studies of nonbehavioral marital and family therapy (Gurman & Kniskern, 1979). The conciliation courts counseling studies utilize reconciliation as a positive outcome variable and thus are not representative of divorce therapy per se. Only the divorce education studies employ meaningful personal adjustment criteria. Higher measures of self-esteem and significant increases on divorce adjustment measures, such as the Fisher Scale (Fisher, 1976), are reported after participation in such groups.

With few exceptions, the handful of studies on divorce therapy are weak methodologically. Client variables such as socioeconomic status and race are ignored. Important situational and temporal variables such as stage of the dissolution process rarely are analyzed for effect. Few studies employ alternative treatment groups or follow-up data. Despite these methodological weaknesses, the outcomes reported generally are more positive as a result of some therapeutic intervention, compared to no treatment.

There is little or no controlled research on divorce therapy per se, that is, on those interventions specifically designed to help divorcing individuals and couples achieve more constructive outcomes and better personal adjustment. In prior research studies, divorce usually has been either an unintended outcome of marital therapy or a negative consequence of reconciliation counseling. This negative bias appears to have affected the research designs as well as the choice of outcome variables. Few dependent variables have been designed and used in research to tap constructive aspects of divorce and its aftermath (Kressel & Deutsch, 1977).

REMARRIAGE

There are those who would argue that the best predictor for adjustment after divorce is remarrige itself. Remarriage is felt to indicate psychological mastery of the stress associated with separation and divorce. It also means the cultural stamp of approval is received again; one is part of a couple, one fits in again, is "adjusted," and is not seen as deviant within the society. Remarriage, by implication, means the winning again of a love object and the visible proof that one is loved and wanted once more. Not only do symbolic rewards accrue, but secondary gains result, for example, an increase in earnings and possible income available, companionship, and the help and support of another person. Level of education, income and outside the home employment appear to affect remarriage, particularly for women. Divorced women are most likely to remarry sooner if they have relatively little education, are not in the labor force, and especially if they have preschool children (Glick, 1980).

Despite the slight decline in remarriage rates for divorced individuals over the past few years (Glick, 1980), remarriage may be viewed commonly by mental health professionals and lay people as proof of readjustment. There is recent emerging evidence that the remarried appear similar to first-marrieds in most aspects of current perceived well-being and marital and parental role adjustment (Weingarten, 1980). Such evidence indicates that the remarried have mastered the crisis of divorce and have developed or regained an adaptive pattern of psychological functioning.

CULTURAL ASPECTS

In discussing the causes and consequences of divorce, the influences of the cultural and community context have been noted repeatedly. Society's emphasis on achievement, mobility, consumerism/replacement, self-realization, individualism, and narcissism appear to have contributed to the readily available solution of divorce as a response to marital discord.

Those communities and subcultures that tend to reinforce such values would be expected to produce higher rates of marital dissolution, and that appears to be the case. Divorce rates are higher in those areas of the country, such as the West Coast, that traditionally have been associated with high mobility, transition, and an emphasis on individualism and self-fulfillment (Bloom *et al.*, 1978; Glenn & Supancic, 1984).

The changes in the traditionally fault-based legal system also reflect cultural values and have made it possible for divorce increasingly to be sought as a viable solution to marital problems. Despite the presumption that no-fault divorce decreases the amount of animosity, tension, and polarization in the divorce process and thereby eases adjustment, other cultural attitudes may intervene to mitigate against facile adjustment to divorce. There remains considerable negative valence attached to divorce, and society exerts considerable pressure on the individual to stay in the preferred state, that is married.

Not only is divorce regarded as somewhat negative in our culture, but there are no established role models, norms, or rituals for the divorcing individual or for persons who must relate to him or her. Some authors have proposed going through some kind of ceremony or ritual to demarcate divorce, as happens with the death of a loved one, and also the sending of announcements, as is done for a birth or a marriage (Johnson, 1977).

Perhaps even more important than the lack of ritual itself is the lack of kinship structures and social mores within our society that would enable the individual to know what to expect and how to act after a divorce. Not only does one lose a spouse in divorce, but also a certain degree of one's identity, as society has defined it. Part of the kinship structure and friendship network disappears. This network is often dependent upon the status of being married and is not, as in other cultures, based on one's previous status. The loss of a spouse, father-in-law, mother-in-law, sisters and brothers-in-law, married friends, and possibly even one's own children, are a combination that can lead easily to much distress over identity and to isolation and anxiety about how to act as well as what to expect from others.

The law specifies some commonly accepted social procedures, but promulgates no mores for the complicated kinship system that results from divorce and serial marriage. Furthermore, in American culture, unlike others, it is considered psychologically healthy to break away from one's original family before starting one's own, that is, to "divorce" emotionally from one's parents in order to commit emotionally to a spouse. We speak pejoratively of the 30- to 40-year-old married person who is still a "mama's boy" or "girl." Having severed these primary identities, usually it is not feasible or culturally approved to return to one's parents for succor and/or reestablishment of identity after divorce. Such behaviors, however, are common for individuals in those cultures that do not break the original kinship tie (Burch, 1971).

Divorce then cannot be understood except in relation to the culture of which it is a part. In American culture, which values strongly the affectional and emotional bonding between spouses and increasingly downplays and devalues the economic ties, it seems likely that divorce will continue to be a painful process. Emotional commitment is demanded in marriage and breaking the bond after having once been strongly felt is not an easy task. Divorce therapy is designed to ease this process and is a uniquely western invention, arising out of a cultural context that promotes self-realization and narcissism, as well as intimacy and emotional bonding.

CHRISTIANITY AND DIVORCE

Across the world, historically one can find many examples of how religious, social, and economic forces have interacted to create norms within a culture that affect how divorce is viewed and its personal consequences for the individual. Practically all societies make some cultural provision for the dissolution of marriage through divorce. Historically and globally there have always been societies with relatively high and relatively low rates of divorce. In some societies there is a high frequency of divorce for recently contracted marriage, but the rate dwindles to a rarity after a union has lasted a year or more or after children are born. In other societies the rate of divorce remains high throughout the lifespan. In some cultures, divorce is not particularly emotional and the outcome is institutionalized; in contrast, for American society divorce is highly emotional and the psychic outcome often unpredictable.

The fairly negative view of divorce traces its roots to the influence of Christianity on western culture. The whole western conception of divorce has been conditioned by the religious sanctification of marriage. If marriage is believed to be indissoluble spiritually, within the culture divorce is likely to be seen as wrong. It may be viewed as a punishment, penance for a failure not just in one's own eyes, or those of the culture, but also in God's. The strong, pervasive influence of the Christian sanctification of marriage is witnessed by the fact that, across time, there have been far more benevolent and less punitive attitudes toward divorce in cultures that do not bring the diety into the marriage bond to make it a sacrament (Burch, 1971; Cohen, 1961; Murdock, 1964). Other cultures humbly and pragmatically recognize the imperfection of the human condition, the influence of many mitigating factors, and the ultimate frailty of human bonds in their understanding and acceptance of divorce. This book has been undertaken in such a spirit and is hoped to represent a more benevolent and compassionate conception of divorce.

The causes and the consequences of divorce have been reviewed in order to provide a historical and cultural perspective for therapists dealing with individuals in the divorcing process. The next chapter focuses on the therapeutic approaches likely to be helpful in this situation and reviews various therapeutic modalities in terms of their applicability to divorce therapy.

Chapter Two

The Origins of Divorce Therapy

Divorce therapy is only beginning to define itself as a specialized form of therapy. An exploration of the historical and therapeutic antecedents that have shaped current thinking and application of divorce therapy is helpful in understanding this type of treatment. While a growing literature on what divorce therapy purports to do has emerged, there is almost a total absence of writing that analyzes its theoretical underpinnings from related disciplines and other intervention strategies. The purpose of this chapter is to uncover the roots that have contributed to the formation of divorce therapy. Chapter Three will then outline a theoretical formulation of divorce therapy that is largely based on a developmental perspective, but is also related to psychodynamic, behavioral, and educative approaches.

Preparation for therapists who treat individuals and couples in the process of divorce follows numerous routes of training: individual, family, or marital therapy, child psychology/psychiatry, social work, and educational counseling are the most common. The practice of divorce therapy is based on concepts often derived and borrowed from the more established fields of family and marital therapy as well as the newer areas of grief therapy and crisis intervention.

One author has indicated,

> At a minimum, [a divorce therapist] needs a thorough knowledge of growth and development of the individual; concepts of union, separation and intimacy; communications and systems theory; dyadic relationships; power and conflict; family theory and therapy; loss, grief, and mourning; and stages of the divorce process and accompanying feelings. Intervention skills should include individual, marital and family therapy, plus crisis intervention and breadth of familiarity with a variety of techniques from different schools of therapeutic thought to incorporate judiciously in accordance with the needs of patients. (Kaslow, 1981, p. 694)

Such a compilation led the editors of the *Handbook of Family Therapy* to speculate that there seemed little that was unique to divorce therapy training or that was strategically or technically unique to divorce therapy itself. "Nonetheless, specialized knowledge of the common patterns in the divorce process does seem central to effective clinical work in this area" (Gurman & Kniskern, 1981, p. 694).

Divorce therapy does owe a heavy debt to marital and family therapy in particular, as well as to individual therapy, in terms of specific intervention strategies. However, the view promulgated here is a relatively new conception which views divorce in developmental terms and as a predictable stage of personal and interpersonal development for some individuals, with its own unique attendant problems, crises, and treatment implications. In the past, divorce has been seen and treated largely as aberrant behavior, as a deviation from the norm. In fact, helping people explicitly to divorce rather than to marry or to stay married still raises many value-laden conflicts and concerns on the part of those therapists who adhere to certain cultural stereotypes and religious viewpoints about marriage. There remain therapists who implicitly measure psychological maturity by the criterion of being married only once and being able to sustain that union for life.

TRACING THE THEORETICAL/STRATEGIC ROOTS OF DIVORCE THERAPY

There are essentially four areas from which divorce therapy as currently conceived and practiced has derived: (1) marital and family therapy; (2) crisis intervention treatment; (3) grief and bereavement counseling; and (4) educational-supportive counseling. Contributions from the family-marital field are commonly organized along the lines of the four major theoretical positions: psychoanalytic, intergenerational, systems, and behavioral. Divorce can also be viewed as a part of individual, marital, and family life cycle development; this approach will be elaborated in the following chapter. Dealing with issues of object loss and subsequent mourning and depression have led many investigators in the field to use elements of grief theory to define the stages of divorce, as well as to guide accompanying treatment strategies. Wiseman's (1975) use of the labels, "denial, loss, anger, reorientation, and acceptance," to define the stages of emotional response to divorce, closely parallel Kubler-Ross's (1969) elucidation of the stages of death and dying.

Because the possibility of divorce, as well as the process of divorcing, can precipitate severe stress of crisis magnitude, some individuals in the field have tended to view divorce therapy as a form of crisis intervention. Therapeutic techniques are designed to reduce anxiety and to remove stress inducements, such as in issues of custody, effectively and promptly. Divorce mediation is an approach derived in part from this genre of active short-term interventions. Such specific interventions ameliorate conflict and significantly lessen stress and hostility through highly structured management behaviors and the use of mediation.

Educational approaches that are based on theoretical models of learning and relearning have also found favor in the divorce therapy literature. Using groups to teach social, interpersonal, and assertiveness skills is a common strategy promoted as effective in helping divorced individuals to regain confidence and to learn coping behaviors needed to adjust to the realities of being single and alone.

Should divorce therapy deal primarily with short-term, educative efforts and mediation approaches based on support, advice giving, and problem solving? Or does effective divorce therapy by necessity include psychodynamic and psychotherapeutic strategies aimed at long-term behavioral and attitudinal change, perhaps including some basic personality reorganization? It is the position of the authors that effective divorce therapy does need to move from problem solving to unraveling the basic antecedents of the individual's personal and interpersonal development and to apply that information to present and future behaviors. This critical part of divorce therapy, often accomplished postdivorce, is in some ways the preventive part of divorce therapy, aimed toward insuring that the individual can move on developmentally into future successful relationships. Psychoanalytic and intergenerational approaches to the study of family therapy have provided a rich tradition that underscores the importance of looking backward as well as forward, understanding and using family history to predict current and perhaps future marital conflict.

MARITAL/FAMILY THERAPY CONTRIBUTIONS

PSYCHOANALYTIC APPROACHES

Psychoanalysis is the original theoretical source from which much of present-day psychotherapy has emerged. Thus, it represents a natural and logical starting point for reviewing the theoretical and strategic roots of divorce therapy. A basic premise of most psychodynamic approaches to the treatment of marital and family conflict is that partner and family difficulties are often seen as symptoms of unresolved childhood conflicts (Meissner, 1978). A family can be viewed as suffering from developmental failures across several generations, paralleling the idea of "fixation" at, or "regression" to, early oral, anal, or pregenital developmental levels. A parent who lacked a loving, guiding mother or father may behave inappropriately when required to provide a nurturant marital role for which one had an inadequate model. The internalization of an adequate role model into one's own psyche is viewed as critical to later successful parenting in such a conceptualization.

Within the marital union, this model assumes that each partner will bring expectations and fears closely corresponding to the level at which some aspect of their own developmental unfolding was blocked. The marriage itself then represents, in this view, another opportunity to work through the earlier conflict, to recreate a situation where the necessary experience can be relived and mastered (Skynner, 1981). If, however, the earlier conflict is not mastered within the marital situation it may be relived again and again, even with new partners. A wife, for example, complains that she is not getting her needs met by her spouse. A behavioral analysis of the problem might point to a dysfunction in the communication system between the spouses. A psychodynamic perspective on the situation might indicate that, at a different level of analysis, the source of the problem lay in repressed anger toward her mother for her refusal to gratify dependency needs in childhood. Such an interpretation would lead to psycho-therapeutic attention to the wife's personal development and differentiation quite apart from therapeutic interventions designed to improve communication transactions between the spouses.

A central feature in psychoanalytically oriented couples therapy is its attention to early conflictual childhood experiences that are experienced and played out within the marital union and may operate at unconscious levels. Unconscious processes are presumed to play important parts in the original, unverbalized aspects of the marital contract (Sager, 1981). The contract or script between the partners reflects the way they operate together to fulfill their individual expectations, conscious and unconscious. Each partner typically unconsciously "colludes" in the marital interaction system, impliciting acting out a variety of maneuvers that serve to maintain the system and the marital contract without changing it or going too far in any direction that would destroy it. For example, a husband may complain that his wife is not affectionate enough with him and periodically withdraws emotionally; the wife may present a very similar complaint about the husband. Neither spouse may consciously realize that their original marital contract was based on the premise that neither spouse would violate intimacy barriers. When one moved closer, the implicit responsibility of the other was to withdraw, in effect maintaining the desired degree of emotional distance between them. Unless the equilibrium is seriously disturbed or the terms of the original contract seriously questioned, the marital interaction patterns remain relatively consistent.

Another defense presumed to function to maintain the system and to prevent dissolution and divorce is the unconscious use of projection by one or both partners. For example, some part of the conflict or dysfunction in the marriage may be projected onto a child or other third party. This has been referred to as "triangulation" (Minuchin, Rosman, & Baker, 1978). Marital conflict is avoided by focusing on fighting with the child, the school, or the in-laws. In such cases the task from a psychodynamic perspective is to refocus attention from the environment back to the couple, eventually shifting once again back to earlier individual experiences.

Separation

A common view in the psychodynamic marital literature is that the root of most couple problems can be found in the failure of one or both partners to have mastered the key developmental task of separation-differentiation (Ables & Brandsma, 1977; Mahler, 1968; Meissner, 1978). This conception, perhaps more than any other, has had an impact on the theory and practice of divorce therapy. A classic psychoanalytic perspective on the trauma engendered by marital separation and divorce would presume that the divorce experience and event will be shaped for the individual by all of his or her prior experiences with separation-differentiation.

Spira (1981) wrote,

> The separation experience precipitates both internal and external changes . . . it requires the withdrawal of cathexis from the internal representation of the object to make energy available for future reinvestment. . . . The withdrawal of cathexis from the former partner is gradual and similar to the process involved in mourning. . . . Although the affective reexperience of divorce is activated by the marital separation itself, a person's reaction must be seen as a reactivation of feelings from earlier life experiences that involved separations. Earlier experiences with separations are colored by the attitudes of the particular developmental phase in which they took place, by maternal attunement or its lack, by innate ego endowment, and by cultural norms. (p. 259)

This therapeutic approach requires that an individual response to divorce be explored in such a way that one's history of separations is illustrated and worked through. For example, at first glance the extreme ambivalence and grief many people experience during divorce can be puzzling to a therapist who views the end of what appeared to be an extremely destructive union. But the great difficulty many people experience in successfully separating from a "bad" marriage can be more easily understood and appreciated by understanding such an inability as a reenactment of earlier conflicts. The marriage may have replicated the individual's original experience with an ungratifying object (person), with whom he or she was unable to separate even though basic needs were unmet (e.g., a cold, punitive parent). If later object choices, such as one's mate, implicitly are asked to fulfill those unresolved wishes and cannot, the person hangs onto the frustrating object as long as possible to avoid separation anxiety and accompanying anger. Thus, the earlier anxiety surrounding the possibility of separation from an unsatisfying object has never been successfully resolved and repeats itself in the person's extreme anxiety, ambivalence, and grief over the divorce from a later unfulfilling relationship.

Psychodynamics of Divorce

Spira (1981) provides a number of illustrations how a psychoanalytic perspective might be applied to the various other reactions a person might experience in divorcing: self-criticism, depression, anger, guilt, deprivation, as well as relief, elation, and omnipotence, and how a divorce therapist would work with and understand these feelings from such a dynamic perspective.

1. *Self-criticism.* The individual believes that if he or she were really lovable, the mate would have stayed and fulfilled their needs. Blaming oneself for the failure of the union may replicate an earlier disappointment in a parent who failed to fulfill narcissistic needs for enhancement of self. The placing of blame on oneself again protects the object from the person's anger and thus also serves to deny both the fear and the expression of that rage.

2. *Depression.* A central developmental task is to come to terms with one's own strengths and weaknesses as well as the strengths and limitations of others, to achieve a realistic assessment of that balance, and then to accept it successfully. These processes are referred to as "self-constancy" and "object constancy" (Mahler, Pine, & Bergman, 1975). Where object constancy has not been achieved, the divorcing person may feel particularly depressed over the loss of the individual who was unrealistically thought to be able to meet important basic emotional needs. The person describes himself or herself as feeling empty, and sometimes engages in a series of quick, unsatisfying liaisons that may shore up defenses against feeling depressed.

3. *Anger.* From a psychoanalytic perspective, anger toward the spouse or the therapist actually may be displaced hostility and in part belong to an earlier period or object. A therapeutic goal would be to help the divorcing person understand this transferential perception and to use the current experience in order to unravel anger related to prior separations from the current affect. Such feelings would be explored in the transference relationship with the therapist and not in terms of the ex-mate.

4. *Guilt.* The partner who initiated the separation and/or divorce may feel quite guilty and identify with the ex-spouse, who is perceived to have been abandoned. The guilt and projective identification with having been abandoned can prevent or interfere with the forming of new

emotional investments and can lead to a pattern of periodic cyclical separation and reuniting.

5. *Deprivation.* Divorcing individuals may speak of feeling cheated within the marriage and question their ability to ever have a subsequent satisfying relationship. Such feelings might be interpreted psycho-dynamically as having resulted from failure at an earlier developmental stage where the person felt deprived emotionally. Part of the therapist's task is to help the individual realize that in reality he or she has more options available for ego gratification than presently seems to be the case.

6. *Relief/Elation.* A person after divorce may experience feelings of elation and euphoria, fantasizing the fun, suitors, and lovers expected with the freedom of being single again. These expectations may disguise the desire for an all-loving powerful parent figure who can fulfill unmet ego needs. The therapist in such a case would be seen as critical in stimulating adequate reality testing and ameliorating the disillusionment that can accompany such unrealistic fantasies.

7. *Omnipotence.* A final psychodynamic example is illustrated by the person who feels a sense of elation and omnipotence after a divorce, not due just to grandiose fantasies about available love objects, but also because the separation represents an earlier triumph over an unresolved and unsatisfy-ing parental relationship. In such a case the spouse unconsciously represents the parent. By divorcing, the person feels a sense of mastery over a previous childhood dependence on and inability to separate from the depriving parent. The sense of omnipotence is illusionary, however, if the person has never solved the conflict with the internalized original source (Spira, 1981).

Presuming Developmental Deficit

The theme of all these interpretations and therapeutic strategies revolves around understanding how earlier conflicts are manifested in the marriage and later in the divorce. Such an approach has been criticized on several grounds (Wile, 1981). Discrediting an individual's feelings and reactions by attributing them to developmental deficits may be missing important situational determinants, the cultural context, and other current factors that operate to shape and reinforce those feelings. The intrapsychic approach also can be seen as somewhat accusatory and moralistic in that it places blame again on the shoulders of the client(s). Failure to master developmental tasks is viewed as the responsibility of the person and such interpretations may reaffirm self-criticism and self-denigration (Wile, 1981).

The view of divorce from a perspective of intergenerational transmission, as previously discussed in Chapter One, clearly derives from a psychoanalytic framework that posits the transmission and interplay from generation to generation of family patterns of projection and introjection. Exclusive focus on this historical dynamic can, however, lead a therapist to presume that divorce is necessarily the result of key developmental deficits. Marital therapists often work with couples who appear to be relatively unconflicted at the conscious level yet experience great stress due to conflict at the conscious level that is a function of sociocultural and situational factors. For example, a couple may share a fairly mature object relationship and have similar interests and tastes, but be jointly and very significantly stressed by cultural and familial pressure about their different religious, racial, or ethnic backgrounds (Gurman, 1978). To say that divorce was the result of a lack of self-differentiation from their respective families, while ignoring the actual cultural and situational constraints and pressures on such relationships, can represent a narrow, unidimensional perspective on the meaning of divorce.

Marital conflict, and divorce, can occur in the absence of significant individual psychopathology in either or both spouses. That is, marital conflict and ultimate marital dissolution can be the result of the *interaction* between the partners, a view more consistent with a social learning perspective on marriage and divorce. In terms of the goals of divorce therapy, however, such a view does not necessarily mean that understanding and insight into the nature of the interactional conflict is not helpful or integral to therapy. For the strictly behaviorist or family systems therapist the genesis of the conflict would not be seen as critical as the current organization of the interaction. Divorce therapy that goes beyond supportive educational counseling owes a debt to both psychodynamic and developmental views that posit the important role of understanding past interactional patterns to better deal with present and future ones. Some divorce therapists would go even further and ask that the person's family be brought into therapy to unravel, illuminate, and resolve core personality conflicts.

INTERGENERATIONAL APPROACHES

Marital therapy began to borrow extensively from family therapy in the late 1960s when Boszormenyi-Nagy and Spark (1973) as well as other therapists, explored the therapeutic advantages of using a transgenerational approach. Applying a contextual view to marital therapy involves combining couple sessions with sessions where family of origin members are present. Such an approach has become an accepted mode of treatment by individuals who believe that most marital conflicts are metaphors about original family conflicts. Correspondingly, most problems of children are seen as metaphors about the quality of the relationship between the parents. From this viewpoint, a typical pattern of intervention would involve some initial conjoint diagnostic sessions, moving fairly quickly into family therapy with children and/or grandparents or any other extended family members present (Boszormenyi-Nagy & Ulrich, 1981; Framo, 1981; Whitaker & Miller, 1969). Some work in couples groups may also precede the family therapy, but the main goal is to bring into the therapy session as many members of the family as possible and, if not possible, to treat the marriage in a contextual framework. In this model, individual therapy is conducted as though more than one person of the nuclear family were present and the therapist is committed to helping not only the individual or couple, but also significant others interlocked with the patient's basic welfare and interests.

The roots of the transgenerational approach can be traced in part to psychoanalytic thinking wherein core historical conflicts are seen to be present in contemporary behaviors. Intergenerational approaches also borrow heavily from systems theory, viewing the whole as greater than the sum of its parts. To understand the part clearly one must perceive the interaction of the part within the system in which it operates. Just as the individual is part of a couple system, the couple system is part of several family systems. From this viewpoint, all psychopathology is interpersonal, and interactional insight is most valued. Whitaker and Keith (1981) speak then of "exploding the myth of individuality."

Divorce and Family Therapy

The intergenerational approach is also beginning to make its way into the thinking of those divorce therapists who desire to go beyond supportive therapy, to goals of deeper personal and interpersonal integration. Divorce can be treated as part of a larger system problem, and the therapist may see not only the divorcing spouses together, but bring in the children and even the couple's parents and siblings at appropriate stages (Framo, 1978). More often than not, this approach has found favor either in the beginning stages of divorce therapy or in postdivorce treatment. In the former situation, the therapeutic objective is to help the couple decide whether to divorce or not. Intergenerational sessions can help reveal how past family problems are being acted out in the present and *who* is really being divorced.

A clinical paradigm derived from Boszormenyi-Nagy and Ulrich (1981), reframed here as applicable to divorce, serves to illustrate this phenomenon. An ambivalent father abandons his wife, who, in turn abandons their son. The father rescues the child, and gains custody only to abandon his second wife and his now adolescent son. The stepmother is the only person with whom the now grown-up son is able to have a trusting relationship. However, in order to exonerate the mother and have a relationship with her, the son must divorce the father (you are no better than she). Furthermore, to excuse the mother and father, he must divorce the stepmother (you are no better than they are). He marries, and the same unresolved cycle of destructive hostility continues, but is now directed toward the son's spouse and children: "How can I treat my spouse better than my mother treated me without being disloyal to my mother?" The commitment to preserve the parental relationships and to exonerate the generations before is accomplished at the cost of new relationships. The son divorces his wife with the implicit message being "you are no better than they were."

The Myth of Individuality

At the point when a couple divorces, a therapist treating the couple might move from the intergenerational context or couple therapy to individual therapy. Again a theoretical orientation that disputes the "myth of individuality" might predispose the clinician to continue to see the couple and, at one extreme, even to bring in boyfriends, girlfriends, and lovers (Keith & Whitaker, 1977) or ex-in-laws. The premise underlying such an approach is a strongly promarital one: that is, the marriage, although broken legally by divorce, never really does end.

> The craziest thing about marriages is that one cannot get divorced. We just do not seem to make it out of intimate relationships. It is obviously possible to divide up the property and to decide not to live together anymore, but it is impossible to go back to being single. Marriage is like a stew that has irreversible and irrevocable characteristics that the parts cannot be rid of. Divorce is leaving part of the self behind, like the rabbit who escapes the trap by gnawing one leg off. (Whitaker & Keith, 1977, p. 71)

By including such family outsiders as lovers in the therapy, it is presumed that the basic integrity of the biological (parental) unit will surface and perhaps be reconstituted when placed side by side with the more tentative, short-lived, "nonbiological" love affairs. Related to the notion that marriage does not end psychologically with divorce is the premise that family of origin conflicts also do not end with marriage or necessarily with the divorce; that divorce is at least three generational. Thus in this view one can never escape one's psychic baggage, positive or negative, not only from the marital union, but from the original family.

While the intergenerational approach is used occasionally in the predivorce stage of divorce therapy, many divorce therapists would choose not to bring in spouses, in-laws, parents, or even lovers once the decision to divorce has been made and whatever terms can be negotiated are dealt with in conjoint therapy. It would be more common at this point to switch to individual therapy, ending the couple and/or family sessions. The rationale is that continuing to see the spouses together can artificially reinforce the fantasy of their still being in a viable marriage and can contribute to, rather than defuse, the emotional bonds. Thus usually the separation is acknowledged symbolically by treatment in individual rather than conjoint therapy. The goal is to disengage rather than to constitute, and to individuate, rather than to couple.

Some divorce therapists are beginning to write about employing family therapy on a postdivorce basis (Baideme, Hill, & Serritella, 1978; Goldman & Coane, 1977; Goldsmith, 1982; Storm & Sprenkle, 1982). Typically, in such a format the symptomatic child is the initial focus and the therapist quickly moves in to get both ex-spouses as well as stepparents into therapy. This unique kind of intervention grew out of the fact that most divorces involve children and that the parenting function remains, although the spouses have legally terminated their relationship.

It is difficult to work on a marital relationship in individual therapy, with one spouse behind the scenes and outside the therapy. Similarly, it is often nonproductive to see in individual therapy only one ex-spouse, who is having difficulty handling the children of the former union, without the cooperation and inclusion of the "silent" partner. The first task in such a therapeutic context is to redefine the family as existentially including all members, despite the divorce. Another goal is to free the children from being surrogate parents and spouses, a process intensified by one parent's physical absence. The surrogate roles are reduced by reestablishing the viability of that parent's role in the family despite the divorce. An opportunity is provided in this type of treatment to correct whatever distortions remain about the divorce, to facilitate mourning the loss of the intact family, and to complete the process of emotional divorce. The therapeutic task is difficult and somewhat paradoxical, for although one wishes to foster the emotional divorce, simultaneously one does not want a coparental divorce.

The premise underlying this approach assumes that the symptoms of the children reflect the unfinished business and conflict between the divorced parents. Moreover, there are believed to be real differences in feelings and behavior associated with being the biological parent or the stepparent (Sager, Brown, Crohn, Engel, Rodstein, & Walker, 1983), but these differences can become obscured or distorted, resulting in symptomatic children. Bringing in the absent parent, the stepparents, and even grandparents postdivorce, in order to finish unfinished business, essentially reflects a systems point of view about the family, intact or divorced.

SYSTEMS THEORY APPROACHES

Family systems theory developed in part as a reaction against the psychopathological labeling of individuals; instead the couple or the family is seen as interacting within a system of operation (Hoffman, 1981; Jackson, 1977: Satir, 1971). Family systems theorists have proposed that it is possible for a marriage to be nonfunctional without the partners having significant individual psychopathology. The therapist then focuses on how the spouses view themselves and their significant others: how they perceive their problems together, their needs and gratifications and expectations of the marriage and the presenting problems. Individual and/or family history is not as relevant from such a perspective as the current symptoms and precipitants of the therapeutic contact. Family systems therapy, as it has been applied to marital and divorce therapy, is probably more a series of loosely connected concepts than an actual theory of marriage and its dissolution, more a style of thinking than a body of theory or a comprehensive model (Steinglass, 1978).

Perhaps the main contribution of systems thinking to a perspective on the theory and practice of divorce therapy is the recognition that it is limiting and unwise to consider only the individual and his or her reaction and behavior as he or she goes through the process of deciding, accomplishing, and working through divorce. The process and the outcome of divorce will be significantly affected by the network of significant others related to the individual. The divorce therapist who considers this contextual system, by philosophy, method, or by mode (utilization of conjoint, individual, and/or family therapy at appropriate stages) is likely to make more informed, realistic assessments, to employ a more powerful form of intervention, and to better insure the possibility of longitudinal change within the individual and within the future blended family.

Homeostasis

A key operating principle of family systems theory is circular causality, that is, that each spouse's behavior is a reaction or adjustment to the behavior of the other. One major way that circular causality operates within a family is through the principle of homeostasis. Homeostasis is the tendency of couples and families to resist and counteract all forces (including the therapist) that threaten to disrupt their achieved equilibrium, however fragile or pathological it may be (Jackson, 1957). Family systems theorists who apply the homeostasis principle to marital therapy have found it useful for enabling the therapist to spot sequential patterns in a couple's functioning. By studying the principles of homeostasis and how it is repeated within a system, one can also make useful predictions about the recurrence of certain response patterns in families and how therapy can change those patterns (Hoffman, 1981). If divorce is viewed as a radical change that disturbs the homeostasis of a system, then the problem is how to account for such change?

Second-Order Change

Systems theory prescribes that the system does not really change when more of the same is tried or prescribed, or when the reverse, less of the same is tried or prescribed. Surface changes, labeled "first-order" changes, may occur that allow for differences in movement within the system; for example, a husband begins to help more with the household work because his wife has returned to school. While the wife is appreciative of the more equitable distribution of labor, hostility and distancing behaviors remain at the same level.

Second-order change requires a shift that actually alters the system itself and not just its surface operations or manifestations. Such a transformation occurs when a new and radical shift takes place, usually to a new level of functioning (Watzlawick, Weakland, & Fisch, 1974). As applied to the above example, as the wife returned to school, she might also begin personally to explore, grow, and differentiate enough to disturb the equilibrium in the marital union. The dyadic system might be upset enough that the husband attempts to discount her efforts of personal change; he may voice approval of her fledging independence, but covertly sabotage individualism by ambivalent messages. If the wife resisted reestablishment of the equilibrium in the marriage, both in terms of power and differentiation, then ultimately the second-order change that might occur within the system would be a divorce. Divorce in this manner can be seen as a second-order change, not as the breakdown of a system, but as a potentially positive change in a system, its part and its interaction.

From this perspective, divorce has the power to alter radically the relationships of the individuals within a system and thus to change the nature of the system itself. If emotional divorce has been accomplished, and both parties have successfully separated and achieved better personal individuation, their relationships with important others in their families also will likely change.

> Furthermore, new mature relationships may be established between and among extended family members as a result of the divorce experience. Initially, the psychic upheaval may cause them to reach out toward the distraught person—offering to listen to or be with the person in whatever ways they are needed. This can lead to breaking down existing barriers to closeness and affection and allow for sharing of confidences and the deep rooted loyalties felt by various members of the divorced person's family of origin. Or, the converse might be true. Members of the extended family may have occasion to learn to respect the divorcee's need for privacy and aloneness; this can reverse a family ethos of over-intrusiveness. (Kaslow & Hyatt, 1982, p. 119)

On the other hand if ex-spouses continue to play out old games and dyadic strategems and never truly divorce emotionally, then the family system itself may not be altered radically. Although there has been a change (divorce), triangulation and parentification of children continue and every opportunity, however inconsequential, becomes an opportunity to act out the old conflicts. The system may perpetuate itself by the inclusion of new spouses and stepparents into the basic conflict areas. From this perspective, divorce can be conceived of as potentially both a first and/or a second order change phenomenon, depending on how it is accomplished.

The Strategic Approach

Both structural (Minuchin *et al.*, 1978) and strategic (Aponte, 1974; Haley, 1973; Todd, 1984) approaches to family therapy owe much to systems theory, yet lean very little on the cybernetic paradigm (Stanton, 1981; Hoffman, 1981). Haley coined the term "strategic therapy" to describe therapy in which the clinician actively designs interventions to match the presenting problems. Strategic therapists tend to be quite pragmatic and symptom focused. In contrast to more psychodynamic approaches, insight is not seen as critical for personal change, nor is the expression of feelings or emotions per se encouraged as cathartic or releasing. The therapist does not offer a different view about underlying motives or patterns to bring about insight or understanding, but attempts to shift views about reality, to relabel and reframe behaviors within a family.

The concept of transference similarily has little place in strategic therapy, as the therapist encourages little or no dependence upon him or her and quickly directs such feelings back to individuals within the person's system. Despite the eschewing of the role of the therapist in terms of bringing about insight and transference, the therapist as perceived in such a context is actually quite powerful. The structure, process, and almost all decisions about therapy are the responsibility of the strategic therapist (Stanton, 1981). The therapist takes responsibility for the course of therapy and, if therapy fails, the fault is more likely to be attributed to the failure of the therapist than to poor motivation on the part of the client or family. Families and couples typically are seen as locked into very stable, powerful systems of operation and homeostasis that may require quite active intervention and paradoxical strategies on the part of the therapist. These strategies have been sometimes criticized as manipulative and unnecessarily devious (Wile, 1981). However, therapeutic change within a system is thought to come about only when a therapist intervenes actively and directly in the family, in the process setting off interactional processes and "shaking up" the system (Haley, 1971).

The Values and Power of the Therapist

Applying these concepts to divorce therapy leads to some interesting observations. The catalyst function served by the therapist with a couple considering or on the edge of a divorce may well tip the system toward divorce whether or not the therapist professes the usual stance of apparent neutrality: "I will not take sides. Divorce is for you to decide. I want what you want." Given the stress of a situation such as divorce, however, clients may interpret such neutrality as support for their own private decision making. Each spouse may pick a side for the therapist, put him or her on that side, and act as if he or she had said "okay," even though the therapist does not know what side he or she has been put on (Whitaker & Miller, 1969).

A more active stance by the divorce therapist, such as suggesting separation or changing to individual therapy might also act to change significantly the process and the system. The therapist then finds himself or herself in the role of an "alternate mate" for many spouses on the verge of divorce. Therapeutic intervention in the decision-making stage of divorce has important consequences that will be more fully explored in Chapter Six. "Therefore, the therapist should be aware that he (she) may be intervening and changing a process that, when nature takes its course, will heal" (Whitaker & Miller, 1969, p. 616).

Therapists of different persuasions have questioned the assumption that people are so resistant to change and family psychopathology so ingrained that one must employ methods of paradox, and indirect, but powerful control over the course of therapy (Jacobson, 1981). Wile criticizes the strategic approach as implicitly assuming a kind of adversarial relationship between therapist and family, that may account for the dramatic techniques sometimes used. He feels that while such therapists do not talk about regressive infantile impulses, their approach is similar to depth analysis in the denigrating terms by which people are described and in the assumption that individuals function in an immature way that is below the level of rational dialogue and problem solving (Wile, 1981).

Paradoxical techniques are probably least applicable in situations of crisis or extreme instability, such as acute decompensation, acute grief reactions, attempted suicide, and loss of employment (Papp, 1980; Rohrbaugh, Tennen, Press, White, Raskin, & Pickering, 1977). In the case of possible or imminent divorce, when stress, grief, anticipated loss, and acute anxiety are all likely to be high, such interventions may not be appropriate or particularly useful.

Yet the core of a paradoxical prescription, that is, the positive reframing of the symptom, can be extremely useful in divorce therapy as the person begins to heal. Here the therapist "reframes" the traumatic experience of divorce as not just loss and disaster, but as a positive opportunity for change and growth. Such cognitive restructuring helps the person perceive the possibility of an eventual increase in self-esteem through the transcendence of the loss.

BEHAVIOR THERAPY CONTRIBUTIONS

While systems theory and structural or strategic approaches proposed by marital and family therapists have had less of an impact on our thinking about divorce than about marriage, the behavioral models applied to marital therapy have had a considerable influence on divorce therapy and mediation. There are some limited parallels between the systems and behavioral approaches. Both operate under assumptions of little interest in the role of past unconscious conflicts and both place emphasis on the viability of the presenting problems and see the goal of therapy as successfully dealing with the presenting problems.

Psychoanalytic approaches to divorce view accompanying depression, stress, ambivalence, and feelings of guilt as reflective of unconscious individual and dyadic problems. A systems viewpoint might treat such reactions as being a product of faulty communication or faulty problem definition. From a social learning perspective, such problems would probably be seen as learned behaviors, amenable to relearning and to social reinforcement. Behavioral approaches to marital therapy are based on operant and cognitive learning principles and a focus on the marital relationship in term of mutual behavior shaping (Bandura, 1969; Jacobson & Margolin, 1979; Stuart, 1976; Weiss, 1978).

Conflict Management

Behavior change theory has provided useful frameworks and strategies not only for marital therapy, but also for divorce therapy. Perhaps the greatest contribution of learning theory and behavioral methodologies derived from these concepts has been in resolving and managing the intense interpersonal conflict commonly engendered by divorce.

Divorce can be viewed as a conflict-management tool, providing a welcome relief and end to discomfort and hostility. In fact, as the divorce rate has risen, the rate of murders within the family has decreased (Brown, 1976). Intense conflict usually precedes, accompanies, and in some cases lingers insidiously after divorce in disputes about, for example, child custody and money. Most divorce therapists utilize behavior management techniques to control conflict within the divorce process and to deescalate postdivorce conflict.

Divorce Mediation

Divorce mediation has borrowed heavily from conflict management techniques largely based on behavioral change approaches. The major goal of divorce mediation is to help couples become rational and reasonable enough to cooperate in making compromises acceptable to both partners in such conflict areas as child support, division of economic resources, custody and visitation. The divorce mediation movement grew up in reaction to the adversarial nature of the legal system, which specifies a winner and a loser in divorce, if not in actual attribution of "fault," then in deciding who gets the leavings and how much (Coogler, 1978; Irving, 1981).

Divorce mediation is not therapy per se, but may be therapeutic for both parties involved; it is a method constructed to resolve disputes by providing management and resolution paradigms. The focus is on problem solving. In the initial phase of mediation, conflictual areas are identified and clarified, and an agenda is mapped out. The second phase involves discussion of alternatives and their consequences and efforts at compromise. Increasing the flow of accurate and nonhostile dialogue and insuring that both parties participate equitably and actively in the negotiating process are other goals. In the final phase of resolution the mediator makes structured attempts to assist the couple in selecting solution alternatives to the problem and in developing an agreement about the steps to be taken to insure the success of the chosen alternative (Irving, 1981; Kressel, Jaffe, Tuchman, Watson, & Deutsch, 1980). The process is very task oriented and borrows heavily from behavioral change therapy as well as labor mediation techniques.

Structural mediation is highly oriented to the situation and seeks to provide participants with specific skills needed to deal effectively with areas of conflict. Skill training in problem solving, negotiating, and contracting are hallmark strategies of the behavioral marital therapist (Weiss, 1978). That such an approach has found favor with and been incorporated into the work of mediation therapists in mediating, for example, issues of money, custody, and visitation in divorce, is not surprising. Divorce therapists who attempt to help couples define, negotiate, and contract the conditions of a structured separation also have employed a behavioral framework (Granvold & Tarrant, 1983; Hight, 1977). The popular use of marriage contracting, either verbal or written, grew out of the notion that mutual equitable reinforcement of individually desired behaviors can be effected through the structured use of behavioral exchange.

Behavioral Exchange

In one form of behavior contracting, "quid pro quo," spouse behavior changes are cross-linked (Jacobson, 1981). The contract is written so that if one partner performs in a certain desired way, he or she will be rewarded by the other partner changing behavior also in the desired manner; for example, Margo helps Stan figure out the monthly budget, in return for Stan maintaining the automobiles. One can readily see how the concept of behavioral exchange might be employed particularly in the middle phase of divorce, after a decision to divorce has been effected and part of the therapeutic task is to negotiate and mediate desired exchanges and behaviors. For example, Harold will agree to pay for the 1st year of their older daughter's college, if Yvonne cooperates by agreeing to a lowering of child support payments.

A second form of behavioral contract, now more favored in marital therapy, is the "good faith" contract; in this case the reward for the desired behavior is not contingent on behavior on the part of the party, but linked to some desired individual reward for oneself. For example if Stan takes care of the children for an evening each week while Margo attends a dance class, then he is also entitled to a weekly evening of private time for himself away from the family. One can see how after a couple has split, the nonreciprocal nature of this type of reinforcer would have little potency, for the rewards have to be either internal or self-provided (Harold is happy his daughter will be able to go to school; Harold gets to feel he's a generous guy), or from other sources than the partner (Harold's daughter is pleased and treats him better; Harold's friends think he's generous). In reality underneath most so-called "good faith" contracts are behavioral linkages. The private time Stan desires after pleasing Margo can only be accomplished with her cooperation, for example, by leaving him alone and taking care of the kids. The cooperation is the link and the reciprocation.

In divorce therapy, a good faith contract might read something like this: If Harold agrees to put money away for his 15-year-old daughter's college expenses, he is entitled to have the final decision on the choice of the college. The implicit reward, while not a quid pro quo behavior on the part of the ex-spouse, is agreement and cooperation by the ex-spouse to effect this reward.

The Point of No Return

A behavioral framework based on principles of operant conditioning and social exchange theory can be employed in divorce therapy to decide the so-called "point of no return," the point at which the losses outweigh the gains from the marriage. At this juncture, divorce is implicitly or explicitly the preferred choice for at least one of the partners, and the therapist needs to make a critical diagnostic assessment, often moving then from marital therapy to divorce therapy. Social exchange theory has proven to be a useful concept for explaining marital stability (Johnson, 1977). It can be utilized by the therapist to assess whether marital dissatisfaction outweighs possible satisfaction. Federico (1979) notes that an important clue for the therapist in diagnosing this balance is to realize that someone who desires to leave a marriage will use a series of exquisitely rated behaviors whose goal is to put progressively increasing distance and dissatisfaction within the partner and in the relationship.

In exchange terms, the partner alters the spouse's gains versus cost ratio by lowering the gains, raising the costs, and in effect pushing the spouse, who is ambivalent, toward divorce. Accommodation by the ambivalent spouse to restore harmony and defuse conflict are negatively reinforced with escalating demands and more unreasonable behaviors. The following sequence is illustrative:

> The Provoker begins spending less time at home, saying that s(he) needs to spend more time at work and then also needs a corresponding amount of relaxation time. The spouse objects but eventually accommodates. The Provoker then begins sleeping on the couch. The spouse objects but eventually accommodates. Then the Provoker takes a lover . . . and invites the spouse to join with the lover for a ménage à trois. At that point, the spouse is beyond the point of accommodating and files for a divorce. (Federico, 1979, p. 100)

Thus the partner who says, "I want a divorce," may not necessarily be the one who most desires a divorce. Similarly, a statement of "I still love you and I don't want a divorce," may suggest a closeness that is contradicted by the partner's actual distancing behaviors. From a behavioral perspective, the actual behavior, rather than the verbal expectations, may be the most potent indicator of where the partners actually are relative to the point of no return.

The Issue of Motivation

The behavioral framework is largely instructive and educational, rather than depth therapeutic in approach, and as such has provided a useful paradigm for divorce mediation work. Behavioral approaches can also be quite helpful in brief therapeutic interventions, a common condition both in marital and divorce therapy. In contrast to much of individual therapy, the conjoint phase of divorce therapy, like marital therapy, does not tend to be a long affair. As such it requires an active therapist, and one who can apply a good deal of technical flexibility. Even when working from an essentially psychodynamic posture, the eclectic marital therapist, and the divorce therapist, might also utilize behavior modification methods (e.g., a communication exercise) within the same session.

While variants of behavioral exchange theory and practice have found their way into divorce mediation and structured separation counseling, behavior therapists have not yet addressed the critical issues of grief, loss, anger, and revenge inherent to divorce and the dissolution process (Gurman, 1978). Some behavior therapists ignore the underlying collusive conflicts between couples, blame noncompliance with the therapist change efforts mainly on salient skill deficits, and maintain that it is the job of the therapist to teach such skills (Weiss & Margolin, 1977). Along these lines, a historical criticism of behavioral therapy has been that it overlooks important motivational factors (both at an individual and dyadic level) that mitigate against straightforward behavioral contracting and change. More recent cognitive behavioral approaches, however, have attempted to account for the motivational variable.

People may politely adhere to the imperative of the therapist by making surface changes that subsequently they sabotage. This is experienced by mediation counselors who attempt to work with divorcing couples experiencing a high level of emotional stress surrounding the dissolution process. The simple application of mediation, conflict management, and rational problem solving has had poor results with couples who exhibit high levels of prenegotiation conflict and non-mutuality of the decision to divorce (Kressel et al., 1980). This pattern manifests itself clearly in those postdivorce cases where visitation, child support, and/or division of property continue to be issues of continuing dissatisfaction for years after the divorce. Postdivorce counseling services for such families have sprung up in a number of cities under the auspices of the family courts. Writers in this area have noted that it is apparent from working with such couples that custody and visitation problems are usually not the real issue, but represent "Old wars being fought on new battlefields" (Elkin, 1977, p. 56). Unless the underlying motivation is addressed no amount of behavioral contracting is likely to solve the presenting problem.

Weiss (1978), taking a behavioral perspective, notes that problem solving cannot happen if one individual is seeking support while the other is problem solving. In divorce therapy, problem solving cannot occur when one person is seeking revenge while the other is problem solving. Successful behavioral exchanges in marital therapy require that partners place the relationship above absolute individual gain (Kimmel & Havens, 1966). Successful behavioral exchanges in divorce therapy also require the couple to put the welfare of their children above personal gain, and furthermore that the adults act like adults and not like children. Therapists who are prepared only to work with the "adult," may find it difficult to deal with divorcing or divorced individuals, who have well-established patterns of childish coping mechanisms (Bancroft, 1975).

Successful divorce therapy often needs to go beyond educative efforts and mediation counseling, incorporating a developmental perspective that allows for understanding motivation and eventual reconstruction in terms of personal and interpersonal unfolding. Succeeding in this regard is not easy, since predivorce therapy generally begins with crisis. When the crisis is finally "resolved" by a decision to divorce, many people end therapy prematurely. They are not interested in further exploration or change, since the major anxiety and conflict leading to the decision to begin therapy ostensibly has been resolved. The fact that a substantial number of individuals seek out therapy months or years later, in order to deal with unfinished divorce business, speaks to some of the inherent dangers in employing *only* a crisis intervention model.

CRISIS INTERVENTION

Divorce therapy, in theoretical orientation and in practice, is indebted both to marital and family therapy. Divorce therapy also has roots in crisis intervention theory. "Whether one views divorce as 'disaster' . . . or as 'development,' divorce is a crisis and should be approached accordingly" (Sauber & Panitz, 1982, p. 207). Divorce is born out of stress. Whether one views the stress in positive terms, as conducive to future personal development, or in more negative ways, as engendering individual regression and/or societal instability, acute stress generally is experienced as part of the divorce decison and process.

Divorce is a form of emotional crisis that produces the opportunity for positive outcome and growth concomitant with pain and conflict. In this respect, it is no different from any other intense emotional stressor that brings people to therapy. The status quo by definition does not produce growth. Some anxiety and conflict generally are necessary to motivate change. However, intense stress and overly high anxiety can engender emotional paralysis, confusion, and nonfunctional disorganization not conducive to positive rational change. In such a state one's usual equilibrium is grossly upset and preferred coping mechanisms often are far less effective. Crisis theory provides a conceptual definition for dealing with upset in an individual's usual steady state (Rapoport, 1965; Sauber, 1973). In accord with crisis theory, a real advantage to intervention at this time is that the chances for effecting change in a fluid system are greatly enhanced (Wallerstein & Kelly, 1977).

EFFECTS OF ACUTE STRESS

General principles of crisis management include assumptions about the importance of immediacy of treatment, proximity of treatment to home, and positive expectancy of the therapist (Hill, 1965; Parad & Caplan, 1965; Thweatt, 1980). These principles are based on the hypothesis that experiencing a crisis producing event, such as divorce, is likely to place a person in an acute state of personality disorganization in which prompt, active, readily available intervention is desirable. Many investigators in this area have cautioned against the danger of mistaking and mislabeling acute personal stress and disorganization experienced in the early stages of divorce as manifestations of deeper psychopathology.

Wallerstein and Kelly (1977) note "while divorce constitutes a time-limited crisis in the life of the child and the adult, during which the usual coping and adaptive mechanisms are in disarray," yet, ". . . many people underestimate the vicissitudes and difficulties of the transition. Our study confirms findings that we may reasonably expect a period of several years of disequilibrium before new, more gratifying job, social, and sexual relationships can become stable enough to provide comfort and a renewed sense of continuity" (p. 5). There is the issue of what defines "time limited." If one talks about a moderate degree of disequilibrium, not for months, but for years, this goes beyond the parameters of the usual crisis intervention model. The short-term emotional reactions associated with divorce need to be clearly differentiated from the long-term consequences of coping with a crisis (Kraus, 1979).

While crisis theory can provide a useful intervention construct for the analysis and treatment of acute emotional reactions, the divorce therapist must go beyond such a conception in order to deal adequately with the long-term consequences of divorce for the individual. One of the major criticisms of crisis intervention treatment is that its practitioners frequently focus too quickly on enabling individuals in situations of interpersonal loss to resume task-oriented behavior as rapidly as possible (Hassall & Madar, 1980). Problem solving takes precedence over emotional expression, but it is also important that the therapist subsequently refocus from problem solving to an expression and working through of loss and the accompanying feelings of grief, depression, and anger.

Initial applications of crisis intervention treatment to divorce therapy were predicated on a very brief clinical intervention (approximately 6 weeks). Experience has suggested that a 3-month period is more realistic and effective. In one treatment format each parent and child are seen three to six times by the same therapist for an average of 14 hours for each family (Wallerstein & Kelly, 1977). Optimum intervention time is hypothesized to be from 1 to 6 months following parental separation. After 6 months, therapy is believed to be less effective in that the system is no longer as fluid, with symptomatic behaviors present and parent-child alignments consolidated and strongly defended. Brief treatment can meet some of the special needs of divorcing individuals, but actual intervention strategies need to consider the catalyzing of longitudinal change as well as short-term amelioration. Intervention strategies may range from those predominately educational in nature, such as teaching divorcing parents how to alleviate the stress of the children, to others decidedly more clinical in nature and impact, such as using interpretations that defuse a parent's projective identification with a child and support self-differentiation (Wallerstein & Kelly, 1977).

From a more psychodynamic perspective, it is also recognized that the crisis of separation and/or divorce "awakens unresolved key problems from both the near and distant past, and revives old feelings of upset and conflict which are linked with previously unresolved crises" (Caplan & Parad, 1965, p. 67). Applying crisis intervention theory and techniques in a group setting, Hassall and Madar (1980, p. 593) present eight steps to crisis resolution that are decidedly psychodynamic in character and goal:

1. Identify the emotionally hazardous situation.
2. Identify defenses you create to avoid grief.
3. Give up these defenses to permit yourself to experience your emotions as intensively as possible—begin to mourn.
4. Obtain new information about your relationship with the lost person, e.g., what were all the reasons for the marital conflict.
5. Learn to manage your feelings by becoming more and more aware of your emotions.
6. Verbalize and experience the feelings which lead to discharge of tension.
7. Identify the early-life crisis in your life you have not solved.
8. Problem solving—restructure life.

The frenzied activity that divorcing individuals typically experience is interpreted supportively by the therapist as a normal, external manifestation of the inner stress they feel in a crisis situation. Clients are presented with an intellectual understanding of themselves and their particular situation. Following this, they are encouraged to give up defenses against emotional expression of their loss and to begin the cathartic mourning process. Finally, developmental principles are incorporated as clients are supported in rethinking critical incidents of their earlier lives and identifying earlier separation crises and conflicts that may have an impact on the current one. The crisis situation and loss that precipitated it offer an opportunity not only for restructuring and adaptation, but also for change and growth.

ASSESSING MAGNITUDE OF STRESS

A crisis such as divorce has the potential to be a major disruptive force in the lives of the people who must experience it. Perhaps second only to the death of one's spouse, divorce requires the most severe demands for personal and interpersonal reorganization faced by an adult in our society (Holmes & Rahe, 1967). Crisis theory predicts that the magnitude, character, and longevity of the reaction and the ease of the reorganization will be directly related to individual and situational variables. While it is not possible to differentiate clearly the impact of particular individual and situational factors on short-term emotional distress or eventual long-term adjustment, researchers have hypothesized about the effects of such factors on divorce adjustment outcome. From a clinical standpoint, it is important for the divorce therapist to make a careful assessment of the individual and situational factors that may have an impact upon the client's reaction to the divorce and ultimately on his or her long-term adjustment.

Individual factors such as age, gender, education, vocational status, financial resources, psychological state, social support, philosophical belief system, and decisional control operate to affect the outcome of long-term adjustment to divorce (Kraus, 1979). Many of these factors were discussed at length in Chapter One, including the sociocultural values and mores of the particular society. These variables may also affect the client's short-term reaction to crisis. Other situational variables like the presence of additional high sources of stress, for example, small dependent children, ailing parents, death in the family, loss of income or job, pregnancy and birth, and change of residence are other stressors that may accompany the divorce itself. The difficulty of immediate practical functioning is compounded by such multiple stressors, changes, and losses.

In our society, the divorcing individual is faced not only with one loss, the spouse, but typically with a multitude of others, including economic loss, loss of prior friendships, loss of kinship structure and role status, and loss of assigned place within the community and society. Viewing divorce in terms of loss permeates the literature on divorce therapy. This has led to the incorporation of concepts from grief counseling.

GRIEF COUNSELING

Bereavement counseling has developed largely in the context of working with the terminally ill, with death and dying, and with the survivors of the departed. A component of grieving involves dealing with separation anxiety, that is, facing the fears of aloneness and the meaning of loss of attachment (Switzer, 1970). The stages of the grief process and the working through of loss in part by experiencing grief have been conceptualized to fit a temporal paradigm proceeding from shock and denial to acceptance. The tasks of grief work have been described as (1) acceptance of the reality of loss; (2) surrender of emotional ties to the deceased; and (3) formation of new relationships (Clinebell, 1966). The parallel to the successful resolution of and ultimate adjustment to divorce is apparent.

Therapists writing about both grief and divorce use essentially four stages in their conceptualization of the process; the terms and sequence may be slightly different, but similar concepts occur with regularity in the literature (Bowlby, 1977; Kressel, 1980; Kubler-Ross, 1969; Thweatt,

1980; Uroda, 1977). The basic four stages are (1) denial; (2) anger or protest; (3) mourning or despair; and (4) detachment or readjustment. Sometimes the despair/mourning stage is postulated to come before the anger/protest stage and sometimes vice versa.

STAGES OF GRIEF

In the first stage of grief, a person refuses to face the reality of the person's death, the parallel in divorce being the possibility that the marriage is dying or is dead. If an individual's primary defensive mode of operation is repression and denial, getting beyond this initial stage may be very difficult. Divorce therapists usually can recall an instance when one spouse, in the very face of a divorce, continues to act as though the other spouse will stay and the marriage bond continue. Even after a divorce, the parties may continue to have sexual relations or occasional "dates," just as a bereaving person, for example, may preserve the room of the deceased exactly as before or may set a dinner place. The task of the therapist in both cases is gently, but firmly, to help the person accept the external reality of the loss and gradually come to terms with the actuality of one's changed role and status.

Many individuals have noted that the norms of our society regarding divorce do not aid in this process. Instead, societal mores may contribute to the maintenance of denial. As a culture, we tend to deny divorce, as we deny death; we encourage those who experience loss to be brave, to maintain emotional control, and praise those who return to productive activity as quickly as possible. As a consequence, our cultural expectations may subvert going beyond the stage of denial to the next normal, crucial step of anger and mourning, a progression necessary before reaching the phase of acceptance. It is as though one would like to skip these intervening stages, because they involve difficult, painful feelings that are not easy for the participants surrounding the grieving individual to deal with: namely, anger, protest, and betrayal, as well as withdrawal, perceived failure, and confusion.

The "protest" stage is usually the most difficult for others to accept. Intense hostility may be directed toward other members of the family. Anger may result from the narcissistic injuries experienced in divorce, the rage at abandonment, the blow to one's ego that a love object would leave and the inner fear that one is not lovable. Sustained anger and blaming following divorce may be in the service of keeping from awareness the portion of responsibility one shared for the breakup of the marriage. There is greater cultural tolerance for the expression of anger after divorce than after widowhood. In this context, it is interesting to note that individuals who were depressed following divorce were significantly more likely to show irritability and recurrent thoughts of death or suicide than those who were depressed following the death of a significant other (Briscoe & Smith, 1975).

The third stage of grief work, involving despair, mourning, and the clinical features of depression, is perhaps the most well known. Sadness, unresponsiveness, fear, withdrawal from others, feelings of personal failure, and confusion characterize this stage and can also be seen to parallel the classic signs of unipolar depression. From a developmental perspective, the person no longer is trying to deny the detachment, or to reattach, as in the stage of anger and protest, but gradually is coming to terms with the reality of the separation through active mourning.

The final stage of detachment involves emotional acceptance and behavioral readjustment. The person feels emotionally divorced from the ex-spouse and begins significantly to restructure his or her life to reflect the new realities of single status. New energy is felt to be available for reorganizing practical aspects of life and recreating a new life-style, similar tasks for both the bereaved and the divorced.

ATTACHMENT THEORY

The predictable four phase sequence of behavior (denial, protest, despair, and detachment) that follows separation is derived from attachment theory (Bowlby, 1960, 1977). Attachment theory proposes that there is a strong tendency to form intense affectional bonds in the young of almost all species of birds and mammals. In humans this propensity is felt to persist into and throughout adult life. Attachment behavior can also be seen on a developmental continuum, varying from primitive smiling, clinging, and crying of the infant to more advanced and sophisticated sympathy, patience, and altruistic love of an older adult.

In divorce there is often extreme ambivalence about separation from a spouse. Weiss (1978) explains this ambivalence by making a distinction between attachment and love. Love may erode, but attachment persists and resists dissolution even in the face of hurt and anger, once people have been bonded together. Hancock (1980) notes that basic to all the losses sustained in divorce is the loss of the sense of meaning and belonging. This sense of belonging was largely defined by attachment to a significant other and to a system of significant others. As a marriage and family dissolves, an unstable dependence on this old structure may still persist. Adjustment to divorce will depend in part on how successfully the person can detach from the old marital structure and role and the sense of meaning and belonging provided by that role.

The clinical and empirical literature suggests the relevance of attachment theory in explaining the often strong persistence of emotional involvement between ex-spouses. In a longitudinal investigation of postdivorce adjustment, Hetherington, Cox, and Cox (1976) found that 2 months after divorce, 17% of the ex-husbands still helped with home repairs, 8% babysat while their ex-wives went out on a date, and 13% had sexual intercourse with their former wives. Seventy percent of the women and 60% of the men said that the spouse was the first person they would call in a personal crisis, and that the divorce had either been a mistake or that they should have tried harder to resolve their differences.

Denying or attempting to skip, abridge, or otherwise dilute the mourning stage of grief work may only serve to perpetuate unrealistic attachment to the ex-spouse. Among a group of middle-class women with preadolescent children, Wise (1980) characterized the responses of these women postdivorce as indicative of a disturbed mourning process. One to 4 years postseparation, all of them were experiencing some feelings of depression, anger, preoccupation with loss, feelings of being incomplete, and reconciliation fantasies. Many of them continued an intense, ambivalent involvement with their ex-spouse.

> With only one exception, they expressed wishes to find a new mate quickly and reestablish an identity defined by attachment to a man and a household based on the traditional man–woman roles. Although all had considerable training and skills, and several had new jobs or had returned to graduate school, they did not define their work as a significant part of their lives. Nor did they seem to derive much gratification from their achievements at work. In other words, they wanted the role they had lost and were not thinking in terms of alternatives. (Wise, 1980, p. 154)

These women did not express sadness or mourning at the loss of their attachments, but continued to protest and rage at their ex-spouses or to be fearful and preoccupied with reunion. They had not resolved the ambivalence toward the ex-spouse or realistically and nonpunitively recognized their contribution to the demise of the marriage. Nor had they been able to change appropriately their perception of themselves and how they could function positively within a new meaning system.

The ability to mourn may also be critical to the ability to love, as many analysts have noted (Bak, 1973; Kernberg, 1974). Love is a state that seeks to reunite, to undo loss, and it may be through the experience of grieving that a person learns the value of attachment (Charlton, 1980). Perhaps grieving is essential, not only to detach successfully, but also to successfully attach again.

> I have seen several patients who as children were denied opportunity to mourn losses and who subsequently formed inadequate and dry marriages that inevitably came to divorce. In their divorce experience, however, they were once again offered an opportunity to mourn their losses and in some cases, with therapeutic support and interpretation, were able to use the experience to resurrect their imprisoned abilities to love. (Charlton, 1980, p. 20)

Although the mourning process that is presumed to be integral to both divorce and bereavement links the two events conceptually, there are differences in the actual death of a significant other and the symbolic "death" that characterizes the divorce event, process, and aftermath. Applying grief theory and therapy and its temporal stages per se to divorce as though it were an actual death has some limitations in light of these important differences.

DIVORCE AND STAGE THEORY

In discussing the process of divorce, many authors have employed some kind of temporal sequencing or "stage" theory to describe the divorce process. Less a theory, and more a description based on the sequence of events, "stage" theory categorizes common phases of divorce. The categorization may be psychological in nature, proceeding from "disillusionment/erosion" to "detachment" to "hard work/recovery" (Kessler, 1975; Storm & Sprenkle, 1982). Frequently the psychological stages used to describe the divorce process have paralleled those previously conceptualized for the grieving process and have utilized similar terminology, for example, shock, denial, depression, anger, mourning, and acceptance (DeFazio & Klenbort, 1975; Froiland & Hozman, 1977; Kaslow, 1983; Krantzler, 1974; Kressel & Deutsch, 1977; Wiseman, 1975).

Table 1 represents a summary of the temporal stages postulated for divorce by various authors in the past decade. The conceptions vary from Weiss's simple two stage process, "transition" and "recovery," to Kessler's elaboration of seven periods. The influence of bereavement counseling is noticeable in the terms employed, yet the previously mentioned caveat with regard to the ready application of the grieving process to divorce must be reiterated. The important differences between divorce and bereavement will be detailed in the following section on divorce and reactive depression.

Despite the differences in the number and labeling of the stages, basically all the temporal conceptions refer to three phases: (1) a predivorce period (shock, denial, disillusionment, erosion); (2) a transition period (decision to divorce, separation, negotiations); and (3) a recovery period (reorientation, restructuring, reequilibrium). Thus, the stages postulated may refer less to psychological sequelae than to the usual structural decisions and tasks involved in the divorce process. A relevant example here is how Kressel (1980), in a later conceptualization, has changed the labeling of stage 3 from "mourning" (a psychological term), to "negotiations," (a structural one). Bohannan's (1971b) conception of "legal divorce," "economic divorce," "coparental divorce," and so forth, is also essentially based on defining divorce in terms of tasks, for example,

TABLE 1
Conceptions of divorce in terms of stage theory

Author(s)	Stage(s)					
Bohannan (1971b)	1. Emotional divorce	2. Legal divorce	3. Economic divorce	4. Coparental divorce	5. Community divorce	6. Psychic divorce
Fisher (1973)	1. Predivorce	2. Divorce	3. Postdivorce			
Krantzler (1974)	1. Shock	2. Restoration of equilibrium	3. Mourning			
Kessler (1975)	1. Disillusionment	2. Erosion	3. Detachment	4. Physical separation	5. Mourning	6. Second adolescence
DeFazio & Klenbort (1975)	1. Shock	2. Depression/ rage	3. Separateness			
Wiseman (1975)	1. Denial	2. Loss/ depression	3. Anger/ ambivalence	4. Reorientation	5. Acceptance	
Weiss (1976)	1. Transition	2. Recovery				
Froiland & Hozman (1977)	1. Denial	2. Anger	3. Bargaining	4. Depression	5. Acceptance	
Kressel & Deutsch (1977)	1. Predivorce decision	2. Decision making	3. Mourning	4. Reequilibrium		
Kressel (1980)	1. Predivorce decision	2. Decision making	3. Negotiations	4. Reequilibrium		
Storm & Sprenkle (1982)	1. Decision making	2. Restructuring	3. Recovery			

Note: Bohannan (1971b) includes a 7th stage: 7. Hard work.

63

obtaining legal counsel, determining economic division, and deciding custody, an approach taken by divorce mediation specialists.

Although stage theory presumes fairly well-defined and predictable periods in successfully detaching from a love object, this view can be misleading to the therapist who wishes to do effective divorce therapy. Emotional detachment is seen in this book as a continuous, multileveled and multiinteractional process that therapist and client must deal with throughout divorce therapy. While there are discrete and fairly predictable tasks defined by the legal system and the society that every divorcing party must endure, using these tasks (physical separation, economic settlement, custody) to define the therapy of divorce gives us only a superficial, surface framework with which to understand effective divorce therapy. The personal adjustments prescribed by the legal system do not delineate the underlying therapeutic tasks nor necessarily prescribe the temporal process of divorce therapy. The important psychic processes in divorce, as explained in the following chapters, are better conceptualized as developmental in nature and therefore continuous and multileveled.

DIVORCE AND REACTIVE DEPRESSION

Recently, divorce therapists have been cautioned not to mistake the acute grief, personal distress, and disorganization accompanying divorce as indicative of more serious underlying psychopathology or endogenous depression. Similarities noted in the coping processes of a variety of stress situations, such as those caused by bereavement, terminal illness, and divorce, have led to the suggestion that the reactive process in divorce can be viewed as part of a general human adaptive mechanism rather than as a neurotic response (Kressel, 1980). The natural symptoms of the mourning experience, tearfulness, fatigue, sadness, reunion fantasies, and idealization of the lost object, must be carefully differentiated from the more chronic emptiness and loss of self-esteem that accompany an endogenous depression (Charlton, 1980; Thweatt, 1980).

In the attempt to see divorce in more benign terms, because of its increasing prevalence, and to "normalize" the process by conceptualizing it as though it were like "normal" bereavement, professionals in the field have minimized the important differences between divorce and bereavement. Briscoe and Smith (1975) compared depressive symptomatology as manifested in divorce, bereavement, and nonreactive depression. They noted many important differences between the symptoms of the divorced and the bereaved, particularly in affect manifestation. The divorced individuals displayed significantly more anger in the form of projection, irritability, and suicidal ideation. Significantly more of the divorced depressives saw a psychiatrist as an outpatient or were hospitalized for their depression then did the bereaved group. In direct contrast to those who would see divorce as the grief response to a crisis situation, these investigators concluded that no distinct syndrome, such as bereavement or grief reaction, could be identified for divorce.

An important distinction is that, while the death of a spouse very likely precipitates depression similar to bereavement, divorce can be the cause or the result of depression, as was discussed in Chapter One. If the latter is the case, one can see how carefully presumed assumptions break down in regard to the temporal phases predicted for separation and attachment loss. The personal and interpersonal problems an individual brings to a marriage are not necessarily solved by a divorce. Nor are confusion about identity, depression over presumed personal and interpersonal failure, and anxiety and unhappiness with oneself and one's life necessarily resolved through the stages of mourning and object loss.

The object loss in divorce may be more conflictual than that experienced in the death of a spouse because typically it involves a purposeful and active rejection by another person. The person who did the rejection and abandonment does live and remains a daily symbol of the rejection (Bohannan, 1971b). Moreover, with that individual remains a possibility for reunion and for reunion fantasies, particularly for children, but also for the spouse. Divorce, unlike death, allows for the continued availability of the parent for intense living out of both conflict and longing.

In bereavement one is allowed to idealize and romanticize the former spouse or parent and still detach. With divorce, there is a need to focus on the negative aspects of the spouse and the self in order to separate psychologically. While one can rationalize the separation caused by death as "God's will," "his time," "for the best," divorce is still perceived as "something that should not have happened" in the eyes of the participants, the society, and the church. The state and the church provide the bereaved with a formalized funeral ritual, society's way of symbolically recognizing that the loss and the grief is acknowledged and acceptable. The lack of a divorce ritual or socially sanctioned ceremony underlines the lack of societal and cultural support for divorce and the disapproval for its occurrence.

All these factors contribute to making the adjustment process for divorce more complicated and sometimes more extended than the process of grieving the death of a significant other. The stages of grieving proscribed by attachment theory may have relevance for divorce, but may not fit so neatly. Denial, anger, and mourning may be stages with much longer fixation due to both the symbolic availability of the object and because divorce can be the result rather than the cause of a depression. While stage theory in one form or another has been a popular paradigm to explain the process of divorce, other findings support Goode's (1956) original conclusion that there appears to be no one time period in which the majority, much less all divorced individuals, undergo intense personal disorganization and depression (Dasteel, 1982).

The common denominator in divorce and bereavement is adjusting to loss and the new status of being independent. Crisis and attachment theories have helped to provide an understanding of the psychodynamics of the divorce process, from the perspective of dealing with the stress engendered by separation and loss. Therapies dealing with crisis intervention and bereavement incorporate both psychodynamic and behavioral interventions, often in the context of a fairly brief therapeutic encounter. Other researchers and therapists would take this approach one step further and employ treatment methods for dealing with divorce that are essentially more educational than therapeutic, particularly with postdivorce adjustment. The assumption is that divorce is a temporary stress reaction demanding behavioral change, relearning, reeducation, and the acquiring of new skills and coping abilities.

STRUCTURED EDUCATIONAL INTERVENTION

Many researchers and clinicians contend that the trauma of postdivorce adjustment can be effectively eased by using structured intervention approaches (Granvold & Welch, 1979; Kessler, 1978; Langelier & Deckert, 1980; Morris & Prescott, 1975; Welch & Granvold, 1977). The assumption is that individual, family, and/or group psychotherapy may not be the only means of diminishing postdivorce distress. Systematic educational interventions such as assertiveness training, communication skills training, and cognitive restructuring can provide benefits. The format typically employed is a small group or seminar over a period of several weeks duration, each session lasting 2 or more hours, with a specific topic area, in-class exercises, and assigned homework.

Some counselors have employed an unstructured approach within these groups, not initiating topics, but following the conversation and tone of the group, intervening only for clarification (Morris & Prescott, 1975). Such groups might be considered more support groups than educational groups. They provide participants with a sense of commonality, opportunities for mutual problem solving and sharing, and the supportive ventilation of feelings. Education comes from the participants themselves, who act as therapists as well as teachers for one another in regard to new ways of coping with their shared stress. More often, a fairly structured, short-term treatment is utilized, with the counselor(s) clearly in the leader–educator role. There is some evidence for the superiority of the structured approach over the unstructured one in skill-building interventions designed to enhance positive self-assurance and identity (Kessler, 1978).

SKILL BUILDING

Developing interpersonal, communication, and social skills in divorce adjustment groups can involve such procedures as role playing, nonverbal exercises, directed reading, writing, keeping a journal, and giving feedback as well as the use of problem-solving and decision-making exercises plus value clarification vignettes (Langelier & Deckert, 1980; Thiessen, Avery, & Joanning, 1980). Members are asked to participate actively in the exercises and afterwards to discuss them.

Films and tape recordings may also provide the stimulus for discussion. Kessler and Whiteley have developed an educational package for this kind of structured skill-building approach to postdivorce adjustment. For example, one film vignette portrays a mother chiding her daughter on the phone: "As your mother, you know all I care about is your happiness. I haven't told you this before but your Dad and I have had rough times. But we took our marriage vows seriously. Why don't you stick with him . . ." (Kessler, 1978, p. 211). The film illustrates the guilt-inducing encounters with parents and in-laws often faced by a divorcing person and is designed to trigger feelings and memories in the group. This leads into a structured assertive training exercise where the members can practice assertive responses to the vignette, as well as role play other conflictual situations they have had with family or friends, again practicing assertive responses (Kessler, 1978). Another typical format is to use a short introductory lecture, followed by facilitators giving experiential and didactic training in particular skills, for example, communication, empathy, or self-disclosure (Thiessen *et al.*, 1980).

The social and communication skills approach was designed to help the divorced person regain self-esteem and acquire a new social network. Building skills in other specific areas of concern for the divorced, such as managing finances, budgeting, job hunting, and dealing with children as a single parent also can be addressed. Educating divorcing individuals in regard to their legal rights, having them prepare weekly and monthly budget outlines, referral to continuing education and vocational resources, singles associations, for example, Parents without Partners, and the use of bibliotherapy to help clarify the divorce process are all special educational, didactic strategies designed to meet specific problem areas.

COGNITIVE RESTRUCTURING

Other structured, educational approaches for dealing with divorcing individuals emphasize the cognitive reorientation that must accompany behavioral changes. The rationale underlying this approach presumes that postdivorce adjustment inherently involves emotional accommodation and cognitive restructuring, as well as behavioral change (Granvold & Welch, 1977). The paradigm is derived from cognitive-behavioral therapy, but is presented in a more educational than therapeutic format, employing a seminar as well as small group process, modeling, behavior rehearsal, and the use of homework assignments. Topics for the weekly seminars might include the emotional impact of separation/divorce, the continuing relationship with the ex-spouse, the impact of family and friends, relationships with children, work, dating, and sexual adjustment. Utilizing Ellis's (1962) rational–emotive therapy (RET), the seminar goals of cognitive restructuring involve altering negative cognitive set, as well as dealing with irrational assumptions and dysfunctional internal verbalizations.

The modeling process involves the facilitator–leader assuming the role of the participant whose problem is under consideration. The participant plays the role of interactor while the remaining group members either play significant others in the situation or observe the interaction. Irrational components of one's responses and irrational assumptions about the world are actively confronted and challenged in this approach, for example, the erroneous assumption that it is a dire necessity to be loved by the ex-spouse. A key assumption in this approach is that nearly all instances of unhappiness are due to internal thoughts as well as to external events, and that understanding the tenets of rational judgment is a requisite for corrective mediation and resultant behavior change (Granvold & Welch, 1979).

This chapter has attempted to trace the theoretical roots of divorce therapy as practiced today. Family and marital therapy, as conceptualized in analytic and intergenerational modes, have provided a developmental perspective from which to address the fundamental issues of separation and identity that divorce raises. Systems theory views divorce, like marriage, in a contextual as well as an intrapsychic framework; one can literally never "divorce" oneself from the culture and larger system in which divorce derives its meaning. Crisis intervention theory has been useful for understanding the divorce process as a reactive response to intense stress, and attachment and grief theory help predict the sequence of emotional responses to object loss and eventual detachment. Structured educational interventions emphasize the skill building and cognitive restructuring that can be helpful in achieving a successful adjustment to divorce.

In the following chapter an approach to divorce therapy is presented that finds its roots in several theoretical perspectives. This approach basically is a developmental one and the specific model is derived from family life cycle development. The restructuring of identity following loss, particularly in terms of role theory, is a key element in this perspective. Understanding the narcissistic injury that results from object loss and the accompanying loss of self-esteem are other key components. While elements of crisis intervention, grief therapy, and structured behavioral change are to be found in the actual implementation of this model, the approach is a therapeutic rather than an educational one and emphasizes psychodynamic as well as cognitive behavioral factors in therapy.

Chapter Three

Divorce and the Life Cycle:
A Developmental Framework

In marriage one expects love, loyalty, and commitment from a highly invested loved object. From the significant other, a person also expects to receive a basic confirmation of self-worth, ability to be loved, and life meaning. The dissolution of the bond and the explosion of the fantasy of marital continuance can generate intense feelings of betrayal, failure, and the loss of self-esteem. The greater the emotional investment in this dream, in marriage as an institution to fulfill personal identity, the greater the potential stress and conflict in divorce.

It is not surprising then that divorce and its psychic aftermath commonly have been perceived in fairly negative terms: as stressful, conflictual, problematic, and as a crisis, loss, break-up, or dissolution. The divorce therapist may employ techniques of mediation to deal with the conflict, crisis management to deal with the stress, grief therapy to help with the loss and depression. However, in emphasizing the conflict and the stress of divorce and its management in divorce therapy, too often the potential for positive change and personal developmental transformation is minimized. Divorce is a marker event like other key powerful crossroads in one's life, such as leaving home, marrying, committing to a life's work, or the death of a parent. It involves very significant stress, but it also offers important, if not unique, opportunities for understanding previous growth or its lack, and for resolving prior personal and interpersonal conflict. Divorce can lead to the transformation of key paradigms, basic lifetime developmental tasks that are redefined and renegotiated, permitting the individual and/or a family to move on developmentally.

A life cycle developmental perspective offers a promising approach to understanding the psychological predispositions to divorce. Divorce therapy based on such a perspective helps people to traverse the difficult passage of divorce successfully and to use the experience for personality transformation. This approach emphasizes the interaction of individual and interpersonal change and the working through of problems and conflicts associated with such change. It assumes, however, that these problems will be worked through again in different form down the road, and emphasizes the benefits of that constant working through process.

The underlying premise here is that key developmental milestones are never simply grappled with, solved, and put to rest once and for all, simply because one leaves home and becomes self-supporting. Nor do you solve the basic task of experiencing intimacy by finding a nice person to marry who says "I love you." Similarly one does not necessarily solve identity issues of becoming a separate person simply by divorcing the person you believe is holding you back from autonomy. As will be outlined later, the two key life cycle tasks, intimacy and identity, are grappled with continuously throughout the life cycle, and any marker event such as marriage or divorce has the potential to redefine and transform both of these tasks.

The view of divorce presented in this chapter is based on the premise that divorce can be integrated into individual, marital, and family life cycle expectations and processes. Some adult development theorists do not agree with the use of a psychopathological framework to describe the conflictual period and stressful tasks of divorce. Nonetheless a promarriage bias remains in much of the developmental literature, for example, the notion "that marriages that continue are more likely to be contributing to adult unfolding, and marriages that end are less likely to be contributing to adult unfolding" (Vines, 1979, p. 12). These views are based on the assumption that divorce is most likely to be the product of psychological disturbance that leads to marital dysfunction. Another implicit assumption is that the decision to stay married has more potential for adult development than the decision to divorce. A more value-free approach would be open to the possibility that both marriage and divorce can generate adult unfolding or, conversely, block individual development, depending on a multitude of factors.

Much of the family life cycle literature assumes that the typical nuclear family continues unbroken through all its various normal stages, until one parent dies. When one considers how very few families today fit this normative presumption, the model seems inadequate. Messinger and Walker (1981) note that the development of a family life cycle model incorporating the stages of divorce and remarriage would be a tremendous help to those who work with families. Carter and McGoldrick (1980) are to be commended for beginning efforts in this direction. Yet even these authors characterize divorce in largely negative terms, listing it along with illness, disability, death, and catastrophe as a "paranormative event," in the family life cycle.

[Normative events] occur regularly in the vast majority of family units, arising directly from procreative and childrearing functions. . . . [Paranormative events] are mediated by conflict, illness, extrinsic circumstances or combinations of these and include a) miscarriage, b) marital separation and divorce, c) illness, disability and death, and relocations of household, e) changes in socio-economic status and f) extrinsic catastrophe with massive dislocation of the family unit. (p. 41)

As the incidence of divorce approaches half of all new marriages in the society, perhaps we need to rethink what is "normative" behavior. Nor of course are the "normative events" arising from procreative and child-rearing functions conflict free as contrasted to other stressful family life events like divorce and separation. Therapists, educators, lawyers, health professionals, and others who work with families, as well as families themselves, need to better understand these particular milestones, to predict them, and to help themselves and others traverse them successfully.

THE MARITAL PATTERN: OLD AND NEW

A more realistic appraisal of divorce in the developmental life span begins from an examination of when marriage typically occurs in the individual life cycle, and how the marital and individual tasks are uniquely intertwined. Cultural, socioeconomic, and biological forces have interacted to influence the place and the timing of marriage in western culture.

In our society people generally marry in the early to postadolescent years, from about ages 19 to 24. This pattern has maximum biosocial benefits in terms of being the best physiological period for safe gestation and reproduction. Marrying in this period has served most efficiently society's need for procreation and cultural maintenance and survival. Medical advances, better nutrition and health care, and more women having work commitments have acted to delay and extend the safe period of first pregnancy. Nonetheless the safest optimum biological time for pregnancy is still in one's 20s, and maximal fertility for both males and females occurs at age 24 (Hook, Cross, & Schreinemachers, 1983), which in part accounts for the likelihood of marriage at this time.

Marriage during this developmental period also serves the function of a convenient and socially approved place to go when one is no longer a child, when there are younger children who are more demanding of the parents, and when the parents have "had it" with parenting, desiring a separation and independence from their children. The institution of marriage also provides a socially sanctioned milestone that signals emergence into adulthood. Traditionally it is part of the rite of passage into adult responsibility and independence.

Social, biological, and cultural factors have acted to propel people into marriage typically during postadolescence. Yet this period is hardly a developmentally stable one, conducive to future relationship longevity and best mate selection. People marry in their early 20s, but still have a major portion of their growing up to do. The subsequent process of individuation and personal change often results in the two individuals growing apart.

In the past, significant economic considerations, cultural norms and ethnic, social, and religious sanctions prohibited people from seeking separation when they grew apart psychologically, morally, or socially. Both partners may have realized that their original mate choice, while perhaps appropriate at the time of marriage, was no longer a positive one. Yet, people stayed in a unfulfilling marriage despite personal unhappiness and the blocking of their own psychological growth. Less devastating economic consequences, particularly for women, and the culturally approved goal of seeking individual fulfillment have led to reduced legal or social prohibitions regarding divorce.

Divorce, like leaving home and separating from one's parents, can be viewed as a further opportunity to move toward ego differentiation and individuation. While it is true that some partnerships end because of psychological dysfunction in the individual and/or neurotic interaction in the dyad, all divorce cannot be blamed on individual or couple pathology. Nearly half of all first marriages currently can be expected to go on to a divorce and a remarriage. It seems more realistic and less biased to come to terms with the fact that our society is experiencing a widespread sociocultural phenomenon and a very common, stressful, but critical human experience that has developmental impact. Divorce then must be integrated theoretically and experientially into our ideas about normal life cycle development.

There is rarely a divorce without significant personal stress; facing and working through conflict and stress can represent the path to personal growth. If the person has gained greater understanding into his or her functioning, values, attitudes, morals, interests, traits, and/or goals in life as a result of the decision to uncouple, then the developmental benefits can be significant. Furthermore, if the individual has attained a historical appreciation of the impact of early developmental building blocks, then the decision to recouple can lead to further personal and interpersonal gain.

The second match is also more likely to be a closer one and perhaps a more lasting one as the person moves into a more stable period of adulthood. During this time personal insights can be deeper, goal achievement more realized, and personal limitations more accepted. A crucial task for the divorce therapist is to maximize the potential of this decision and this period for differentiation and positive separation, viewing it, like the separation from parents, as another stressful, but crucial step in the process of individuation.

IS SEPARATION NECESSARY TO DEVELOPMENT?

Two caveats are in order. The notion that all people must divorce in order to continue to grow psychologically, and that all divorce necessarily represents the right solution in terms of fostering personal and interpersonal growth, is not being advocated here. With regard to the first point, it is interesting to consider how in western culture we have come to believe almost universally that the leaving of parents and generational separation is a sign of adulthood and psychological health. Separation from parents, a "divorce" in a sense, or "firing" one's parents from their job, is considered mandatory to further development into adulthood. Yet historically and cross-culturally a somewhat different picture emerges. Children in many parts of the world have been and still are expected to live with and pay deference and subordination to the primary family for much longer periods, even after marriage. One might be "adult" in terms of productivity and economic contribution; however, the full status of adulthood, as defined by independence of decision, action, and respect, does not accrue until one becomes the actual oldest adult in the household, typically in one's 50s or later. Even then, separation by leaving the extended family is not necessarily a mark of more mature development in certain cultures.

By leaving one's parents physically at a much earlier age, one is expected in our society to attain full independence of action and decision, as well as cultural respect, in one's 20s and 30s. Despite physical separation, which may involve a city block or thousands of miles, emotional separation may not be nearly as effective or apparent. In divorce, the physical act of separation, while symbolizing independence of action, does not necessarily also herald an emotional autonomy and a corresponding developmental milestone.

It will be argued later in this chapter that separation is a key task of development necessary to identity formation. However, there are many forms of separation at various points in the life cycle, and in each period the meaning of separation is redefined and transformed. Separation also can be fully understood only in juxtaposition to its dynamic opposite, communion, that is, a coming together.

Separation and individuation do not have to mean rejection. In other cultures, a psychologically healthy person may be expected to retain and to incorporate most of the parental values, goals, and attitudes, subordinating individual hopes, aspirations, or ideas to the family or societal good. The benefit that enabled many people to accept prohibitions on individual differentiation (against family, racial, ethnic, gender, or class lines) was a sense of belonging and security. There have also been societal punishments for breaking those traditions. The price of obtaining social stability, family lineage, ethnic or gender identity, and class distinctions has been decreased individual differentiation and choice.

Similarly, the maintenance and promotion of the marital bond, like the original parental bond, has largely acted to serve the greater good. Intact marriages promote societal welfare. They help maintain class lines, parental lineage, economic status, and religious power and influence within a culture. Likewise an intact family has greater influence, status and power as a subforce within a society. The trade off for submerging individual identity in the marital dyad, like the parental dyad, is a sense of security. In return for adherence to the promotion of couple welfare or family good, perhaps at the expense of individual benefit, one is promised emotional and economic security as well as societal and institutional approval.

In the ideal adult development paradigm, the individual would not have to reject parents or spouse in order to "grow up." One could incorporate values and learnings from any key experience. This inoculation would include incidents from childhood, where one is under parental aegis, and those from postadolescence, where one seeks further development in the accompaniment of a spouse figure who alternates between peer and parent. Ideally, one could handle both these developmental experiences not through damaging rebellion (in the sense that leaving home or getting a divorce may represent an acting out or escape), but by transcendence, wherein prior experiences are incorporated and transformed into a new maturing experience.

GROWING IN OR OUT OF MARRIAGE

People who divorce and those who decide to stay married may do so for neurotic as well as for healthy reasons. Some people manage to change in tandem with their spouses, for example, growing up together if they have married young. It is a tricky business to explore successfully one's own identity through the personality of another. To do so requires several necessary and fortunate conditions. The first is the positive circumstance of having enough personal flexibility and adaptation to permit both partners not only to recognize and value change in themselves, but also to encourage it in their spouse.

Vaillant (1977), in his longitudinal study of 95 men and the process of their adult development, concluded that adaptation equals health. The ability to move adaptively through transition periods differentiated the men who were able to sustain happy long-term marriages from those who were not. Related requirements are that one have enough ego-strength not to be threatened by the necessity of change and transition, and the desire, once seeing change and growth in one's spouse, to also desire to change oneself. A most crucial and sometimes fortuitous circumstance is that both spouses change in directions that are not antithetical, if not parallel or complementary. Necessary compromise that does not inhibit personal integrity can then be achieved at modest cost to the individual development of both partners. Such compromise permits them to continue to commit and couple while not blocking further individual or dyad autonomy and unfolding.

A second group of married couples stay together perhaps for less positive reasons. Cultural, economic, or religious prohibitions act to inhibit dissolution, or their denial defenses are so strong that the marital distancing is not recognized. They rationalize their marriage in terms other than its existence for growth, happiness, or fulfillment. Individuation is either mutually blocked in collusive efforts, or one or both persons grow outside of the marriage, but not in tandem. Individual psychotherapy with one partner may act to promote this state of affairs.

A growing number of people, for the reasons discussed in Chapter One, refuse to rationalize the distance or lack of personal fulfillment in their marriage. Marital expectations tend to be high in our society. One wants and feels entitled to both personal and marital fulfillment. When a marriage comes apart because two people do not grow together, move in noncompatible directions, or are frozen in an iceberg of stagnant inertia, then divorce indeed can be a powerful and ultimately positive release of energy and development.

When there are significant interlocking developmental blocks, the decision to divorce is more problematic. Unless the individual and dyad dysfunction is explored and worked through, divorce may offer no long-term solution and the person is likely to repeat the scenario in future relationships. Perhaps the most difficult and critical task of the divorce therapist is to appreciate and sensitively assess this state of affairs. It consists of two parts. The first involves the assessment of whether the marital difficulties are seen as involving significant interlocking psycho-pathology. Secondly, the therapist needs to ascertain whether the individual developmental blocks might be transcended successfully within the marital system, or whether indeed separation may represent the best choice for the future growth of both individuals.

One does marital therapy as long as one is working toward the understanding and removal of such blocks with the goal of improving the marriage. During such a time there should still be sufficient good will, affection, and the modicum of trust and hope necessary to work toward rebonding rather than dissolution. When these feelings have eroded to the point of sustained intense anger or to indifference, the direction of therapy changes. The therapist now is helping the person to make the decision of whether to divorce and how to do so successfully. The goal of therapy then becomes understanding the dissolution of the marriage and transcending the experience developmentally. At this point one is doing divorce therapy, although the critical work of the predivorce therapy period may technically still be marital therapy.

In reality the transition to divorce therapy is often shifty until one partner decides to ask for the divorce and or to move out. A less common scenario is for both partners, already having made the decision to divorce, to come to a therapist for help in easing the transition. Even when an individual or a couple comes in specifically asking for help in mediating a divorce or dealing with a hostile ex-spouse or children, the task of the therapist is not only to provide behavioral tools with which to ameliorate the hostilities and make the decisions, but also to help each person in the family move along developmentally through this transition. Therapeutic strategies in the decision-making period of divorce therapy will be discussed more fully in Chapter Six.

SECOND-ORDER CHANGE AND DIVORCE

It is important for divorce therapists to adopt a developmental framework and incorporate principles of individual developmental change into their work. If divorce therapy is defined simply as involving the mediation of interpersonal conflict or the working through of grief, one has basically only a first-order change situation. That is, the surface manifestations have changed; for example, economic and/or custody issues are settled on the surface. However, no significant change in the individual's personal functioning or interpersonal system may have been effected. The person is either still struggling with a particular developmental task and redefinition or is in a state of repeating with other people scenarios that reenact the developmental struggle.

Divorce represents second-order change only when the person is able to redefine and transcend the developmental task of separation. To achieve second-order change the divorce therapist needs to attend not only to immediate needs for conflict negotiation and crisis intervention, but also to personal and interpersonal restructuring that permit the individual to transcend the experience and to learn from it. "Reframing" the divorce for the client, as not a failure but as a positive step toward risk and change, can lead to significant second-order change.

In summary, separation and divorce can be realistically viewed by the therapist as increasingly common milestones in adult development that bring the potential for both stress and growth. The decision to marry and the decision to divorce frequently come in life cycle stages of development where attachment and commitment are key issues. Either choice has the potential to enhance or to disrupt the resolving and redefining of these developmental tasks. In the next section of this chapter an attempt will be made to integrate divorce as a developmental marker event in the life cycle, from an individual, marital, and family perspective, and to view such perspectives in terms of their key developmental tasks, separation and communion.

LIFE CYCLE THEORY AND DIVORCE

Recent writings on adult development, the marital life cycle and the family life cycle all owe a heavy intellectual debt to the pioneering work of Erik Erikson. Sociological conceptions of the developmental tasks of the family and marital life cycle (Duvall, 1971; Rodgers & Hill, 1964; Vines, 1979) as well as certain therapeutic applications (Haley, 1973; Minuchin, 1974; Rapoport, 1965; Rhodes, 1977) tend to be essentially Eriksonian in nature. The premise is that successful completion of early developmental tasks leads to successful completion of later ones. A parallel correlate is that failure to complete early stages leads to problems with later ones. The work on adult development by Levinson and coworkers (1978), Gould (1978), and others (Lidz, 1968; Neugarten & Datan, 1974) has flowed from Erikson's theories of psychosocial development.

Erikson's model is based on the concept of epigenesis, borrowed from embryology. During human physical development each organ has a particular time frame and origin. Different organs undergo a growth spurt at different times during the life of the embryo. If development fails to proceed at the genetically determined time, the organism will fail to develop properly. If the organ begins to develop at the appropriate time but its growth is stunted or modified, its essential nature will not be destroyed. Normal development of each organ is interactive; for example, the heart and lungs are balanced in size and development (Erikson, 1963).

This analogy is used to explain personality development. The theory is basically psychoanalytic in nature; all of the stages of personality growth are presumed to have their origins in early childhood. The main "growth spurts," Erikson's "Eight Stages of Man," are spread out over the life span. Each stage involves the solving of a particular life crisis, which is never solved completely but lays the foundation for the successful coping with the next stage and task. The tasks that characterize the particular life stages have what are known as positive or "syntonic" features as well as negative or "dystonic" tendencies. Both qualities are necessary to full functioning and it is the balance of these two aspects that is important (Erikson, 1983). For example, in old age, ego integrity, the acceptance of one's life, is contrasted with despair, the feeling that time is too short to try out alternative life paths.

It's exactly a matter of balance, but we avoid the terms "positive" and "negative." Sometimes what we call the "dystonic tendency" can have positive aspects. For example, during old age the life crisis involves the conflict between integrity and despair. How could anybody have integrity and not also despair about certain things in his own life, about the human condition? Even if your own life was absolutely beautiful and wonderful, the fact that so many people were exploited or ignored must make you feel some despair. (Erikson, 1983, p. 27)

The eight stages of personal development as explained by Erikson are (1) trust versus mistrust in infancy; (2) autonomy versus shame and doubt in early childhood; (3) initative versus guilt in childhood; (4) industry versus inferiority in children of school age; (5) identity versus role confusion in adolescence; (6) intimacy versus isolation in young adulthood; (7) generativity versus stagnation in middle adulthood; and (8) ego integrity versus despair in old age. Erikson's emphasis was on the early years of development, which are much more detailed than the later years. The first six stages describe what is now the first half of life, while only two are devoted to the second half. Levinson and colleagues (1974) expanded these notions, delineating seven stages to the years between postadolescence (18-21) and older age (60 and over). The last 20 years of life, which now may represent a whole quarter of one's life, are still not that detailed or well defined by any of the life cycle theorists.

MARITAL LIFE CYCLE AND DIVORCE

Individual and marital development are very closely entwined. Berman and Lief (1975) have attempted to relate the marital life cycle to individual developmental tasks, based on Levinson's stages of adult development (1974). In stage 1, "pulling up roots," 18 to 21 years of age, the individual task is to develop some personal autonomy, and the marital one is to shift from family of origin to a new interpersonal commitment. The original family bonding may conflict with adapting successfully in this stage. In stage 2, "provisional adulthood," 22 to 28 years, the individual task is to gain entry into the adult world by developing intimacy and some work identification. These two stages strongly parallel Erikson's formulation of his stage 5, "identity versus role confusion" in late adolescence and stage 6, "intimacy versus isolation" in young adulthood.

Berman and Lief's "transition at age 30" marks stage 3 (29 to 31 years) when one must decide whether to commit to work and/or marriage and doubts about one's choices come into sharper conflict. Stage 4 (32 to 39 years) represents a "settling down" period; the individual task is to deepen one's commitments and to plan and pursue long-range goals, while the marital task is one of meshing commitments to children and spouse and productively fulfilling both responsibilities (not unsimilar to Erikson's notion of generativity).

The fifth period of "midlife transition" (40 to 42 years) is another brief, but critical stage. Here the individual searches for the fit between his or her aspirations and the reality of the environment. Maritally, there is a summing up, and evaluation of the successes and failures of the relationship. Both these tasks lead into the next period of "middle adulthood" (43 to 59 years) when one needs to restabilize, to reorder priorities and, maritally, to resolve conflicts and stabilize the marriage for the long haul. Finally at stage 7 "older age" (60 years or more) the person must deal with aging, illness, and death while retaining a zest for life and, in the marital relationship, support and enhance one another in that struggle.

In this paradigm, while provision is made for the shift from the family of origin to the new marital commitment, this is the only individual separation that is developmentally marked and approved. For example, in stage 3, "rates of growth" may diverge if one spouse has not successfully negotiated stage 2 because of parental obligations (Berman & Lief, 1975, p. 586). No other major individual separation like that engendered by divorce is integrated into this model of adult development.

The model also presumes one major lifetime relationship, one marriage, one commitment. Indeed the successful passage from stages 2 and 3 of the marital life cycle into the later stages of development is predicated on the assumption that a lifetime commitment will be successfully negotiated and implemented. The individual and marital tasks of establishing autonomy, intimacy, commitment, and generativity are defined mainly through bonding, rather than through a cycle of bonding, separating, and rebonding, a common phenomenon in society today. A similar state of affairs can be seen in an examination of the family life cycle literature based on Eriksonian principles.

THE FAMILY LIFE CYCLE

Haley (1973) is the family theorist who originally articulated the importance of the concept of the family life cycle to the therapist. He describes six stages through which families pass: courtship, marriage, childbirth and child raising, middle marriage, launching children, and retirement and old age. The demarcation of these periods is not dissimilar to the individual and marital life cycle paradigms discussed previously. The family life cycle stages overlap many of the individual and marital ones, but they are defined primarily by the presence or absence of children and the state of the child's development, for example, "child raising" and "children leaving home." The family developmental tasks of these periods also have been elaborated by Rhodes (1977). The courtship and marriage stage of Haley's family life cycle embody the "intimacy versus idealization or disillusionment" struggle. The major task of the dyadic family prior to the advent of children is the formation of a relationship durable enough to withstand later stresses. The formulation parallels Erikson's idea that the essential task of the individual in young adulthood is to achieve intimacy in love and friendship, as opposed to isolation. "Idealization" refers to the childlike projection of unrealistic qualities onto the partner in the flush of being in love. "Disillusionment" means the gradual abandonment of those fantasies. One must work through both idealization and disillusionment to achieve intimacy.

Child bearing and raising apply to the second stage of the family life cycle beginning with the birth of the first child and ending when the last child enters school. The theme of the period is termed "replenishment versus turning inward," referring to the struggle to nurture family members without either an abandonment or imperviousness to one's or the family's needs. With the last child entering school comes the third period of the family life cycle, middle marriage. Here the task is to balance the individuation of family members against pseudomutual familial organization.

Pseudomutual families are characterized by the fear that the individual differentiation of family members is fairly dangerous. One can survive in the outside world only by a suffocating attachment to the family at the expense of independence. As the children become teenagers, the pertinent task for both the children and parents rests on their ability to develop companionship outside and inside the family. The alternative to developing friendships with peers and/or through a revitalized marital relationship is to suffer isolation and an invasion of the adolescents' lives, impeding their natural disengagement.

The next two stages of the family life cycle are defined by children leaving or having left home. The launching stage describes those families whose children are leaving home to establish their own lives apart from their parents. The family task is to negotiate "regrouping versus binding or expulsion." Maturing children are allowed to depart without premature excommunication for their rebellion, or overprotection that would bind them even further. After the last child departs, the family task involves the theme of "rediscovery versus despair." Rhodes (1977) notes that rediscovery refers to the couple's renegotiating their relationship divested of the parenting role, and redefining the relationship with the children, now adults. The family that has restabilized by developing new relationships with their adult children does not feel amputated or depressed by their disengagement.

The last stage of the family life cycle, "retirement and old age" refers to the period from the parents' retirement to their death; the parents are now likely to be grandparents and the children to be parents. The developmental theme and task, "mutual aid versus uselessness" is similar to

Erikson's "ego integrity versus despair," an opportunity for intergenerational support and help.

THE BIAS OF FAMILY LIFE CYCLE THEORY

Current family life cycle theory is based on the premise that there are children born to the marital union. Very little has been written about the family *without* children, perhaps implying that it is not a family at all, for family is defined as consisting of more than an adult dyad. The typical labeling of the stages, for example, "beginning families," "child-raising families," "families as launching centers," and "aging families" (Carter & McGoldrick, 1980; Hughes, Berger, & Wright, 1978) are all defined by presence or absence of the children. Thus the traditional family life cycle model has little to say about the childless couple or the person who may "parent" in nonbiological roles.

The traditional family life cycle model also does not adequately address the situation of serial marriage, divorce, and the remarried family. A key assumption is that the successful family is one in which the intact original family raises and launches the original set of children step by step through the previously outlined stages. In reality such families are decreasing in number and the family is more and more likely to be a blended or reconstituted family through death, separation, and/or divorce. A more useful approach to understanding the family life cycle would be to think of a conceptualization that is (1) less dependent on the implicit presence of children; (2) not necessarily defined by the presence and interaction of the original participants, and (3) less based on the assumption that successful family life development means unbroken movement through a series of struggles defined largely by the birth of the first child to the leaving of the last.

The assumption of epigenesis breaks down when it is unilaterally applied to the remarried family. The stages of family life may not be nearly as discrete, well defined, or definitively linked and dependent on preceding developments. A blended family may return to the child-bearing stage with a new child born to the union, despite one spouse being at the "launching stage" that is, having a teenager from the prior marriage. The parent may successfully launch the teenager, but have problems raising the new child from the present union. It is also possible that the previously unmarried stepparent might help to complete the launching task with the teenager successfully without having prior experience in the child bearing and rearing stages. Also the divorced parents themselves may not be in tandem in family life cycle tasks as assumed by the model. For example, one parent may be "in retirement," that is, having finished with raising adult children. In another case, one parent may never have wanted or had children and preferred to abdicate or minimize the parenting role. In both cases, the other spouse in the blended family essentially rears the children from his or her former marriage alone. The family life cycle tasks for these two individuals are not necessarily the same nor are they parallel, as in an intact original family.

INTIMACY AND IDENTITY

A more useful approach to delineating a life cycle model applicable to the divorced and/or remarried, as well as perhaps to the married, would be to use, incorporate, and explicate general concepts of development such as separation/union and individuation/communion instead of stages of child rearing. These key developmental tasks are ones that all family members must accomplish at various points within the different marriages and families, but they may recur and need to be reworked and redefined in different temporal order. Like the first marriage and the divorce, the next marriage and/or family may represent both a threatening, fearful situation, blocking further personal development and an opportunity to go on to new levels of individual and interpersonal growth.

While an Eriksonian framework has been extremely valuable in better understanding individual adult development, it is less useful in explicating marital and family life cycle development. A major difficulty with this approach as originally articulated and applied to contemporary ideas about marriage and family life is the basic assumption of multiple discrete and different tasks for each period of development. The assumptions are that a viable lifetime partner choice is made, children are born and raised and an unbroken family concludes its individual, marital, and family tasks and changes in logical, linear order, for example, trust, autonomy, initiative, industry, identity, intimacy, generativity, and ego integrity. Yet the family is a complex system and changes within the family are more likely to occur in discontinuous leaps than in a smooth, unbroken line (Hoffman, 1980).

A NEW DEVELOPMENTAL FORMULATION

A more parsimonious model of life cycle development is based on the assumption that there are but two key tasks of all human development, and that they recur over and over again, but with different meanings at each period of life. These two key concepts will be labeled *intimacy*, where the key task is *communion*, that is, being able to be close to another individual, and *identity*, where the key task is successful *separation* or individuation. Intimacy depends largely on successful communion with others, based on trust, respect, compassion, communication, and cooperation. Identity is defined largely by separation and differentiation of self from others through autonomy, independence, industry, and ego integrity. These two tasks appear to supersede and subsume the other tasks. They are basic to all human development. The goal is to be close, yet separate; to be intimate, yet autonomous; to find the "self," yet merge with the "other."

At each period of life, these two concepts, intimacy and identity, and their core tasks, communion and separation, occur again and again, with different meanings at each period. At each stage they are reworked, redefined, and transformed. The adequate solution for one period of life may not be the best one for the next. Each period of life can require a redefinition of intimacy, moving from the intense dependency on and love for and from a parent, from selfish love to peer love, to committed love for a nonfamilial figure, to generative love for one's biological children and finally, to a sense of global intimacy, a feeling of love for the world and the species.

The individual, marital, and family life cycle tasks that take their unique meanings from these two key concepts are interwoven throughout the lifespan. One affects the other and vice versa. It is necessary to appreciate fully the place and tasks of marital and family development before one truly can understand the individual. Similarly, the individual's place and tasks in the life cycle influence the development and task of the marital and family life cycle.

Key marker events such as marriage, divorce and remarriage can be viewed and appreciated from a perspective that considers the two basic life tasks, communion and separation, and how these tasks take on different meanings and have different solutions in the individual, marital, and family life cycles. Each marker event brings both stress and conflict, as well as the potential for further development and refining of the two key tasks. Divorce, like leaving home, marriage, childbirth, retirement, and death, is a marker event, one in which the individual and the family must grapple with and redefine the meaning of intimacy and identity and transform it. Hoffman (1980) notes that a period of stress and disruption is the prelude to what we call a "transformation."

At each of these marker events the interaction between the key tasks of separation and communion must be appreciated and transformed to fit the requirements of the stage of life. For example, at the beginning of a marriage, one's identity often is merged with that of another. The ability to be intimate in a sense primarily defines one's identity, at least in this particular developmental phase. Communion at this stage takes precedence over separation. Identity is defined more by communion than by separation, yet paradoxically in the prior stage of adolescence and postadolscence, identity is defined more by the ability to separate.

This model is not a linear one as is the life cycle approach that has been adapted from the Eriksonian framework. It is assumed, for example, that while successful prior completion of developmental tasks likely aids the completion of later ones, the sequence is not rigid. The interactional process is more important than the task, and the task does not have to be begun in one particular developmental period and worked through in another. The tasks of finding intimacy and identity, of blending communion and separation, are lifetime tasks, to be reworked, redefined, and transformed over and over in the lifespan.

The Eriksonian framework is essentially a psychoanalytic one and a key premise regarding development is biologically based and deals with the absolute influence of early childhood experiences and mastery; trust needs to be achieved before autonomy, identity before intimacy. In the framework being proposed, the tasks may interchange; there is some room for flexibility or multidimensionality. The best adaptation may require just such interchangeability, depending on the life stage. For example, as a child the intimacy one develops with a loving parent is a likely and necessary precursor to later successful individual identity formation that begins in adolescence and develops more fully in young adulthood. The temporal sequence of these two key tasks would be intimacy before identity; communion with one's parents leading to separation from one's parents. In the next period of life, young adulthood, the most productive sequence of tasks is the reverse. A separate identity is usually thought of as the best prerequisite to being able to couple and be intimate without threat and conflict.

Paradoxically, in divorce it is the very breakdown of intimacy, of the task of communion, that may lead to a better defined individual identity. The key developmental task of separation in divorce is utilized to achieve differentiation of self. Divorce is likely to be most beneficial when one does not seek immediately to replace another partner with whom to be intimate, but instead begins to understand and to define oneself alone. A very common mistake people make following divorce is a hasty and premature recoupling and remarriage, never allowing themselves the crucial time to complete needed developmental tasks of individuation. The therapeutic implications of this phenomenon will be discussed in Chapter Eight.

Table 2 summarizes this model of life cycle development, based on the two concepts of identity and intimacy and their related and interacting tasks, communion and separation. Secondly, the table indicates how these tasks are perceived, redefined, and transcended by the key marker event of divorce. To understand Table 2 it is necessary to keep in mind the following basic assumptions of this model:

1. There are two global concepts in all human development: intimacy and identity. The key task in achieving intimacy is communion; the key task in achieving identity is separation.

2. The basic themes of intimacy and identity recur over and over again, but with different meaning in each period of life. During each period they are redefined, reworked, and transformed, the adaptive solution for one period of life may not be the best one for the next.

3. Intimacy and identity, like communion and separation, are always interrelated; one influences the other. Intimate communion with significant others is closely related to how well one has achieved a separate sense of identity, and, conversely, the healthy sense of separateness that one uses to define individual identity is affected by one's communion with others.

4. Individual, marital, and family life cycles are closely intertwined throughout the life span. The individual, marital, or family task of any period of life takes its unique meaning from the interaction of the two key concepts, intimacy and identity.

5. Marriage, divorce, and remarriage are marker events in the life cycle that have the potential for blocking or impeding individual development in intimacy and identity and, conversely, for stimulating and aiding further development in these areas.

6. The model proposed here is nonlinear and multileveled. While successful prior experience in a life cycle task such as communion or separation may aid successful coping with a later task, the sequence is not rigid, or necessarily additive. Communion and separation and their changing interaction are lifetime tasks. There are opportunities at any stage of the life cycle for successful development in these areas, and the processes involved are worked and reworked over the life span.

7. The meaning of separation and communion and how they are translated on an individual basis is influenced profoundly by historical and cultural variables. The content of the task of separation/communion depends on the society, the time within the society, and how biology and culture interact to define the tasks.

Table 2 summarizes the nature of the intimacy/communion and identity/separation tasks in each major developmental period of the life cycle and indicates how divorce in that period affects the two processes. The periods themselves are defined primarily by the nature of the task of intimacy or identity. As one moves into a new period, the task must be redefined, negotiated, and transformed. The boundary age ranges accompanying each period, while representing convenient guideposts, are very flexible. For example, one commonly thinks of the communion task of young adulthood to be the experience of reciprocal erotic love for another outside the family, yet that event may not occur until later adulthood, if ever. Many women in midlife accomplish the separation tasks

TABLE 2

Definitions of intimacy and identity: Interaction of these two basic developmental themes in the life cycle and the effects of divorce

Developmental period	Intimacy/communion	Effect of divorce on intimacy/communion	Identity/separation	Effect of divorce on identity/separation
Childhood: 1 to 12 years	Intimacy defined by attachment to parent; loving, receiving and feeling love from a parent is the critical task in communion.	*Danger:* Child is cut off or blocked from receiving love from biological parents; natural communion with both parents impeded; intimacy with stepparent expected. *Task:* Both parents must reassure child of their love and not use divorce to impede that communion or distort it. *Development:* Opportunity for communion with other loving parental figures; intimacy with stepparent is redefined as friendship.	Emerging identity begins through exploring the outside world. Separation of self defined through testing one's boundaries against the world. Successful communion with parents aids process.	*Danger:* Child is propelled into premature separation from parents and expected to grow up more quickly and take upon adult tasks and responsibilities. *Task:* Child must be allowed to maintain identification with natural parents and be aided in feeling secure and trusting enough to continue to explore his or her world. *Development:* Child's discovery of boundaries is enriched by presence of extended family or new ways and experience of seeing old family.
Adolescence: 13 to 19 years	The task of communion in this period is redefined by feeling acceptance from people outside the family, peers; gradual disengagement from parental intimacy/communion aided by adolescent's separation efforts.	*Danger:* Adolescent expected to replace love object, ex-spouse, just when he or she needs to detach and is self-preoccupied. *Task:* Allow for rejection of parents and stepparents and don't demand pseudointimacy. *Development:* Attachment to peers and benevolence toward family and stepfamily.	Further development of identity redefined by partial separation from parents; seeing self as different than parents, but like peers. Separation uniquely defined in this period as blending into peer group, but blending out of family.	*Danger:* Overidentification with one parent; rejection of parent and/or stepparent. *Task:* Nonhostile contact maintained with both parents to facilitate realistic appraisal and separation from both. *Development:* Healthy separation from family enhanced by the parents' growing individuation stimulated by divorce.

(continued)

87

TABLE 2 (*Continued*)

Developmental period	Intimacy/communion	Effect of divorce on intimacy/communion	Identity/separation	Effect of divorce on identity/separation
Young adult: 20 to 29 years	Intimacy defined in this period by giving love to a significant other outside the family. The task of communion is to successfully give this love and to feel its reciprocation. There is an exclusive emphasis in the way intimacy is perceived.	*Danger*: Divorce is a response to unrequited narcissistic love expected from parents. *Task*: Come to terms with fantasies of omnipotence, permitting the giving of love and intimacy with another. *Development*: Achieving reciprocal intimacy.	The task of separation from family more fully completed by physical leaving and economic self-sufficiency through work outside the family. For women in particular, identity often subsumed in intimacy and defined through it.	*Danger*: Divorce represents a continuation of the unfinished task of separating from one's parents. *Task*: Separate spouse from parent figure. *Development*: Intimacy task is differentiated from the identity one. Self is seen as separate from parent or spouse.
Adult: 30 to 39 years	Intimacy is further redefined in this period in a deeper meaning; the task of successful communion becomes not just to love, but to commit to another person. Successful separation from original family aids commitment.	*Danger*: Divorce represents a running away from commitment. *Task*: Working through fears of intimacy as defined by commitment. *Development*: Intimacy needs become more realistic, permitting compromise, commitment, and communion.	Identity further redefined by commitment to work and goals outside the family; self-differentiation from new family as well as original family.	*Danger*: Divorce is an exaggerated escape into identity exclusively achieved through work and industry. *Task*: Explore and understand the need for balance of separation and communion, as expressed in work and relationships. *Development*: Enhanced sense of positive separation of self.

88

Midlife: 40 to 54 years	The meaning of intimacy again further redefined; communion becomes going beyond loving and committing to sharing. Autonomous intimacy comes through the simultaneous working through of individuation. Spiritual communion can also be important in redefining the meaning of intimacy in this period of life.	*Danger:* Divorce is a response to the inability to share the intimacy in the relationship or to permit the autonomy of the spouse. *Task:* To become secure and individuated enough to redefine intimacy to mean autonomous sharing and communion. *Development:* Mature relationship that blends communion and separation now possible. Relationship intimacy not critical to self-love.	A deeper level of identity can be achieved through full realization and acceptance of one's ultimate aloneness and responsibility for self. An important and related task is to come to a healthy appreciation of one's achievements and one's limitations.	*Danger:* Boredom with self projected to others. Lack of self-acceptance and dissatisfaction with self and achievements lead to divorce and seeking of another partner to complete identity. *Task:* Peaceful acceptance, compromising with self and others. *Development:* Divorce permits the loosening from binding relationship, permitting individuation and realistic self-appraisal.
Late adulthood: 55 to 70 years	As family members leave and die, the task of communion becomes increasingly that of friendship outside the parental and nuclear families. Intimacy no longer means exclusive affectional preoccupation or bonding, but sharing oneself with others.	*Danger:* Inability to adjust to empty nest, growing old, others leaving, and redefining intimacy with spouse leads to divorce. *Task:* Redefine expectations from others and self. *Development:* The development of intimate relationships beyond the original marital one, based on friendship and companionship.	The task begun in midlife is further refined; paradoxically, one begins to realize the truth of simultaneous oneness and aloneness and yet to feel comfortable with the ultimate aloneness and yet to know and appreciate a sense of oneness with the world. This process is aided by the redefinition of intimacy to more broadly mean a closeness to all living things.	*Danger:* Never coming to terms with ultimate separateness and oneness. Feeling incomplete and unfulfilled. *Task:* Identity begins to transfer out beyond one's person, family, or immediate significant attachments. *Development:* Divorce aids in the redefinition and transcendence of the meaning of identity, identity not based on affiliations or achievements, but simply on being, and the satisfied acceptance of being.

(continued)

TABLE 2 (*Continued*)

Developmental period	Intimacy/communion	Effect of divorce on intimacy/communion	Identity/separation	Effect of divorce on identity/separation
The full being: 70 to ?	An ultimate refinement of the meaning of intimacy comes in feeling love for the world and all living things. Paradoxically, a detachment occurs gradually to those individual persons we originally intensely loved as we prepare for the ultimate separation, death.	*Danger:* Divorce is infrequent, but can be a response to detachment, hopelessness, and abandonment. *Task:* To come to terms with whatever level of communion has been achieved and to redefine intimacy to include a more positive appreciation of the benefits of detachment. *Development:* Comfort, relief, freedom from old definitions permits healthy preparation for ultimate separation, and spiritual intimacy of self with world.	Perhaps the more cosmic task of separation is to no longer feel a separate identity, to feel oneness so intensely that one's identity becomes merged with a greater global, spiritual, or cosmic consciousness, whatever one chooses to call the infinite sense of space and time.	*Danger:* Divorce intensifies fears of death, aloneness, uselessness. *Task:* To come to terms with one's life and whatever level of individuation that has been achieved and to retain hope by redefining identity in cosmic terms. *Development:* Peace, contentment, cosmic identity.

leading to identity formation commonly expected to occur in adolescence and young adulthood. Their family, original or acquired, formed the basis of their identity. Only after their children have left home do they understand the necessity for an identity based on separation from others. Such women can and do successfully complete the separation tasks at 40 that are usually thought of as appropriate for 20.

INTEGRATING DIVORCE IN THE LIFE CYCLE

The first two developmental periods in Table 2 summarize intimacy and identity conceptions during these periods, and how parental divorce affects the child or teenager. The latter five periods discuss the effect of divorce on the divorcing parties themselves. The first column summarizes how the concept of intimacy is defined and redefined for each developmental period in terms of how one manages to commune with others and also how the separation task may interact with the communion one. The second column summarizes the effect of divorce on intimacy and the communion task. Columns three and four on identity and separation are similarly organized. Listed for each period is the danger of how divorce can impede, delay, or block the developmental task of the period; the specific objective of the separation or communion task that needs to be accomplished in the divorce process; and, finally, the ultimate positive developmental effect that can occur through divorce and its transcendence.

The model presented in Table 2 does not seek to oversimplify the complexities of human development over the lifespan. The mere description of the concepts themselves belie their enormous, rich complexity and interaction. One cannot understand either intimacy or identity in isolation from one another. Their interaction is an intricate and fascinating interplay throughout one's life. In each developmental period of life, one understands a little more about their interplay and multidimensionality. Nonetheless, some basic understanding of these concepts helps to appreciate development as a continuous unfolding of rather basic themes, themes that have always had historical, cultural, individual, and interpersonal meaning. Furthermore, these themes can be applied to any person regardless of race, sex, age, ethnic background, or culture; they are universal. The advantage to therapy of the approach presented here is that the model involves common developmental problems faced by all adults (communion, separation) as they deal with a variety of ego needs. The strategies based on this model can be modified appropriately in therapy to help individuals from a variety of backgrounds who are considering divorce.

Two other observations might be made about this model of development and divorce. The first is that it reflects the assumption that one moves in ever-increasing progress from the finite to the infinite, from identification with the micro to the macro. This is a distinctly eastern influence, but one that ultimately makes sense in the increasing smallness of the world in which we live. Secondly, all things, living and nonliving, experience cycles and this is true of human relationships. Leaving and moving on from something that is destructive can be difficult and stressful, but may be as important as committing to someone or something. The choice is always a difficult one. Like every important life choice, it is balanced by the consequences not only for the self, but for others, such as children and family of origin. The decision to divorce clearly affects both separation and communion. In the following three case studies, elements of all the various developmental periods are discussed from the perspective of the key tasks of separation and communion and how they are affected by divorce.

Case Study 1: Judy and Eric

Judy (age 27) and Eric (age 34) were married 6 years ago when Judy was a sophomore at the local technical college and Eric had returned to technical school to obtain an associate degree in accounting. Eric had had a brief earlier marriage, when he was 19, that lasted only a year and a half. For the first 2 years of their marriage, while they were still in school and Eric was working part time and then was laid off, the couple lived on and off with Judy's parents. Lisa (age 5) was born a year after they were married.

Eric was an only child whose parents lived in another state. They had doted on him, and his mother in particular had favored him and lived her life around his needs as he was growing up. He continually felt smothered and angry about her need for him and his early first marriage essentially was based upon his rejection of his parents' overinvolvement. Carmilla had been a vivacious, popular, young Catholic girl from a Mexican-American family; he had been intensely attracted to her flamboyance, socialness, sensuality, and the easy camaraderie of her family. She pressed for marriage once they became sexually involved. It seemed a logical escape from home for Eric, although he did see it in those terms at the time.

Early in the marriage their basic personality, ethnic, and background differences emerged, and both agreed reluctantly that they had made a mistake in coupling. They divorced and remained fairly amicable toward each other. Although he hated to admit it, Eric felt his parents had been right about the hastiness of the marriage and the difficulties engendered by their religious, economic, and personal differences. Eric also knew there was more to the dissolution than their background disparities. He realized that he still had a lot of growing up left to do and vowed not to repeat the same mistake.

Eric moved from the small town in which he had grown up to a larger city where he worked at various jobs; he found it somewhat difficult to take orders from superiors and experienced several job changes. At 26 he felt troubled about the lack of a clear career path and, after some investigation, entered technical school to study accounting. He had always worked well with figures and hoped he could eventually be self-employed. He had dated several women when he met Judy, who was attending the same school taking some business courses and working part time as a receptionist. Despite her relative youth, he felt she was very stable and responsible, a contrast to his first wife, yet also fun loving. Like his own mother, she had a strong nurturing side, but during their courtship appeared to permit him the freedom he desired to go out with his male friends.

Judy was the only girl and third born of a family of four children. She was quite close to her parents and middle brother, "parented" her youngest brother and felt ambivalent about and "parented" by her oldest brother. Judy's family was a working class, traditional one, much like Eric's. Her parents treated her somewhat protectively, as the only girl in the family. Her father differentiated her by gender less than did her mother, who relied on Judy for female companionship and communication. Judy admired Eric's ambition and felt he needed her. She wanted a family and her expectations growing up were to work for a while, but to soon settle down and raise a family much like her mother had done before her. Eric was older and seemed more settled and goal directed, like her father whom she idolized. They were married, and Judy quickly became pregnant.

Eric finished school and had difficulty finding a job. His aspirations always seemed higher than his realizations and his desire to be on his own financially and vocationally seemed like a far-off dream. Eric began to accept his fate and settled into a relatively low-paying, but comfortable position as an assistant accountant for a chain of gas stations. Judy reluctantly had to return to work to make ends meet when Lisa was two. She resented the lack of financial security that prevented her from staying home and wanted another child, which Eric opposed. Her parents offered shelter and loans to tide them over but felt increasingly disenchanted with Eric and fed into Judy's frustration about Eric's future.

Eric felt unhappy and chagrined that the warm, loving person he had married now seemed to be a nag. He was angry about her attachment to her parents, especially her mother, whom he alternately blamed for all their woes. Their mutual resentment turned into cold hostility and bitterness. Eric spent more and more time with his friends to escape the negative atmosphere of home, and Judy finally asked for a separation.

Eric moved out and during this time he returned briefly to his parents' home. They had found out about the impending divorce through Judy and offered to put Eric up for as long as he liked. They encouraged him to leave the city and start his life again in his home town. Upon arrival he went to his old bedroom, which for many years had been used as a guest room/study, but retained a few of his high school pennants and other mementos. Something new had been added. Now sitting on his bed to greet him were all his stuffed animals that had been saved from childhood. Disgusted, he quickly returned home and he and Judy agreed to try marriage therapy as a last desperate attempt to salvage the relationship.

Marital therapy soon turned into divorce therapy during the second session. It became clear that Judy wanted out and could not see any future with Eric whom she felt had betrayed their original marital contract. Her smouldering anger toward him had turned to indifference. Eric reluctantly went along with her decision, not really wanting out of the marriage, but not wanting it either, a situation of hostile dependency not unsimilar to what he had felt toward his own parents.

During the separation prior to their divorce, Lisa stayed with her mother in the home. Eric's contact with her was sporadic. He had been fairly close to his daughter, but found their contacts conflictual, as he increasingly felt distant from the marriage, anger at Judy, and associated Lisa with Judy. Seeing Lisa was avoided, as was seeing Judy. The infrequent, unnatural contacts with his daughter were also a painful reminder of how close they once had been. Judy complained in therapy of Eric's lack of interest and responsibility for Lisa, saying she would never agree to joint custody. Lisa became more withdrawn, had problems adjusting to first grade, and began exhibiting some signs of regression, like sporadic bedwetting, moodiness, and clinging. She did not understand her father's departure, and projected her anger on her mother who in turn found it difficult not to blame Eric.

Initial divorce therapy focused on making the decision to leave the marriage less stressful and on helping to implement the separation. Much of the therapy during this time centered on Lisa's problems. Eric began to realize that his avoidance of his daughter was not beneficial and that the impending divorce had propelled Lisa into a premature separation from her father. Eric reestablished regular contact with Lisa by negotiating a mutually acceptable parenting schedule with Judy. He rented a larger apartment with a yard where he could have Lisa overnight. Most of Lisa's distress symptoms disappeared as her world again became more secure. She also appeared to benefit from the additional contact she had with her maternal grandparents, who were very loving toward Lisa and helped her mother obtain some free time by babysitting. They felt less inhibited with their granddaughter now that the divorce decision was finally made. Judy's decision to leave the marriage also forced them to take a closer look at their own marriage, their lack of involvement with each other, and their overinvolvement with their children.

Judy began to explore in therapy her own fantasies of being cared for by a man, first her father and older brothers, and now a spouse. She increasingly saw the childlike part of herself and how her dependency on her parents had never been resolved, and her own identity had not been explored. Judy decided that she would have to make a life of her own and sought a better job. She also began slowly to establish a separate network of friends. She read more about women and their roles, and began to feel a new sense of healthy separation and enhanced self-esteem in her fledging efforts at self-support.

There was less blame on Eric for her dilemma and for the divorce. Judy understood better that she needed to change and grow herself and that, with her original expectations of the marriage, she had been unable to do so. Yet while Judy no longer used Eric as a scapegoat, neither did she feel any lingering guilt over the decision to divorce. As she began to know herself better, she appreciated that she was a fairly ambitious person who could realize her aspirations on her own without submerging them in another's achievements. She desired a similar individual for a partner and realized Eric's passive stance toward life would have precluded true compatibility. She also came to appreciate that she could no longer define her own identity solely by the capacity to be intimate with another person.

Two years later Judy remarried a man who was similar to her in personality and values. He sensitively did not demand immediate devotion and affection from Lisa and allowed her to develop a trusting friendship with him slowly. Lisa maintained her relationship with Eric while obtaining a very valuable new relationship with her stepfather. Her stepfather often was able to be more objective and fair in relation to her as a teenager than was her own mother.

Following his second divorce, Eric initially felt quite disillusioned about love and marriage. He had not been able to obtain the kind of intense, unconditional love he experienced from his parents. However, he began to realize that the price of that love was his own individuality. He had sought to resolve his hostile dependence on his parents by a precipitous early marriage and then by leaving the state. Central questions about the meaning of intimacy still troubled him. Eric thought he had achieved reciprocal love in both his marriages, but he did not realize the strong narcissistic component in his expectations of intimacy with both his former wives. As long as he felt that Judy selfishly would not give that unconditional love, he withheld commitment to the relationship. After the divorce from Judy, he changed jobs again and drifted for a while, avoiding any close relationships and seeing mostly his male friends.

The death of Eric's father a year and a half after the divorce and Judy's subsequent remarriage finally put him in touch with his own grieving and sense of loss. These feelings of loss surrounded not only the death of his father and the death of his marriage, but more significantly the death of his dream to be loved forever. At this point he returned to the therapist he and Judy had seen as a couple to do some individual therapy. He finally was able to confront his core dilemma with the communion and separation tasks in his life. He dealt with how the fear of intimacy and its definition, as being smothering and all consuming, had colored his responses to the significant others in his life. This fear had impeded his committing not just to relationships but also to his work and other important things in his life.

Divorce helped Judy and eventually Eric to confront key issues of intimacy and identity in their lives. They were also able to help Lisa successfully negotiate the parental separation and to use it positively in her development. The divorce had an additional unexpected intergenerational effect. Judy's parents and siblings came to appreciate and respect her courage and growth in establishing a life of her own. They were encouraged by her example to look more closely at their own marriages and their individual and interpersonal development. Judy's mother confided to her that she had also thought of divorce. Her generation, background, and upbringing, however, did not lead her to consider seriously leaving Judy's father, despite feeling many times excessively subjugated and psychologically abused. As her father approached retirement, her mother began to do some volunteer work, got a driver's license, and, despite her husband's protestations, began to develop some interests and contacts of her own outside the home. When Judy's father died, her mother continued to make changes in her life and did some traveling on her own for the first time. Judy philosophized, "It took my father's death to make my mother finally grow and it took the death of my marriage to make me grow up."

Eric, now age 40, was in a loving and very different relationship with a teacher, who was also divorced. He felt some forgiveness toward his parents. He visited his mother, and achieved a limited rapproachment. He brought Lisa, 13, along with him and for the first time she was allowed to establish a relationship with her paternal grandmother.

Judy and Eric illustrate how divorce (1) can interrupt the usual developmental cycle of communion and separation, as it did initially with their daughter; (2) can act as a catalyst to a redefinition of developmental tasks, as it did immediately for Judy and later for Eric; (3) can represent symbolically many meanings of separation and communion for all parties involved; and (4) can be used to redefine, work through, and transcend issues of intimacy and identity by the divorcing parties, their children, and the extended families. The process of developmental change catalyzed by divorce can be very stressful, however, and the outcomes more costly or even incomplete, as illustrated in the following case.

Case Study 2: Meredith and Gerald

The family underwent a profound transformation when at age 45 Gerald began having an affair with another woman. Gerald and Meredith (age 44) had been married for 21 years and had three children, Jeffrey (age 19), Susan (age 17), and Jonathan (age 12). Gerald was at the peak of his career. All his life he had been enterprising and vocationally successful. He had the knack of never letting an opportunity go by that somehow might further his career. In elementary school he peddled pencils to his classmates who had forgotten them, and in high school he put in stints of everything from soda jerking to selling magazine subscriptions. He quickly acquired the reputation of being a man who could sell anything.

Almost by chance Gerald got into what would make him eventually a fairly wealthy man, selling biodegradable cleaning products and organic health and dietary supplements, a field that was just getting off the ground. With the few savings he had accumulated and a loan he became the junior partner in a franchise to sell the products in a Midwestern area. Over time his territory grew larger as he expanded his network and gradually moved into managing the selling of other franchises.

Meredith and Gerald had been high school sweethearts; they had weathered a relatively smooth adolescence together. Their respective families had known each other through local service clubs and approved of the match. They married at 23 and 24 when Gerald was beginning his first franchise and Meredith was teaching junior high. Children followed as Gerald's career in sales progressed. Meredith regarded her husband as a "workaholic" and felt that his work probably meant more to him than she or his family. She tolerated his long hours and frequent traveling by busying herself with raising the children almost single-handedly, substitute teaching in her limited spare time, and then returning to teach full time when Jonathan was in first grade. She was as busy as Gerald and perhaps even more preoccupied with the contingencies of her separate world.

The marriage was regarded as ideal and they were seen as a very compatible, comfortable, well-situated couple, respected by their peers, community, and family. For a long time they focused on feelings of well-being and approval, and denied and minimized how distant and separate their worlds and interests had become. Despite the emotional distance, they still shared a good deal in common regarding the family; water skiing and boating on the weekends were the focus of their closest interactions with Jeffrey and Susan. Gerald and Meredith would no more have thought of having separate friends, hobbies, or interests than they would have thought of blending their careers.

They had thought their family was complete when, at age 32, Meredith became pregnant again. It was a crossroads in the marriage. Meredith was just beginning to let herself feel and complain to herself about the lack of closeness with Gerald. Although an abortion was briefly discussed, they decided they could manage another child and, in effect, the pregnancy diverted Meredith once again from the emotional poverty within the marriage. It made her even busier as she continued to parent, to teach, and to manage the household.

When Jonathan, their youngest, was 10, Gerald was asked to become vice-president of one of the company's regional offices, an advancement that would have required a move and even more traveling. Near the peak of his career, Gerald began to question what he was doing, why he was doing it and he began to experience increasing dissatisfaction with his life. The fruit of his labor became less meaningful and he resented the easy, affluent life of his teenagers, feeling they were spoiled and ungrateful.

He also thought that Meredith, while a good wife and devoted mother, was more involved with the children than with him. He resented the love she lavished on Jonathan and the retarded children with whom she worked. Life seemed less fulfilling, his work boring and meaningless, and he feared growing old. He felt somehow he had missed out, never having had any other significant relationships or sexual experiences with a woman other than Meredith. Now at middle age, Gerald began to feel depressed and old.

Gerald met a younger woman, Gretchen, on one of his trips. She worked as an advertising director for a firm with whom they did business. He "immediately fell in love" not only with her, but with what she represented: freedom, youth, art, a more bohemian existence, sexuality, vitality, and unpredictability. He began to lose weight, to jog and play tennis. He grew a stylish beard, and changed his clothing. Meredith noted all these changes with suspicion and irritation, but was especially disturbed when Gerald began to wear bikini underwear instead of his usual boxer shorts.

Gerald found it increasingly difficult to maintain his secret from Meredith and was alternately guilty and angrily self-righteous, feeling he deserved this new lease on life. Meredith finally confronted him when she found a letter from Gretchen while unpacking his suitcase. His daughter Susan also guessed what was going on when she unexpectedly took a phone call for her father from Gretchen. Meredith threatened divorce and reluctantly Gerald agreed to stop seeing Gretchen and to go into couple therapy. After several sessions in which Meredith expressed how she could not accept the affair and Gerald protested her lack of trust, it was revealed that Gretchen had been in town over the weekend and she and Gerald had seen each other. The revelation served to destroy the uneasy truce in their relationship and Meredith filed for divorce.

The family had varying reactions. Susan, who had discovered the extramarital relationship on her own about the time her mother did, was enraged at her father and strongly allied with her mother. She refused to see or have anything to do with Gerald after he had renewed the relationship with Gretchen. Their oldest son, Jeffrey, was more tolerant and less judgmental. A sophomore in college at the time, he had suspected how distant his parents' marriage was. He was not especially surprised that his father had had an affair, yet felt some disappointment in his father's behavior. This knowledge helped him take his father off the parental pedestal and to view his parents more realistically, as two human beings with their own set of problems. The following summer Jeff cancelled plans to go to Alaska and stayed home, feeling his mother needed his support.

Meredith's secure world had crumbled. She became extremely depressed and made an abortive suicidal attempt with some barbituates, but refused to get into therapy. During that summer, she relied heavily on her children, especially Jeff and Susan, to provide her with emotional support and comfort. Jeff even drove the boat like Gerald used to do on their weekends at the lake, and took over some of the parenting of Jonathan.

Jon seemed to be the least affected by the separation and impending divorce. A popular boy at school, he continued to water ski competitively and won several trophies that summer. He did not blame or reject his father for the marital breakup, as Susan did. Jon did not try to overcompensate by being a companion for his mother or a pal to his father as did Jeff. Approaching 13, he was at an age developmentally when he was eager to separate, and the advent of his older brother on the scene and the modeling of his father seemed to aid his own separation and individuation. Jon maintained relationships with all of the family without a good deal of stress. Jeff, in contrast, became quite disenchanted with staying at home and revealed to his mother that he was planning to spend August traveling in Alaska with a friend, an announcement that sent her back to the pills and threats of suicide.

At this point the family came into therapy to help them deal with the stress of the divorce and the changes it had engendered. Jeff was the most articulate of the children and quickly gained some insight into how he had been futilely trying to replace his father and "save" his mother. Instead he opted to carry out his plan to go to Alaska without feeling guilty and to extend his stay into the fall. Meredith reluctantly agreed that he needed to leave and that she could not lay claim to a pseudointimacy with him. However, Susan's allegiance was harder for her to give up. In therapy Susan and her mother colluded against Gerald, labeling him a "regressed adolescent," a man who had had a "psychotic break" and who irresponsibly had left all the security and comforts of a happy home.

Through therapy Meredith made some efforts, half-heartedly at first, to face up to her own personal developmental conflicts. Her own feelings of inadequacy had led her to settle for a nonreciprocal love in her marriage, in return for the security of the marital contract. Her task was to redefine intimacy based less on security and more on choice. Her own conflicts about identity had been ignored as she had focused on Gerald's identity crisis, refusing to acknowledge as positive his attempts to regain a sense of meaning, self-esteem, and vitality. She gradually began to feel at times both less judgmental about his changing and less guilty that she had not been "enough" for him so he would not have wanted to change.

The therapist reframed for the family her role in his dilemma, suggesting that despite what Meredith might have done, Gerald would eventually have had to face his own developmental issues, just as she did. As Meredith became less depressed, her focus on Gerald and the loyalty of her children ameliorated and her work improved. Later she decided to return to school and obtain an advanced degree in special education. After the divorce, she still found it difficult to accept the affair. She was conflicted about the sharing of intimacy, but found peace in deciding that sexual fidelity was the bottom line. Meredith felt that she could permit some separateness and autonomy in future intimate relationships if she were secure about fidelity.

As Meredith grew more objective about the divorce, Susan's anger toward her father also lessened. Father and daughter began to talk, though not without ambivalence and uneasiness. Susan's developmental task of successfully separating from her parents was delayed and complicated by the divorce and she was thrust temporarily into an overidentification with her mother and a unilateral rejection of her father. Her father's subsequent marriage to Gretchen further complicated the picture. Susan had finished high school and obtained a part-time job near where her father now lived. Being short on cash she decided to live with him temporarily until she could move out and get a place of her own. Gerald was realistic enough not to expect Susan's ready acceptance of Gretchen as a surrogate mother, especially since a mere 7 years separated them in age and Susan was well on her way to adulthood. Gerald did hope that they would become close friends. The expectation was shattered during a confrontation in which Susan accused Gretchen one day of being a "home breaker" and Gretchen threatened to move out if Gerald didn't do something about Susan. At this time, Susan was dating a young Afro-American student and had been hiding his identity from her mother whom she did not think would accept him. In fact, she had moved to her father's house in part to be closer geographically to this young man and to escape her mother's watchful eye.

The night of the blow-up between Gretchen and Susan, Meredith called; she had found out about Susan's relationship with her boyfriend, was very upset, and made that known to Susan. Susan felt doubly rejected and late that night found herself unexpectedly pouring out her grievance about her mother's conservative attitudes to Gretchen who listened sympathetically and, probably because of her generation and background, without judgment. The incident was a turning point for Susan who began to see Gretchen with more benevolence and less resentment. Communion outside her biological family had occurred not only with the young man, but with someone she would have never expected or thought possible, a young stepparent who was actually more like an older sister.

After his marriage to Gretchen, Gerald still attended some family therapy sessions that included both Susan and Meredith and, at one point, Gretchen. He did not realize that his boredom and dissatisfaction with himself had been in part projected onto the marriage and his former spouse. He appeared to lack the insight that at age 45 he had sought another partner to complete the holes in his own identity, just as at age 35 he had used work exclusively to define his identity. After the initial newness of the marriage to Gretchen wore off, he again felt somewhat restless and dissatisfied, and began to wonder if he had done the right thing by divorcing.

As can be seen in this case study, divorce as a marker event in life has both the capacity to aid development through the redefinition of life tasks, as in Meredith's case, or to postpone it, as in Gerald's case. Divorce can also retard development, as in Susan's case, advance it, as in Jonathan's case, or do both sequentially and simultaneously, as in Jeffrey's case.

Divorce can occur at almost any point in a relationship within the adult life cycle. Statistically it is most likely to occur in very young marriages, like Eric's first marriage (Case Study 1) or in young adulthood, like his second. Currently, three-fifths of all divorces occur between the ages 25 and 39; however, the divorce rate has also doubled for people between 40 and 64 (Glick, 1979). It can happen in midlife when people have married in the usual early 20s, like Gerald and Meredith, or even late in life, as illustrated in the next case study.

Divorce is less likely to occur in late adulthood or old age. People who have made it this far in their relationship may be less likely to risk losing security for the unknown and more likely to have somehow made the necessary emotional tradeoffs necessary to stay in the marriage even if it is not a very satisfying or happy one. Yet not everyone at age 60 or 65 is willing to accept security and the known for unhappiness or developmental stagnation. Some people continue to grow significantly at older ages and divorce is seen as a viable option.

Case Study 3: Angie and Mike

Angie (age 58) was a self-made first-generation American who at age 15 dropped out of school to help support her family. Her father was disabled and her mother was a factory worker. Angie got her Graduate Equivalency Diploma, worked as a typist and began her own direct mail advertising company, employing housewives part time, who typed out of their home. It was very successful and helped to finance her daughter's higher education and provided a down payment on her son's first home. Angie's first husband, a career Army man, tolerated her work involvement. He never really approved, but realized it was the reason they were able to live in middle-class comfort. They had a fairly happy marriage and raised two children, Sandra (now 32, single, and a lawyer in another state) and Walt (age 36, a commercial artist, married, with two children, and living nearby). When Angie was 45, her first husband was killed in a freak accident at the end of his last tour of duty. His death was a shock, but her basic independence and gregariousness helped her survive, as did the success of her work, the comfort of friends, and her children.

Mike, also a military man, had known Angie through his casual friendship with her late husband. They began seeing each other and were married a year later, when Angie was 46 and Mike, 49. Mike at the time was at a crossroads in his life and about to retire from military life. He gratefully accepted her proposal to become a business partner as well as a marital partner. A quiet, taciturn man, he had never married, preferring the discipline and single life of the military. Angie provided him with a ready-made family and a midlife career. In return she felt she had acquired companionship and a helpmate for old age. The marriage lasted 12 years. It broke apart for various reasons.

Mike's late adulthood grappling with the direction of his life had not been solved by the marriage, despite the comfort and security it provided. By nature and values, he was never really happy with the demands of the business world. Before he had enlisted, he had studied for the ministry for a couple of years, even thinking he might become a chaplain, and increasingly he found himself drawn back to that life. However, he thought it unrealistic to make such an occupational change, given his age and circumstances. He was happiest on the weekends when he served as a lay minister, but was afraid to be open with Angie about his desires. He feared she could not accept the drastic change in income and life-style, or the move that would be required should he try to finish the seminary and become a minister. Yet his values kept pushing him in that direction.

Angie was troubled when Mike finally made his decision. At first they tried to compromise; she would sell the business and, with those funds and his pension, they would be able to finance a move to the state where Mike could finish his training and find a congregation. The realities of the "costs" of heading her life in this direction placed Angie in great conflict. Her roots were in the city where they lived. Her grandchildren were at a delightful age and she thoroughly enjoyed the frequent easy contact she had with them. Her lifetime friends were there and the business was flourishing.

Angie and Mike talked with a friend who was a therapist and minister, to help them sort out their values and, ultimately, to make a decision to separate. Although it was difficult and extremely painful for Mike to leave, he found a new life and sense of purpose in his second career. Developmentally, he slowly began to come to terms with his ultimate separateness from his immediate family and friends. Yet, paradoxically, in exploring himself, his spirituality, and his mission of service, he felt a sense of greater closeness to all people than ever before. He had feared that divorce would be a symbol of his detachment and hopelessness. Instead he found that the separation freed him to do a realistic self-appraisal and to redefine the meaning of intimacy and identity in his life and to reach a place where he felt more fulfilled.

While she, too, went through very intense periods of anger and grief, Angie realized painfully that she could not compromise by remaining married to Mike, following him on a life path that was not in real harmony with her own. Her realization along these lines was similar to Mike's. Angie found satisfaction in the sense of generativity she gave to her grandchildren and children. Like Mike, she concluded that the meaning of intimacy in her life had to be redefined beyond that provided by immediate family, spouse, or children. Unlike Mike, whose solution was more existential and spiritual, Angie began to deepen her attachments to her friends. Intimacy no longer meant exclusive affectional bonding, but communion and sharing with her friends. She became a mentor and inspiration of sorts to her grandchildren and their friends.

Four years after the divorce to Mike, at age 62, Angie decided to sell the business, but this time it was for a very different reason than that of following a spouse. She wanted more time and greater freedom to do many of the things she had not been able to pursue in her youth and early adulthood. She had worked continuously since she was 15 and had little extra time for the pursuits she loved: music, being outdoors, and gardening. She did not marry again, but lived amicably with a compatible retired salesman for many years. Mike remained one of her many friends.

When Mike was 74 and became ill with cancer, he had become the well-loved pastor of a small congregation. He again faced a developmental crisis. His marriage and divorce had helped him to accept the reality of his aloneness in the world, but being critically ill without the comfort of spouse and biological family to comfort him was a difficult test of his powers of adaptation. Old feelings of hopelessness and abandonment came to haunt him, and it was Angie who helped him to accept his dying. Mike had been a loner and self-contained person all his life. Angie's friendship, which had been maintained at a distance over the years postdivorce, meant a great deal to him. He also admired her acceptance of his leaving to take a separate path and her spirit of survival that led her to rebuild her life and redefine her tasks with each separation: her first husband's death, her children's departure, and the divorce with Mike. With some other friends, Angie helped Mike get into a hospice where he died with dignity and in peace.

In turn, Mike's death and his example influenced Angie to think beyond her own boundaries. Her provincial attitude about the rest of the world and its problems was modified by the example of his life and values. She realized that the divorce was instrumental in permitting them both to develop separately and, paradoxically, to appreciate each other's achievements in a new light, years later.

In this chapter, divorce has been presented as a marker event in the life cycle that has the potential to affect key developmental tasks of separation and communion positively and negatively as they occur and are redefined in each period of life. The next section will focus on the two main psychological processes involved in divorce, object loss leading to narcissistic injury and role loss accompanied by role disorientation. These two concepts help in understanding further the specific impact of divorce on development, and the therapeutic strategies necessary to assist its resolution. Both will be discussed in relation to how working them through affects one's self-esteem in divorce.

Theoretical Focus:
Divorce and Self-Esteem

Chapter Four

Object Loss and
Narcissistic Injury in Divorce

The way one deals with the life tasks of separation and communion directly affects self-esteem. Self-esteem is defined here as the feelings and regard one has for one's self and about one's self. As has been discussed previously, divorce can act in a positive developmental way through the redefinition and transformation of identity and intimacy issues. Divorce can lead eventually to an increase in self-esteem through greater individuation and the negotiating and resolving of separation and communion tasks. However, the immediate consequence of divorce is likely to be a decrease in self-esteem. The process of divorce inherently engenders and reawakens conflicts about identity and intimacy that usually lead to a temporary, but significant, loss of self-esteem. There are basically two mediating processes in divorce that contribute to an individual's loss of self-esteem: the *object loss* that produces *narcissistic injury* and the *role loss* leading to *role disorientation* (see Figure 1).

The latter involves the loss of the marital role and the difficulty in taking on new roles or restructuring old ones. This often results in feelings of role disorientation, confusion about identity, and feelings of inadequacy and ambivalence. Such feelings usually are accompanied by a perceived loss of self-esteem. Individuals in the process of divorce often complain about the loss of role status within the community as well as among their friends and family. They question and worry about whether they are capable and competent enough to restructure their lives and assume new, fulfilling roles.

The blow to one's self-image and the narcissistic injury engendered by the object loss and rejection of a spouse can also lead to a significant decrease of self-esteem. Not only does the person intensely grieve the loss of a significant love object, but it is also easy to feel that one has failed at being lovable, and to doubt one's capability for receiving and returning

107

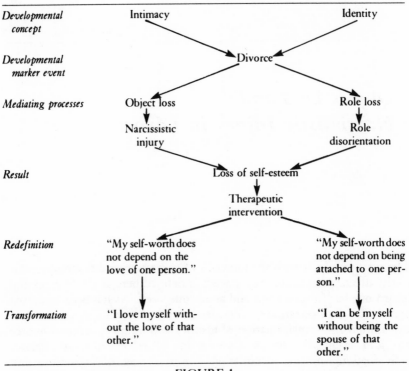

Developmental concept	Intimacy			Identity
Developmental marker event		Divorce		
Mediating processes	Object loss			Role loss
	Narcissistic injury			Role disorientation
Result		Loss of self-esteem		
		Therapeutic intervention		
Redefinition	"My self-worth does not depend on the love of one person."			"My self-worth does not depend on being attached to one person."
Transformation	"I love myself without the love of that other."			"I can be myself without being the spouse of that other."

FIGURE 1

Psychological model explaining the loss of self-esteem in divorce and the therapeutic implications

love. After suffering such a narcissistic injury, divorcing clients may complain that they feel worthless and unattractive to others. They may doubt that anyone would ever find them a lovable partner, and question whether they will ever experience intimacy with anyone again. Their fears of being permanently alone may lead to a desperate search to immediately replace the old spouse, a phenomenon that can short-circuit the crucial period of healing, aloneness, and self-reflection that can be most beneficial in the divorce.

A figurative conception of the relationship between key developmental concepts, the mediating processes involved in divorce, and the loss of self-esteem is presented in Figure 1. The therapeutic task in divorce therapy is to help the individual redefine and transform issues of identity and intimacy, ameliorating the loss of self-esteem accompanying object loss and role loss. This task involves both emotional and behavioral restructuring.

EMOTIONAL AND BEHAVIORAL RESTRUCTURING

Divorce therapy has tended to focus on the behavioral tasks associated with object and role loss. Underlying the real and necessary behavioral tasks, changes, and decisions that must be made in divorce are attitudinal and emotional changes and redefinitions concerning intimacy and identity. For example, the divorced person must face decisions about custody, closeness to children, and problems of economic survival and division. He or she must also learn to create a social network, a new kinship system, and perhaps a different place and role within the community as well as in the family. However, accompanying these behavioral changes and tasks are the corresponding emotional ones relating to intimacy and identity. These attitudinal transformations are an important part of the divorce therapy process.

In essence, the person who divorces successfully must come to understand and internalize a new conception of identity and intimacy. In the first stage of redefinition the internal message is akin to this:

1. My sense of being lovable does not depend on the love of or closeness to my former spouse.
2. My sense of who I am or my sense of self does not depend on being married to my former spouse.

As therapy progresses and as the client achieves a greater degree of individuation and maturity, those conceptions also achieve a higher degree of abstraction:

1. My self-worth is not defined by being intimate with any one person.
2. My self-worth is not defined by being identified with any one person.

And finally:

1. I love myself. I can love myself without the love of another.
2. I am myself. I can be myself without being the spouse of another.

Divorce therapy can thus trigger developmental change in which individuals begin to integrate, accept, and finally to enjoy the fact that ultimately they are with themselves, whether or not they are in or out of any relationship, and whether or not they are loved by any one significant person. In other words, individuals come to love themselves for what they are apart from the role of "loved spouse" or "loved one" in general. Redefining the latter role of "loved one" is a more difficult transcendence.

It is a task that one may never complete in a lifetime; one continues to learn, define, and ultimately love oneself apart from what others think of and define for one and whether they deign to give their love.

In sum, there are basically two mediating processes by which divorce can engender a loss of self-esteem: (1) the actual *object loss* and accompanying *narcissistic injury*, which can change the perception of one's self as lovable and capable of intimacy, and (2) the *role loss* and *role disorientation* experienced through the loss of the marital, parental and/or other associated statuses. This chapter will discuss object loss and the process of narcissistic injury in detail, outlining various defenses employed by the divorced to deal with such a blow to perceptions of intimacy. The following chapter will focus on therapeutic issues of identity and role loss in divorce and the effect on self-esteem. Section III of this book discusses therapeutic strategies for dealing with the object and role loss in divorce through efforts toward *ego reparation* and *role restructuring*.

DIVORCE, SELF-ESTEEM, AND NARCISSISTIC INJURY

Each step in the termination of an intimate relationship and the loss of a love object can leave a person vulnerable to narcissistic or self-esteem injury (see Figure 1). No matter how well one has prepared for separation, the actual parting is likely to arouse feelings of guilt, failure, and inadequacy, which can lower self-esteem. Even a quite healthy personality can be seriously stressed in the process of marital dissolution. Dealing with object loss and narcissistic injury then is an important psychological task in successfully completing the divorce process.

For most individuals, the initial pain of separation and divorce heals in time. However, the psychic components of the divorce experience are not totally self-resolving. One does not always survive a narcissistic injury simply by waiting for time to pass. The former partner, or at least his or her reminders, are around to arouse lingering, unresolved feelings and emotional memories. This continuing awareness of the prior marital bond is especially strong when the couple has children. There are biological reminders, conveyed by similar physical attributes in parent and child, as well as psychological similarities in manner and temperament. The presence of children usually requires continuing negotiation and deliberation between ex-spouses and, through this process, issues from the prior marital relationship frequently are kept alive.

Postseparation dealings hold the potential for continued insult to one's self-esteem. The amount of money each spouse has available to live on usually is diminished significantly after a separation. The situation is conducive to feeling that one is either an inadequate provider and/or poorly provided for financially. Both emotional states affect one's sense of self and can aggravate self-esteem wounds caused by the fact that the marriage did not work out. In this manner, the conditions for perceiving injury to one's self-esteem remain throughout the divorcing process. Time alone usually will not resolve completely the damage to self-esteem resulting from divorce and object loss. A brief or extended period of psychotherapeutic intervention can be helpful for dealing with these self-esteem issues (Rice, 1977).

Mental health professionals are fond of stating, "What's the use of having a crisis if you are not going to get something out of it?" Directly facing the pain and uncertainty resulting from postseparation narcissistic injury can lead to potential growth and positive psychological change. In the present chapter, different psychological defenses employed to cope with narcissistic injury and their elaboration in the divorcing process are explored. Later chapters focus more extensively on the therapeutic process involved in the restoration and enhancement of self-esteem.

DEVELOPMENT OF SELF-ESTEEM

There are several psychological processes that are involved in how one comes to regard and value oneself. Two of these processes have been termed the grandiose self and the idealized parent imago (Kohut & Wolf, 1978). The grandiose self is related to the early valuing of and investment in oneself, and contains attributes reflecting early childhood feelings of omnipotence. The idealized (parent imago) self is composed of internalized conceptions of oneself that result from the investment in and valuing of esteemed others. Parents are the prototypic figures in this regard. Early in life, other people via their behavior and reactions acquire the power to markedly influence one's self-esteem.

If the sense of being positively valued by important others characterizes one's general developmental experience, positive self-valuing is the usual result. The failure to have one's actions or attributes appreciated by valued others can lead over time to low self-esteem. The positive and negative reactions of others remain part of the individual's self-concept, even when the important other is no longer present.

The process of feeling loved and subsequently chosen for marriage by another person is a powerful reinforcer of self-esteem. In this process, through the emotional investment that follows and that may continue over the duration of the marriage, one's spouse becomes a highly significant "other." Many components of self-esteem that had their precursors in early self development are rearoused in the formation of the marital bond. "Falling in love" usually is accompanied by some grandiosity and overidealization of one's chosen partner. Indeed, such mutual valuing undoubtedly is necessary to overcome natural feelings of ambivalence that enter into an interpersonal relationship that lacks written guarantees and a road map of the future.

Even though early notions about one's partner are modified over time, certain internalized conceptions, based on a sense of being valued previously by an idealized other, tend to remain. A marital partner thus retains a good deal of power to affect one's self-esteem. The coming apart of a marital (or other significant) relationship requires a powerful reckoning with the loss of being valued by an important other. Felt narcissistic injury is usually the result. The anxiety occasioned by the process of marital dissolution can be dealt with by a variety of defensive operations designed to soothe the pain resulting from the insult to one's self-esteem. Dealing with these defensive reactions forms an important part of the psychotherapeutic treatment process with separated and divorcing individuals.

PSYCHOLOGICAL DEFENSES TO OBJECT LOSS AND NARCISSISTIC INJURY

Few marriages dissolve with little injury to self-esteem. This can be the case, however, for relationships lasting only for a short time and/or entered into for primarily ulterior motives. A short-lived marriage of two people who marry "to get away from home" is a common example, as illustrated in the following case study.

Case Study 4: William and Beverly

William (age 19) and Beverly (age 18), a young black couple, came to therapy after having been married for 8 months. They indicated they were there primarily because in Beverly's words, "William's mother thinks we need help." The couple had known each other for approximately 2½ years, but had begun dating only about 1 year prior to their coming to therapy, around the middle of their senior year in high school. They felt like they quickly became "good friends" and William stated, "We thought it would be a good idea to get married in June, right after high school." Beverly planned on working and had taken distributive education classes. William had anticipated entering college in the fall and had already been accepted by the time their relationship became serious. Both felt that these educational/vocational plans had been "set" for some time and had lost much of their luster or excitement as "new" ventures. In contrast, the thought of getting married (after having dated for such a short time) did seem new, "unanticipated," and exciting.

Both William and Beverly came from middle-class backgrounds. She perceived her parents as "strong willed" and her father as "judgmental," despite her long-standing efforts to please him. Beverly had attempted the college preparatory curriculum in high school, as father had suggested, but made only marginal grades and eventually switched to a vocational program. She believed that her father favored her younger brother, age 16, and perceived her mother as being more sympathetic to her, but indicated "my mother would never cross my father."

William saw his parents as somewhat passive and compliant. He said "they pretty much let me do what I want; but I haven't embarrassed them." Whatever feelings they had about their son's "early" marriage were not voiced, and William felt he had their implicit support. They seemed to like Beverly. William had an older brother in college and two younger sisters. He thought that having four kids had been a draining experience for his parents and sensed that they were tired of actively intervening in the children's lives, and thus let them do pretty much as they wished.

The summer months after the marriage were described by Beverly as being "full of fun." They both had a fondness for animals and bought several pets, which they kept in their small apartment (against stated regulations). Fall arrived and the routine of work and school set in. William had found high school to be "easy" and was not prepared for the academic demands and self-discipline necessitated by his college curriculum. Beverly objected to his evening pattern of watching TV, playing with the pets, and then beginning to study around the time she was getting ready for bed. However, she rationalized this behavior, and their increasingly infrequent sexual encounters, as the price one pays for having a husband in school. Her concerns increased when William spent most of his Christmas vacation trying to catch up on his studies, in preparation for final exams. Beverly had been hoping that their first Christmas would recapture some of the good times of the summer, but this did not happen. She became more involved with the pets ("her babies," as William called them), fantasizing how "they" would like to have Christmas and buying them each presents.

William survived the first semester and began to get more interested in his courses, buoyed by having made it over the initial hurdles. He felt he had achieved a greater sense of self-discipline. Beverly completed her 6-month probationary period at work and was given a salary increase, which she proceeded to spend largely on clothes and things for the pets.

By the time they entered therapy, the therapist perceived a good deal of emotional distancing in the marital interaction. Both partners appeared to have more emotionally involving things in their lives than one another. The process of looking at their relationship in therapy felt painful to William and Beverly only in that it distracted them from the more pleasant things in their lives. Neither spouse was particularly introspective. It seemed clear to the therapist that Beverly had picked William as a partner because he was accepting and not judgmental, in contrast to her father. One got the impression that any number of young women could have satisfied

William's needs for female companionship and therefore could have been chosen in place of Beverly.

After approximately eight therapy sessions the couple began to talk about separating. Beverly found she was enjoying going out with her women friends more than being at home. William did not object to her absence because it "gave me more time to study." He accepted their diminished sexual interaction by explaining, "It could be good, but we don't take the time." William stated at one point, "Maybe it would be more honest if we split." They agreed tentatively to separate at the end of the semester, when the lease on their apartment was due to expire.

Choosing to leave the marriage appeared to be preferable to facing underlying feelings of depression and disappointment that the relationship did not work out. The therapist's attempts to help the couple get in touch with such dysphoric feelings, if only to enhance self-understanding and facilitate future relationships, were of little avail. The therapist felt caught in a marital process whose ultimate course had already been determined. It appeared as if Beverly was concerned primarily with getting out on her own and away from the unfavorable judgments of her father. William apparently had married because it felt like something to "try" and see whether he liked it.

The couple saw very little of each other during the summer, after separating. The decision arousing the most feelings between them concerned how to divide up the pets, due to the fact that, as Beverly stated, "they're so used to being with one another." It was decided that William would take a favorite cat and Beverly would keep the rest. A girlfriend moved in with Beverly and William moved into a campus rooming house. In October, they decided to see a lawyer at the Community Legal Services and begin divorce proceedings. They saw each other approximately once per month, at Beverly's apartment, to talk out details and in order for William to see the pets. The talks were civil and no extensive attempts to induce guilt or blame were evident in the follow-up therapy sessions. Beverly and William seemed satisfied in general with their situation. Both were dating, though William relatively infrequently. Both sets of in-laws accepted the divorce, with William's mother apparently satisfied that "therapy had been tried."

A phone call to Beverly from the therapist, 1 year after the last session, revealed that Beverly was functioning fairly well. She thought that William was, too, although she rarely saw him. Beverly had a steady boyfriend, but indicated "no plans for marriage." She expressed no rancor or bitterness over the marital break-up when questioned in this regard by the therapist.

The dissolution of William and Beverly's marriage is, of course, atypical from a psychological standpoint. It is unusual for a couple to separate as comfortably and with as little psychological trauma to self-esteem. An unplanned pregnancy did not dictate marriage in this case, as so frequently happens in early marriages. Beverly's divorce was from her family, at least psychologically, rather than from William. His marriage was primarily to his studies, rather than to Beverly. A bond tenuously formed is more easily broken. Neither spouse needed to blame the other in order to justify leaving the relationship. Neither chose to have an affair while still married, as a way of rubbing salt into the wounds of dissatisfaction. Both protected the other's ego and the uncoupling was relatively smooth. Feelings of object loss and narcissistic injury were minimal. The far more common situation in marital separation, however, is the antithesis of that experienced psychologically by William and Beverly. As in the case of this couple, some denial may be present and employed as a defense against felt narcissistic injury. Typically, other defensive reactions tend either to take the place of or supplement the use of denial over time. These response patterns are discussed below, accompanied by illustrative case studies.

DEPRESSION AS A DEFENSE AGAINST NARCISSISTIC INJURY

Although depression usually is thought of as a clinical syndrome, it can also serve as a psychological defense against anxiety. In such a conceptualization, depression acts as a "lid," to shut in or cover anxiety and other painful feelings. It is natural to feel a certain degree of depression and grief subsequent to marital break-up, as an affective response to the loss of a significant other. Depressive feelings often represent the internalizing of angry feelings felt toward the spouse because he or she left, or did not meet one's needs or did not measure up to one's expectations. In the usual course of working through the divorce psychologically, being able to be angry at one's former partner and feeling comfortable expressing such feelings often is helpful in dealing with depression. There may remain periods of dysphoria that persist long after the separation; however, most individuals do not feel generally depressed after time has passed since the separation. This normative process usually takes about 6 months, but may last for as long as 1 to 2 years (Gray, 1978). Therapeutic strategies to deal with the initial grief and depression accompanying the loss of a relationship are discussed in Chapter Seven on healing psychologically from a divorce.

When depression is sustained in postseparation and divorce, it can be utilized as a defense against the pain and anxiety accompanying object loss and narcissistic injury. In this case, feelings of depression are more acceptable or tolerable to the individual than facing the pain resulting from significantly diminished self-esteem. Yet a sustained period of depression prevents one from beginning the process of ego reparation and reintegration that ultimately will facilitate a more adequate psychological adjustment to the aftermath of separation and divorce. A case study will illustrate the use of depression as a defense against perceived narcissistic injury and the pain of object loss.

Case Study 5: Sarah and Timothy

Sarah (age 34) sought therapy to help deal with a generally unsatisfying 6-month on-again, off-again relationship with Rob (age 33). Sarah had been married at age 23 to Timothy, who was 24 at the time. The marriage lasted 6 years. Sarah had been divorced for about 1 year before she started dating Rob, who had not been married previously. She and Timothy did not have children. Sarah catalogued a variety of problems and dissatisfactions in the marriage. She indicated that the final straw that broke up the marriage was Timothy's desire to take a job on the West Coast. Sarah, whose family were all in the East, did not wish "to be so far away from my roots." Furthermore, Sarah was also in graduate school at the time Timothy received the job offer and did not wish to interrupt her studies. It was an agonizing decision for Sarah, but she decided to stay and finish her academic work, despite the pressure from Tim. Within 6 months they realized their commuter marriage was not working. Emotional distance between them had grown enormously and they reluctantly decided to divorce.

Sarah reports feeling very sad at their parting and said to the therapist, "I'm not sure I'm over it yet. I really owe a lot to Tim. Not only did he help me feel okay about myself and God knows my parents didn't do much in that regard, though I love them dearly, but he really gave me the support and confidence to go to graduate school." She went on to rationalize the loss of time as follows, "But I knew I wouldn't be happy in Oregon and I knew he wouldn't be happy if he gave up the opportunity, so you can see it just had to be . . . I mean, I didn't see how we could work it out so we could both get what we wanted."

Because Sarah perceived the decision to part as mutual and the actual parting as relatively friendly, she did not initially report feelings or behaviors particularly indicative of diminished self-esteem. She put her energy into her graduate studies and received support and praise from her professors. She began to date several men on a casual basis but had not had a sustained, serious relationship until she became involved with Rob.

At the time therapy began, Sarah was working for a publisher and feeling somewhat bogged down by the lack of opportunity for advancement, which she blamed in part on a stagnant economy. She complained of apathy, of feeling depressed much of the time, and little sexual interest. There were also some vegetative signs of depression including mild insomnia and loss of appetite. She said: "I know I take out my depression on Rob and that really isn't fair, because it's not his fault. I also know I push him away, until he leaves. Then I miss him and I get over feeling depressed and then I want him back. So far he has come back but I don't know how long that's going to go on."

When asked about the differences between her relationship with Rob and her previous marriage with Timothy, Sarah responded: "Well, I don't get the degree of support from Rob that I got from Tim. Tim made me feel special, like he believed in me. Rob cares, I know that, but he expects me to do more on my own . . . and he's not as verbal as Tim was, but I know he cares or he wouldn't come back like he does."

For most of the early sessions Sarah's preference was to meet with the therapist without Rob present. Much of the time in these meetings was devoted to exploring Sarah's relationship with her family. Her mother's parents had emigrated from eastern Europe and settled in the small town where Sarah grew up. They lived with Sarah's family during her high school years. Her grandparents both died within a year of one another while Sarah was a junior in college. Sarah's grandfather held a "traditional" view of women and subtly berated his daughter for not having married a more competent and prosperous man.

Sarah's father was sensitive to these negative feelings, but rarely confronted his father-in-law, both parents preferring instead to "keep the peace." They rationalized that this was necessary since everybody was living together. Sarah apparently took the brunt of her parents' frustrations in this regard, being subtly apprised of the many ways in which she didn't measure up to their expectations. She had a brother, 3 years younger, who was generally left alone and not expected to help very much around the house. Sarah had felt guilty spending more time on her homework than on household chores, since she perceived her mother to be in a difficult, tiring situation. The praise she received at school helped to balance out, in part, the negative messages from home. In therapy she did not seem cognizant of underlying feelings of anger when describing past difficulties, particularly the lack of acceptance and emotional support she experienced while growing up.

The therapist hypothesized that Sarah's initial attraction to Timothy was based, in part, on seeing him as someone who could provide her more consistent emotional support. The divorce resulted in a withdrawal of this important psychological sustenance and left Sarah feeling depressed. In therapy she realized how she had been unable to express directly the intense hurt and anger she felt toward Timothy for having frustrated her support needs by his leaving. Instead, the present relationship with Rob had assumed a pattern of Sarah's withdrawal into depression and accompanying hostile, indirect punishment of him (when he didn't take care of her needs for dependency), followed by reconciliation (so that she could be reassured he had not really left her).

The therapist felt that much of this process was a displaced expression of her continuing hurt and anger toward Tim and an attempt to undo the damage to her self-esteem that resulted from losing him through the break-up of her marriage. The indirect behavioral patterns used to handle conflictual feelings in Sarah's family of origin probably "set up" the subsequent defensive reactions manifested in her responses to Tim and to Rob.

Therapeutic efforts were directed toward helping Sarah gain insight into and come to terms with the continuing influence of Timothy's leaving and the divorce on her subsequent relationships. In order to do this, it was necessary for Sarah to deal with feelings of pain and anger surrounding the narcissistic injuries she received from her family of origin and the object loss experienced from break-up of her marriage. Expressing anger directly helped to moderate her depression and enabled Sarah to see that Rob's expectations of her becoming more independent and assertive could be interpreted as evidence that he cared about her. The relationship with Rob began to stablize, their commitment deepened and they decided to start living together.

FEARS OF INVOLVEMENT RESULTING FROM NARCISSISTIC INJURY

The damage to self-esteem following marital separation and divorce may lead one to employ a variety of self-protective psychological defenses, such as the avoidance of subsequent meaningful relationships. This is epitomized by the saying, "Once burned, twice shy." A certain degree of interpersonal reticence is a natural response following the break-up of an unsatisfying relationship. When an individual sustains a hesitancy to get involved in potentially meaningful relationships, it can indicate a continuing inability to deal with the psychological correlates of narcissistic injury. This interpretation should be considered when the expected temporal course of reinvolvement in relationships postdivorce is not being followed by the individual.

A failure to get into subsequent meaningful relationships is not the norm for most people who have been married and then divorced. Such individuals, for the most part, do not show a schizoid-like personality pattern of avoidance of relationships over their lifetime. Thus avoiding reinvolvement in meaningful and sustaining ways with other adults suggests a defensive response, often part of the sequelae to perceived narcissistic injury stemming from the break-up of a marriage. The following case study illustrates this process.

Case Study 6: Monique and Paul

Monique (age 38) entered therapy approximately 5 years after the break-up of her 11-year marriage to Paul (age 40). Monique and Paul had joint custody of the couple's three boys, James (age 15), Charles (age 13), and Rick (age 10). Paul was with his sons usually two weekends per month, one of the school vacations, and for a longer period each summer. Monique reported Paul to be a concerned and caring father. He was engaged to Carol, whom he had been seeing for about 2 years.

Monique reported a generally unsatisfying picture regarding relationships with men since her divorce. She said early in therapy: "I just don't understand it. I know I'm attractive and I don't look my age. It's not that I don't attract men. But I seem to find some way that they disappoint me and that's that . . . I break off the relationship. I know it hurts the guy . . . because I've been able to show the loving part of me . . . well, he's got to be confused, if you know what I mean." She continued: "I think I'd really like to get married again. I think it would be good for the boys and, although I'd never admit it to him, I'm jealous of Paul and Carol . . . the way they seem to care for each other, at least from what I gather."

When the therapist inquired as to why she felt "it would be good for the boys," Monique replied, "We're real close, they've really been good to me . . . good for me. I'm worried that I'm getting too attached to them. Jimmy will be leaving home before long. I've come to depend on them and I truly miss them when they're at Paul's. I mean, it's not too healthy, don't you think . . . I'm worried in my frustration I turn to them instead of to somebody else. But they still need me, at least Rick does."

Upon more detailed questioning, Monique indicated that she had had one "intense" relationship, approximately 9 months after she and Paul separated. In retrospect, she felt the relationship was based largely on mutual physicial attraction. She had met Dan at an office party, although Monique indicated "we had previously known who each other was." He was a salesman in the same firm where Monique worked as a personnel coordinator. Dan had been divorced about 2 years and was, in Monique's words, "playing the field." She said they both "had a little too much to drink" and "ended up in bed." She continued "I was relaxed and felt free . . . surprise! . . . Paul used to give me the message that he thought I was too uptight. This wasn't the first time I had sex with someone after Paul and I separated, but it was the best. How do you figure that? I really didn't know the guy . . . it's not supposed to work that way, from what I've read. Anyway, it was more than sex, we both liked being outdoors, and we started seeing each other regularly, until I decided after about a year that it wasn't going to work out. I don't think he wanted to settle down and I didn't want somebody who couldn't be there for me."

As Monique talked more about her relationships since the divorce, it became clear to the therapist that the ending of her marriage had left a marked injury to her self-esteem. She described the coming apart of her relationship with Paul along the following lines: "Well, I always thought we'd just go on . . . doesn't everybody think that? I was happy, at least I thought I was. I got signs here and there that maybe he wasn't real satisfied with things, but doesn't everybody get those? I can see now how much we grew apart . . . even then I was probably too involved with the boys and I think he felt neglected. We started fighting more, not physical fights, but he said some really crappy things to me. I couldn't believe that was coming from *him!* (*Pause.*) I think he realized it was over before I did. He couldn't respect me and say the things he did. We waited until after Christmas and he moved out. At first, we were just going to try being apart. God, it was hard on the boys; I couldn't explain it to me, much less to them. Paul and I tried dating after he left. It just didn't work; I expected the love to come back and it didn't. And then he thought we should start seeing other people . . . maybe he already had . . . and that was it for me. I just didn't feel he cared for me in the way I needed. I still can't understand what I did to make him say what he did . . . before we split."

Monique grew up in a small town. Her father owned a general store, and everybody in the family took turns working there. The store apparently was not very successful financially. Monique attributed this to her father letting people buy things on credit and then not being able to bring himself to collect the money he was owed. The family was quite religious and Monique indicated, "Dad never thought stores should be open on Sunday. He was dismayed when everybody would drive 25 miles just to go to a shopping center." She describes her family as close and loving, but it seemed clear to the therapist that conflict was never dealt with openly. Monique remarked, "Well, we all had to get along, since we all worked together. Father said, 'How would it look to the customers to yell at one another?' That sort of carried over at home, too. Philip [her younger brother] and I would never get into it when Dad was around. It didn't bother Mom too much . . . she just went right on doing what she was doing, unless we started hitting or calling names. Then she'd threaten to tell Father, though she never really did. She let us be kids and I'm glad of that."

Monique met Paul during their 1st year of vocational/technical school. They started dating and eventually "got serious." Their family backgrounds were similar. His father was a small-town minister, who married the couple after both graduated, at the end of their 2nd year of school. The courtship was smooth; both had had limited dating experience in high school. Generally, conflict was avoided in courtship and early marriage, consistent with the "rules" in both families of origin. Monique reported feeling irritable at times but indicated, "I could usually explain it as being that time of the month, or the weather was bad, or something like that. Paul wouldn't talk about it, if something was bothering him, so I just tried to be understanding and he'd get over it after a day or so. The kids could get us away from feeling down. They were really good boys and Paul liked being a father."

The pattern of conflict avoidance during the early and middle phases of the marriage ill-prepared Monique (and probably Paul) for the disillusionment and distancing that happened over time in the relationship. Monique had become used to feeling "loved" by significant others and had not built up ego defenses to cope with perceived rejection. The break-up of the marriage left a strong narcissistic injury from which she had not recovered at the time she began therapy. In some ways the inability to let herself get meaningfully reinvolved, and to struggle through the inevitable, healthy ambivalence and conflict of an adult relationship, was consistent with her life-long pattern of conflict avoidance. This previously adaptive pattern, which promoted domestic harmony in her family of origin, had become dysfunctional. Monique could not achieve what she now felt she wanted from a relationship, in terms of intimacy and commitment.

Therapeutic consideration focused on helping her to deal with the pain of her injured self-esteem, as well as letting go of some of the unexpressed anger she had felt toward Paul. She gradually began to accept that conflict was inevitable in a close relationship and that dealing with it more directly could indicate psychological strength. To achieve these changes, it was necessary to explore in therapy how conflict had been handled in Monique's family of origin. She came to see that feeling anger and frustration was not incompatible with feeling love toward significant others. She learned that one can accept negative feelings from another person, and even rejection, without necessarily suffering great damage to one's ego. In this process, Monique's defenses against narcissistic injury were strengthened. The likelihood of a meaningful involvement with another person was enhanced, since paradoxically she could accept more comfortably the possibility of rejection.

Monique ended therapy after 6 months. She was dating several men and was optimistic that one of these relationships could become more intense. She came back to therapy for a brief period approximately a year and a half after the prior termination. Monique was going through the ending of a close relationship and sensed some "old wounds" were being reactivated as she faced another loss of a love object. However, she felt better about having been able to care in this relationship, even though it was not working out. Monique accepted responsibility for her role in the break-up and, with some support from the therapist, was able to deal with the pain and feelings of rejection in a healthier manner then previously.

ACTING OUT AS A DEFENSE AGAINST NARCISSISTIC INJURY

The opposite response to an avoidance of meaningful relationships is shown by some individuals during and after a divorce. Such a pattern is characterized by an overinvolvement in relationships and is usually accompanied by some sexual acting out, frequently beginning shortly after the separation. One tries to heal the narcissistic wounds caused by perceived rejection from a spouse by engaging in at times frenetic attempts to relate to other potential love objects.

These relationships sometimes have a strong component of "limerance" (Tennov, 1979); that is, the individual feels consumed and obsessed with the experience of "being in love." One is reminded of a recent television commercial in which a man excitedly tells a group of friends in a bar, "I have met *the* perfect woman!" The bartender, with a wry smile, replies, "Again?"

Among the implications of this pattern of behavior is that very strong doses of caring and special attention are necessary to heal the ego pain inflicted by the break-up of the marriage. The short-lived nature of many of these intense, but basically transitional, relationships and the attempt by one or both parties to ascribe to them a greater degree of commitment than is usually the case suggests strong defensive operations at work. These defenses are directed at restoring lowered self-esteem.

Often such relationships are begun before one has truly dealt with the painful psychological responses to marital break-up. The new partner then becomes inevitably triangulated with the former spouse. In the process, the two individuals in the new relationship often do not get a "straight shot" at relating to one another, given the many agendas that remain from the previous marriage(s). The outcome is frequently an eventual series of rejections and disappointments that further assault one's diminished self-esteem rather than bolstering it, as hoped. A case study will illustrate defensive acting out in an attempt to deal with narcissistic injury.

Case Study 7: Richard and Betty

Richard (age 29) initially contacted the therapist asking for an appointment for himself and his wife Betty (age 30). Richard explained that Betty had told him recently that she was having an affair with another man and that she wanted a separation. He felt it urgent to seek therapy before proceeding with such a serious decision. Richard was genuinely perplexed over Betty's recent disclosures. He felt he "had been a good husband" and that he had worked hard and successfully to provide for the family. They had been married for 9 years and had a daughter, Ruth, age 7.

Betty was relatively quiet during the initial session. She had begun working as a social service worker in the community on a half-time basis approximately 1 year ago. She had become involved with one of her supervisors, a man named Alan, who was separated and in the process of getting a divorce from his wife of 11 years. She described Alan (despite Richard's pained expression) as warm and giving and felt attracted to him "because he seemed to know a lot about life." She continued: "It hasn't been easy for him, going through the break-up . . . he has two kids . . . but I admire his courage in doing what he felt he had to."

Betty did not hold out much hope of staying in the marriage. The therapist did not sense a true commitment on her part to working on the marital relationship. She was upset about the hurt she had inflicted on Richard by her revelations, but also felt relieved. She said, "I knew I had to tell him. I was afraid he'd find out from someone else and I didn't want that. I think I tried to let him know what was going on but he didn't get the message . . . and anyway I knew we couldn't run away from this."

At the second session, Betty indicated that she had made up her mind to leave the marriage. Richard was angry with the therapist and appeared to project onto him the same degree of impotence and helplessness that Richard himself was feeling. He appeared to have misread Betty's willingness "to see somebody" in therapy as a sign that she had not yet made up her mind. The therapist began the session by attempting to gather some additional information on each spouse's family background. Betty mentioned that her parents divorced after 25 years of marriage. Neither had remarried. Richard's parents remained married up to the time of his father's death from cancer 3 years before. His mother had recently remarried.

Richard did not see the relevance of the therapist gathering more information since "it looks like things are inevitable . . . I think she's gonna leave, doctor. I think she's just here for me." The therapist acknowledged Richard's feelings of despair and frustration that the therapist could not do more to help. In the absence of any indication that Betty wished to alter the course she had decided upon, the therapist proceeded to ask the couple if they had talked about financial and custody arrangements and whether he could be of any help in this regard. Richard said, "Well, she knows I'll take care of her, I always have. And I would hope we could work out a way to share Ruth . . . I don't think it's good for a child to lose a parent." Betty felt receptive to negotiating things in this regard and indicated she wished to minimize conflict.

As the session was almost over, the therapist offered to work further with them, either conjointly or separately, dealing with issues in the separation or other individual concerns. They decided to talk about this and let the therapist know if they wished additional sessions. Two months later, Betty left a message that she needed a letter to the Family Court Commissioner saying that she had completed the one counseling session required by the state for individuals who are petitioning for divorce.

Approximately a year later, Richard called for an individual appointment with the therapist. He said over the phone, "I feel it's time I came in and talked about things. I've been divorced for nearly a year now and it's just not working out." The anger and frustration he had felt previously toward the therapist seemed noticeably absent this time, somewhat to the therapist's surprise, as he had not expected to hear from Richard again.

During the initial session, Richard described a pattern of intense involvement with a series of women, which he began almost immediately after Betty moved out. At first gratifying and ego boosting, he felt his satisfaction with this pattern of relationships had reached a point of diminishing returns. The following dialogue is taken from this session:

Richard: It really hurt me, what Betty did. I don't know if I showed it or not, but I really felt low. Like I wasn't enough for her. That's the only way I could explain her getting involved with somebody else. (*Pause.*) At first, I was out for revenge. You know, to show her I could have somebody too. I was nervous at first . . . Betty did a number on me . . . but you know it happened easier than I thought. You're not going to believe this, but you know who I went out with first . . . my secretary. That's classic, isn't it, a businessman and his secretary. Well, we went out, she was interested, and we went to bed. But I had a sense things could get sticky, so we agreed not to see each other any more. It wouldn't have worked, anyway; I was already comparing her to Betty . . . I mean, it just wasn't what I was used to. But it felt good to be wanted, and she seemed satisfied, though we didn't go on. Besides, she was between boyfriends.

Therapist: What happened after that?

Richard: Well, basically a lot of one night stands. Some girls I went out with more than once, but as I look back now, I was using them the way two people use each other in a one night stand. (*Pause.*) About 3 months ago, I realized how miserable I was, you know, down on myself. I hadn't really found anybody I could really fall in love with; believe it or not, I was still comparing them to Betty. Damn her . . . I think I'm still hurting.

Therapist: Do you think you've been trying to avoid dealing with some of that hurt . . . covering it up with so many relationships?

Richard: Yeah, it sort of looks that way, doesn't it? But I don't think it's working.

Therapist: Because you're depressed?

Richard: Yes . . . not feeling real happy. I didn't find someone like Betty did.

Therapist: As you look back on the marriage and its ending, what's been hardest to deal with?

Richard: Feeling rejected . . . by her. That's what I can't seem to get over thinking about.

Therapist: Then perhaps not getting too involved with anyone is a way of not getting rejected again, not having to go through that again.

Richard: (*not quite agreeing*) Well, I wouldn't want to go through it again.

Therapist: I think we need to explore why the rejection was so painful. Tell me, was that the first time you had felt rejected by a woman, when the marriage broke up?

Over the next several sessions, object loss and unresolved feelings from the divorce were explored further. Richard generally had felt loved as a child and had been given the message that, if he wanted something bad enough, and was willing to work hard, that he probably could have it. His business success was in keeping with this belief system. He had three semiserious relationships with women before getting involved emotionally with Betty. However, Richard protected himself against rejection in each case by ending the relationship first, when it became clear to both parties that things weren't working out.

It appeared to have taken Richard a long time to make a true commitment to Betty. He remembers: "After a while, I knew I had to trust that she loved me and it would be okay. And, anyway, it was time to think about getting married. I felt like I was ready to settle down. I thought she'd make a good wife . . . at least she was good to me. I wanted to make it work and I believed it could. (*Pause.*) I just wasn't prepared for what happened."

In reviewing the marriage, Richard could now see some of the signs of Betty's growing unhappiness. His defenses against rejection, as well as fears of failure, appeared to prevent his dealing with her frustration and disillusionment, usually conveyed via her question: "Do you have to work so much?" Richard indicated: "She was quite involved with Ruth. Now I see maybe that wasn't completely by choice. I mean, she probably got more back from Ruth than she was getting from me."

It became clear to the therapist that few experiences in Richard's past had prepared him for the ego wounds inflicted by Betty's choosing another man and the subsequent divorce. He returned to his old pattern of having relationships with a tenuous commitment; these were temporarily ego gratifying but ultimately unfulfilling. He was once again spared the pain of rejection by virtue of limiting commitment. However, his recent feelings of depression served to signal the need for a change in this relationship pattern. He began to understand in therapy that he no longer needed a constant stream of ego replenishment in the form of transitory encounters with a variety of women.

By realizing he could survive rejection, Richard was able to risk true involvement. After 5 months of therapy he began dating Laura, who had been divorced for 2 years and had a son, age 3. The fact that she was looking to settle down in a long-term relationship did not make Richard wary, as formerly. He began to see that they had common goals and he liked the way she related to Ruth. He left therapy after 7 months (20 sessions) and was fairly optimistic that the relationship with Laura might lead to a long-term involvement.

In summary, three psychological patterns shown by individuals who are dealing with narcissistic injury resulting from marital separation and divorce have been described: (1) sustained depression, (2) avoidance of meaningful relationships, and (3) overinvolvement in transitory relationships, usually accompanied by sexual acting out. The dynamics involved in these strategies and some treatment considerations have been elaborated through case studies.

Both the person who decides to leave and the person who is "left" need to deal with issues of lowered self-esteem. When an intense emotional investment of the magnitude experienced in a marriage does not work out, both parties suffer pain, disappointment, and doubt in regard to their judgment and capability for sustaining a meaningful intimate relationship. The temporal sequence for feeling self-esteem injury may differ. The person who is "left" may suffer such feelings more acutely. However, over time, the "leaver" must also deal with wounds to self-esteem that result from marital dissolution and accompanying loss of a love object. Being in another meaningful relationship at or near the time of separation does not insulate one completely against narcissistic injury. Eventually, each individual must come to terms emotionally with the ending of the marriage and its accompanying pain. This means the "owning" of one's own contribution to the break-up, as well as focusing on the shortcomings of one's partner. Only in tenuously bonded individuals is this emotional process minimized and, as illustrated in the case of William and Beverly, this may happen because the marriage was entered into basically for motives other than the building of a strong, primary relationship with a significant other.

Chapter Five

Role Loss and Disorientation in Divorce

Intimacy issues related to object loss and narcissistic injury are an integral part of the loss of self-esteem experienced in separation and divorce. Also critical to self-esteem, however, is the role loss and disorientation experienced at this time and the many related issues having to do with one's sense of identity.

DIVORCE AND DELAYED IDENTITY FORMATION

By the time people reach their 30s, usually they have begun to grapple with issues of redefining self-esteem and self-worth as dependent less on what others think, do, or feel for them and more on criteria that are internal and self-validated. The developmental antecedents of defining one's identity apart from others have usually begun in adolescence, where one begins to separate from parents. However, it is fairly common for many people not to negotiate this process successfully, not to finish it, and in some cases perhaps not to even really begin it.

Many people marry before they individuate. It would be unrealistic to expect that one must become a fully self-actualized person before one couples. On the other hand, most therapists would agree that successful coupling requires each person to have individuated to some degree, that is, to have developed a separate identity. Some successful separation needs to have occurred before successful communion can take place in marriage. Yet it has been commonplace for people, particularly women, to leave their original family and to marry soon after, beginning a new family. There may never have been a period of being alone, on one's own, during which the individual painfully, but positively, grapples with issues of "Who am I?" "Do I love myself as I am distinct from others?"

127

Personal identity is often subsumed within the marital relationship. This process can happen to men as well as to women. Even when a person has had a period in young adulthood of leaving home, and gainfully supporting himself or herself, marrying may initiate many demands for sublimating individuality and the ways in which one has previously defined one's identity through special and separate interests, activities, and friends.

The long-term consequences of delayed identity formation or subsumed identity in the marital relationship may be an insidious, progressive loss of self-esteem. Divorce in such cases may represent a positive attempt to regain self-esteem through separation, individuation, and self-definition apart from the spouse, parent, or significant other. Premature replacement of a significant other with a hasty rebound relationship or remarriage can short circuit this positive developmental opportunity. It is similar to replacing the parent with a spouse. In this case, the spouse is replaced with yet another lover or spouse, but the underlying issues about identity are never confronted. The case of Luke and Cindy illustrate these ideas.

Case Study 8: Luke and Cindy

Conflict between Luke and Cindy reached epic proportions when Luke's mother revealed that she was diagnosed as having lung cancer, with a 50% survival rate after treatment. At this point Luke told Cindy they would have to see his parents every weekend and spend most of their free time with his mother, including the couple's upcoming 2-week vacation. Throughout their marriage Cindy had resented Luke's attachment to his parents, particularly to his mother. While she sympathized with Luke's sense of impending loss and his guilt feelings, the prospect of increased in-law contact in an already intolerable situation led Cindy to consider leaving the marriage.

Cindy had met Luke when she was 20 and attending a local junior college. Luke was barely 18 and finishing high school. They married 6 months later when Cindy became pregnant. Cindy subsequently miscarried and then quit school, obtaining a job as a teller in a bank so that Luke could begin college.

Cindy was the youngest of four sisters. She was abused psychologically by her father, as were two of her older sisters. She was very anxious to leave her unhappy home life and begin a home of her own. Luke was an only child and the indulged son of a devoted, long-suffering mother and an immature, gregarious, heavy drinking father. Despite the alcohol, Luke was as attached to his father as to his mother and felt very protective of both. Luke indulged his father's adolescent whims, irresponsible spending, and binges. He put himself in the role of the buffer for his mother, thinking he could protect her from his father's ranting and irrational demands.

A condition of Luke's marriage to Cindy was the continued close involvement of the couple with both his parents. Despite his occasional criticism of his parents, Luke essentially modeled his emotional functioning after them, alternating between the martyr-like posture of his mother and the childlike explosions of his father, during which he would irrationally demand that Cindy take care of all of his needs. He had no other really close friends, had regarded his mother as his best friend, and now perceived Cindy in this light.

Cindy increasingly felt smothered by Luke's expectations of nurturance and dependency, angry at his involvement with his parents, and particularly aggrieved at his ambivalence in regard to having another child. She talked about quitting her job, becoming more openly angry about her feelings. Luke in turn became more demanding and volatile. At this point, Cindy (now age 25) became pregnant. Her preoccupation with the pregnancy, and later with her son, Benjamin, provided a temporary refocus for her. She plunged into motherhood with a vengeance, attended Lamaze classes and later helped to teach them. She loved taking care of Benjamin as much as she had begun to resent taking care of Luke. In angry response to her emotional unavailability, Luke became involved with another student at the college he was attending. The affair for him, like the pregnancy for Cindy, served to stave off some of their conflict, until Luke's mother became so gravely ill.

The open warfare ignited again by the illness of Luke's mother and his overinvolvement with his parents led Luke and Cindy to seek couple therapy. They were seen for 15 sessions over the course of a year. Luke became more involved with his girlfriend and finally told Cindy about the relationship. They could not resolve their personal and interpersonal conflicts within the marriage and decided to divorce. Luke married his girlfriend 7 months after the divorce. His mother weathered treatment for her carcinoma and began to return to normal life. A year later Luke's new wife was complaining of his overinvolvement with his parents.

After the divorce, Cindy found herself in a very difficult position. As a single parent of a young child, with little economic or psychological support from her ex-husband and none from her family, she was hard pressed to make ends meet. Her sense of self-esteem plummeted. There were limited dating opportunities in the small town where she lived, but she finally met an older, divorced man who appeared financially to be quite solid and who took a genuine interest in her son. She almost married him. Fortunately, through the prodding of a good friend, she realized that she neither loved this man nor knew enough about herself to attempt another marriage. Another union at this point would have been a repeat of the subsuming of her identity in the marital relationship and a premature replacement of her marital role loss; but it was difficult to trade the discomfort and growth resulting from being on her own for the security and status of being "safely" married to a stable man. She began painfully and slowly to rebuild her self-esteem and to redefine her self-worth separately from the man with whom she was attached.

This case illustrates how divorce can be related to delayed identity formation, as illustrated by Luke, and to subsumed identity, as shown by Cindy. Divorce helped Cindy struggle with and begin to transform and resolve issues of identity; however, in Luke's case, it only served to replace or substitute the participants. The underlying issue of individual separation has yet to be confronted by Luke. Perhaps the dynamic between him and his new wife will aid in this developmental process in a way in which it was not possible with Cindy. His mother's death could ultimately serve as a catalyst or marker event for change, the way divorce did for Cindy.

The remainder of this chapter will discuss the concept of role loss as it affects identity and self-esteem in divorce. Included in this discussion will be four kinds of defenses or strategies employed by individuals to deal with the threat to self-esteem imposed by perceived role loss in divorce and by the necessity for role restructuring. A brief case study will serve to illustrate each example.

The four defensive postures that people typically employ to deal with role loss and role disorientation in divorce are (1) overcompensation; (2) self-denigration; (3) withdrawal; and (4) projection. A caveat is in order, namely that these various defenses against the loss of self-esteem accompanying object loss and role loss in divorce are not orthogonal. Elements of denial and depression, for example, can be found in most of the defensive postures.

PSYCHOLOGICAL DEFENSES TO ROLE LOSS AND ROLE DISORIENTATION

LOSING A ROLE

Sociologists generally define the concept of "role" in functional terms as denoting the set of activities and attitudes intrinsic to a given status or social position. For example, the marital status refers to one's position within the family structure or within the society. Assuming the marital "role" can involve behaviors such as cohabitation, monogamy, procreation, and engaging in any or all of the other activities expected of a spouse. "Status," by contrast, is a more structural concept, indicating one's position within a social structure or social institution.

Rosow (1976) delineates the difference between role and status in terms of the relative ambiguity of status and role prescriptions. In the social institution of marriage both status and role are clearly present and are closely linked. "Tenuous role" situations are those where one's status is well established but the role is unclear. Uncertain status, but clear role expectations characterize "informal role" situations, whereas a "nonrole" exists when neither clear status nor role prescriptions are present.

Being divorced is an example of a tenuous role, where the status is clearly defined, but the role behaviors are unclear. One has to reformulate new roles with little outside support and few normative guidelines from a society that is geared primarily to being married and part of a family. In the period of limbo before one is legally divorced, yet not living with one's spouse in marriage, the individual may experience the situation of a "nonrole." In this often conflictual period, clients frequently are not sure whether they are married or divorced, emotionally or functionally. Neither clear status nor clear role prescriptions are present.

Both before and after actual legal divorce, there is "role loss" and "role disorientation," that is, the loss of former, structured roles associated with being married and having a family and/or children, and the sense of confusion about one's place and identity. There is also the demand to adapt successfully to the loss of the relationship itself. Depending on the individual case, divorce is likely to involve the following factors: (1) the loss of the attachment to and identity associated with one's spouse; (2) the loss of the familiar role status as a married person; (3) the loss of corresponding roles such as homemaker or wage earner; (4) lower socioeconomic status because of loss of income; (5) the necessity to assume new, perhaps unfamiliar and undesired roles such as "single person," "head of household," or "welfare recipient"; and (6) changes and losses in one's social support system as a result of these role and status changes (Brown & Foye, 1982).

The loss of the role of wife and mother can be especially difficult for women who have been raised to view marriage and motherhood as their ultimate "careers," in the process not developing autonomous coping skills. Divorce may stimulate an identity crisis aggravated by the loss of the "occupation" of housewife (Lopata, 1973) and the necessity of meeting the practical, economic, and emotional changes demanded in supporting oneself as a single person. In successful role changes, the person both relinquishes an old role and adopts a new one (Riley, Foner, Hess, & Tobly, 1969). However, the process is aided considerably when there is a socially valued and rewarded role to replace the old one and when the person is prepared for the new role. Neither condition generally is true for divorce. Despite its prevalence, the stigma attached to divorce continues to make many people reluctant to admit their new status. Occasionally a spouse has been getting ready for divorce and a new life for many years. The wife who returns to school for further training and then waits to divorce until her children are grown and her skills are marketable is a case in point. But this kind of preparation generally comes after the fact.

Because the new role of being divorced is so little valued and because divorce is associated with undesirable role losses rather than with positive opportunities for role transformations, increments, and restructurings, there is almost always a temporary, but very significant, loss of self-esteem as one divorces. People generally do not prepare for or expect divorce and thus do not integrate it into their expected or possible life plan or consider it as a potentially positive part of their developmental process. One expects to leave home and parents and, although such a separation may bring conflict and loneliness it is usually expected that, in the long run, the personal growth engendered by greater independence and self-definition will bring an increase in self-esteem. It is critical in divorce therapy that the individual redefine the divorce in such terms, working through the stress, conflict, and problems associated with separation and ultimately moving on to a new chapter of life with an increase in, or at least a restoration of self-esteem.

Unfortunately, instead of rationally recognizing the role losses that divorce brings and the opportunity for positive change, many people react to the potential self-esteem threat accompanying role loss by defensive maneuvers and strategies. These are designed to deny the loss and to salvage one's self-esteem. A common pattern, particularly for a woman who has identified strongly with the mothering role, is to react to the role loss by overcompensation.

SUPERPERSON

The tale is all too familiar. For example, take the single, divorced woman who has tried to divide herself into many whole pieces, attempting to be a full-time wage earner, a head of household, both father and mother to her children, a dutiful daughter, and a faithful friend. The psychic theme in part is denial; one pretends there has been no loss. Everything will go on as before, all the children's hundred and one activities will be managed and the household and style of living maintained, whatever the personal cost involved. The divorced superperson feels he or she must do everything perfectly and better perhaps than before the divorce, to make up for presumed failure. Underlying guilt motivates much of the frenetic activity and overcompensation. The weekend father who compulsively drags his children to one activity after another and showers them with material goods to "prove" what a good father he still is, is yet another common example of how this phenomenon works to salvage self-esteem.

Case Study 9: Al and Betsy

Al (age 33) and Betsy (age 33) were divorced after ten years of marriage. They had two children, Bill (age 9) and Jessica (age 8). Both Al and Betsy had been good parents, probably better parents than marital partners. It was difficult for Al to change jobs after the divorce, because his new work took him and his new wife out of town, away from his children. However, he had not been able to find work in the economically hard pressed area where his former family had lived. He had been laid off from his old job as a welder, and was unable to keep up with child support payments to Betsy.

Betsy worked as a nurse, taking the late night shift from 11 to 7 so she could be with her children during the day, before and after they went to school. She was very fearful that the children would blame her for the divorce. Other than work, all her activities centered about the needs of the children; she was determined that their lives would not change very much because of the divorce and Al's leaving. She chauffeured them after school to soccer, ballet lessons, activities at the YMCA, and to their friends' homes. On the weekends she ferried them off to parks, the zoo, and places that didn't cost a lot of money. Betsy felt the evening meal and their lunches had to be home prepared. Although she disliked baseball, she dutifully sat at Bill's Little League games in the evenings before she went to work.

On those rare occasions when she did leave the children she was unable to enjoy herself or get rid of guilt feelings. Her frenetic efforts to be a "super mom" increased when Al remarried. She felt angry and bitter and handled these feelings indirectly by becoming a martyr. She drew comfort by telling herself how well the children were doing and salved her self-esteem by thinking of herself as a good and devoted mother. Betsy's efforts at overcompensation for her lost role as wife and new role as single parent sometimes failed her and she would become depressed and discouraged, feeling trapped, unappreciated, and frustrated about how narrow and circumscribed her life had become. Her friends encouraged her to date, to go out socially, but she offered the excuse of having to be with her children.

The children saw Al one weekend every month. He would become very anxious before these visits and treated them as special events, tests of whether he was still loved by his children and was still their "father." He refrained from disciplining them during these times, fearing their disapproval. He showered them with whatever money he was able to come up with, much to the dismay of his new wife, Elaine, who felt that when his children were with Al, she, the marital relationship, and her own son were ignored. Elaine resented his preoccupation with his children's needs and desires, his generosity with presents and special favors, and the tension that he felt, which affected their relationship.

Both Al and Betsy are examples of people who acutely feel role loss in divorce. In this case the family and parent roles were threatened and tested. The threat to Al and Betsy's perceived loss of status and love from their children led to overcompensation in their perceived roles as parents, after the divorce. By acting in ways they thought a perfect parent would act, Al and Betsy managed to fend off the threat to their sense of self-worth, and assuage their guilt for perceived failure in maintaining the old roles.

Exaggeration of the parental role in some ways reduced the threat of losing that role or of its changing negatively. Whatever pain, cost, or sacrifice was entailed in the exaggeration and overcompensation was perceived as the price to be paid for the "sin" of the divorce. Tenacious indulgence of the children was not seen as being overly permissive or ultimately detrimental to their independence, but as living proof of parental love for children and the maintenance of their status as beloved and lovable people. ("What a good mother I must be; I am always with you, even more than I was before. You cannot blame me for any loss.") The overcompensation also soothed self-esteem loss for Betsy, ("How good I am to be both mother and father to you; I am so needed now") and similarly the role loss for Al ("I am really still a good father and a good person even though I left. You can have anything; I am so generous with you, you must see me as good").

While Betsy reacted to the threat of role loss by redoubling her efforts and activities with the children after the divorce, some people respond to impending or actual identity loss with confusion, disorganization, and inactivity. The surface message to others is one of a lack of understanding and comprehension of the changes and losses in their lives ("I don't understand what is happening or what is necessary to change"). The underlying defense used to cope with the role loss and decrease in self-esteem is self-denigration. The cognitive message to one's self is, "I am too dependent on my former life and roles to be asked to restructure my life."

SELF-DENIGRATION AS A REACTION TO ROLE LOSS

Case Study 10: Miguel and Thereza

Miguel and Thereza grew up in Puerto Rico and immigrated to the United States shortly after the birth of their second daughter. Thereza had a good job in Puerto Rico as an executive secretary in an American importing firm and had taken advantage of an opportunity to be transferred to the United States. Miguel's dream was to open his own garage. He was an excellent mechanic, though not formally educated. The move proved to be very difficult for the family, especially for Miguel whose sparse English blocked him from obtaining the kind of work he desired. He wanted to return to his homeland but Thereza did not, feeling the opportunities here were greater for their daughters. They separated for 1 year, with Thereza alternatingly deciding to return to Miguel and then changing her mind. The separation increased her dislike of his complaints about his inadequacy and difficulties in making it in America and she found herself losing respect for him. She coped with the cultural shock and barriers by adapting to certain new ways and rejecting others in favor of her own cultural heritage. She enrolled her children in an inner-city magnet school that offered a bilingual curriculum. She became active in local Hispanic politics and community affairs. Miguel, in contrast, became more anxious and complained of the changes in her, blaming them on her Anglo assimulation. Their eventual divorce compounded his confusion.

In therapy, Miguel complained that he did not understand why his wife wanted to divorce him or what had happened to change their relationship. He could not see that any good could come from the divorce, nor that change within himself was possible. Suggestions to look for a better job, to make new friends in the Hispanic community, and to reach out to some relatives in America were met with anxiety and fear. Underneath his surface bravado, he felt quite inadequate to deal with all the role loses and changes the divorce entailed, particularly since he was still dealing with felt cultural, family, and identity loss subsequent to leaving Puerto Rico. He was a bright and competent man, but the way he dealt with his wounded ego was to announce to the world that he was not capable of change, nor did he understand it. He would do nothing and thus in effect also not acknowledge the role loss.

Miguel gradually regressed into an even more dependent stance in which he would claim he did not understand the changes before and after the divorce and that it was up to Thereza to make things right again. If she would only have quit her job working for the Americans and stayed at home, if she would only have returned to Puerto Rico with him, if in essence she would only have stayed put and not changed, things could have been and still would be fine between them.

The implicit message underlying these complaints was that since Thereza was the strong one, it was within her power to make things fine; she could not expect him to adapt or to change before or after the divorce. The theme was again that of self-denigration. He saw Thereza as "stubborn and strong willed." She had decided to divorce Miguel, but felt sadness and empathy for him, which Miguel believed she was not capable of feeling. Miguel's defensive posture of self-denigration eventually led him to another way of coping with his loss. He began to mourn and withdraw, dropping out of therapy and subsequently returning to Puerto Rico, "to find a new life."

WITHDRAWAL AND ROLE LOSS

Some people respond to any change, positive or negative, by asserting defensively that nothing good can come from change. ("Nothing good can come from this divorce. There is only loss.") Such individuals often manifest the clinical symptoms of depression: passivity, hopelessness, apathy, sometimes even suicidal feelings. Suicide represents the ultimate withdrawal and escape from the situation and the suffering of role loss and loss of self-esteem. The posture of hopelessness can serve an important function in coping with the aftermath of role loss in divorce. In essence, the person believes: "I don't have to face my losses or the difficulty in replacing them if I stay hopeless and inactive."

The confusion and disorganization Miguel initially displayed in coping with the role loss gave way to withdrawal and despondency after the divorce. He was particularly distressed when Thereza began dating her boss. He complained to the therapist that since the divorce he did not feel "like a man" anymore. By her leaving, he felt Thereza had emasculated him in the eyes of his family, friends, and community; he was no longer a breadwinner, a husband, a father, a lover, or indeed a person.

The decrease in his self-esteem engendered by these perceived role losses in his identity left him feeling not only inadequate, but hopeless. He mourned the losses and soothed his self-esteem by heavy drinking, which temporarily relieved his depression, but only acted to increase his withdrawal from life. His parents and family in Puerto Rico became very concerned for him and encouraged him to return home, which he eventually did, but not before making an abortive suicidal gesture by driving off the road in his car, after drinking.

Thereza also exhibited some withdrawal and feelings of hopelessness after the divorce, but in contrast to Miguel, they were not nearly as extreme, since developmentally she was "further along" than he. She mourned the loss of the relationship. She felt anger and pity for Miguel that turned more into indifference and a detached compassion once he returned to his homeland. She was able to restructure her life more easily than Miguel, having several personal and situational assets that he did not. Her ability to adapt and the increase in self-esteem her job and community activities gave her helped. Her daughters provided some comfort and familial continuity was maintained in part by the presence of her sister in the same city. Finally, despite the losses incurred by way of the divorce, separation from Miguel had given her an economic and personal independence she had not known before. Thereza's social withdrawal was temporary. She began to date again and eventually remarried.

Miguel reacted to Thereza's changing by blaming her for the divorce. Some individuals carry this scenario further by insisting on punishing the spouse for the divorce. One defensive response to the threat or the reality of role loss is splitting and the projection of blame. ("You have changed; I have not. I am good; you are bad.") The person in essence salvages or maintains their threatened self-esteem by adopting postures that proclaim, "I am still the good spouse (father, mother, etc.); you are the bastard who left."

The corollary to this defensive posture is: "You deserve to be punished and it makes me feel better to punish you." The person tries to find ways to remind the ex-spouse what a bad person he or she was to leave, thus depriving the spouse of marriage and the marital identity. Every simple encounter or negotiation can become an opportunity to play out this scenario. The ex-spouse may be called angry, abusive, uncooperative, the very postures the person himself or herself is feeling and exhibiting, openly or covertly.

There is another underlying dynamic in this stratagem. By asserting essentially that the other person is to blame for the divorce and must be punished, the person maintains that they themselves have not changed. Furthermore, one may feel psychologically still married to the ex-spouse, even though divorced, and this is another way of saying that one has not changed. ("I did not want this divorce; it was not my fault. I have not changed; in my mind we are still married, and because we are still attached, I will continue to punish you and find opportunities to remind you of the mistake you made and the bad person you are for leaving me.") One or both partners may use projection to deal with role losses, as in the case of Grace and Bill.

USE OF PROJECTION IN RESPONSE TO ROLE LOSS

Case Study 11: Grace and Bill

It was difficult to say whether the prelude *or* the aftermath of Grace and Bill's divorce was more conflictual. Indeed, they developed to a fine art the needling of each other with various barbs. Any negotiation or possible mutual encounter, item or issue, however small, became ammunition for their continuing engagement after the divorce. Bill (age 52) was the dentist and a prominent man in the small town where they lived. The family also maintained a country home on some farmland in an adjacent county where on the weekends Bill played the gentleman farmer. His practice was reasonably successful; however, much of their comfortable lifestyle was provided by Grace's personal wealth, inherited through her family.

Grace (age 51) spent most of the years of their early marriage raising their three children. Two adopted sons were grown, married, and living away from home. A 16-year-old daughter, Jenny, was loved and pampered. Grace was a passionate gardener and golfer, who provided all the flowers for their local church year round from her bountiful garden. She improved her golf game at the country club to the point where she frequently won in local competitive events. Their marriage was comfortable, but boring. Particularly after their sons left home, each spouse expressed a dissatisfaction with the other's lack of enthusiasm or input into the marriage. Their sexual encounters decreased to the point where they no longer had sex nor talked about it, privately blaming each other for the lack of initiative and desire. They fought frequently and destructively.

Bill was ambivalent about the prospect of leaving the marriage; for years he had perceived their love as waning and he questioned whether the original match with Grace had been a good one. However, their daughter, his place in the community, his family's potential negative reaction, his religion, and his personal values all contributed to his long delay in actually seeking a divorce. As he approached midlife, he finally decided he could not face the emotional poverty in their marriage for another 20 to 40 years, and asked Grace for a divorce.

Grace was equally, if not more, dissatisfied with their marriage but was more adamant about staying married than Bill, for similar as well as for additional reasons. She did not relish the thought of losing her role and status in the community and among her friends and family. Her strong religious beliefs also made her against divorce from a moral standpoint, however miserable one was in a marriage. On the other hand, she realized privately that she was more fortunate than most women in an unhappy marriage, being economically independent of Bill by virtue of her family's wealth. Grace preferred to maintain the facade of a happy marriage to the outside world and to find her satisfactions in her ability to maintain her affluent life-style, play golf, see her friends frequently, travel for pleasure, and visit with her children. She also thrived on feelings of being respected, admired, and envied in her community. She opposed the divorce throughout their marital therapy, but finally went along with it after Bill stopped coming home and began to sleep, live, and work in his dental office.

Grace's opposition to the divorce increased Bill's animosity toward her. He came to believe that her conservative ways had "held him down" all his life. He thought of her as a snobbish prude, as old before her time. In contrast, Grace called him "immature and irresponsible."

While the divorce ended some of the hostilities, it provided new opportunities for further confrontations over economic, social, domestic, and sexual issues. Rationalizing that Bill did not contribute equally from a financial standpoint to their partnership, Grace unilaterally removed the savings from their account at the bank. Bill responded in kind by not making the house payments for several months, until he was ordered to do so by the court. Division of their financial assets was a long, stressful, and protracted affair. Bill claimed that he had contributed substantially to their economic growth by helpfully advising Grace on investing her inheritance and making it grow. However, Grace portrayed him as an economic sycophant.

A small fortune was spent on lawyers, who would hammer out various proposals, only to have either Grace or Bill refuse to sign the stipulation. Finally, it seemed that they were at least agreed on a reasonable settlement, which Bill signed, and Grace said that she would, also. Several weeks passed, however, with no response from Grace. Bill then received a short note from Grace's attorney explaining that Grace could not sign the stipulation because it was incomplete. The note was accompanied by a list of a half-dozen small household items that Bill had taken, which Grace felt belonged to her, including two pairs of pot holders, a tea strainer, and a barbecue fork.

In therapy, Bill didn't know whether to laugh at or explode over the absurdity of the list. He insightfully commented that Grace would find any excuse, however, trivial, not to divorce him in order to maintain the facade of their relationship and her role. Secondly, by not divorcing he felt she would continue to make life miserable for him. He knew he would "pay" for leaving her.

The therapist, however, pointed out Bill's role in maintaining their interaction and how he, too, had continued their interaction by behaviors designed to provoke Grace, thus prolonging their continuing contact. For example, Bill could easily have bought a new small lawn mower to take care of the little bit of lawn around his office, but he continued to borrow the mower left with Grace, a maneuver that never failed to lead to greater hostilities. Furthermore, he flaunted his new girlfriend by showing up with her at a large party given by their close friends, where Grace had also been invited. This made Grace furious.

Grace felt that by getting a divorce Bill robbed her not only of companionship and security, but also, and more importantly, of a multiplicity of roles, particularly the family role. She very much enjoyed being the respected wife and mother of a successful man and successful children and the admiration she received from her father, various relatives, and her in-laws. Actually, she liked her parents-in-law better than her own father and stepmother. Grace had lost her mother when she was 17. She had grown close to her mother-in-law, who did not have a daughter. Since the divorce those contracts decreased markedly and she felt the loss acutely, again blaming Bill.

Just as important to Grace was her social role in the community. She no longer received frequent social invitations related to their status as a prominent couple in the small town. Even her close women friends seemed threatened by Grace's single status. Bill's social encounters with their old friends, accompanied by his new woman friend, only heightened Grace's loss. She called the friends, intimating that his girlfriend had been "a homewrecker." She thus succeeded in alienating these friends and others subsequently against Bill. Even those individuals who refused to take sides pulled back, not wanting to be embroiled in the middle of the conflict.

Sex had always been the couple's most troublesome area. It was not surprising that sex provided the most potent ammunition postdivorce. The plan had been that Bill would live in their country house, having daughter Jenny with him on weekends. One weekend, soon after their divorce was final, Grace learned that Bill's woman friend had also stayed in the house with Bill and Jenny. Grace's conservative morality was deeply disturbed and she berated Bill about his loose morals and the negative impact on their daughter. She went to her lawyer and took Bill back to the Family Court. She demanded a stipulation that Bill not be allowed to see their daughter in the presence of his woman friend or have her overnight. The court said that Grace would have to be satisfied with the latter requirement.

Concern for her daughter was claimed to be her motivation, but Grace was threatened by several real and symbolic losses through this event. She feared both a diminution in her daughter's affections and the possibility that the woman friend eventually would become another mother figure. Most deeply she felt a loss of self-esteem in regard to her sexuality. As long as she had been Bill's wife, there at least had been the public assumption of her adequacy as Bill's lover. The presence of his new lover and the felt confirmation by her own child of the reality of her replacement was difficult for her to accept. She reacted by projecting her anger onto Bill, ("He is punishing me and our child"). In reality, she punished him by prohibiting easy contact with their daughter.

When divorce does not substantially decrease the emotional engagement and when conflictual identity and intimacy issues continue to involve the whole family, as well as friends, lovers, or extended family, a good therapeutic strategy is to bring as many of the participants of the social network as possible into therapy (Speck & Attneave, 1973). An attempt is made both to sort out the dynamic and developmental issues and to promote conflict resolution. Fortunately, the key participants in this case were willing to meet with Bill's therapist and a cotherapist, who was brought in specifically to help with the family therapy. One of Grace and Bill's sons also returned home and participated briefly, but helpfully, in the negotiating of a ceasefire between his parents.

In coping with the role losses she experienced in the divorce and with the need for role restructuring, Grace had to make both behavioral and attitudinal transformations relating to intimacy and identity. Grace's particular therapeutic task was coming to accept that her identity could not revolve about Bill ("I can be myself as I am, unmarried; I value myself as a single person/parent"). She had to find new, satisfying ways of defining her identity through separation as well as through communion ("I know who I am apart from what others tell me I am"). As she began to value her intelligence, generosity, loyalty, athletic, and social skills, she realized these were her "gifts," married or not.

There were also intimacy issues that needed transformation and development. ("I can make close, satisfying, and at times erotic friendships; I can love myself as I am, unmarried"). This process involved coming to terms with her sexual inhibitions, dealing more openly with her need for affection, requesting it from others, and also beginning to love herself, thereby being able to provide for herself some of the affection and self-love she craved.

Bill had feared the divorce, but courageously had separated when he was convinced the relationship was dead. He made several developmental strides as a result of the marital dissolution. The most important of these was the realization that he could make close, satisfying erotic and nonerotic relationships ("Just because my spouse does not love me does not mean others—children, parents, friends, colleagues—do not love or respect me"). His fear that he would lose the esteem and good will of his family and the whole community proved to be unfounded. While there were a few people who ostracized him, he received compassion and understanding from most people, including his parents and children. Paradoxically through the task of separation he had discovered that he was capable of successful communion, a discovery that in the long run considerably helped his self-esteem.

In this chapter, the second of the two mediating processes by which divorce engenders a loss of self-esteem has been discussed, namely, role loss and disorientation. The corresponding need for role transformation and restructuring was also addressed, and will be explored more fully in Chapters Eight and Nine.

Four kinds of defensive postures or strategies that people employ to deal with the threat to self-esteem imposed by role loss in divorce and the need for role restructuring have been summarized: (1) overcompensation stemming from guilt and denial; (2) self-denigration related to feelings of anxiety and inadequacy; (3) withdrawal as a response to mourning and hopelessness; and (4) projection that serves to protect oneself from anger while permitting punishment and abuse of the ex-spouse.

Any or all of these strategies may be utilized by a person who is dealing with divorce and experiencing diminished self-esteem. All serve in some fashion to aid the person temporarily in repairing his or her self-esteem, but at the cost of denying reality and postponing change and possible growth. It is the task of the divorce therapist to help educate, catalyze, nurture, and support the divorcing individual's efforts toward rebuilding, maintaining, and finally increasing his or her self-esteem. Part of this is accomplished by necessary role restructuring. Therapeutic strategies designed to aid role restructuring and ego reparation after divorce will be discussed in the next section.

Therapeutic Strategies for Ego Reparation and Role Restructuring

Chapter Six

Divorce Decision and Implementation

It is relatively rare for a couple who has made the decision to divorce to seek divorce therapy. Probably because spouses have been imbued with the idea of saving a marriage at all costs, the public has been educated to seek therapeutic help in saving a marriage, but not in dissolving it positively. An exception is when a divorcing couple, usually because of bitter disputes around economic or custody issues, is required by the court to seek help through divorce mediation. Other couples in desperation may seek out a divorce mediator to help them negotiate and settle such practical issues as property division, child custody, and visitation. The literature on divorce mediation, however, points out that while the mediation process may have therapeutic benefits, it is not therapy per se, nor is the divorce mediator necessarily a trained therapist (Kersey, 1982; Silberman, 1981). Issues of conflict negotiation and resolution are likely to be addressed in divorce therapy and the therapist may well find himself or herself temporarily involved in some mediation, but the distinguishing characteristics of divorce therapy are its psychological emphasis on dealing with developmental issues of one or both partners and the need for emotional as well as behavioral restructuring.

It is usual for a couple to be involved in divorce therapy only after having first sought marital therapy. As the partners decide to divorce, the process becomes "divorce therapy." Another common occurence is for an individual to seek help sometime after the legal divorce is over, to deal with issues of lingering distress about the divorce. Opportunities for therapeutic help in the divorce process are becoming more available.

As society institutes other mechanisms to help people divorce with more compassion and less stress, it is more likely that the personal and interpersonal outcomes of divorce will be more positive. People then may come to perceive this difficult period also as an opportunity for personal development, a crossroads in which therapy can significantly aid the parties involved to make the transition in a positive and useful fashion. Too often what has happened in marital therapy is that once the decision has been made to divorce, the parties involved assume that therapy is over. The only thing left to do is to divide up the property and decide about the children and that usually means a trip to one's lawyer.

Thus a first priority in therapy after a divorce decision has been made is for the therapist to help educate the spouses about the important tasks left to be accomplished that revolve about their individual developmental issues. The couple is usually receptive to the idea that help might be obtained in negotiating the practical, necessary issues of separation, such as custody. Individuals in this situation often do not perceive immediately how it is important to understand:

1. why this relationship did not work, in order not to repeat the dysfunctional pattern;
2. that emotional disengagement can be a long process, and if it is not successfully accomplished, partners may continue to maintain a conflictual relationship with each other and with their offspring long after the divorce;
3. that the decision to actually make a final separation may trigger acute stress, disorganization, and bereavement in one or both partners that therapy can help relieve;
4. that divorce offers an important opportunity for facing personal developmental conflicts and making positive developmental strides if one is willing to risk such change, and that therapy can be a key element here in this redefinition and transformation;
5. finally, that the decision to divorce has important repercussions for a system of significant others. Family therapy involving the biological parents and/or the stepparents may be important in resolving the object and role loss, promoting role restructuring necessitated by divorce, and ameliorating narcissistic injury felt by the partners.

DECIDING TO DIVORCE

A critical part of divorce therapy is the predivorce period in which the partners decide whether or not to terminate the marriage. Prior to this period, the therapist frequently has been involved in marital therapy with the goal of attempting to salvage the marriage or at least to discover whether it is possible to transform and/or repair the relationship. In such therapy the premise is that the participants desire to see if they can maintain their relationship. The therapeutic focus is on the potential for the rehabilitation of the union. In divorce therapy proper the premise is that a final decision has been made to dissolve the marriage. The focus of therapy becomes the disengagement of the partners. Therapeutic strategies at this point in the divorce therapy process are designed to promote dissolution with a minimum of pain and humiliation, and to encourage developmental growth through facing identity and intimacy issues. The period between marital and divorce therapy per se is a transitional one. The therapist may find himself or herself functioning as both a marital and a divorce therapist as the clients act out their ambivalence about divorce, commonly vacillating between wanting to maintain and wishing to dissolve the marital relationship:

> The first period, predivorce therapy/counseling, centers around the imminent decision whether to divorce or not. It can be at times a long period of indecision whether to divorce or not. One or both spouses may seek therapeutic help. A marriage and divorce therapist should be ready to help whichever way the final decision goes. As a result the therapist frequently must alternate between being a marital therapist and a divorce therapist during this stressful period. This role-change follows the changing needs of the clients as they explore whether to divorce or not. (Fisher & Fisher, 1982, p. 9)

Some therapists would define the predivorce period as beginning whenever there is increasing marital dissatisfaction, tension, or stress. This is usually followed by a decline in intimacy, sometimes with desperate subsequent attempts to recapture a sense of love and closeness. The couple may fight more openly, frequently, and bitterly, or may withdraw into increasing silence and isolation. A lover may be taken for "psychological insurance" (Kressel, 1980), and the couple may enter marital therapy for the first time.

A more precise definition of the predivorce period may be made, however, by considering it as the time when divorce is first mentioned seriously by either spouse as a choice meriting sober consideration. The two parties make the subject a topic of actual discussion or debate. At first the alternative may be alluded to in therapy by one spouse: "If things don't get any better, I think we need to consider divorce." Such a statement is not uncommon, and is not necessarily the precursor to a serious consideration of the divorce alternative. More often it represents a realistic and healthy recognition that all alternatives of conflict resolution are possible, and that a good marriage must be based on viable choice. Statements such as, "I think we should divorce," "I can't stand the conflict (indecision, stress) anymore," "I've reached the end of my rope," "She doesn't want to split, but I see no other alternative," "I just don't have the feelings anymore, I can't see how we can go on this way," indicate a significant break in marital solidarity and attachment that has led the partner(s) to actually consider dissolving the bond.

MIXED MESSAGES

The therapist needs to be aware that the couple's communication patterns or the "marital dance" (Whitaker, 1970), may involve convoluted minuets. The "I want to divorce" message may be the means to shape up or manipulate the other spouse. Similarly, the "I don't want to divorce" message may conceal a wish to separate, but to remain the "good guy." One partner here attempts to force the other to make the decision and "do the dirty deed." Such a strategy allows the spouse to feel the victim, dissipate guilt and/or act out angry feelings. Sometimes the "I want to divorce" message appears to be stated by one spouse prematurely, without significant recognition of that person's contribution to the marital discord or an appreciation of the positive personal changes that could be accomplished to restore marital harmony.

The task of the divorce therapist in this critical period is a difficult one. He or she must not only sort out the seriousness and intent of the divorce messages or threats, but make some diagnostic and prognostic evaluation of the decision, should it begin to be implemented. It is not suggested here that the divorce therapist play God in terms of responsibility for making the decision to divorce. Obviously the clients themselves must always have this final responsibility. Nor can the therapist foist his or her values on the client by suggesting that the *best* thing to do is to stay married, or to be divorced, be it for any reason. What the therapist can do is to carefully, rationally, and skillfully help the clients consider all the alternatives, their consequences, and their important meanings for intimacy and identity.

This is a period in which the therapist must be exceedingly patient. The persistence of attachment in the marital relationship, however dysfunctional or no longer growth enhancing, is well known (Hancock, 1980; Weiss, 1976; Wise, 1980). In some cases the decision may take years to make, with sporadic contacts with the therapist in between the ups and downs. Clinical experience suggests that a better adjustment to divorce often is associated with a clean break. The separation is neither a hasty or premature one in which the alternatives have not been thoroughly analyzed, nor a long drawn out one of agonizing seesaws.

In the authors' experience, a period of 6 months to 1 year spent in such exploration and decision making is usually required in order to guarantee sufficient time for thoroughly analyzing the situation psychologically and therapeutically. Economic or family considerations, however, may well act to keep the person in the marriage much longer even when the decision has been firmly made to leave. In such a situation the therapist may find himself or herself in a position that demands a good deal of patience. Supportive therapy in which clients are helped to "keep a finger in the dike" until they can feasibly leave the relationship becomes the modus operandi in this therapeutic situation.

WHY DON'T YOU LEAVE IF YOU'RE SO UNHAPPY?

Perhaps the single most common therapeutic pitfall of the novice divorce therapist during the predivorce period is for the therapist to become impatient or intolerant with the client's indecision to divorce or to stay married. In such a situation, the therapist may project his or her own values onto the client(s) and implicitly or explicitly urge that they leave the situation. The therapist may imply that the individual is "stupid" or "sick" for staying in the relationship, particularly if they are being abused. The client who picks up this judgment is likely to leave therapy or, if he or she stays, to receive the message as simply more confirmation of helplessness and incompetence for being unable to separate. A corollary may be the feeling that "I deserve this abusive marital relationship because I am so inferior, dependent, and hopeless," and an even further supposition may be made; "You [therapist] *should* criticize me and I deserve it. I am so stupid and helpless."

The therapist needs to point out the destructive consequences of staying in a psychologically unhealthy marriage and the client's responsibility for moving toward a resolution of the situation. The therapist, however, must not become overly involved personally and thus set up a situation in which the client feels judged for his or her action or inaction. The case of Joe and Selma illustrates these points.

Case Study 12: Joe and Selma

Selma was a 28-year-old woman who had been married for 11 years. Her husband, Joe (age 29) was a factory worker. Selma and Joe had been involved since their early teenage years. They had five children, ages 2 to 12 years of age. The oldest child, Josie, had been named for Joe, but actually had had a different father, which Joe suspected and which Selma denied. Joe married Selma in the middle of this pregnancy and began physically abusing her shortly after Josie was born. She recalls that, at the time she seriously considered leaving Joe, but she became pregnant again with Everett (now 11) and felt there was no way she could leave. Besides, despite their conflicts and his abuse, she still felt in love with and deeply attached to her husband. Other children followed with mounting debts. Joe would disappear periodically, but Selma took him back each time.

Selma came into therapy on referral from the Family Court when, in one of Joe's rages, Josie also became the target of his anger and suffered a broken arm. A teacher finally got the true story of what had happened from Josie and subsequently confronted Selma. At first Selma denied Joe's involvement, but tearfully and reluctantly admitted it in a session with the school's social worker. Joe refused to come in for therapy, but Selma saw a therapist and started to explore her feelings about herself, her family, and the relationship. Over a period of a year Selma poured out her anger and bitterness toward Joe, and her desire to leave him. These expressions alternated with feelings of apathy and passivity about her situation, as well as hopefulness and well-being when Joe was once again being nice to her. She rationalized that, with the exception of the incident with Josie, Joe never had abused the children, and that the kids needed his presence, however unstable.

Selma seemed to be helped the most from several family therapy sessions with her children and occasionally with Joe and by contacts with a group of battered women who supported her fledging efforts at assertiveness. The therapist was encouraged when she decided she could make it on her own, got a job as a file clerk, and asked Joe to move out, which he subsequently did. All the children except for the youngest, Dawn, age 3, were now in school and Selma's sister, Tess, moved in with her to take care of Dawn. The first "separation" lasted 5 months before the couple agreed that Joe would move back in. During this reconciliation the same pattern of discord and abuse was renewed, whereupon Selma again sought out the therapist. Several months intervened with many stormy ups and downs in the relationship; Joe would move in and out. Selma now suspected he also had another woman. Still, she was very reluctant to divorce and fearful that she could not make it on her own. The therapist continued patiently, but repeatedly, to point out to Selma the destructive consequences of her situation, not only for her own self-esteem, but also for the psychological health of her family.

Selma: He just don't give a damn. He couldn't just shack up with that woman if he did. And, God, when I think of what I've put up with from him. . . . (*Cries softly.*)

At this point the therapist had a choice of several responses. The first would have been to reflect the abuse and rejection Selma felt she had suffered.

Therapist: You feel there's no way he could care about you and treat you as he has.
Selma: No, no he can't, and yet . . . I know he does.

The therapist had reflected those feelings many times. While they helped Selma feel support and understanding, this kind of response was certainly not news to her, and furthermore may have acted in the long run to increase her self-pity and ambivalence.

Another alternative used by the therapist under similar conditions would have been to reflect the second part of her statement involving her persistence in the relationship:

Therapist: You've taken a lot for a long time in this relationship.
Selma: I don't know why I do—I must really love him, or I can't live without him.

Again, the therapist felt that such a reflective response, while initially helpful in establishing rapport, now only seemed to reinforce Selma's irrational belief that if she stayed this long in the marriage, there was no way she could leave him; moreover, persistence in the situation had come to be equated with love, despite how intolerable or costly.

The therapist decided to respond in a more confrontative manner, hoping her inquiry would inspire Selma to look into her fears about separation.

Therapist: Then why do you put up with the situation?
Selma: I don't know. I just don't have no guts, I guess. I'm just a mess. I can't make up my mind. I tried to leave him and I can't. You think I should leave him, don't you? I'm so weak.

Selma had used the therapist's confrontation as a confirmation of her own incompetence to handle the situation and to separate, and further, had projected her own anger with herself onto the therapist. Yet she had also probably realistically surmised that the therapist was becoming impatient and somewhat disgusted with her indecision.

There is another therapeutic strategy that is useful in a case such as this, when the predivorce decision is long and agonizing and when the ambivalence brings increasing stagnation for all parties. The response of the therapist is based on a developmental view of divorce and focuses on any positive moves the person has made toward personal individuation in the ambivalent marital relationship. In this mode, the therapist first gently, but firmly, puts the onus of the decision where it belongs, back on the client:

Therapist: I'm afraid it's not my place to make that decision for you, Selma; you are the only person that can make the choice. Nor do I agree that you are a weak person. It seems to me that anyone that could survive the adversity and stress that you have experienced has a lot of strong inner resources. Finally, I think you are forgetting that you did indeed survive successfully when you separated from Joe, and you also managed to do a lot of positive things for yourself and the children as a result. You got a good job and supported them and yourself. You held the family together and Everett and Josie both did better in school. You became close to your sister and made some new friends. You felt happy and strong.
Selma: Yeah, I did. I felt better about myself during those few months than I have in a long time, but at first the loneliness almost killed me.

Therapist: Yes, it was rough all right, but it got better and you felt better. [Once again, the client is being reminded by the therapist of her inner resources and her potential for healing and change.]

Selma: Yeah, I know, it did get better. (*Long pause.*) But I guess I never did give myself a real chance to . . . to make it go . . .

Therapist: . . . to completely heal.

Selma: Yeah, but more than that, cause I had started to feel better. Actually I felt lots better after 3 months away from Joe, but I never gave myself long enough to see if I could really do it, to do it, to separate once and for all.

Therapist: Separations have always been hard for you. [The therapist is referring back to an earlier discussion about Selma's father, who deserted her mother when she was 10 years old.] Remember our talk about your Dad?

Selma: I felt the same way about him as I feel about Joe; there just gotta be something I could have done to make him stay.

Therapist: And so you always go back and try to make it right.

Selma: Yeah, crazy, isn't it? (*She begins to laugh.*) You know, I really don't feel like going back this time.

Therapist: You don't have to. You can move forward again, just as you did before.

In this vignette the client is apprising on both cognitive and emotional levels that she has a choice about separation, and furthermore that there is hope that she can come to terms with her conflict about separation, in part because she has already demonstrated the capacity to take care of herself and her dependents. Both behavioral and attitudinal changes are referred to in this exchange as both are necessary to effect a successful decision to divorce. Selma had come to terms with the original narcissistic injury she suffered by her father's leaving and the realization of how vulnerable she was to accepting abuse from anyone, particularly in an intimate relationship. Her already low self-esteem was dealt another blow by the thought that she again had failed to keep an important man in her life.

The loss to Selma's self-esteem also raised issues of her personal identity, causing her to question whether she was adequate and competent to take care of herself. Issues of identity and adequacy in intimacy were closely tied together and had to be explored and understood before she could feel capable of, as she put it, "giving herself a chance" to see if she could separate.

In Selma's case, the more difficult part of the divorce turned out to be the predivorce decision. The therapist's strategies in the predivorce period involved five important principles: (1) a recognition of the client's pain and what she had suffered, but not a constant rehashing of that litany of abuse;

(2) a leading her away from the victim posture, by emphasizing that she had viable choices and the inner resources to implement those choices; (3) an exploration of the behavioral consequences, positive and negative, of those choices; (4) a cognitive and emotional understanding of the antecedents of her present behavior; and (5) active reinforcement of the prior positive behaviors she had effected in her efforts to separate successfully.

THE THERAPIST'S VALUES AND COUNTERTRANSFERENCE

The predivorce period is a time when clients are most in need of an objective, patient helper, a listener for the cathartic expression of their ambivalent feelings, a bearer of hope for their pessimism, and an objective clarifier for their confusion and indecision. The position of the therapist as consultant or mediator is perhaps more common and appropriate after the decision to divorce has been effected; at this point the therapist usually either sees the couple to help make decisions regarding separation and division or sees one or both of the individuals to help effect disengagement. In the predivorce period, however, the therapist typically is involved in couple therapy and, as such, functions in an impartial role for both clients, not only in the decision of whether or not to divorce (as in the previous case with Selma), but also in terms of being the therapeutic agent for both partners.

The therapist can become impatient dealing with the couple's ambivalence, as illustrated in the previous case, but can also allow values, personal conflicts and/or countertransference to influence the couple's decision negatively. The therapist may harbor prejudice against divorce that can lead implicitly to steering the couple away from discussion about separation. He or she may emphasize only the stress and problems that a divorce can bring, thereby reinforcing the client's tendency to focus on the negative aspects of a potential actual separation. Part of this prejudice can emanate from more than a healthy and realistic appraisal of the difficulties of divorce, which every therapist needs to appreciate. It may be more deeply rooted, for example, in an unhappy personal experience with divorce on the part of the therapist or his or her close associates. In such a case the therapist again implicitly projects personal pain and anger onto the client.

Another way therapist bias can operate in therapy is when the therapist's unresolved conflicts about marriage and divorce become entangled during therapy with irrational feelings about one of the spouses. Here the therapist may unwillingly ally himself or herself with one of the spouses, encouraging that spouse or the couple to separate because the therapist believes the one partner is sick, or wrong, or no one could live with him or her (she's just like my former wife, or the friend of my former wife, etc.). The therapist's own values, conflicts, or countertransference feelings may preclude being the objective, patient helper of both the clients in the critical period of predivorce therapy.

The therapist can also lose his or her objectivity in this situation by unwittingly becoming the substitute spouse of the favored client. This is more likely to happen if the therapist strongly identifies with one of partners. A similar phenomenon can occur in the common case where one partner decides to divorce and then implicitly leaves the spouse in the hands of the therapist, in essence saying, "You can now take over for me and I won't feel so guilty." Therapists who fall into this role can lose whatever bargaining power and objectivity they had as a helper of the relationship (Rice, 1981; Whitaker & Miller, 1969). While this loss may not be critical in the case where one spouse goes on to do quite well without therapy, the lack of credibility with the other partner may hamper further dyadic work that may be important, such as in the period of negotiation or if some family therapy is advised. One way to help overcome these limitations is to use a cotherapist in divorce therapy. This strategy will be more fully explored in Chapter Ten.

THE "FLIP-FLOP"

The predivorce decision period of divorce therapy typically lasts for several months, but the decision may be made in a matter of weeks, or it may take years with no resolution, change, or coming to a final decision. The decision to divorce typically is preceded by more open declaration of the breakdown of the marriage. Lawyers are contacted, friends and family are advised of the imminent dissolution. Marital therapy may be tried as a last ditch effort. Older children may become confidants, as may lovers. The couple's dissatisfaction becomes "community property" as they go public with their feelings and decision. The actual decision may produce a temporary state of relief and even mild euphoria, leading to a short-lived renewal of marital intimacy and "trying it again."

This cycle, deciding to split, feeling better, becoming closer, seeing each other again only to experience renewed conflict and once again deciding to split, finally leads the couple (and likely the therapist) to the inevitability of divorce as a positive and/or perhaps the only, rational solution. The "marital flip-flop" (Kressel, 1980) finally stops as both parties realize the pattern and the futility of the pattern of alternately pushing for and opposing the divorce. The therapist's critical role in the healthy ending of this cycle is to realize that it often must be played out at least a few times to convince everybody of its ultimate futility. The therapist needs to explain the dynamics of the cycle to both parties and how it is not getting them anywhere:

Therapist: (*to couple*) It's interesting how you seem to be repeating a pattern here. In December you decided to split, after months of bitter fighting. You both had had it. Frank left for a couple of weeks and you both felt better, happier, more hopeful, hopeful enough to try it again. But by spring you were back to where you were in December, fighting, criticizing, berating each other for not giving you what you want. So you decided again to divorce 2 weeks ago at our last session. And today you've said that after that session, you both felt a little better, enough so that you stayed together over the weekend, and made love, but things ultimately ended in another bitter fight. Getting together seems to have led you back to the same place you were in December and March.

Husband: Only now it doesn't take so long for it to happen.

Wife: Yes, the flip-flop now happens in a matter of days, even hours, instead of months.

Therapist: Right, you both seem more aware about how the cycle operates and how it seems destined to end.

Husband: It seems pretty futile.

The ambivalence inherent in the "flip-flop" of the predivorce decision period may be helped through the use of an extremely useful therapeutic tool in divorce therapy, the structured separation (Granvold & Tarrant, 1983; Hight, 1977; Toomin, 1972).

STRUCTURING SEPARATION

Many terminating marriages experience some form of separation prior to a final dissolution. Weiss (1975) estimates that between 45% and 60% of the marriages currently being formed will sustain a separation at some point. A separation initiated by one or both partners can be highly conflictual and stressful, particularly if it is abrupt, sudden, and unplanned. It may be used as a negative, manipulative tool for gaining control or serve as the threat of a more permanent abandonment by the unhappy partner. Even in cases where there is no purposeful intention to wound or to control the other partner, the separation may be initiated in desperation and panic as a flight from a situation that is felt to be intolerable and unresolvable. The lack of forethought, planning, and mutual consent is likely in this case to exacerbate the conflict, even if there is some momentary relief for one or both partners.

The purpose of therapeutically structuring a separation during the predivorce period is to use separation as a positive, therapeutic tool. The object is to interrupt the conflictual marital interaction and to facilitate the decision of whether to divorce or to maintain the marital union. The success of a period of structured separation cannot be measured by whether or not the parties involved decide to reinstate the marriage. The few studies in the literature on the use of this method have reported varying results. The extreme is represented by one divorce therapist who noted that 92% of a sample of 25 couples who used this method reestablished a viable marriage (Hight, 1977). The author goes on rightly to caution that such outcomes cannot be offered as documented proof of the effectiveness of the structured separation. Other authors report that between one half and two thirds of their clients go on to effect a divorce after experiencing a structured separation (Granvold & Tarrant, 1983; Toomin, 1972). Whether or not they make the decision to divorce, most of these clients report that the experience was quite helpful, both in making a more rational decision about divorce, and in facilitating their personal growth.

A divorce therapist needs to make a careful appraisal of the couple's motivation, interaction patterns, and individual and joint objectives regarding the marriage and its possible dissolution before suggesting a structured separation. There are several helpful guidelines in making this assessment culled from more than a decade of clinical practice during which the structured separation method has been used in divorce therapy. The two main considerations in using structured separation as a therapeutic tool are the degree of conflict and tension in the marital interaction and secondly, the degree of ambivalence about dissolution.

Structured separation is most useful in the case where the degree of marital dysfunction has resulted in extreme tension, conflict and/or anger between the spouses. There are few positive exchanges and any marital interaction very frequently leads to more hostility, fighting, greater distance, or an escalation of the conflict. The scales may have tipped for the couple. In social exchange theory terms, the cost of living together seems clearly to outweigh the benefits. Yet, despite the extremity of the conflict or tension, the couple is not ready to make the final decision to divorce. There is still sufficient ambivalence about leaving that the spouses continue to stay, although they appear to be at an impasse and their continued interaction and even their simple physical presence is perceived to be quite stressful to both parties.

Under these two general conditions, high tension and conflict coupled with high to moderate ambivalence about dissolving the marriage, a structured separation can offer an "environmental conflict management tool" (Granvold & Tarrant, 1983). Structured separation can serve another important function. Besides providing both some relief to the warring parties and a mutually structured period for the decision making, such an arrangement offers an extremely valuable opportunity for personal growth and experimentation that may not be possible under the intense conditions of marital conflict.

The structured separation also represents a developmental therapeutic strategy. It is based on the theoretical premise that separation can promote the dealing with and transcending of intimacy and identity problems (as outlined in prior chapters). For this to happen, the two parties involved must be willing to risk some experimentation. Frequently, although the conflict is intense and the ambivalence is great, the partners are not yet ready to risk the new experiences that a separation is likely to bring. Nor may the spouses be willing to face the very real possibility that the separation may be a structured preparation for divorce. The therapist needs to discuss all the possible ramifications of this decision with the clients, pointing out their alternatives, and the risks as well as potential benefits of separation. The following issues may be addressed in explaining the function, goals, difficulties, and benefits of a structured separation.

1. When there is intense conflict and tension, the separation affords a respite, a "vacation" from the dispute during which each party can more objectively assess the situation and their individual feelings once given some peace and privacy.

2. When there is considerable ambivalence, the separation provides and validates a structured time-limited period for decision making. The separation forces a change in the relationship and may effect a break in decision-making dilemmas.

3. Where one person greatly fears dissolution and refuses to let go while the other wants to leave and is feeling "smothered," the structured time-limited separation offers both a compromise. Both parties are involved in the choice; there is no "leaver" or "leavee," no abuser and victim. The model is one of honest recognition of the impasse and a mutual compromise to give each other some space before any final decisions are made. Both parties are afforded a period of education and a chance to appraise what realistic, nonconjugal living would be like.

4. Both parties may seriously consider or want divorce, but likely have fears about their ability to make it on their own. The structured separation offers a "successive approximation" strategy that minimizes the shock of dissolution, permits a realistic "role play," and offers the opportunity to adjust to the new contingencies of being on one's own.

5. Where there is considerable denial of the conflict and/or fear of exposing the marital dysfunction to significant others, the structured separation can serve as a public announcement of the significance of the marital problem. During this period the parties involved and their network of significant others can work toward accepting the reality of the situation, supporting and facilitating resolution and change.

6. When one or both parties feel stifled or stymied by the marital conflict and impasse, a period of separation affords opportunities for

valuable new learning and personal development. The key word here is choice. Perhaps for the first time since they were married, the partners are permitted a choice of where, when, and if they want to be together. The effect of experiencing such a choice may be quite liberating and lead to the wish for renewed intimacy unbound by mutual neurotic dependency. Choices can lead to experimentation and this period also may be one of reassessment in one's vocational and social spheres. Some people may choose to return to school, to change jobs or careers, to begin a career or to experiment with a new work direction. Others may seek out new friendships or attempt to strengthen old ones, or try some sexual experimenting not previously permitted in the marriage.

The period is one in which there is a lot of value clarification about what is really important to the individual. For example, relationships with children may take on different meanings, particularly for fathers who were in peripheral roles. In sum, a separation can provide a meaningful time for preliminary role restructuring as one prepares to deal with the possibility of role loss.

In the process of living alone, one usually also learns more about one's dependency and control conflicts and how well one has dealt with issues of intimacy and identity. Perhaps for the first time, a woman may learn in a structured separation how much her identity was based on the subsumed identity of her spouse. A man may learn how dependent he was on his wife to meet all or almost all of his nurturing and intimacy needs, thus stunting his own growth in these areas. Such realization may produce developmental growth as one now is offered the chioce and opportunity to explore and to understand oneself better.

Choices, however, may be fearful. One can confront the fear of loss in this period as well as the fear of freedom (Toomin, 1972). It is a challenge for both therapist and client to use the freedom of the structured separation period to deal with loneliness and aloneness, to learn not to fear these conditions, but to use the time for reassessment, introspection, and exploration. As one confronts one's ultimate aloneness and learns to accept it as a positive condition permitting reliance on and respect for self, one can better make choices about whether to couple and to be intimate. Such a choice is less likely to be based on childish needs or fears of abandonment and inadequacy.

ISSUES OF STRUCTURE

The success of a therapeutic separation is closely tied to how well it is designed. It is important in therapy to discuss all the important areas of possible interaction and concern and to come to a concrete mutual understanding of the ground rules of the separation. Implicit assumptions in the premise of a structured separation should be reiterated. These generally are (1) that the parties involved will not live in the same residence for the duration of the separation, and (2) that no lawyers will be brought in or any divorce proceeding instigated during this time, nor will any permanent economic division or custody agreement be effected. Given these premises, the couple and the therapist will need to discuss the purpose, length, and benefits of the separation, the mechanics of separating their residences, and finally the ground rules with regard to contact with each other, their children if any, their families and friends, sexual intimacy and outside relationships, and the general issues in maintaining privacy.

With regard to the length of separation, most therapists who have dealt with this strategy recommend at least 6 weeks and preferably, about 3 months. The latter is felt to be a sufficient time period for the parties to make a more realistic appraisal of their feelings, allow for some change and experimentation, and defuse the hostilities enough to permit more rational dialogue.

It is generally expected that during this period the couple will meet on a regular basis with the therapist to discuss their progress. Individual sessions may be scheduled to deal with personal developmental issues that may arise. The couple usually chooses to have one person stay in their domicile and the other obtain different housing such as a temporary apartment or moving in with a friend. Sometimes for economic or other reasons, one party has no choice other than to move in with a parent. This option is generally not advised, as it may only act to encourage dependency rather than to promote mature independence. Most couples with children will choose to disrupt their children's lives as little as possible and usually during this period the children will live with the parent in the original domicile, although there may be some overnight and/or weekend habitation with the other parent, by mutual consent.

It is critical to set up mutually agreed upon guidelines for contact between the parties. While some couples desire no contact at all during this period, it is helpful for the therapist to point out that one of the main purposes of the separation is to facilitate their ability to relate again comfortably. Even if they ultimately decide to divorce the ex-spouses will need to be able to talk to each other about a variety of issues, particularly if there are children involved. Furthermore, the couple needs to reassess their feelings about one another periodically as they change and experience the ramifications of the structured separation. However, too much contact can mitigate against an effective separation, providing no opportunity for privacy and choice or experimentation. In the authors' experience, one or two weekly in-person contacts is generally a good compromise. It may be contracted that this is to be a social time, with conflict resolution generally reserved for the therapeutic interaction. The amount of telephone contact should also be discussed. Unplanned drop-ins or calls can act to invade privacy and breed resentment.

The couple also needs to decide if they will maintain their sexual relationship and whether each spouse can initiate sex and the other have the right to accept or refuse. Expectations in this area need careful clarification. The whole area of other relationships, especially sexual ones, must be dealt with directly. Generally most couples will agree whether or not they want this mutual option. Where one does, and the other does not, the party desiring this option generally acts on it, and the other partner must be made aware that he or she ultimately cannot control the other partner's sexual choices. This can be a highly threatening topic for some couples and must be approached therapeutically in a matter-of-fact way designed to encourage honesty and clarification. Even when both partners desire and agree to explore other relationships with the possibility of sexuality, they may decide not to disclose the specifics of their activities, for such disclosure is likely to increase distance and promote feelings of rejection. In any case, the couple needs to work toward a mutual agreed upon set of ground rules in this sensitive area.

Issues regarding contact with children and significant others also need to be clarified. Not only must the parents learn to adjust to the separation but the children as well, need to face the new exigencies of the relationship with their now separated parents. Their reactions will vary, of course, depending on a variety of circumstances, but in general the guideline of constancy applies. The more the parents can build in regular, predictable contact that is organized and scheduled, the quicker the child will know what to expect and the more secure he or she can feel about the continuation of the parental relationships.

It is important for the therapist to encourage the partners' cooperation in arranging smooth and regular access to both parents. The therapist should be sensitive to manipulative efforts by either party designed to use access to the children as a means of forcing more contact with the other spouse. Visits with the children by the spouse that is living away from the home are generally not advised to take place within the home, as this situation can destroy privacy and reawaken ambivalences and hostilities (Granvold & Tarrant, 1983). In some cases where the couple has managed to cooperate and function well as parents despite other areas of conflict, the two parties may be able to handle occasional family outings or activities successfully. An operative agreement concerning the positive continuation of parental contact and responsibility during the time of the structured separation can serve as excellent preparation for establishing parent–child relationship patterns that will continue after a more permanent separation through divorce.

Agreement concerning the contingencies of the structured separation may be formalized in a separation contract (Hight, 1977), or more simply reiterated and summarized verbally in therapy and renegotiated in subsequent sessions as various new experiences or implications come into play.

There are couples for whom any kind of separation is taboo; a viable marriage and a "healthy" relationship are more rigidly defined for such individuals by minimal separation of the spouses in daily life. Any type of separation, much less a prolonged, physical one, is viewed negatively. For those people, intimacy does not contain a positive element of autonomy. This rigid view may have been in part what precipitated the marital conflict, yet the partners are locked into their conceptions of intimacy that are ultimately destructive to them personally and to the growth of their relationship.

Despite educative efforts by the divorce therapist to untangle these irrational expectations of marriage and to present alternatives and options, such individuals may adopt an "all or nothing" view. No trial separation or period of change can be tolerated; "either we are together or we split." With no gradual period of separation for the actual physical parting, the shock and distress of dissolution may be great for such people, despite the fact that there may well have been a long period of emotional distance or "psychological separation." All couples need to recognize that there is obviously the risk that in choosing to separate, one will choose to divorce and that, in fact, learning to adjust well to separation may hasten a final divorce decision.

THE FINAL DECISION

A final decision to divorce may be reached after a period of separation that is structured in therapy or initiated by the parties prior to therapy. In some cases the decision to divorce is made with no actual experience of what separation will be like. Despite preparation in terms of emotional detachment and/or role restructuring, the final decision usually generates feelings of grief and loss with the recognition that the marriage indeed is over. Relief and respite are likely to be mingled with feelings of depression as one comes to the final realization that the relationship loss is likely to be permanent.

The following chapter will explore more fully therapeutic strategies that can help divorcing individuals adjust to object loss and narcissistic injury, and to gain insight about themselves in relation to the divorce and its meaning. Before the divorce therapist can help one or both individuals understand their loss and go on developmentally, the practical exigencies of effecting the final divorce decision must be faced in therapy. Just as the divorce therapist can aid the parties in relieving the tension in an unresolved marital struggle through structuring a working separation, the therapist can help the couple ameliorate tension and conflict that works against solving the practical problems and decisions involved in dissolution.

LAWYERS AND THERAPISTS AND THEIR SPECIAL JOBS

The divorce therapist has a unique and important role that is different from the role of the divorce lawyer and mediator. The long-term success of the work done by the divorce attorney and divorce mediator may well depend on how effective the prior divorce therapy intervention has been. It is very difficult to negotiate the practical problems of property division, custody, and support in a rational, equitable manner when the two parties involved are still so emotionally entangled that these issues simply become further ammunition in the unending battle.

It was noted previously that the effective practice of divorce mediation is directly dependent on the degree of lingering emotional conflict between the partners. Agreements about practical problems of dissolution made through a mediator, lawyer, or judge are less likely to be upheld peacefully and cooperatively when there is underlying angry attachment between the ex-spouses and the maintainence of a "blame mentality." In addition, the degree of the success of the custody arrangement appears to be most directly dependent on the degree of conflict between the ex-partners (Clingempeel & Reppucci, 1982). The postdivorce clinics mandated and referred to by the courts for mediation and arbitration of prolonged disputes over custody bear witness to the phenomenon (Elkin, 1977; Sheffner & Suarez, 1975; Suarez, Weston, & Hartstein, 1978).

Thus divorce therapy has a very important function in facilitating rational and equitable problem solving and compromise on such practical divorce issues as custody, support, and property division. Successful compromise is immeasurably aided if the couple is helped to work through irrational and projected anger, to disengage emotionally to the point of distance and neutrality, and to make their own separate, healthy development and that of their dependents paramount.

A therapist may confront two divorcing, warring parties about attending to the ultimate welfare of the children and remind them that their function as parents will continue despite the divorce. They will usually agree that of course, they will still be parents, and that the "children come first." Yet this reminder can be a futile gesture on the part of the therapist, lawyer, or divorce mediator if the parents harbor conscious or subconscious hostilities toward each other that one way or another will act to sabotage their best intentions. The working through of these lingering hostilities and projections can be accomplished in couple therapy or in individual therapy, if one of the parties does not wish to continue treatment after the divorce decision is made. While the latter option is probably the more common situation, it may not be the most efficient. Only one party is permitted the opportunity of completing the critical work of emotional disengagement and neutrality that will help to insure less destructive interaction in the process of divorce settlement and facilitate postdivorce parental cooperation.

While the remedial approach and work of the postdivorce clinics is important and often necessary, a more preventive approach can be taken by the divorce therapist. He or she can directly suggest to clients who have decided to divorce that the ultimate success of their dissolution for themselves and for their dependents will likely be dependent on how well they can dismantle their respective "blame mentality." Such dismantling in therapy will also directly affect their healing, restructuring, and successful future personal development, and that of their children and significant others.

Clinical experience with divorcing clients is backed up by the growing literature on divorce law, arbitration, and mediation that strongly suggests that it is a tactical error for the divorce lawyer to expect clients to be able to make difficult settlement decisions rationally and equitably and resolve such problems until unfinished emotional business with each other has been dealt with (Elkin, 1977; Kressel, 1980; Sheffner & Suarez, 1975; Steinberg, 1980). The divorce lawyer is still in the most influential position to help divorcing clients in the throes of conflict gain the kind of therapeutic help they need via adequate referral to mental health personnel.

Ideally the therapist would be seen first, but in reality, the lawyer is frequently the first professional to whom a large percentage of individuals in marital distress turn. The therapist cannot function in a lawyer's role or vice versa. Divorcing clients confront the attorney with psychological, social, and economic as well as legal problems. Perhaps in no other area of the law are lawyers asked to give advice on personal matters often having little or nothing to do with the law itself (Fisher & Fisher, 1982). One lawyer articulates the problem as follows:

> If not sharply defined, this expanded role, though well-intended, can erode the foundation of legal counseling, client self-determination, and the legal orientation of the lawyer's counseling efforts . . . Unless the attorney has extensive psychological training and clinical experience, he should not attempt to engage in extensive marriage counseling. He is a counselor at law and not a marriage counselor. There is a substantial difference. The counseling skills required of a lawyer and of a psychologist are not identical. Counselors of the two so-called helping professions help in different ways. The client of the psychologist receives directions on how to help himself; the performance is by the client himself. On the other hand, the client of the lawyer is presented with a selection of alternative solutions: the performance by the lawyer. It is one thing to tell a person what you can do for him, and quite another to tell him what he can do for himself. . . . (Callner, 1977, p. 389)

The skills of the two helping professions are obviously different; the lawyer is a highly trained talker, the therapist, a trained listener. To help his or her client, the lawyer learns how to lay blame most skillfully, the therapist to soften it. The lawyer's methods are adversarial, the therapist's consensual (Hancock, 1982). Both seek to help their divorcing clients, but their premises, aims, and methods may be quite different and likely account for why there presently is such little interface between the divorce lawyer and the divorce therapist. These differences do not mean automatically that there cannot be helpful dialogue, referral, and cooperation between the two professions.

Despite the advent of "no-fault" divorce and the opportunity for divorce mediation, the adversarial process is built into the foundations of our legal system and, as such, is unlikely to change fundamentally. A hopeful strategy for some alleviation of the added conflict the legal system may impose on those who divorce is offered by a team or interprofessional approach to divorce (Duquette, 1978; Korelitz & Schulder, 1982; Perlman, 1982). This would involve cooperative, collaborative efforts by both lawyers and mental health professionals. Steinberg (1980) writes that referrals to mental health professionals are critical for all cases of divorce: "[Such referrals] . . . spare me much of the pressure of dealing with the emotional issues a competent therapist absorbs. And so I refer my divorce clients to a therapist at the earliest possible moment" (p. 262).

The divorce therapist should not presume to offer legal advice. While it is important that he or she be well-informed about the economic, cultural, social, educational, religious, and legal aspects of divorce as well as psychological and therapeutic implications, the divorce therapist's primary function is in the latter area. The therapist's role is also distinguished from that of the divorce mediator, who may be hired by the court and whose primary role is that of advocate for the welfare of the children, and secondarily, the adult clients (Sheffner & Suarez, 1975). The interests of the children are paramount to the mediator, and the interviewing involved is often not unlike that done in cases of adoption, foster care, or child abuse (Irving, 1981). The mediator's role differs from the lawyer's in that the attorney has a power conferred on him or her by the individual client, and seeks to promote the client's interest. The mediator is not interested in the best arrangement for the individual client, but in the best solution for all concerned and particularly for the children.

The stance of the divorce therapist is unique and different from both that of the lawyer and mediator. He or she does not function in an advocate role for either adult or child, but in a more neutral stance that permits exploration of all possibilities and the consequences for those involved. The divorce therapist may in an advisory capacity point out alternatives and consequences and in an educative capacity cite the literature on the best known strategies for insuring the health and welfare of children postdivorce. However, a therapist working with a couple in the divorce process does not make these decisions, directly offer legal advice, or align himself or herself exclusively with one client or the children.

While joint custody and equal property division in divorce settlements are more common today than a few years ago, as these decisions come up in therapy, the ramifications of all alternatives need to be discussed. Joint custody may work effectively for two people who cooperated quite well as parents and who do not have intense postdivorce hostilities. It may be disastrous for the couple who cannot emotionally disengage, or simply unworkable for the partner who is moving out of state or remarrying into a new family with other dependents.

Similarly, while parity in property and monetary division is appealing to many people who work in this area, equal property division may actually function to penalize women. In California, for example, the mandate of equal community property division has resulted in many couples having to sell their one home with the mother and children being forced to rent and faring considerably worse economically than they did prior to the change in the law (Weitzman, 1981). Obviously there are no economic winners in divorce, but women who bear the actual and hidden costs of supporting their families, yet have lower earning power and fewer of the fringe benefits associated with a lifetime of participation in the labor force, tend to be the bigger losers (Fineman, 1983).

There are no simple or best alternatives, and the sensitive therapist needs to be well educated and open to all alternatives. What is fair to one individual or one couple is perceived as manifestly unfair or unworkable to another. Some couples would think nothing of asking their children to move back and forth during the week between two separate houses and, in fact, the children may manage to adjust quite well. Yet still another couple feels this alternative could not even be considered because, by their perception and values, it places an intolerable burden on the children.

If the emotional entanglement and the hostile interaction have been ameliorated sufficiently in or outside of therapy, these practical decisions of dissolution can be made effectively through the help of a therapist, lawyer, and/or mediator. The therapist may well open the discussion and then refer the clients upon their request to a lawyer well versed in family law in order to implement the final settlement. In cases where it is appropriate—that is, where the couple has disengaged considerably, but cannot conclude an agreement over an issue such as custody, visitation, or maintenance—the seeking of a mediator is in order and this individual may be court appointed.

Where mediation and negotiation are found to be impossible, a couple may have three options (Irving, 1981). They may go to the court and use the adversary system as a means of venting their resentments. They may choose "binding arbitration," in which they agree in advance that the arbitrator's decision will be binding on them, as would a court order; or they may choose "advisory arbitration" where they are free to accept or reject the decision of the arbitrator and apply to the court again for final determination. It is possible for a couple to go round and round again in this system for some time, in the process reopening old issues and wounds.

The following case vividly illustrates how unresolved emotional dependency and hostility must be first addressed and worked through before successful practical dissolution can be achieved.

Case Study 13: Martin and Claire

Martin (age 42) and Claire (age 38) had been separated for a year and a half. He had been against a divorce and repeatedly had tried to convince her that they should reunite and try to reconstitute their marriage and family. Martin was a prosperous, well-known attorney in a small town and Claire had delayed a divorce action, fearing that she could not obtain a fair hearing, would be negatively judged by her friends and neighbors, and would suffer financially because of Martin's knowledge of the law. There were many difficulties that resulted from the ambiguity of her situation. The limbo of the unresolved, stressful separation with no significant change in her lack of feeling for her husband finally convinced Claire to seek a divorce. Martin agreed, for the sake of their children, that he would not continue the conflict by opposing her.

The couple had two children, Quentin, 16, and Alex, 13. Both sons had been living with Claire in the family home and had had liberal access and visitation with their father. Martin had bought a condominium in a nearby larger town. Quentin expressed a desire to live with his father in the city so that he could finish high school at the large and excellent city school and participate in the multitude of sports it offered. Claire herself was now in school attempting to finish a college degree and somewhat stressed by the demands of being a single parent and full-time college student. She agreed to the arrangement, provided that she, too, would have unlimited visitation with Quentin.

The arrangement seemed to be working and Claire agreed in the divorce negotiations that, while both parents would share custody, Quentin would live indefinitely with Martin, and Alex with her. Before the holidays Martin contacted Claire and explained that he was planning to take Quentin to Mexico and surely she and Alex would want to go, too. She gave her permission for Alex to accompany them, but refused the invitation for herself.

A week later Martin again persuasively invited her to go along, playing on her fears of loneliness and appealing to her desire to "help the boys have a nice Christmas, by keeping the family together over the holiday." She was reassured that there would be no expectation of sexual intimacy and seduced by the thought of a luxurious week in the sun especially after a year of penny pinching. Upon their return, Martin began calling Claire more frequently and suggesting family activities that they could all do, "so the boys could be together." He also told Alex every time he saw him how much he missed him and how nice it would be if his mother would cooperate in letting him visit more. The implicit message was that if it wasn't for your mother restricting our contact, we could be together having fun. In response to his pressure Claire ambivalently increased the family outings, which left her feeling more unhappy and confused.

Claire also discovered that Martin had been writing and calling her mother, complaining that Claire's selfishness was the cause of their divorce and the break-up of their family, and that not even the two brothers could be together. The separation of their two sons had never sat well with Claire's mother and Martin's complaint only aggravated her disapproval, which she expressed to Claire. "How can you go to school full time and expect to be an adequate mother to that boy?" "Doesn't Alex miss Quentin; how can you separate them?" were all messages Claire received. Armed with the "approval" of Claire's mother and the power of money and status, Martin took the next step and demanded to have custody of both boys. He also delayed her child support checks so that she increasingly felt financial strain and distress.

Claire's lawyer was thoroughly exasperated by Martin's actions, and those of Martin's attorney, who took an equally intransigent position on behalf of his client. It appeared as though the settlement would have to be accomplished by the court. Martin's actions were also personally costly. In his rigid, obsessive, vindictive pursuit of controlling Claire, he had developed numerous psychosomatic difficulties. His migraine problem increased to the point that his physician advised him to seek therapy. In the course of separation, Claire and Martin had had three sessions of marital therapy, at Martin's insistence, in an attempt to "save the marriage." The therapy was aborted when it became very obvious that Claire did not want to continue the marriage nor engage in efforts to salvage it. The therapist suggested the couple continue treatment, in the form of divorce therapy, in order to help them disengage successfully. Martin wanted no part in such a disengagement at the time and therefore rejected the suggestion.

After almost 2 years of separation, Martin sought out the therapist again. The presenting problem was "the difficulties Claire is causing me," although he acknowledged that he had exacerbated their conflict by demanding custody of Alex and Quentin. The following excerpts are taken from an early therapy session:

Martin: It's only for their own good, you know. They shouldn't be separated. Even her mother agrees. Christ, I'm in a much better position to take care of them, after all, with my income and her half-cocked school thing. And damn, they're boys. They need a father more than a mother at this age!

Therapist: They really need you more than her?

Martin: Well, I don't know. I suppose they need both of us. But dammit, they could have had both of us if she'd tried harder to make a go of it.

Therapist: You still sound so angry with her for leaving.

(*Long silence.*)

Martin: Yeah, I'm still angry with her all right, but what good does it do?

Therapist: What good? Probably none. On the other hand, you've certainly done a good job in showing her how angry you are.

Martin: What do you mean?

Therapist: Marty, when you challenge the custody, delay the support payments, and call somebody's mother behind their back, you let them know how angry you are. How many other ways can you find to say it?

Martin: I know what you're saying, and I suppose you're right that some of what I did was because I was so unhappy about what she was doing to me. But I think anybody would get angry if they felt they'd been treated as badly as I was.

Therapist: I think most people do feel considerable anger after a spouse wants a divorce, especially when you thought you could depend on that person being there. Perhaps you were more dependent on her than you even realized.

Martin: I think so. (*Pause.*) And it's funny, because I don't know what I was dependent on her for . . . except, I guess for emotional support . . .

Therapist: And what else?

Martin: Well, there's the feeling of having a family there, even though I couldn't be home much, just knowing they were, she was, there. God, I guess I just never thought she'd actually leave. I mean, have the guts to leave.

Therapist: Why not?

Martin: Well, I mean, you know, the money and the kids, and the house and all that. I know it wasn't that good between us a lot of the time, but to leave all that!

Therapist: It's hard to imagine anyone would trade all that security . . .

Martin: (*Interrupts.*) Yeah, for what? For what?! Some feeling of freedom?

Therapist: Some people feel they have to give up some security, to risk losing some security, if they want to change and to grow.

Martin: But why couldn't she have changed, we have changed together . . . within the marriage?

Therapist: That's ideally what you would have liked. Probably Claire, too. But sometimes that isn't always possible.

Martin: I don't think I could ever have made the choice she did.

Therapist: You know, in a way you're saying that you couldn't imagine that Claire wouldn't be controlled by all those things, the possibility of losing the house, money, the kids, you. It's hard to believe that those things didn't ultimately stop her from divorcing you.

Martin: Yeah. In the end none of those things stopped her.

Therapist: It's hard to accept that in reality we can't control another person's decisions, that you can't make someone love you or stay with you, that it has to be their choice.

Martin: And how the hell can I live with her choice?

Therapist: You're forgetting you have a choice, too, a choice to continue to be angry with her or to get on with your own life.

Martin: You make it sound so easy, but it isn't.

Therapist: I know, Marty. It isn't.

In this brief interchange the therapist used a combination of therapeutic strategies including questioning, reflection, cognitive restructuring, psychodynamic interpretation, paradox, and mild confrontation designed to help the client better understand and come to grips with certain of the key issues that were involved in the prolongation of the divorce discord. In this instance, the wish to maintain a hostile-dependent relationship, unrealistic desires to control and dominate, and the fear of change were touched on as the therapist attempted gradually to lead and help the client to overcome his resistance to change and role restructuring, to explore his fears of loss, and to consider the trade-off of security for growth.

Martin stayed in individual therapy for several months. During this time he and his therapist continued to work on the difficult issues of control and dependency that prevented him from successfully separating from Claire. Several sessions with Claire present and one with the whole family helped clarify and resolve their unfinished business. Martin was now able to recognize how his conflicts around intimacy and identity issues had precluded the successful resolution of the custody issue. They agreed that their original agreement concerning custody was an appropriate one, as did their sons.

The therapy also helped Claire to disengage and to recognize her part in continuing the marital merry-go-round by participating in the "family" vacations and outings and thereby helping to feed the fantasy of reunion and Martin's unrealistic expectations. They both began to heal, but, as Martin had told his therapist, helping and healing oneself was not necessarily an easy process. The following chapter will discuss in detail the healing process in divorce and how the divorce therapist can help clients rebuild and increase their self-esteem after divorce by accepting, understanding and reinterpreting the object and relationship loss.

Chapter Seven

The Healing Process

Following the decision to divorce and its implementation, initial relief or elation often is followed by renewed distress, depression, and the loss of self-esteem. Individuals in this situation are confronted in a variety of realms with the reality of the ego blow or narcissistic injury and the role loss experienced. In therapy, the client may still be confused and unsettled about the reasons for the dissolution and its meaning. The ramifications of the separation, especially as it affects the network of significant others, may necessitate family as well as individual therapy. As one lives with and psychologically accepts the divorce, there is an increasing need to move on developmentally and to do some constructive role restructuring. The remainder of the chapters in this section address these processes. The present chapter will discuss the healing process and its therapeutic ramifications in terms of mourning, making immediate structural changes, gaining deeper insight into the causes of the dissolution and the dysfunctional pattern of coupling, and disengaging emotionally. These therapeutic goals ultimately involve ego reparation. They help to rebuild self-esteem and to heal the narcissistic injury and object loss in divorce.

Chapters Eight and Nine will address specific therapeutic strategies designed to help clients deal with the role loss and disorientation experienced in divorce, how to move clients toward self-individuation and independence, and ways of rebuilding and increasing their self-esteem through work, education, and new relationships. Finally, Chapter Ten explores how the therapist needs to deal with such structural issues as the appropriate therapeutic mode to use, for example, when individual divorce therapy is preferred over couple therapy or family therapy, how to combine these modes, and issues of cotherapy in doing divorce therapy.

THERAPEUTIC STRATEGIES FOR EGO REPARATION

In studying how people adjust to divorce, Pino (1980) notes that the most frequently used coping pattern was the one labeled "narcissistic." This pattern parallels the classic grief reaction after a relationship loss, with the individual exhibiting depression, somatic symptoms, and preoccupation with self. The ego reparation necessary in healing the narcissistic injury engendered by divorce can be accomplished through several therapeutic processes and goals: (1) supporting and allowing for the client's initial grief reaction and reactive depression; (2) facilitating the client's dealing with the practical, immediate consequences of dissolution; (3) helping the individual gain a deeper understanding of why the relationship did not work; (4) facilitating disengagement and letting go of the relationship; and (5) supporting the reemergence of hope and change for the future. The therapeutic processes and strategies involved for the first four of these healing goals are discussed in this chapter and the latter in Chapters Eight and Nine on role restructuring.

MOURNING THE OBJECT LOSS

It is relatively rare for the couple who has made a decision to divorce to experience any more than transitory feelings of relief or elation initially. Feelings of euphoria and more long-lasting feelings of happiness, well-being, and confidence in the future are much more likely to occur later in the postdivorce process, after the person has completed some of the other healing goals noted above. Generally, the first therapeutic task is to support the normal and predictable feelings of grief, mourning, and depression likely to accompany the client's increasing awareness of the permanence and irreversability of the marital dissolution. During this period the individual may exhibit many of the classic responses associated with reactive depression to a relationship loss. He or she may experience feelings of dysphoria, insomnia, appetite decrease, anxiety, inability to concentrate, decrease in libido, confusion, disorganization, and obsessive preoccupation with the loss.

There may be mood swings, as one alternately feels more hope and confidence and then renewed despondency. The divorce therapist needs to help the individual anticipate these feelings, to accept them as part of the normal grieving process, and to put them into some temporal framework that will help the client anticipate eventual relief and healing. During this period the therapist continues to reinforce the reality perception of the loss as final, reframes the depression and grieving experience as acceptable and cathartic, and facilitates the individual's reaching out to support people and structures in his or her life.

It is important that the client realize, even while intensely grieving, that this period will pass, but cannot be skipped. The therapist needs to stress the normality of intense and prolonged feelings about the relationship loss. Clients need to know that it is not at all uncommon for the intense period of grieving to last 6 weeks to several months and the whole process of adjustment 1 to 2 years. The therapist can also help the individual understand that there is important emotional, cognitive, and behavioral role restructuring down the road that one can gradually begin to do that will shorten, ameliorate, and eventually, it is hoped, end the intense feelings of abandonment and loss and the depression and/or anxiety accompanying such feelings.

In this period the therapist also must attend to any physical and somatic discomfort, as well as to the emotional distress of the client. An evaluation of the need for antidepressant or other psychotropic drugs to help the individual get through the initial grieving period may be in order. The therapist needs to ask about eating and sleeping patterns, encouraging the client to maintain healthy behavior in these areas and to engage in regular physical activity.

Inquiry about the client's support network is also important. The individual may wish to be alone in this period, and some introspection can indeed be helpful. However, it is also important in therapy that he or she be encouraged to reach out to significant others, to maintain old friendships where possible, and to allow family, friends, and colleagues to be of help and support. Some research on postdivorce adjustment has suggested that the degree of social interaction outside the home is important (Spanier & Casto, 1979). Clinical experience also suggests that postseparation adjustment is facilitated significantly by an intact network of friends. This variable, along with the type of separation (sudden and unexpected versus prepared or more structured), appears to be even more important for postseparation adjustment than the effects of lingering attachment to one's former spouse. Thus, the importance of maintaining a social network and reaching out to significant others who can aid and support the grief work and healing during the initial and later adjustment period needs to be addressed and facilitated in therapy. Another method of therapeutic intervention at this time is for the therapist and client to assess not only the network of support, but to solidify remaining intact structures in the person's life that can act to maintain stability and security.

GETTING ORGANIZED

Changing residences, jobs, friends, daily time schedules, surrounding objects, familiar environments, and family contacts all at once is to be avoided in the period after making a decision to divorce. Too many simultaneous stresses can produce significant overload and the therapist can help the client assess what situational changes must be made immediately and what can wait until the gradual return of a more normal mood and elevated confidence. The expected confusion and disorganization a person experiences in acute loss can be exacerbated by too many changes, which can come to be perceived as losses rather than as positive alterations. Some of the immediate consequences of the decision to divorce must be dealt with, despite the anxiety, depression, and inadequacy the individual may be feeling. Too often therapists shy away from helping people deal with the behavioral and practical living decisions they need to make in the process of divorce that can ultimately have a significant effect on the individual's adjustment.

Three areas of immediate consequences that can be discussed in therapy are: who needs to know about the separation or divorce and how to break that news to them; who will move, how, and when; and how to assess and divide the joint contributions and assets accumulated during the marriage. Because these decisions often must be made at the peak of grieving, it is imperative that the therapist help the individual(s) sort out irrational expectations, look at all alternatives, and maintain a flexible posture in regard to future renegotiation. Despite the difficulty inherent in making these decisions, the process of doing so helps the client to heal. It reaffirms in a concrete way that the relationship is indeed over and that one must heal and go on.

The therapist can encourage clients to help their children and families deal with the news of the dissolution by presenting it in a honest, matter-of-fact way that emphasizes the continuity of their personal relationship with their kin, and the alleviation of any irrational blame. Children especially need to be reassured that the decision is not their responsibility and that the parental relationship will continue despite the demise of the marital one. Support can be requested, but should not necessarily be expected, from friends and relatives. In the authors' experience, most families are more supportive and less condemning of the decision than the spouses initially expect. Preparation is a key word. A structured separation can help prepare a spouse for the possibility of a permanent separation. So also can the divorcing spouses help prepare their families and friends for the adjustments they may need to make as a consequence of the divorce by being honest about the decision, discussing its ramifications, and admitting their need for help and support.

The decision of where to live often is a particularly stressful one for the person who decides to move out. If the individuals have already had the benefit of a structured separation, one or both may be familiar with the feelings and practical issues involved in such a change. However, if this is the first separation, relief and excitement may be either diminished or mingled with fear and anxiety. Part of the decisions involved at this time may be made primarily on convenience, economic, and equity grounds, part in respect for the needs of any children involved. The therapist needs to help the person(s) carefully explore the various options and the personal consequences to the children and family as well as to the individual.

Another immediate decision is likely to be the division of some of the jointly owned belongings and assets and the deciding of child support, at least on a temporary basis. The economic and legal concerns of clients in divorce therapy cannot be ignored by the therapist. As noted previously, decision making in the acute phases of grieving can be impaired, necessitating therapeutic help and intervention. Furthermore, it is critical to sort out which major life decisions must be made immediately and which can and should probably be postponed, for example, changing jobs, starting a new significant relationship, and moving to a new location.

> A willingness to engage the client in discussions of the pros and cons of various practical financial and related arrangements and a strong bias in favor of deliberation and slowness of decision-making and planning can be of inestimable value to a patient in the throes of the divorcing process without in any way resulting in an abdication of the therapeutic role. It is not necessary that the therapist possess the expertise of a CPA or a lawyer to be useful in these matters, although a general familiarity with the issues to be resolved in divorce settlements and the kinds of tax and other considerations that are typically involved will be helpful. (Kressel, 1980, p. 239)

Therapists can help one to appreciate better that there are no hard and fast rules regarding what constitutes an equitable or reasonable settlement in divorce. Each couple/family is different and brings a unique set of needs, values, and contingencies that must be weighed and considered. A first step is obtaining the correct facts, if this is at all possible. It is important for the therapist to encourage both parties to have full access to all of the information in a given area. This is relevant particularly to the woman, who may have reduced negotiating power if she has little of the relevant financial knowledge and picture at her disposal. Because postdivorce adjustment is so significantly influenced by social and economic resources, having full knowledge about existing tangible resources and the prospects for economic security becomes an issue for therapy, particularly for women. Therapists can also encourage a flexible posture of compromise with regard to these decisions, pointing out when the client appears to be taking an unreasonable, punitive stance, as in Case 13 (Martin and Claire) presented in Chapter Six. The following case illustrates the dealing with grieving, reactive depression, and practical decision making likely to occur once a decision to divorce has been made.

Case Study 14: Emily and Nathan

This was Emily's (age 32) third marriage and Nathan's (age 36) second. Emily's first marriage occurred when she was 19 and ended in divorce 2 years later. Her second marriage at 23 was a far happier one, but ended tragically when her husband, Jack, was killed in a motorcycle accident. She married Nathan, Jack's second cousin, a year after the accident, when she was 27. Emily had come from a large Catholic farm family and was the oldest daughter and second born of eight children. Most of her late childhood and adolescence had been spent in helping to raise her brothers and sisters in order to alleviate the burden of her frail, sickly mother. Emily decided early in life that she did not want any children. There were bitter arguments with her first husband over her decision that she would be happier without children, particularly when, despite her husband and parents' protests, she had an abortion.

Emily felt much more compatible with her second husband, Jack, who also preferred a more independent life-style. They enjoyed going out frequently, partying, and socializing. His death was an enormous blow to her, but she threw herself into her work and tried at all costs to contain her grief. Her friends and family complemented her on how well and easily she picked up the pieces of her life.

Emily had known Nathan for many years through Jack's family. Nate had been divorced for 3 years when he and Emily began to see each other. He had an 8-year-old mildly retarded daughter and a 6-year-old son from his first marriage, both of whom lived nearby with their mother. He saw them infrequently, being preoccupied with the full-time demands of maintaining a large dairy farm. Emily was impressed with Nate's ardent courting and attention; his devotion to her helped soothe the wound of Jack's death and, with some ambivalence, she decided to give marriage another try. She was wary of moving back to a farm, but Nate suggested that they renovate the 100-year-old farm house he had been living in on the farm. Emily had worked outside the home most of her adult life, first as a nurse's aide and then as a successful beautician. With the help of a small inheritance from her grandmother and her savings, she had planned to open her own salon. Instead she took the money and invested it in building a new house on the farm for herself and Nate.

Emily's ambivalence about marrying Nate increased as the years went by. His early attention to and time spent with her soon changed, as he again devoted himself to the long days of labor the farm demanded. Emily disliked the commute to town and resented the isolation and lack of social life. She increasingly felt bitter that she had not opened her salon and that she was working for someone else. It seemed to her that every penny they made was plowed back into the farm. She and Nate began to have many arguments about finances.

Four years into the marriage Emily had a brief affair, did not tell Nate about this, and subsequently felt very guilty. Nate complained about her lack of sexual interest and affection. She found herself seriously considering having another affair when she realized she could not go on in the marriage as it was and asked Nate for a divorce. Nate was shocked and openly demonstrated his profound unhappiness about her decision. He threatened that he could not live without her. His dependent response seemed to reinforce her own independent one; she would have to be the strong person to compensate for his weakness. She moved out, sought out a lawyer, looked for a new job, and began dating several men. Three months after leaving Nate she came into therapy complaining of feeling hopeless, confused, and very anxious. She was fearful of losing her job after she began having days where she could not work and periods where for no reason she would start crying uncontrollably. The therapeutic exchange reported below occurred in the third session:

Emily: I don't know what's wrong with me. I've never been out of control like this before or felt so bad. It's not as though I didn't realize I'd feel bad, but not this much pain. I try to force myself to work and it doesn't seem to work. And I can't even think straight. I thought I knew what I wanted. I mean, I made the choice to leave.

Therapist: You didn't anticipate how much you would hurt or that you'd feel so vulnerable and out of control.

Emily: No, no, I didn't. (*Suppresses some crying.*) I don't understand this. I went on OK after Jack's death . . . (*Starts to cry.*)

Therapist: It seems to me you may not have allowed yourself to really grieve Jack's death, just as you are now.

Emily: (*Cries for several minutes.*) I think you're right. Everyone expected I'd do it again, just like with Jack . . . but I can't. I can't. Right now I don't know even who I'm crying for, but I know can't keep it all in.

Therapist: You don't have to. When you experience a loss of a loved one, you need to spend some time letting yourself grieve that loss, to be sad, to share that sadness with others. It's part of letting yourself heal and coming to terms with the reality of the loss.

Emily: Well, I can accept that. But it seems so . . . so extreme. I mean it's not just being sad, but feeling so out of control and so tense as well, like I can't do anything right anymore. Is that normal?

Therapist: Uh-huh. Most people do experience some very intense disturbing feelings after deciding to divorce, no matter how unhappy they were in the marriage. Panic, confusion, disorganization, depression—in short, it can be a very stressful time and some people feel like they're losing control mentally.

Emily: Yes, that's how I feel. But how long will this last? I don't know if I can take much more of this.

Therapist: It generally takes a good year or two to adjust completely to a divorce, but you can expect that the really intense mourning you're doing right now will get better in a matter of months, maybe weeks, depending on a variety of factors.

Emily: Months. God, that sounds like a long time . . . but at least if I could believe there was an end in sight . . . and what do you mean by factors?

Therapist: Well, for instance, how well and quickly you'll be able to reach out to your friends and family to help you during this time.

Emily: That's about the last thing I feel like doing. I've lost all interest in seeing people now. And my family, well, I can imagine how they'd feel about a second divorce. Their little prodigal daughter, married three times and the last two outside the Church!

Therapist: So you haven't told them?

Emily: No. But I finally did tell Mark [her youngest brother]. And he was pretty good about it. Even better, I guess, than I thought he would be, especially since he liked Nate so much. We had a really good talk.

Therapist: Mark surprised you, and you got more support than you thought you would. Did it feel good?

Emily: Yeah. I'm glad I did finally talk to him. I should more.

Therapist: Your parents might surprise you, too.

Emily: Well, I doubt that.

Therapist: It's also important to let your friends know you need their support, Emily.

Emily: Yes, I know I should. But it's hard to talk about it. For one thing I'm afraid I'll cry again like at work and won't be able to stop. And also I feel like such a failure. It's so hard to tell people this one didn't work out either and expect they'll be sympathetic.

Therapist: Emily, you're feeling like a failure right now, but those are your feelings, and not necessarily those of other people. But you're projecting those feelings onto other people. In fact, I suspect your friends would be more compassionate toward you than you are now being toward yourself.

In this exchange Emily was reassured that her emotional reactions to the reality of the marital dissolution and the relationship loss were normal, to be expected, and time limited. It was also suggested that there were ways in which she could help herself transcend the throes of the separation process by reaching out to her family and her friends, as she had begun to do with her brother. In the subsequent weeks Emily did talk with her family and also with a couple of women friends, whom she found very helpful. Her parents were not condemning as she had expected. They expressed disappointment, but told her she ultimately must do what she thought was best.

In this session, Emily also began to realize that she was actually grieving the loss of two relationships. She had shortened the mourning she needed to accomplish following Jack's death and instead had impulsively thrown herself back to work and into a rebound relationship with Nathan. She had never worked through the meaning of that prior object loss and the separation from Nathan again evoked it. Her rebellious, independent nature led her to negate the need to acknowledge losses and endings, to mourn, to be vulnerable and thus open to the positive changes that eventually can come from such an experience. Subsequent therapy focused on helping her to gain a deeper understanding of the causes of the divorce and meanings of separation in her life. However, the next session focused on more immediate practical problems and decisions that had considerable bearing on her postseparation adjustment. These included where she would live, her work, and how these matters would be affected by the division of the assets in the marriage. Nate was brought into these subsequent sessions in order to help both parties resolve their differences and negotiate a compromise that would meet their individual needs.

DECISION MAKING

Emily: Well, it doesn't help to live in that little flea hole.

Nate: You were the one who had to have a separate place right away.

Emily: You know very well this isn't "my place." It's what was available at the time, Nate. You have the house as well as the farm right now. And you're pretty damn comfortable.

Nate: Come on, Emily, half the house belongs to you.

Emily: By right the house should belong all to me. If it wasn't for my money, Nate, there never would have been any house! If it wasn't for me being so stupid as to put it in to begin with!

Nate: And I contributed nothing, right? Nothing! Why you never lifted one finger on that farm. (*Looks away disgustedly.*)

Therapist: It seems to me you're both being a bit unfair with each other. You contributed the down payment, Emily, but Nate contributed the land for the farm. Without the farm, there would have been no house. And while Emily didn't work on the farm with you, Nate, she certainly helped support the household with her own full-time work.

Emily: That's right. OK, so we both contributed, but now the money's all tied up in both the house and farm, and what am I supposed to do? Demand that Nate sell the farm and house so that I can get some capital? Where would he go and what would he do? How would he ever get another farm again? And his kids, I know he doesn't see them much, but when they do come in the summer, it means a lot to them to have the place. And yet what does it mean for my future? I don't want to go on working for someone else all my life and living like this with no real future.

Therapist: What are your alternatives, Emily?

Emily: Alternatives? I don't seem to have any.

Therapist: Or maybe in your anxiety you're not able to work them out, maybe not even see them. Have you people explored other options, like Nate making gradual payments to you, taking out a loan, maybe a second mortgage . . . could he borrow from his parents?

Emily: Well, I don't know if he'd be willing to do that . . . (*Looks at Nate.*)

Nate: I don't know. If there was only some way to get the money out of that house without giving up the farm.

Therapist: People explore a lot of options in a situation like this. Like selling the house and a small parcel of land with it, or renting the house and realizing some income from it that could go back to you.

Emily: (*surprised*) Well, I never thought of that. Nate might be able to rent it out. I really think you preferred that old wreck on the property anyway; you never seemed really comfortable in the new house, Nate.

Therapist: (*Pause.*) So far we've talked about options that Nate could explore, Emily, but what about you? What could you do?

Emily: Well, I suppose I could insist on my share right now . . . but I hate to see Nate lose the farm. Your mentioning a loan a minute ago, I suppose I could try and apply myself for one of those small business loans. I don't know if I'd even qualify. And I could take Mark up on his offer to help me . . . I hate to do that though. I've never borrowed money from anyone, but he knows I'd pay it back.

Therapist: It seems there are more options than perhaps you originally thought. What else?

Emily: Well, I guess . . . (*Pause.*) There's always changing jobs and trying to make more money. I know I could make a hell of a lot more money waitressing at the Lodge, but I'm not sure I'm up to it. The wear and tear . . .

Therapist: The personal cost to you doesn't seem like it would be worth whatever more money you'd make.

Emily: No, I don't think so. And besides I really do love my work; it's just that I always wanted to be my own boss, and I know I could really make a shop go if I just got the chance.

Therapist: Maybe you'll have to make your chance, by taking some risks, and exploring a lot of alternatives.

In the former exchange Emily and Nate are beginning the process of assessing the various options that are open to them in dividing up their assets and in compromising so that both can have vocational and other opportunities that are important to them and their future development. The therapist encouraged this process by suggesting that it was important to explore all alternatives carefully, to maintain a realistic, nonpunitive appreciation of the needs of both parties and to try to be open to creative individual solutions.

Some of the alternatives involved taking risks and making changes and the therapist helped them sort out which of the risks were reasonable and which were too costly, as well as which changes needed to occur right away and which could be delayed. As it turned out the solution involved a combination of alternatives. Nate was able to refinance the farm, which enabled him to give Emily a partial cash settlement. Emily used this money and a loan from her brother to launch herself into her own salon. This involved moving to a different town with a better and larger market of customers, but by the time this important decision was made, Emily was further along in adjusting to the divorce and in feeling more self-esteem and confidence in her decisions.

INSIGHT AND REEVALUATION

Divorce therapy also helped Emily and Nate by permitting them to reanalyze the marital dynamics and interaction, to reassess their individual roles in the dissolution and to free themselves of a blame mentality that would work against long-term emotional disengagement. The healing process of regaining self-esteem and repairing the narcissistic injury was facilitated in therapy not only by working through grieving and struggling with decision making, but also by the gaining of a deeper understanding of why the relationship did not contribute to their mutual growth. Much of this understanding was based on a better appreciation of their individual needs, values, and personal development, and how their decision to get married had been based on an unrealistic assessment of the successful meshing of those needs and values. This kind of analysis is similar to what had been called the "marital autopsy" (Pino,1980).

The marital autopsy concept was derived from the technique of psychological autopsy used for analyzing death in an aged population and in suicides (Weisman, 1968). Such a technique is useful in helping individuals understand the precipitants and antecedents to the demise as well as in aiding them to obtain some closure and to move on psychologically. Similarly the participants in a marital dissolution need to have a clearer picture of the dynamics of their conflict and an appreciation of why the separation was necessary in order to help them developmentally in their own lives and in any future relationships. Such an analysis can also promote the healing process in that it offers some closure about the object and relationship loss and acts to reduce emotional and cognitive confusion and disorganization. A more rational assessment can act to help dissipate the blame mentality in which one or both individuals continue to project their anger onto the other unrealistically, thereby maintaining the emotional engagements and repeatedly reopening the narcissistic wounds.

The marital autopsy as a research tool was developed by Pino (1980) and involves giving a structured questionnaire covering five areas based on the temporal phase of the marriage and divorce: postmarriage, dissolution phase, preterminal phase, the course of the marriage, and the premarriage situation. In divorce therapy, however, the broad concept of reassessment can be employed without recourse to an actual questionnaire or attempting to define discrete phases, an analysis that may be somewhat artificial or not meaningful to the client. The emphasis can be on process and *themes*, rather than on rehashing what events occurred and precisely when and how they occurred.

The following excerpt is taken from the sixth session of divorce therapy with both Emily and Nate present. They had begun to make some progress in arriving at the practical decisions necessary to dissolve the marriage, but were both still actively mourning the loss of the relationship and trying to make sense of why it had not worked. Being more articulate and introspective, Emily was further along in this process than Nate. This probably was aided by the fact that she had been the initator of the separation. Nate still was prone to fall into the victim posture although he, too, was beginning to appreciate their basic incompatibility and why divorce was probably the best alternative.

Nate: I still sometimes think we could have made a go of it.
Emily: I don't think so, Nate.

At this point the therapist could have chosen to reflect Nate's wish that the marriage hadn't ended, but such a response may not have helped Nate overcome his ambivalence in the long run and could have acted to intensify such feelings. Instead the therapist decided to reinforce the reality of the break for Nate by addressing Emily and inviting her to elaborate.

Therapist: Why not, Emily?
Emily: I've given it a lot of thought, and I think it was doomed from the start. I was still so hung up on Jack. And I really hadn't come to terms with his death.
Therapist: Emily and I talked about that once, Nate. In an earlier session . . . how she had never really permitted herself to grieve Jack's death.
Nate: I know that. In fact, you're still not over Jack. But when we got married I really thought you were. You can't say we didn't talk about it. Remember I even told you I couldn't be Jack for you.
Emily: I know. I didn't expect you to, at least I didn't think I did, but in a way I did. It was too soon, Nate, like a rebound situation.
Nate: But would it have made any difference if we would have waited?
Emily: No, I don't think so now, because I really wasn't ready to get married again and I married you for . . . for . . . (*Hesitates, afraid of hurting Nate.*) . . . the wrong reasons.
Nate: (*Looks away.*) I don't know what you're talking about.
Emily: It doesn't matter now . . .
Therapist: Well, I think it does matter now in that it's important that you both have a clearer understanding of what went on in your

relationship and why, if only so that you don't repeat the same pattern in the future. Emily, you seem to be saying that you married Nate prematurely, for reasons that perhaps in the long run were not the best. What did you mean?

Emily: Well, I think I was really insecure. I mean on the surface everybody got the idea I had it together because I'm so damn good at that. But I was scared. I really didn't know what to do after Jack's death. It was so empty and I didn't know what would happen to me in the long run.

Therapist: How did Nate fit in?

Emily: He was just *there,* and he's so . . . so, I don't know. He seemed so stable, and he was comforting. And I wasn't sure what I was going to do and he offered a . . . like a ready-made future. I certainly didn't want to go back home, even temporarily.

Nate: And yet you chose to live on a farm again, Emily. Why? You never were cut out for it.

Therapist: You didn't want to go back home, and yet you did.

Emily: What? (*Pause.*) Oh. Yeah, I guess I did. I never thought about it that way until now, but it's true.

Therapist: Marrying Nate was like going home again.

Emily: Yeah, it's funny, I could hardly wait to get off the farm when I married Eddie [her first husband] and yet I put myself right back in that situation with Nate. Why would someone do that?

Here the therapist might have reflected Emily's puzzlement or reiterated that during her bereavement she was seeking the security of an earlier time. Instead, the therapist decided to plant the seed that a key developmental issue was at stake, an issue that would require some work for Emily.

Therapist: Well, it seems to me that separation is a key issue here. And how you separate and choose to develop your own identity at various times in your life has a lot do to with when and how and why you form relationships.

Nate: It was dumb of me to expect that you'd adjust to my life.

Emily: I wish you wouldn't say that, Nate, it's . . . it's like you're feeling so damn sorry for yourself . . .

Nate: (*Interrupts.*) I'm not feeling sorry for myself, Emily! I'm just saying the truth! It was stupid. We were both stupid.

Emily: Oh, I don't know. You're being too hard on yourself, Nate. (*Laughs.*) That's what you [the therapist] always tell me, isn't it? I mean I think we did and made the decisions we thought were right at the time. Maybe we wouldn't make the same ones now.

Therapist: I think what Emily's trying to say, Nate, is that it's important to forgive, not just others, but yourself, to be compassionate.

To understand that at a given time in your life you may make a decision you think is the right one, and it may be for the time. It serves a purpose. But people change, and what they want changes and how well they understand themselves. So it's important to be accepting of the change even if it's painful, and compassionate with yourself. At the time you chose to marry Emily, you thought it would work out. (*Silence. Nate looks sad.*) (*To Nate.*) You look pretty down.

Nate: Yeah, I am. I did think it'd work out, and I'm still not sure why it didn't.

Therapist: Emily has said she doesn't feel like she was truly ready to get married again and that she was confused and fearful and you represented a lot of security to her. What about you, Nate? Why do you think you married Emily at the time?

Nate: I don't know. I liked her . . . I mean it was a lot of fun to be with her. We could talk. She was . . . you know, (*turns to Emily*) you've always got along with people, made them laugh . . .

Emily: I'm more outgoing than you. My friends were your friends.

Therapist: You both seem to agree that Nate was attracted to you, Emily, because you were sociable and you found it easy to talk. And those are things you find hard to do, Nate?

Nate: Yeah, I've always been more or less a loner. I probably should never have married in the first place. It's hard for me to, to a . . . a . . .

Emily: Relate to people.

Nate: You know, there's one thing that bothers me. All this business about security . . . Emily being insecure, marrying me for that. I never saw her that way. In fact, I liked how independent she was; she wasn't like my first wife that way. She'd always speak her mind.

Emily: That was also part of the trouble though, Nate. I'd speak my mind and you'd clam up.

Therapist: You say you liked Emily's assertiveness, Nate, just as you liked her sociability.

At this point the therapist chose not to reflect and reinforce Emily's mild attack on Nate's passivity and withdrawal. Such a response would probably have made him more defensive and ended up in another replay of former marital skirmishes. Instead the therapist chose to help Nate focus on unraveling and understanding the dynamics of his marital choice, by reiterating the reasons for his attraction to Emily.

Nate: Well, sometimes she was too assertive, but basically, yes, I did.

Therapist: Did you ever wish you could be as assertive as Emily?

Nate: Well, I don't know. I suppose sometimes I have. Basically she gets what she wants.

In the past marital encounter, this kind of exchange would have pressed Emily's button immediately, and she would have defended herself and accused Nate of feeling sorry for himself, yet at the same time being protective of him. She had come along far enough in her own healing that she was able to make a less attacking response, though a confrontative one that had the potential to help Nate.

Emily: (*agreeing*) That's because I've learned to say more of what I want. If you want to learn to do that, Nate, you're going to have to be willing to take more risks with people, not withdraw. It isn't easy. I couldn't do it for you. Nobody can do it for you, but yourself.

This latter exchange occurred near the end of the session and Nate did not immediately respond to Emily's observations. It was obvious from his pained, thoughtful look that she had struck a chord in regard to his basic conflict with intimacy and identity issues.

Nate: I know what you're saying. (*Pause.*) . . . and there's truth in what you're saying . . . but you also have to remember, I'm not you.

Intimacy for Nate had been represented by an assertive parental figure who could read his mind about what he needed. This was something Nate had come to expect in other people who were close to him. His own mother had done this, as had his first wife; however, issues of identity were also involved. Nate vicariously had identified with Emily's gregariousness. The identification provided feelings of communion with others that he felt he missed. It helped to modulate his own feelings of inadequacy about his potential to relate, to be intimate with others, and to receive satisfaction of his needs.

At the same time Nate resented Emily's assertiveness and petulantly protested that "she always got what she wanted." In order to separate successfully from her he had to redefine his own expectations of what others could provide him as well as accept what he was capable of and willing to give. His statement that "perhaps I should not have married at all," was a beginning, though incomplete, recognition that he may not have been willing to give to a relationship as much energy as he was to his work. Nate still needed to come to terms with who he was and that his basic identity and feelings of self-worth came from his intense involvement with the farm. As long as he did not recognize that he was unwilling to work at being intimate and could tolerate only a mild degree of intimacy in a relationship, he would likely have difficulty healing the narcissistic wounds from the divorce, and would instead continue to maintain a posture of self-pity and hurt. He needed to accept responsibility for his priorities and choices.

The "marital autopsy" in the case of Emily and Nate involved a better mutual recognition of the dynamics of their choice and who they both were at the time of their marriage and at the point of dissolution. Both had projected an image of strength and invulnerability to the other, for different reasons. As noted previously, Nate needed to see Emily as competent and confident both personally and interpersonally to help fill gaps in his self-image. He denied her fears of making it on her own, needing to see her as strong and independent. He also had minimized her feelings of loss and grieving over Jack, her second husband, thereby reinforcing her denial and helping to abort her grief. Correspondingly, Emily initially projected an image of strength and invulnerability onto Nate, defining his intense involvement with his farm as evidence of his emotional stability and independence. He was someone you could count on, someone who wouldn't leave you.

LETTING GO

In the course of the individual and couple treatment, Emily had gained a much fuller understanding of why she had coupled with Nathan and why it did not work for her. Her first forays in unraveling the picture led her to realize that the choice to marry Nate was a premature one and that she "was not ready," having aborted the grieving process over Jack's death. A second level of understanding was achieved when it became clear to her that despite her facade of competence at that time, she was confused, afraid, and anxious. Nate represented a good deal of ready-made security, and that such security had earlier antecedents related to her best memories of growing up on the farm and the stability it had meant for her. Nate's association with the farm was a symbol of that security. His early devotion to her in their courting and his single-minded pursuit of his vocation had acted to convince her of his loyalty. This was a very powerful attraction because she interpreted it as meaning he would always be there. He would not leave her abruptly, as Jack had. This realization helped her let go of Nate and the fantasies of what he represented and what the relationship had meant to her.

After four conjoint sessions with both Nate and Emily, they decided that whatever unfinished business they had together was settled sufficiently enough to terminate the joint therapy. Emily continued in individual therapy with the therapist. The following excerpt is from the eighth individual session:

Emily: I never blamed him [Nate] for his first divorce, you know.
Therapist: How so?
Emily: Well, Helen [Nate's first wife] was the one to leave him, and he made it very clear to me that he wasn't the one to initiate the divorce,

although it was apparently mutual in the end. But he didn't start it, make the final decision I mean, which is so typical of Nate. But anyway, I think that was important to me in that he wasn't the one to leave, you know? I couldn't see him leaving me either. And after losing Jack, I think that was pretty important.

Therapist: You really wanted to see him as always being there, didn't you?

Emily: Yeah. That was really important, because when I think of sometimes how his passivity irritated me, . . . and yet it was his very inability to leave, to make a decision, that drew me to him.

Therapist: His passivity meant he probably wouldn't leave.

Emily: Right. I was in control. Of course, I really wasn't. He controlled me a lot by just withdrawing and threatening to withdraw. He [Nate] called yesterday, you know.

Therapist: Why?

Emily: Well, he wanted to know what I thought about what color the inside of the house should be painted. Can you believe it? And whether or not I'd be willing to pay for part of it. I said I'd have to think it over, but then he wanted to get together to talk and I said I didn't think that would be such a good idea. That I'd call him back, but he didn't like that and he said what was wrong with just talking together and trying to be friends, and why couldn't we see each other now and then when we had to talk about something, or if something came up.

Therapist: You're not so sure that's a good idea.

Emily: No, I mean, sometimes I get lonely and there's no one around and it's tempting to call him or just to do something with him, not really because I want to be with him. Maybe I want him to be there for me.

Therapist: And every once in a while it's like you check out if he's still there by taking him up on his suggestion that you get together.

Emily: And when I do, it never works out. It's still too painful. I don't know if we'll ever be able to be friends. Maybe someday, years, months from now, if and when seeing each other doesn't still arouse so much . . . ah . . . stir up feelings again.

Therapist: It's like you just get a little scab on the wound, and then you see him, and it's peeled off again and raw.

Emily: Does that mean we shouldn't have any contact?

Therapist: Lots of people find in going through a separation and divorce that any kind of contact is painful and only serves to delay the healing. To heal successfully you need to disengage and that probably means minimizing any kind of contact unless it is necessary. And when you have contact, structuring it so that it's brief and task oriented. It means the contact is business-like, to the point, impersonal, like it would be with someone at work. Somebody you didn't particularly want to see, but for one reason or another you had to work with this person for a brief time about a work-related issue.

Emily: I suppose I'm just going to have to tell him that. That I don't want him to call and suggest we get together. And that he needs to make some of these decisions by himself. I mean he could decide about the paint, jeeze, it's just an excuse, I know. But I fall into it, too.

Therapist: You reinforce it.

Emily: I shouldn't have told him what to do. I just told him to paint the whole inside white so that any buyer could do anything with it they wanted! But he could have figured that out himself. (*Laughs.*)

Therapist: Have you ever told him not to call?

Emily: No.

Therapist: Hard to be that forceful?

Emily: Well, he thinks I'm assertive, but I still have a hard time sometimes being assertive with him. I still protect him, both because I feel guilty for leaving and because like I said before, part of me still wants to . . . to hang on by some slim thread I guess, just the ace in the hole of knowing he's still there. Even though I know I have to give that idea up. I recognize that when he talks of never marrying again, that in some way that's comforting and reassuring to me, even though I know I should be encouraging him to find someone else and to move on.

Therapist: Really hard to make a final separation. To let go, to let the fantasy go.

Emily: The fantasy?

Therapist: Yes, the fantasy, that he'll always be there for you.

Several important therapeutic processes have occurred in this exchange. Emily realized that her fear of loss and separation strongly influenced her decision to marry a person whom she felt she could control. Her desire for Nathan's allegiance extended beyond the divorce and was perpetuated by periodic postseparation contact that ultimately proved costly to Emily's own growth and disengagement. The therapist reinforced her rational assessment that it was unlikely she could maintain an objective, detached view of the relationship nor heal the wound to her self-esteem if she continued to engage emotionally with Nate. The last exchange between the therapist and Emily touches on an important therapeutic strategy in the latter phases of divorce therapy that helps the person to effect a lasting separation. This involves the deeper understanding that letting go of one's spouse also means letting go of a particular fantasy and symbol. The divorce therapist helps clients understand fantasies they have about what they hoped the marital relationship would do for them and what the relationship symbolized in terms of intimacy and identity tasks.

Emily's first marriage at age 19 clearly helped her to separate physically from a basically unhappy, exploitative home situation. She felt used by her parents, having served as a surrogate parent for her sickly mother. Through leaving home and working, she began to establish a fledging identity for herself. The attention and affection she lacked from her parents was sought from her peers and her postadolescent lover, ultimately her first husband. The communion and success she felt with her peers, however, did not transcend into a deeper relationship commitment with her first husband, who was unsupportive of her independence and identity.

When Emily married Jack, she was further along in her own personal development, having established a successful career path and economic independence. She chose a partner more like herself. The marriage was not based on rebellion or a need to escape from parental domination, but more on an appreciation of her needs for closeness and commitment to another person. She also began to redefine her notions of intimacy, understanding that it could be blended with a healthy dose of autonomy and separation as both she and Jack pursued their separate work interests, yet closely intersected in other areas, such as their love of motorcycling.

The loss of self-esteem engendered by her first divorce was well on the way to being repaired when Emily was faced with Jack's unfortunate accident and death. The personal and interpersonal strides she had made in her second marriage in terms of a stronger personal identity and a deeper appreciation of the meaning of intimacy were not developed further in her third marriage. Nate had been chosen to replace, to repair, and to redo, but not necessarily to help her move on developmentally. His love for and loyalty to her helped soothe the loss of Jack, but, as she came to appreciate, did not help her deal with a prior loss, that of her mother's love, nor to come to terms with her desire that someone would love her in the way her own mother did not.

The powerful fantasy Emily had to give up was that someone, in this case Nate, would accept and love her unconditionally in a way she had not experienced as a child. The fantasy was that Nate would replace not only Jack, but her mother too. Of course, he could not. Her next task developmentally was to redefine the meaning of intimacy in her life in less parental, dependent terms and to transcend her insecurity over the lack of unconditional love. Emily needed to learn and believe that she could provide more self-validation by and for herself, as she had begun to do in her relationship with Jack. Jack's loss had made her question once again whether she could make it on her own and had set her back developmentally. Through the divorce from Nate and divorce therapy she was able to come to appreciate this process and ultimately to transcend it.

Emily devoted the year after the divorce was finalized to setting up her business. She dated infrequently and reported no interest in remarrying. Two years after the divorce she became closely involved with a man, Stephen, who had been divorced for 4 years and had custody of his 11-year-old son, Adam. They lived together and set up a household. The therapist worked with the new "family" for a brief time to help them adjust to the new relationships, particularly that between Emily and Adam. At the last therapy session, Emily was very happy in her relationship with Stephen, was far more realistic about her expectations of an intimate relationship, and more confident about her own capability for meeting her personal and interpersonal needs.

Prior chapters have noted that the two mediating processes in the loss of self-esteem engendered by divorce are (1) *object loss* accompanied by *narcissistic injury* and (2) *role loss* leading to *role disorientation*. Therapeutic intervention in divorce therapy is designed to help clients adjust to both of these events through the process of *ego reparation* and *role restructuring*. This chapter has outlined the therapeutic strategies and issues most relevant to dealing with object loss and narcissistic injury and promoting the ego reparation necessary after divorce. Four general therapeutic strategies in divorce therapy and their implementation were outlined in the case history presented: first, supporting and allowing for grieving and reactive depression, a process in which the client is encouraged to express verbally the feelings of loss, confusion, anxiety, and obsession, to accept the change as permanent and to reach out to others who will help and support accepting and dealing with the loss.

Secondly, the therapist must simultaneously help the client begin to deal with the practical, immediate consequences of the decision to dissolve the marriage and to help him or her explore in detail a variety of options regarding the mechanics and consequences of decisions concerning economic and familial division. Thirdly, the divorcing client needs help in gaining a deeper understanding of why the relationship did not work and/or did not contribute to further developmental unfolding for the individual. This process involves reassessing the marital interaction and the symbolic meanings of the client's intimacy needs and personal identity. It also means an alleviation of the blame mentality and coming to terms with one's own responsibility for the dissolution. Therapy aids the client to accept that one has a choice to leave as well as to stay in a relationship and to "depersonalize" the loss and rejection. (Instead of believing "it was her fault" or "it was my fault," one comes to realize that "it didn't work for a multitude of reasons that we are beginning to understand in order to help us move on.")

Letting go, the fourth aim of the ego reparation process in divorce therapy, is facilitated therapeutically by both behavioral and attitudinal changes. The client is supported in effecting a physical disengagement and decline in contact. Long-term disengagement is also aided by the therapist helping the client understand the meaning of separation in his or her life and how he or she has dealt with prior separations. A lasting disengagement is more likely to be achieved if one understands that the letting go of the other person is difficult because it involves letting go of particular symbolic fantasies the spouse has behaviorally represented. This understanding helps the individual also understand, redefine, and transcend the related intimacy and identity issues that underlie the fantasy.

A general aim of divorce therapy, which permeates all other goals, is to support the reemergence of hope and change for the future. Instilling hope involves a redefinition of the marital loss and the divorce in more positive terms, a detachment from the victim posture, and a recognition that divorce offers the opportunity for positive changes. Such an appreciation is more likely to come as self-esteem rises and the client begins to believe that he or she deserves happiness, along with other changes and opportunities to seek the things and people that may better contribute to development. It also means a deeper appreciation that one can be alone and provide oneself with sources of satisfaction and happiness and that one's self-esteem can be heightened by better self-differentiation and self-sufficiency gained through divorce. These realizations are tied closely to how successful the person is in restructuring his or her life and in making the behavioral, economic, social, and familial changes that may be necessary for both recovering from the divorce and for gaining from it. In short, hope and belief in the future is strongly influenced by how well the person deals with the role losses and is able to effect methods of role restructuring. These processes will be discussed in the next two chapters.

The general therapeutic strategies of divorce therapy are not necessarily implemented during therapy in any fixed temporal order. As was mentioned earlier in explicating the theory of divorce therapy, stage theory, while somewhat useful for purposes of categorization and organization, breaks down when applied to the therapeutic process in divorce therapy. The therapist may well be dealing simultaneously with issues of grief, attachment, and/or physical division and employing the various strategies discussed in this chapter over and over again as different issues crop up in the process of therapy. The overriding therapeutic aim in divorce therapy remains the same, that is, the rebuilding and increasing of self-esteem through the processes of ego reparation and role restructuring.

Chapter Eight

Reaching Out and Rebonding

The developmental approach expounded in this book is based on the premise that there are two kinds of psychological processes resulting from the object and role loss in a marital separation and divorce, namely, narcissistic injury and role disorientation. Both result in a loss of self-esteem that can be ameliorated by the corresponding tasks in divorce therapy, ego reparation and role restructuring. Both tasks are important and interrelated. It is difficult to accomplish the necessary role adjustments and changes under lingering feelings of regret and anger over the dissolution of the marriage and the wound to one's ego. Conversely, clients who experience extreme legal, social, or economic difficulties in setting up a new life-style and assuming the appropriate roles may find it impossible to feel better about themselves and the decision to separate and divorce.

Some writers about divorce adjustment suggest that establishing a new life-style is more important and problematic for overall adjustment to divorce than is dealing with the actual dissolution of the marriage (Spanier & Casto, 1979). Creating a new life-style involves many role changes across a variety of areas. The present chapter will explore role restructuring in relationships subsequent to divorce. Three areas will be discussed, redefining roles within one's interpersonal and familial relationships, forming a transitional relationship, and committing to a second coupling or remarriage. Chapter Nine will concentrate on role loss and restructuring in the areas of work, school, and avocation.

RESTRUCTURING RELATIONSHIPS

Major marker events such as separation and divorce generally affect all interactional spheres: the immediate family, including any children,

191

parents, and siblings; the extended kinship family; the network of old friends and work associates; the potential new network of friends, lovers, and intimates; the relationship with the ex-spouse; and one's role in the community at large. Another difficult role transition involves being alone and independent and these changes must be accepted and ultimately used for developmental growth. All of the role transitions in divorce are potential grist for the mill in therapy as therapist and client explore felt role disorientation and the implications of role structuring with family, friends, intimates, associates, and with oneself.

1. *Parents and Siblings.* After a divorce there may be a tendency to fall back into the role of a child with one's parent(s). Such behaviors are often reinforced by the parent(s), who tend to side with their child against the ex-spouse. Grandparents may take on new, more salient roles for the client's children, substituting in a parent role.

2. *Children.* Much has been written about the difficulties of the single parent role. Fathers can experience severe relationship loss and more awareness of their dependency on others, as they become weekend parents (Dreyfus, 1979). Mothers can be overburdened with the stressful demands of child rearing, nurturing, disciplining, and providing a home with little social or economic support (Kohen, 1981). Either spouse may face the loss of home and children as well as a relationship loss, and either may have the additional burden of helping the children to accept the parental change in status, family responsibilities, and relationships. The more involved parent generally bears the brunt of dealing with the children's role loss on top of his or her own. Some parents feel conflicted and guilty over any time or energy they devote to their new role as single person and any involvement in new relationships or individual pursuits. They either compartmentalize, ignore, or suppress these roles. An effort is also made to compensate for the children's loss of family by concentrating instead only on the highly involved parent role.

3. *Extended Kin.* The role of "consanguineous" relatives (one's parents and siblings) may take on new salience after a divorce as the person seeks support, attachment, and approval. Relationships with "affinal" relatives (in-laws) are likely to be weakened or eliminated following divorce. Having children present and being female and a mother, a role traditionally symbolizing the "family," may create greater pressure to interact with in-laws despite the ambiguity of the new role (Bohannan, 1971a; Goode, 1956). Once divorced, many people do not consider their in-laws as "part of the family"; yet the former affinal relatives often feel connected to the children by a primary consanguineous relationship (Spicer & Hampe, 1975).

4. *Friends.* Like some members of one's family, friends may implicitly "take sides" in a divorce by remaining the friend of only one of the former spouses. Friends generally are divided up as much as any other

community property. Sometimes friendships fall by the wayside because the friend finds it easier to withdraw and not take part in the conflict or disengagement. It is too difficult or embarrassing to take sides, or the stronger relationship has been with the couple, rather than with the individual. Once the couple's relationship is dissolved there is little basis left for the friendship. For example, where there has been a more intense prior tie to only one of the divorcing parties, a woman may find herself in a new role with respect to the newly separated or divorced individual. The relationship may now take on sexual overtones, real, imagined, or symbolic, all of which may be threatening to any or all of the people involved.

5. *New Friends and Lovers.* The divorced individual is likely to find that it is necessary to expand and supplement one's previous social network with new contacts and friendships. These new friends may be more representative of the individual's current functioning, both in a social and developmental sense. The friends also may be single and divorced, but more importantly they may reflect different personalities, attitudes, and values than those of the individual chosen in the past. One may choose, for example to affiliate with more confident, assertive people or those who are more independent, expressive, or in other ways complementary and supportive of the developmental changes in the individual. It may take much effort, many frustrating attempts, and a good deal of personal change to build successfully a different social network to serve supportively and effectively in one's new role as single and independent.

Another role transition that must be accomplished involves sexual behavior. While some of the newly divorced welcome the opportunity for sexual experimentation and learning about themselves, others may be quite uncomfortable in taking on the role of sexual aggressor, initiator, or sexually available person. Many divorced individuals choose short-term sexual partners in order to gain renewed self-esteem and proof of ability to perform or to attract. However, an on-going monogamous relationship, inside or outside of marriage, is generally the desired sexual goal and eventual preferred relationship role (Cleveland, 1979).

6. *Ex-Spouse Relationship.* The role that is maintained with the ex-spouse can be problematic and ambiguous, particularly if there are children involved. One loses the role of spouse, but not of parent. Guidelines for role relationships with a new mate of the ex-spouse are even more uncertain and problematic. Some cohabitation between separated spouses is fairly common, often serving to confuse the resolution of separation and divorce and raising false hopes of reconciliation for either spouse. Continued family outings or family holidays with the ex-spouse may also contribute to confused role expectations and reunion fantasies on the part of the children. In relatively rare instances, the divorced parties have managed to transcend the expectations of the old marital relationship and

become "friends," mutually supportive and platonic. The new friendship role of the ex-spouse may become salient upon remarriage by either party.

7. *Being Alone.* Role disorientation and the need for role restructuring occurs not just within one's immediate life space, but within the community and society as well. Economically or socially, one is no longer defined by the presence of the spouse, nor does one enjoy immediate entry or access to work and social spheres that are largely predicated upon marriage and tend to serve couples. One's status may change on a credit card, with a bank loan officer, a waiter, the teachers of one's children, as well as the changed reception that one receives in a bar, store, restaurant, or social gathering of any kind. The common theme is that one is no longer seen as attached, as part of a significant other or, in some cases, as wholly identified with the other spouse. Internal adjustments involve the perception of being alone not as a deficit but as a manifestation of growing and evolving personal independence and differentiation. Communion with significant others may occur down the road, but one's basic identity will not be exclusively defined by such a union.

Each of these relationship areas, friends, intimates, and family, including kin and ex-kin, as well as community, and the perception of one's self in relation to these people, involve implications for role restructuring that can be explored and implemented in divorce therapy. Therapeutic interventions designed to aid successful role restructuring in divorce largely flow from a cognitive–behavioral approach that emphasizes the learning of new skills, behaviors, and redefined self-perceptions that emanate from these new role behaviors.

TRANSLATING ANGER INTO ACTION

It has been noted previously that one of the main tasks of divorce therapy is helping client(s) to let go of the "blame mentality," which is shown either through punitively finding fault with themselves or projecting blame onto their former spouse for ending the relationship. As long as these feelings are played out, the relationship is never really ended, and the "marital dance," continues in frenzied polkas of custody battles or devious minuets of settlement sabotage. The more one accepts a mutual responsibility for the dissolution of the marriage, the better prepared one is for beginning and carrying through the accompanying role changes and adjustments that need to be made in order to move on developmentally.

One useful therapeutic strategy is to encourage the client to use the energy of any lingering anger from injury to self-esteem in more constructive outlets designed to further the separation process by independent action. The divorce therapist needs to support clients in taking back control of their life by utilizing anger as a motivational vehicle for behavioral change, instead of as a "present" to the former spouse and proof of injury and continued involvement. Once anger is translated into positive action, the disengagement process and the healing process are considerably strengthened. New behaviors that result from taking back power propel the client along developmentally. As one restructures one's life and receives positive feedback, important changes in self-esteem related to stronger identity and redefined perceptions of the meaning of intimacy and identity can occur.

These processes are interactional; getting rid of the blame mentality, translating the energy of anger into positive action, disengaging, healing, restructuring, and transcending involve a dynamic, fluid interplay. Like the Buddhistic notion of "karma," the therapeutic process is conceived of as nonstatic, in terms of movement, flow, and change. The second therapeutic strategy for helping the client to accomplish necessary role restructuring involves supporting change and role experimentation, and the assertive behaviors involved.

THE TAO OF DIVORCE

Fritjof Capra in his provocative book *The Tao of Physics* (1975) notes that Buddhism teaches that "all compounded things are impermanent, and that all suffering in the world arises from our trying to cling to fixed forms—objects, people, or ideas—instead of accepting the world as it moves and changes" (p. 177). Separation and divorce are manifestations of change, and the pain of divorce largely arises from trying to cling to something that has changed, not accepting the change, or not making other changes accruing from the separation. Trying to help a divorcing client successfully transcend some role change involves several steps. Assessing realistically what change is possible and whether support is available is usually a necessary first ingredient. It will be difficult for a divorced mother who receives little child support, but is wholly responsible for the care of her children, to take on readily and easily the role of available dating partner as she struggles with the new role of single parent. Similarly, an introverted, divorced male who depended on his wife to be the emotional caretaker of the relationship, his social secretary, and ambassador, will not readily reach out to new people and make the new friendships necessary to help him transcend his loneliness and rebuild his social circle.

As client and therapist realistically assess the social, economic, and legal barriers to successful role change and restructuring, the therapist can help the client explore possible external supports that can be mustered and utilized. Participation in community based support groups of other divorcing individuals is often helpful. Members share resources that can aid in managing time, providing emotional nurturance, and rebuilding a friendship network. Community resources like free recreation, low cost childcare facilities, communal housing arrangements, and the help of any extended family can also be utilized.

Although there may be community or family resources and supports that can aid the client in adjusting to the various role accommodations and changes postdivorce, a powerful resource tool can be the therapeutic group composed of like-minded divorcing individuals who are seeking help and mutual support in postdivorce adjustment. The intervention strategies can involve group process (Coche & Goldman, 1979), cognitive and role restructuring, communication skills exercises, modeling, behavior rehearsal, problem-solving exercises, and the use of homework assignments. More didactic information about the typical problems and psychosocial implications of separation and divorce can be given to introduce the topic to the group and launch their discussion and mutual problem solving (Granvold & Welch, 1977).

Structuring the group through strategic interventions such as role playing and other verbal and nonverbal exercises can help the members better master the adjustments, logistics, and coping techniques necessary in the divorce process (Kessler, 1978). The divorce therapy group can become a powerful support resource for the client, perhaps even more salient and useful than that provided by family and friends, who may simply not be able to muster the understanding and practical support derived from first-hand experience with separation and divorce.

The therapist reinforces the client's reaching out to friends, family, new acquaintances, the community, and other individuals who have experienced divorce either in a therapeutic or social context. The client is also reinforced by his or her efforts and by the evolving network of support to make necessary role changes and to take control of one's life. As a person gradually tries on the new role through experimenting with some of the behaviors, the cognitive perception of oneself in the new role is reinforced. The client's growing confidence in the new role is abetted as he or she learns the behaviors, information access, rules, and exigencies of the new role and builds the skills necessary to act out successfully. The better the learning and the stronger the confidence, the more likely others will reinforce the perception of success in the new role, be it as single person, single parent, or breadwinner.

The necessary skill building may involve a variety of therapeutic experiences, for example, parent effectiveness training as one copes with the difficulties of being a single parent and the only disciplinarian, training in communication skills as one attempts to build a social life and reach out to new friends, and going back to school as one tries to acquire the financial skills and vocational training necessary to support oneself and one's family. Whatever the task, the therapist can help set up behavioral hierarchies and priorities to help the client gradually and slowly master the changes, setting the pace at a rate that can be handled emotionally and practically.

In the role change and restructuring accompanying divorce one is always dealing with ambiguity. It is the inherent ambiguity of many of the role changes following divorce that produces role disorientation and can make role changes so problematic and anxiety producing for many clients. Although there soon may be more divorced than never divorced people in our society, there are not well-defined role behaviors, language and appropriate labels and expectations for kinship structures and relationships that would make the transition to divorced status more comfortable and predictable. Some of the role changes faced by a client become more structured over time, such as the evolving change to single parent status. Other roles remain ambiguous, such as relationships with one's in-laws after divorce.

A therapeutic task in postdivorce adjustment and role change is to apprise clients of ambiguity inherent in the role change process, pointing to social contributants as well as intrapsychic ones. This helps one more realistically and rationally assess the difficulties imposed by the lack of cultural norms and structures, instead of blaming oneself for inadequacy in postdivorce adjustment. Society does not readily produce the norms and the structures; for example, there are no "single parent" school banquets; one may not truly have a father-in-law after a divorce, yet a child may still have a grandfather.

To a large extent the therapist needs to help the client develop his or her own structures, links, and networks that define the norms and boundaries of the new familial and friendship roles and kinship structures. For one client, dating after a divorce may be seen as inappropriate, the more comfortable role taken on is similar to that of a widow who mourns a death. For another divorced person, a role transition to "swinging single" is desired and quickly implemented. Despite the best efforts of client and therapist to build the structures and make the role readjustments that will aid one in transcending and learning from the separation experience, there is likely to always be some ambiguity in the process, as well as in the new roles, that must be expected and tolerated. When one can move beyond just tolerating the ambiguity, to accepting it and appreciating the dynamic nature of life and all roles in life, the "tao" in life, so to speak, one becomes less threatened by the lack of permanence and definition and more appreciative of the flexibility and movement possible in a nonstatic role.

REPLACEMENT VERSUS RECONSTRUCTION

Some individuals deal with the role losses and changes incumbent in divorce by attempting to replace the lost object/person with an appropriate person substitute. Postdivorce development involves a difficult process of change and experimentation in which assumptions about prior attachments are explored, and it is hoped, understood. The individual may abort this process by bonding more closely with a child, parent, or lover, who in many respects takes the place of the spouse. The lover taken prior to the separation and divorce, who essentially is "waiting in the wings," represents one such example. This phenomenon will be discussed more fully in the next section on transitional relationships. The divorcing client may move back into the parent's home and the parents may replace some of the security, structure, and closeness of the marital role.

Far more likely, however, a particular child is singled out to act as a replacement for the spouse. Children who are of preadolescent age or are the oldest adolescent and are the same gender as the departed parent may be most vulnerable to being placed in this position. What can occur is a blurring of roles and generational boundaries that help define parent-child roles. This child is usually the child who is closest to the absent parent or the "Oedipal child." Some of the conflict between the ex-spouses will now continue in the new "marriage" between parent and son or parent and daughter, reflecting the ambivalent feelings of both parties.

The divorce therapist can convey the age-appropriate behaviors and role expectations for the client's child or children. He or she can also help the parent understand the motivations for replacement and compassionately aid the parent to seek more appropriate solutions to the role loss than a pseudomarriage with one of the children. Such a "marriage" can also mitigate against the successful later remarital adjustments, as will be discussed later in this chapter.

THE TRANSITIONAL RELATIONSHIP

The initial role restructuring that occurs in adjusting to divorce is likely to center on the relationships with family and friends. Unless the individual already has been involved emotionally and/or sexually with someone prior to the separation, initial disinterest in other relationships gradually changes as one begins to heal and regain self-esteem. After the decision to divorce has been made and the parties have separated for some time, it is common for the individual eventually to become involved in a transitional relationship. This relationship can be termed "transitional" because it is generally not permanent, yet serves many important psychodynamic functions that help one transcend the separation, begin to heal the narcissistic injury and "role play" some new behaviors that prepare one for more major role restructuring.

Although a transitional relationship can provide valuable support to a person healing from a divorce, a danger is that, because of insecurity and projective distortion, the person may prematurely bond with this first significant other, imagining a permanent commitment. The danger is particularly acute when the divorcing person has someone who is "waiting in the wings," that is, another intimate relationship immediately available to replace the spouse. Little or no period of questioning, reworking, redefining, analyzing, or "feeling" the separation and dissolution is undertaken. The critical developmental growth that needs to occur from experiencing aloneness and loneliness is denied, aborted, or skipped.

In our society, as in most cultures, loneliness is usually perceived as a negative state and is avoided. Marriage is seen as bringing a state of attachment and connection that is presumed to counteract loneliness (Woodward, Zabel, & DeCosta, 1980). As divorce severs this sense of identity and oneness, the individual may be unable to deal even temporarily with the feelings of dissociation and potential detachment and may seek a ready replacement, however inappropriate or costly in the long run. The person is "saved" from experiencing these difficult feelings by insuring the presence of a "savior" in the form of another committed person ready and waiting. Yet the divorcing client may run the very real danger of repeating dysfunctional patterns, inhibiting personal growth and change, and eventually ending up with yet another divorce.

The transitional relationship can begin both prior to and after the actual marital separation. It can occur after a lonely period of introspection and withdrawal during a predivorce separation and be motivated by feelings of aloneness. The increasing desire to reach out to others or experiment sexually may culminate in the individual desiring a more monogamous stable relationship, not necessarily a marital one, but a "steady," more exclusive one. Or the transitional relationship may have begun prior to the separation as an extramarital affair or a developing relationship that takes on a commitment to bond during the separation or after the divorce. In all these cases, but particularly in the latter, the individual may not recognize the transitional nature of the relationship, nor its dynamic functions. Here is where therapy can be particularly useful.

In divorce therapy, the therapist can help the individual understand the functions of the first intense postseparation relationship, its advantages, intrinsic nature, and the reasons these relationships are generally transitory. As the client is helped to appreciate the important functions as well as the limitations, he or she is better prepared to recognize when the transitional relationship is no longer developmentally helpful and why. This knowledge is gained in therapy in part by contrasting the transitional relationship with the marital one and looking for covert themes and similarities below the surface contrast. This understanding can enable the client to appreciate the dynamics of the separation as well as his or her own needs and motivations.

The transitional relationship generally helps people with each of the two major tasks that they need to accomplish in a divorce, that is, ego reparation and role restructuring. The wound to self-esteem is soothed by the knowledge that one is again attractive to someone else and that one can be intimate with another person and be desired by that person. Narcissistic need replacement occurs in the transitional relationship, which is often characterized by more intense physical and emotional attraction to a person who symbolically represents either what the spouse was not or what the person would like the significant other to be. The desire to replace the loss of the former marital role of being "attached" and part of a couple, yet somehow also free and detached is also well served by a transitional relationship in which the two parties can maintain closeness without commitment.

In this way the individual is essentially role playing, experimenting with the new role of single person, yet remaining part of a couple. There is substantial comfort and security in being "attached" to another person and many people use attachments to define their identity. Deprived of the relationship with the spouse to define identity, some clients immediately begin a search to find the "other," another person who will help restore self-definition. Identity is supplied by their attachment to another person, by that person's approval, and/or by vicarious identification with the new individual.

The motivation to replace the object and role loss in divorce, however, may also involve the desire for some change and for some role restructuring. The transitional relationship can offer an important opportunity for personal learning. Frequently the individual, perhaps as a form of rebellion, chooses someone opposite to the spouse, someone who offers symbolic surface contrast to the characteristics of the former husband or wife (Taibbi, 1979). A younger person who symbolizes more freedom, openness or sexuality may be a particularly attractive choice in the transitional relationship, as the client hopes to recapture some part of themselves or to reflect an idealized self in the other person.

While a transitional relationship can provide some immediate amelioration in the tasks of ego reparation and role restructuring, it is generally not a long-term solution for resolving and transcending the object and role loss in divorce. The therapist and client need to be aware not only of the functions of such a relationship, but also of its psychodynamic significance.

Perhaps the key variable in recognizing a transitional relationship is in the careful exploration and identification of the common characteristics of the marital and transitional relationships and then isolating the covert theme beneath the apparent surface contrast of the new relationship. The superficial differences between the relationships may be striking, but often there are commonalities in key problem areas of intimacy and identity that mark the similarities between the two relationships. Therapeutic discussion reveals similar interpersonal dynamics with the new individual, in different personal clothing.

A metaphor for the transitional relationship is that it is like receiving a bandage when one needs some new skin. There needs to be some immediate repair to the loss of self-esteem, but the repair tends not to be long lasting. Thus, another common characteristic of the transitional relationship is its feeling of prematureness, of emotional intensity before the issues of grieving, aloneness, and separation have truly been addressed and worked through. The therapist may have the sense that the client is latching on to someone who initially is perceived as very attractive because of strong surface contrasts with the former spouse. Yet the client does not appear to have had the opportunity to transform the experience of the separation into a developmental leap that would ultimately lead him or her to choose a different intimate other based on new self-perceptions. The client may have some sense that the coupling is premature, yet either be seduced by the security of the attachment or in a state of intoxicating "limerance," wherein one projects quite unrealistic attributes onto the loved one (Tennov, 1979).

The transitional relationship has similarities to the so-called rebound relationship that often occurs after the break-up of an intense long-term relationship. Both involve a sense of premature coupling and the avoidance of loneliness and the state of separation. Other identifying characteristics are the temporary state of limerance that accompanies the relationship and the strong surface contrasts, but underlying dynamic similarities, to the original partner. The "savior" theme and the "opposite" theme may work hand in hand to attract the client who may feel: "Ann will save me from being alone because she is the opposite of Mary who left me." The following case illustrates dealing with a transitional relationship in divorce therapy.

Case Study 15: Vicky and Tony

Vicky (age 26) had been separated from her former husband, Angelo, for over a year and was waiting for the final divorce decree. During an initial 6-month period, she had little interest in dating other men and was absorbed in her work and in trying to make the external adjustments necessary to accomplish the separation and divorce. After this period, Vicky began to date sporadically. Usually these were men she met through her friends. An elementary school teacher, she found little opportunity to meet single men through her work, nor was she inclined to frequent the bar scene as did some of her single friends.

After 6 months, her initial grieving of the divorce had abated considerably, and she felt ready to meet someone new, yet still quite hesitant about becoming more than superficially involved with anyone. Vicky had struggled with a weight problem all her life that was reinforced by the criticism of her former husband, Angelo. Thus she also felt some insecurity about becoming sexually involved with men and unsure about her attractiveness. It was safer to go out with her several close women friends who were supportive and accepting than to risk being rejected again by another man.

Vicky's various friends encouraged her to date and offered to "fix her up," which she generally rejected. Her best friend, Bernice, who was unhappily married and had two children, repeatedly told Vicky how lucky she was not to have any kids and to be "free as a bird" to see whom she wanted. Bernie taught with Vicky and on Fridays they would usually stop and have a drink on the way home from school, an opportunity to let down over a friendly exchange about the vicissitudes of teaching 6- and 7-year-olds. On one occasion Bernie suggested to Vicky that they go to a place where the brother of her sister-in-law, whose name was Tony, was bartending, and that Vicky would enjoy a surreptitious look at this "gorgeous hunk" of a young man. Vicky went, intending to enjoy only a vicarious visual experience, but to her surprise talked to Tony for several hours after Bernie had left for home. She was immediately attracted to Tony, not only because of his handsome physical appearance, but because he seemed so warm and interested in talking with her. They spent much of the rest of the weekend together, which included a very positive sexual experience for Vicky.

Vicky was aware that a significant part of her attraction to Tony was the contrast he presented to her former husband, Angelo. In individual therapy following her separation, she had rehashed many times how she saw Angelo as controlling and dominating. He had kept tight rein over the purse strings as well as over her personal mobility. Yet despite Angelo's overt display of dominance, he was quite dependent on her and demanding of attention and nuturing. Vicky had also lamented Angelo's involvement with his large family, which included parents, seven brothers, and two sisters. She felt that his loyalty to them, particularly his parents and twin brother, Alfonso, came first, and this conflict was critical in the dissolution of their marriage.

Tony was a part-time college student, bartending on the side to make ends meet. His easy openness, and his ability to express feelings, greatly impressed Vicky. They began seeing each other more frequently. As he had very little money, they would do things like take walks, chaperoned by Vicky's dog, play racquetball, or just sit and talk for long evenings. He also liked to cook, which further impressed Vicky, and he surprised her with a candlelight spaghetti dinner on her birthday. He seemed of another generation than Angelo, although the two men were only 6 years apart, because of his willingness and comfort in expressing the more "feminine," softer parts of his personality.

Vicky: Can you ever imagine Angelo cooking me a dinner?! Wow, if I didn't have dinner on every night at five, he'd throw a shit fit.

Instead of focusing on the remnants of anger with Angelo, the therapist decided at this point to pursue Vicky's perception of the difference between the two men and the relationship.

Therapist: It really means a lot to you—doesn't it?—that Tony would do something like that for you.

Vicky: Yeah, and you know the really great part about it is that it's not a big deal for him. I mean it is to me because I'm not used to a man doing those things, but to him, it's just natural. No big deal making a dinner, just something he'd do on an everyday night, only it happened to be my birthday. He's just so, so . . . ah . . .

Therapist: Different?

Vicky: Well, yes, but in a good sense. I guess because of all these years with Angelo, I just never thought a man could be so open. He's just not hung up on all that stuff about what a man should be. And he's so affectionate, in an easy kind of a way, like he's never embarrassed about giving me a hug or a kiss around his friends. Maybe it's because he's younger.

Therapist: How do you mean?

Vicky: Well, I think the kids nowadays, lots of them aren't so hung up on the macho stuff.

Therapist: That's interesting you used the word "kids" . . .

Vicky: That's the one thing that bothers me, the difference in our ages. I guess in some ways he does seem like just a kid and I wonder if he's too young for me. When I think of his age, and remember he's only 20, I think "kid." Yet when I think of "Tony," I don't, because he seems so mature for his age.

Therapist: In the way he relates?

Vicky: Yes, he's got so much more on the ball personally than guys with 10 years on him. He's just really, really special.

The therapist had attempted to begin a line of therapeutic exploration with Vicky that would first clarify her perception of strong apparent differences between her spouse and current boyfriend. This would, it was hoped, lead to a better elucidation of the real and imagined differences as well as any underlying dynamic similarities. In the process, two other themes became clearer, one that Vicky was particularly enamoured of what she perceived as Tony's great "specialness," a usual sign of the distortion of the limerance process accompanying a transitional relationship. In this way, Vicky was hoping Tony was the ideal man, strong, yet sensitive, affectionate, and not dominating. Yet another emerging theme was the realization that she was not completely comfortable with the nature of the relationship, admitting that sometimes she wondered if he was "too young for her." The therapist further pursued the seeds of her discomfort, again with the goal of helping her to better appreciate the function and meaning of this relationship at this point in her life.

Therapist: Tony seems so special to you and he seems so much more mature than his age would suggest. Yet you also say at times you've wondered if he's "too young for you." Is there anything here besides the fact of his age that worries you?

Vicky: I don't know. It's just that sometimes I think we're at such different places in our live. Me having been married, almost divorced. He's never had a really serious commitment, nor do I think he would want one at this point in his life. Nor should he have one, really. He's got a lot of time for that. And, of course, I've had a successful career for 5 years and he doesn't have the slightest idea of what he wants to do or what direction he wants his life to take as far as work goes. His main job now is just to manage to stay in school if he can.

Therapist: So sometimes you're concerned that you're at very different places in your life, that indeed you're quite a bit ahead of him as far as some of the critical experiences you've had, like having been married and having a career.

Vicky: Yes. Sometimes I think he's even a little awed by things like my house and furniture and stuff. I don't think he resents that I have those things or that I make more money than he can now, at least I hope he doesn't. But sometimes I notice he's not really comfortable when we go to my house, and he seems to always suggest we stay at his place.

Therapist: Does that bother you?

Vicky: Well, yeah, kind of. It's hard with Mitzi [Vicky's dog]. Mitzi would much rather be at our house where she's got the yard and her squirrels and bones!

Therapist: (*Laughs.*) So Mitzi doesn't much like getting shifted around. But how do *you* feel about the differences between you? [Shifting the focus from the immediate problem with the dog to the more important developmental issues.]

Vicky: Well, I'm not too worried about it. After all, neither one of us is talking about long term . . . or marriage or anything close to it. So why can't we just enjoy what we have right now? This is the best I've felt in years. And Tony's made it all happen.

Therapist: You can also take some credit for your happiness, Vicky.

Vicky: What? Oh, yeah, I know. I know. But meeting him, and . . . and feeling good about myself and good about sex again, well, I wouldn't have without Tony being who he is. Like I said, he's just a very special person.

Although Vicky has some appreciation of the developmental differences between her and Tony, her tendency is to minimize them and instead to revel in the ego-enhancing aspects of the relationship. An important and useful function of the transitional relationship can be its helpfulness in repairing the self-esteem injury and the object and role loss endured in the marital dissolution process. Vicky implicitly states that she is aware of the "here and now," the basic transitory nature of the relationship, but tends somewhat to idolize Tony as her "savior," the special one who was able to make her feel desirable and a sexual person again, in the process underestimating her own role in her healing and regaining self-confidence.

The following excerpt from therapy occurred in the next session 2 weeks later. Vicky had met Tony's parents for the first time. Her mood was clearly less euphoric. The meeting had happened by accident. She and Tony had driven down to his parents' home to pick up some of Tony's things that he had stored there. His parents had returned from their vacation a day earlier than was expected and were there to greet them. Tony's father was a physician. His mother owned a fairly successful antique business and traveled a great deal. Tony was the middle child; his oldest sister was a 2nd-year medical student, apparently destined to join her father in practice; and his younger sister was a freshman and honors student at a prestigious women's college. The meeting was short, cordial, and formal. Vicky had the impression that Tony's parents had not known that Tony was seeing her or who she was.

Vicky: I wish it had been more comfortable, but it was hard with us being so surprised they were there and they were surprised to see us, too, but . . . (*thoughtfully*) more surprised I think to see me with Tony.
Therapist: Did you and Tony talk about it?
Vicky: No, I wish we would, but we took a friend of his back with us and he hasn't called me. (*Looks worried.*)
Therapist: You look concerned.
Vicky: I'm not sure what's gone on between him and his parents. I wouldn't be surprised if something has. I get the feeling he's got a lot of pressure there, from them I mean. His sisters doing so well and all.
Therapist: It's a pretty high powered family to be in.
Vicky: Yeah. And the way his father and mother looked me over, I'm glad I'm not in it! I wonder how much Tony tells his parents. We've been dating for 4 months, and yet I don't think they knew who I was or, if they did, they were sure cool about acknowledging it.

Tony's telephone calls to Vicky became more infrequent in the next few weeks, and Vicky finally confronted him about his withdrawal. He denied the direct involvement of his parents, but admitted that they were less than happy that he was involved with a divorced woman 6 years older than himself, and that their disappointment with him was compounded by his lack of academic direction and the contrast to his sisters' success. Instead of being angry with them, he seemed more conciliatory and penitent, feeling that they indeed had a right to be irritated and frustrated with him. Correspondingly, for the first time Vicky became irritated with Tony, as she realized the extent to which he was still dependent on familial approval. The most important breakthrough in therapy occurred at this point, when the same covert theme that had occurred in Vicky's and Angelo's relationship was recognized in the transitional relationship with Tony.

Despite the strong surface contrasts, Vicky had again involved herself with a child/man who had not separated from his parents' dominance and in the process had triangulated herself in a parent role, against the disapproval of the other parent(s). Tony was "free" only in appearance; when she began to assess him more realistically and without the benefit of limerance, she also realized that he indeed was not a "savior" for the long or short run. Part of her attraction to Tony had been the apparent differences in personality that he presented, compared to her former husband. He also represented some of her fantasized new self: single, free, open minded, sexually and otherwise. It was a new role, albeit a stereotyped one, that she had imagined should occur after a successful divorce. In this respect Vicky had been strongly reinforced by her married friend, Bernice, who vicariously enjoyed her relationship with a younger man, and the implied freedom and rebellion from culturally sanctioned role expectations that Vicky and Tony's relationship represented.

The transitional relationship with Tony also had useful and positive aspects for Vicky, in that it helped her deal with the marital role loss and try out some new roles. She had not seriously imagined a permanent commitment with Tony, implicitly realizing the transitional nature of the relationship, yet at the same time she had idealized it. The relationship had helped her feel desirable again, raised her self-esteem and ameliorated her fears of sexual inadequacy, through permitting herself a relationship with a younger, less threatening person. Her understanding in therapy of the nature and functions of the relationship had also reinforced her appreciation of the dynamics of the marital dissolution process and her need to move on developmentally.

REMARRIAGE

Most people who obtain a divorce eventually remarry. The median interval between divorce and remarriage is about 3 years, and it is estimated that four out of every five divorced persons will eventually marry again. These figures include three-fourths of divorced women and five-sixths of divorced men (Glick, 1980; Norton & Glick, 1976). The high prevalence of remarriage has led to an increasing call for research in this long neglected area as well as a small, but growing clinical literature on dealing with the special problems of the so-called "blended," "reconstituted," "stepfamily," or "remarried" family (Furstenberg, 1980; Messinger, Walker, & Freeman, 1978; Sager *et al.*, 1983; Schulman, 1981; Visher & Visher, 1979; Whiteside & Auerbach, 1978). However, beyond the fact that marriage is still quite popular after divorce, little is known about the return to marriage or treatment of the remarried family. The last part of this chapter will discuss the prelude to remarriage and becoming part of a remarried family in terms of strategies within the divorce therapy treatment process that aid such a change in role.

There is a common conception that remarriage represents strong evidence of postdivorce adjustment. When one remarries, people usually assume that one has successfully traversed the "battlefield" of divorce. The proof is one's new attachment, visible evidence of one's happiness, societal conformity, and desirability. From a developmental perspective, remarriage may represent any point on a continuum of stagnation to progression. A rebonding may reflect a divorced person's gradual, hard won changing self-perceptions and interpersonal communion. However, the second bonding can also be a flight to perceived security with little personal or interpersonal transformation. The more critical key to postdivorce adjustment may not be remarriage, but personal development and how well and how far along the individual has come in redefining issues of intimacy and identity and in making developmental transformations that can accrue from marker events like divorce. This may be why the literature on adjustment and remarriage is somewhat conflicting.

Many studies report that remarried individuals claim they are quite happy, feel well satisfied with their marriages and look forward to the future (Albrecht, 1979; Weingarten, 1980). Other studies report that remarriage after divorce is not positively correlated with enhanced well-being, that there are no noteworthy differences on measures of well-being between those who have remarried and those who have not, and that divorced individuals, whether remarried or not, generally experience a greater sense of well-being over time (Spanier & Furstenberg, 1982).

These latter data reinforce the notion that remarriage is not the sine qua non adjustment criterion for the divorce therapist or client. Successful and rewarding second marriages can reinforce self-esteem, but unrewarding pairings may act to further increase a sense of failure and loss of self-esteem. Economic considerations as well as developmental issues can produce a premature recoupling, and there is evidence that younger, less well-educated divorced women tend to "hasten into remarriage" probably because they are so stressed by the lack of adequate income and resources to manage their families (Spanier & Glick, 1981).

A DIFFERENT EXPERIENCE

Although clinical and empirical data are sparse, it seems evident that (1) personal and familial adjustments in a second marriage are likely to be complex, particularly if there are children involved; (2) second marriages and remarried families are quite different in many important ways from first marriages and families; and (3) because of the potential complexity inherent within a blended family, the "second time around" offers different opportunities for both growth and conflict.

The meaning of intimacy is likely to be changed in a second marriage. Due to their experience in a first marriage, the two parties may view an intimate relationship with more realism and less idealism and distortion. The couple is likely to be a little more tolerant of differences and faults as though one had an altered standard of success and was more determined to make a "success" of the bonding. Remarried couples report that they have a different conception of love and different expectations of marriage than in the first union (Furstenberg, 1980), and that they are more sensitive to their own emotional limitations and those of their partners (Weingarten, 1980). It may be that intimacy takes on a more diffuse quality in a remarriage; limerance is forsaken in favor of maintaining one's identity and perspective. More realistic perceptions and redefined standards of success are also likely motivated by the desire and pressure to make the new relationship work, in light of losing the first one.

Even though there is more pressure to "make the relationship work," paradoxically, remarried couples also concur with the view that they are less likely to stay in the relationship if it is not satisfactory. In fact, the divorce rate for the remarried is somewhat higher than for families of first marriages (Glick, 1980). Having endured, transcended, and perhaps benefitted from a separation, and having learned the mechanics of how to obtain a divorce, divorced individuals may be less fearful and more willing to separate again should the relationship prove unsatisfactory.

Just as intimacy is redefined in a remarriage, so is identity. The stronger identity that is often a result of divorce is not likely to be sacrificed at the marital altar. Hard-won independence may not be compromised by demands to merge identity or to concede to a partner's dominance. This is particularly true for women for whom the autonomy issue was a salient one in the first marriage. Many women report that as much as they are "in love" with their new significant other, they will not again define love as losing one's "center" or identity. Identity then is not defined primarily by love, by being in love, and by having a loved one.

For some individuals, particularly those who are economically self-sufficient, remarriage is not as attractive an alternative as a monogamous, committed, unmarried relationship. Such a relationship does not have the implicit role expectations or the legal and societal role restrictions typically placed on marriage. Such changed perceptions about intimacy and identity are also likely to lead those who have experienced divorce to have different expectations about the proper roles in marriage and a preference for roles that are more autonomous, less stereotyped by gender, and more reflective of parity in the relationship.

Divorced women express a significantly high level of egalitarianism in their marriage role perceptions. However, divorced men report more egalitarian attitudes than first-married men in terms of sharing household tasks, but not in areas regarding authority in the family and responsibility for finances and employment (Maxwell & Andress, 1982). The discrepancy between the sexes regarding appropriate role proscriptions and role restructuring postdivorce may make many women somewhat wary of remarriage. It is not easy to relinquish the autonomy and control achieved after divorce through being in a head-of-the-family role that has given more authority, responsibility, and, consequently, greater self-esteem. Age and a decreasing marriage market may also act to make remarriage a less likely alternative for many older women. Older divorced men are statistically much more apt to remarry than are older divorced women (Cleveland, 1979). Dealing with the possibility of long-term singleness becomes another role restructuring issue, particularly for the older divorced woman.

THE BLENDED FAMILY

Remarried families represent an extremely complex family form that is only recently beginning to be studied and understood. The variety of parent, stepparent, custodial or noncustodial, and kinship relationships makes it difficult both to characterize this type of family and to treat it. Such families are labeled as "blended" or "reconstituted," in culinary terms, as though all one had to do was add water and mix well to create a new functioning family. Children may resent having to change their roles in a new family structure that may involve less autonomy and more subservience to the new stepparent, the loss of a pseudoadult or "parent" role, and a decreased attachment to the natural parent.

The remarried family also involves a situation in which there are no commonly shared role expectations or culturally sanctioned institutional forms on which to rely (Cherlin, 1978). The boundaries between roles are more permeable and open, particularly between stepchildren and parents. Issues of authority, intimacy, and sexuality are more ambiguous. The ambiguity may lead to conflict and frustration, but greater openness and flexibility in such families can also provide children with opportunities for developing different kinds of supportive adult relationships. Such relationships may be based more on friendship than on parental consanguinity and authority. New and shifting coalitions may form within such families between subsets of siblings as the children restructure their roles and relationships within the remarried family (Messinger *et al.,* 1978). Postdivorce therapy can help individuals and their significant others better prepare for and anticipate the very different kinds of roles they will face in a remarried family, and the necessary role restructuring that flows from redefined conceptions of intimacy and identity in these family constellations.

There are several therapeutic issues and strategies that relate to the role restructuring represented in the possibility of remarriage. These issues and strategies flow from the conception that remarriage is a marker event, like divorce and marriage. Such events pose unique developmental opportunities and conflicts concerning separation and communion and their particular meanings at that stage of the person's development. Five therapeutic issues and related strategies will be discussed in regard to their import for dealing with remarriage issues: (1) role replacement as represented by premature bonding; (2) dealing with the ghosts of the ex-spouse and former family; (3) defining dependency and maintaining centeredness; (4) redefining family roles; and (5) exploring long-term alternatives to communion and bonding, other than marriage.

FLIGHT INTO HEALTH AND REMARRIAGE

The kind of premature bonding that can occur in a hasty remarriage has been alluded to several times in discussing the role restructuring that needs to be accomplished in postdivorce development and therapy. The same kinds of therapeutic considerations that apply in the transitional relationship are of relevance here. Again therapists need to be aware of and discuss with clients the dynamics of solving the injuries to self-esteem by choosing a replacement who represents surface contrasts to the ex-spouse or one's projected ego-ideal. The spouse replacement may have been "waiting in the wings" and purposely put into place prior to the separation and divorce with unconscious or conscious intent to avoid the developmental crisis that divorce would precipitate. The characteristics of the transitional relationship and its analysis in therapy apply here. If a person has not allowed himself or herself to experience the separation, aloneness, and loneliness that divorce introduces and the accompanying introspection and redefinition, then a hasty remarriage, like the transitional relationship, is not likely to lead to a developmental leap or change. By understanding generational and bonding themes, exploring fears of separation, and discussing the kind of identity gained through the reflection of another's love and approval, the therapist can help the client understand whether the remarriage represents a progressive developmental focus.

EXORCISING GHOSTS

A common difficulty in relationships "the second time around," is dealing with the role expectations and preconceptions one has learned in the former relationship. One may automatically expect that a significant other will dominate or exploit or withdraw or be selfish, or any one of a thousand different complaints and conflicts that one may have had with the former spouse that are then projected onto the new relationship. These kinds of projections can operate for children as well as for spouses in a remarried family. Children may expect their stepparent to behave in ways that are desirable or undesirable depending on the kind of relationship they have had with the "present" as well as the "absent" parent. Stepmothers face additional difficult role expectations by stepchildren due to the highly negative preconceptions and mythologies we have about stepmothers in our culture.

Thus, an important therapeutic issue becomes dealing with the "ghosts" and expectations from the former marriage in the current relationship and family. The task of the therapist is to help the client or other family members assess realistically such projections and expectations by applying cognitive behavioral strategies such as rational inquiry about motivations and repeated assessment of current behaviors as contrasted to old ones. The individual must be gently reminded in therapy to live within the present relationship and its current on-going functioning. This requires an appreciation of the past conflict and dynamics. It also requires a willingness to rid oneself of dangerous generalizations that can undermine trust and faith in the new relationship. As has been noted previously the divorce therapist can be a bearer of hope, without which there can be little trust and faith in the new relationship. As has been noted previously, the projection and distortion that may prevent living in and building on the present.

DEFINING DEPENDENCY AND MAINTAINING STABILITY

In the prior discussion on remarriage, it was emphasized that remarriages are often quite different from first unions, particularly in regard to role expectations and redefined meanings of intimacy and identity. The therapist must not only help the person deal with and dispel the unrealistic ghosts and projections of former relationships, but also redefine new healthier expectations regarding a potential marital bond in a remarriage or a significant unmarried rebonding. Here therapy can be very valuable in exploring preconceived notions of femininity and masculinity and the qualities and attributes one traditionally expects of a husband or wife as related to gender stereotypes.

Divorced men can gain a new appreciation of the fallacy of the strong, silent, unfeeling male and become more in touch with feelings of dependency and vulnerability. The experience gained in divorce can lead to greater value placed on learning to express feelings and being sensitive to the feelings of others. As they examine their own contribution to the dissolution of their marriage, many men appreciate for the first time how their attitudes about masculinity had significantly inhibited their functioning in marriage, parenting, and other relationship areas. Divorced women may question stereotyped female roles, gaining a new appreciation of the meaning of independence and the self-sufficiency apart from a marital identity and the expectations of sharing overt, rather than covert power within a relationship.

Exploration and reinforcement of these new role expectations based on a more androgynous view of gender and gender relationships may ultimately lead to greater self-esteem and better self-definition within a relationship or remarriage. The therapist must be aware, however, that the premium placed on independence, separate identity, parity, and self-fulfillment can sometimes lead to more problematic bonding. Perhaps in the future there will be less questioning about roles and better accepted guidelines, and less inherent conflict in opting for and expecting relationships characterized by high parity. Reluctance to merge households, families, or finances may have a strong appeal in maintaining the separate identity gained in divorce, but may represent a symbolic separation that ultimately takes its toll on the commitment and intimacy within a remarriage. Helping the client to define this delicate line between maintaining autonomy, without sacrificing intimacy and implementing the kind of complex role restructuring required, is a formidable task for the therapist.

The important underlying issue concerns helping the client to understand that no matter what relationship one has again in one's life, no matter how close, or how intimate, the "self" is never lost. The person one ultimately has is oneself. Intimacy is thus redefined to include "aloneness." Aloneness has a positive new meaning for one's identity in that one now knows that one always has one's self, that person is always there to nurture, to take care of, and to be compassionate. One may go through many separations in one's life, even another divorce, but the individual does not truly separate from one's self. The therapist must continually reinforce the notion that the individual always returns to the personal core within oneself, despite the ebb and flow of relationships, marital and otherwise, in one's life. Helping people stay "centered" requires that they regularly take time for themselves to do the individual things that make them feel good about themselves. This varies from person to person, but generally involves a balance between some meaningful work, hobbies, exercise, relaxation, and friendships apart from the spouse or significant other.

REDEFINING FAMILY ROLES

If the therapist is dealing with a client who is already in a remarriage, family therapy may be the appropriate mode of treatment. The kinds of role change and role restructuring of relationships that occur in a remarried family can have dramatic import not just for the person, but for any and all of the individuals in the merging subsystems, including children and stepchildren. The therapist can be of great benefit to these families in helping them to deal with false expectations of having a "first marriage," or a primary family. Previously unmarried individuals may be sorely disappointed that the children of the divorced spouse do not relate to them as a real "mother" or "father," and that the honeymoon can be quickly dissipated when a ready-made family arrives on the scene. The therapist can help the parties involved to face their disappointments and resentments over discovering that their fantasies about the marital or family roles are quite different than the realities. Children need guidance in regard to the feeling that their new "mother" or "father" will displace or replace the original one. Similarly, stepparents need to be reinforced in their perceptions of the futility of trying to replace natural parents or to maintain the facade of closeness and bonding between all members of the stepfamily. If these conflicting and irrational perceptions are not dispelled, there may be conflict and friction between the spouses. The divorced client is caught between loyalty to the spouse and loyalty to his or her children.

The primary therapeutic task in this situation is to redefine family roles and rebuild boundaries between the adults and children in a remarriage. The boundaries that define the remarried family and its identity will probably be looser and more permeable than in the original nuclear family (Walker & Messinger, 1979). Rebuilding these boundaries involves strengthening the spouse subsystem and creating a new, more salient parenting role for the stepparent. Both these strategies act to dilute the tight original parent–child coalition that works against the formation of the marital bond in a remarriage. At the same time that the bond between the spouses is reinforced as primary, the boundaries for closeness between stepparents and stepchildren or between adolescent stepchildren are better defined to enforce the incest barrier, a common underlying concern in such families. Whiteside and Auerbach (1978) state,

A primary early task of the remarriage (or of therapy if help has been sought), then, is the development of a close spouse relationship, with a way of negotiating conflict without drawing the children in as go-betweens. They must give up some of the closeness across generational boundaries—but without leaving the child in a rejected, unsupported position. Closeness within the new family must have the clarity of incest limits with both parents' support . . . the establishment of a parental relationship between stepparent and child is tricky. If the natural parent remains in contact with his child, this means that parent and stepparents share reality functions. That is, they both provide economic support, a role in major decision making, and so on. With this sharing there is less chance to establish clear role boundaries. For the child an attachment to the stepparent means an inherent disloyalty to the natural parent and may present him with a confusing set of messages about himself. (pp. 278-279)

The stepparent–child relationship, however, offers more than just opportunity for conflict because of the ambiguous role boundaries and potential for divided loyalties. It also presents unique and special advantages in giving a child contrasting and alternative models of identification, value formation, and sources of adult support and friendship that can be reinforced and strengthened in therapy. The therapist helps the client and members of the blended family to redefine their family roles in less traditional terms that involve both strengthening some existing role boundaries, while opening up others.

EXPLORING ALTERNATIVES

The divorce therapist may need to help clients deal with another aspect of postdivorce role restructuring involving the exploration of long-term alternatives to marriage, when remarriage is not the likely or desired alternative. The client here is aided in discovering other avenues for meaningful relationships that will facilitate successful adjustment to a more permanent role of being single. The development of a network of close friends is especially important. Friends come to serve as "family," as one's kin and family dies. The older divorced man or woman may wish to remarry, but have little opportunity. Others may opt for long-term singlehood by choice. Sexually, there are several possibilities open to them. They may find a monogamous sexual relationship that involves a long-term commitment without marriage. Some older divorced women suppress or deny their need for a sexual outlet by concentrating on their parental and grandparental roles, thereby validating femininity in a traditional nurturant occupation. Other individuals define themselves as self-sufficient sexually by establishing essentially autoerotic sexual patterns. Short-term sexual relationships may be available with younger partners. Homosexual relationships may be an alternative (Cleveland, 1979). All these options can be explored in therapy with the client who wants to remain single, chooses not to remarry or who, by virtue of restricted opportunities, is not able to do so. It is important for the therapist to help the client realize the inadvisability of stereotypically and rigidly defining happiness and readjustment solely in terms of the possibilities of remarriage or rebonding.

It helps self-esteem to believe that one has the choice to rebond and that there will be another person available. In most cases of divorce, this is the case and the therapist can realistically reinforce the client's perception of hope and choice. But even when there is little choice because of age, situational, or personal constraints, one still has a choice of how to live one's life, given personal resources. The therapist can help the individual to assess those options, build upon whatever relationship resources are available and to accomplish necessary role restructuring that will facilitate the forming of such relationships.

A case study that incorporated the major therapeutic issues and strategies in regard to remarriage after divorce and involved significant role change and restructuring, is presented below.

Case Study 16: Barbara and Peter

Barbara (age 46) first came to therapy 5 years ago for help with a troubled marriage. She and her former husband were seen for several months in couple therapy and they subsequently divorced. Barbara stayed on in individual therapy to help deal with her grief, depression, and adjustment to the divorce. Barbara was a bright, intense woman who had a doctorate in anthropology and had taught at a private university for several years. Therapy helped her regain her self-esteem and she made progress both in her career and in establishing new relationships. She began to write and publish and do the traveling she had always desired to do. Two years after her divorce she met Peter (age 45) at a faculty grand rounds. Peter was a medical professor and chair of his department; he had been divorced for 3 years. His only daughter, Rachel (age 14), was living with Peter's former wife, Ellen.

Six months after Barbara married Peter, Rachel came to live with them because her mother complained that she could no longer handle her. Rachel was failing eighth grade although she had always been a good student. Rachel's arrival changed the family constellation considerably. Barbara became increasingly upset over the changes and how her expectations of marriage and family were not being met. She returned to therapy for help in sorting out her feelings and wondered who was to blame for the conflict and tension in the family.

In the initial session, Barbara told the therapist that she had very much looked forward to Rachel's arrival. She felt that Rachel's mother, Ellen, had not provided Rachel with the kind of structure and guidance she needed, and Barbara thought she and Peter could help fill the gap. This they had done and during her first year in high school Rachel's grades improved dramatically. However, Rachel let it be known that she considered Barbara to be "uptight" and a perfectionist, and the implicit comparison with Rachel's "easy going" mother grated Barbara. Furthermore, the closeness she had hoped would develop with her stepdaughter had not materialized. Barbara complained to the therapist that Rachel would not talk to her and avoided her, preferring her father. Correspondingly she felt that Peter's sympathies were with Rachel in family squabbles about curfews, allowance, and chores. Not only had she not gained a daughter, she felt like she had lost a husband.

Barbara's initial involvement in parenting Rachel gradually diminished as she grew increasingly discouraged about the lack of reinforcement and the conflictual triangle that was developing within the family. As Barbara withdrew from the family, she also became depressed and her self-esteem plummetted. She doubted her ability to parent and to be a successful member of this family and a good spouse for Peter. Barbara ventilated her feelings in the first session and the therapist helped her articulate her ambiguous role within the new remarried family. She was not a "mother" as such, nor did she feel she was Rachel's friend, having been rejected in her efforts to adopt the role of Rachel's "good" stepmother, who would provide her with the structure and guidance she needed. Barbara felt her expectations for Rachel were reasonable and matched those that had been placed upon herself as she was growing up. Peter complained that she didn't understand adolescents, that Rachel was a good kid who was now making A's in school, with little time for anything else, and that Barbara expected too much.

In the second session Barbara realized that she did not have the benefit of a shared history with Rachel that would enable her to see progressive development and better understand and accept where Rachel was now. It was as though she had been deprived of the "golden years" of parenting and childhood with Rachel. Instead she was presented and initiated into the joys of parenthood by a withdrawn uncommunicative teenager. Worse yet, the ambiguous stepparent role and the lack of a historical role negatively affected the bond with Peter, and she began to feel a change in her role as Peter's wife as well. Barbara wondered if she would have to adjust her expectations of being "in first place" in his affections and loyalities and whether that was simply the nature of a second marriage.

After two sessions with Barbara, the therapist asked her to bring in the family. Peter was quite willing to come; Rachel was apprehensive, but agreed. In the session that followed, the ambiguity of Barbara's parenting role in the family was discussed along with the various expectations and fantasies of "family" that the three of them had based on their prior experiences with other family members. There were clearly "ghosts" about the premises.

Peter: I really feel like I can't win, you know. If I support Barbara, Rachel's mad at me. But sometimes I genuinely feel Barbara's being unreasonable, and I'll try to get her to see that Rachel's just being an ordinary kid and doing the same dumb things her friends do, and then Barbara will fly off the handle at me or get real sullen and it's iceberg city.

Therapist: You feel like you're right in the middle.

Peter: Yeah.

(Silence—Rachel has spoken very little in the session and the therapist tries to engage her.)

Therapist: What do you think of what your Dad said, Rachel?

Rachel: I don't know . . . *(Pause.)* I don't think he sticks up all that much for me. *(Turns to father.)* Like you're always saying we can't play music because Barbara wants it quiet. And we can't make a mess . . . and . . .

Peter: Well, that's true. We do pretty much live around Barbara's rules.

Barbara: *(defensively)* What do you mean?

Peter: Well, it's just that as far as the house goes, it's pretty much your way. I know you can't stand a mess, so I don't fool with the wood anymore, and I'm always on Rachel to tone down the boom box.

Barbara: Well, I'm surprised. I didn't think you liked the noise that passes for rock music either.

Therapist: You seem to have more power in this family than you thought you did, Barbara.

Peter: She has a lot of power.

Therapist: How so?

Rachel: We live like Barbara wants to, that's all.

Therapist: You sound mad, Rachel. *(Silence.)* Do you ever tell Barbara when you're mad at her?

Rachel: No.

Therapist: Why not?

Rachel: I don't know. It would just cause trouble and I'm afraid . . . *(Pause.)*

Therapist: Afraid of what, Rachel?

Rachel: *(obviously very disconcerted)* I don't know . . . maybe . . . maybe I just don't want to cause any trouble between her and my Dad.

Therapist: And maybe she would leave?

Rachel: Maybe.

Peter: Well, I know I'm afraid of that.

Barbara: *(surprised)* You are? Why?

Peter: I suppose it's irrational, but it's there, that gnawing fear.

Therapist: Even though you know it's irrational, you still worry that Barbara will leave you, Peter . . . perhaps like Ellen did?

Peter: I think that has something to do with it. And I suppose that's why I'm always hopping around trying to make sure the place is as she likes it, that she's happy here.

Therapist: I find myself wondering if you and Rachel, having lost one mother and family, are pretty wary of losing another, and maybe you expect Barbara will eventually leave you like Ellen, that she doesn't get some of the anger you both have for Ellen.

Barbara: I've felt that. You've always told me you married me because I was unlike Ellen, and yet when I am, you don't believe it; you still treat me as though I'm going to walk out on you. When will you trust me?

Peter: I do trust you, hon; it's just that after what happened with Ellen, it's hard.

Barbara: Well, can you see how it's hard for me, too? Not only do you guys not really believe I'm going to be around here, but you make it very difficult to win a solid place in this family.

Therapist: What kind of a "place" would you like to have, Barbara?

Barbara: Something better than this limbo. (*Turns to Rachel.*) Despite what you think, Rachel, I really didn't expect to be your mother, but I'm beginning to realize that I shouldn't have expected you to be my daughter either, or that you would make us an instant family.

Peter: (*Laughs.*) An instant *happy* family! I think we all had unrealistic expectations at the beginning, and we're just beginning to grapple with things as they are.

Several important themes that typify therapeutic issues with remarried families have emerged in this session. The therapist helped the various family members deal with concerns about divided loyalties, projected expectations, and ghosts of the former family and marital relationships and the need for significant role restructuring within the family that was more realistic and appropriate to the contingencies of a second marriage. The therapist also aided in uncovering the separation fears for Peter, Barbara, and Rachel. In doing so, they discovered how the projected loss dominated their interaction, setting up Barbara for anger, rejection, and further exclusion from the family and reinforcing the bond beteen Peter and Rachel. Once this threat was faced, the task in therapy became that of strengthening the spouse bond, while simultaneously allowing Rachel to develop more autonomously in adolescence, yet still have some support from the family. Peter and Barbara began to do more things together, as they had done in the first part of their marriage. Rachel began to do things with her friends, taking time out from her studies without feeling guilty that she was letting Peter and Barbara down if she didn't make all A's. The fear of abandonment by her parents subsided as Peter and Barbara's relationship cemented.

The last four sessions of therapy were spent with Peter and Barbara, discussing other significant issues in their relationship, particularly that of parity in roles. Barbara's experience in her first marriage had left her wary of entering into a relationship in which she would not feel like an equal partner. In the flush of initial romance and courtship she had fallen into a more traditional role, for example, cooking special things for Peter and cleaning up afterward. Later, when they were married and she moved into their newly purchased home, Barbara again found herself doing most of the cleaning and upkeep. She did so because her standards were higher than those of Peter and Rachel, because she enjoyed some of the housework and used it as an escape from her work, and finally because she wanted to avoid the conflict that demanding more family participation would bring.

When it became increasingly evident that these domestic activities were now expected as part of Barbara's role in the family, she became more openly angry and rebellious, demanding that they renegotiate their contract. Peter reluctantly admitted that it was not fair, but complained that, as a busy physician, he had little time for housework. This irritated Barbara because it implied that her work was less important than his. She also felt that, despite Peter's acknowledged support and pride in her career, subtly he communicated that her field, anthropology, was less important than his. It was "unscientific" and her field work with migrant workers was less critical than his with seriously ill patients. She compared Peter to her first husband who had deeply resented her scholarship and her career. Peter felt this comparison was grossly unfair.

The remainder of therapy was devoted to helping the couple clarify how the prior marital experiences had left undue suspicion and had acted to prevent the building of trust, and focused on current strategies to help cement that trust. The latter involved negotiating a new marital agreement outlining a fair division of labor. The couple also learned and practiced communication techniques designed to demonstrate the kind of listening and supportive comments they desired from each other with regard to their professional work.

Peter and Barbara were both quite aware that the work they did on this relationship was different in many ways from their behavior in prior relationships. One critical difference was that they readily knew that each had the choice to leave if things were clearly unsatisfactory, and that they might well leave. Because they were trying hard to make it work, they probably would not. As Barbara put it, "I really want this marriage to work, and I'm trying my damnedest to make it work, but if it doesn't, I will get out. Nothing is worth losing my self-esteem." Another way of looking at what Barbara said is that maintaining her core of personal esteem and integrity had become more important than maintaining any single relationship. This theme, common in remarriage, reflects the developmental reality that one must face, surmount, integrate, and accept separation as a part of life and a part of identity.

Chapter Nine

Role Restructuring through Work and Education

Successful role restructuring is critical in divorce, not only in relationships, but in work or education. The psychic energy that has been bound up negatively in a conflictual relationship may be released and redirected to one's career, education, community service, social causes, or self-improvement, leading to increased feelings of competence, assertion, and self-esteem. The experience of initiating, implementing, and completing these pursuits successfully can be quite therapeutic. It is more difficult to feel depressed when one is active. There is a positive correlation between role restructuring and involvement in work or new vocational pursuits and an increase in personal development postdivorce.

One interesting investigation corroborating this hypothesis involves a followup of divorcing couples who were seen at a kibbutz clinic over a period of 15 years (Kaffman & Talmon, 1982). Three patterns of couple adjustment were discovered in the 2nd to 3rd year after separation. About half of the cases reported generally positive outcomes, overall good functioning and general satisfaction in most life spheres; another third were more negative and dissatisfied with the outcome of their divorce and were often still enmeshed with their ex-spouse, depressed or angry and helpless. (In cases such as these seen by the authors, psychic energy has not been redirected or reinvested in new life directions and commitments, and individuals have remained "stuck" in self-pity and previous complaints.) In about 15% of the kibbutz cases, there was significant personal growth and change in the direction of expanded personal maturity.

While it was impossible operationally to define or objectively to evaluate the presumed reasons for the exceedingly positive outcomes, certain beneficial influences and themes occurred over and over again in these cases. All involved significant role restructuring. There was reinvestment of mental energy in new constructive, unconventional directions, actual experience of mastery of difficulties through new behaviors and actions, increased work activity and commitment, a supportive love affair (one might label this a "transitional relationship") and the creation and use of a supportive network. These factors were given more weight than therapy in the client's appraisal of their successful adjustment postdivorce, although divorce therapy may have operated to help and encourage all these influences.

COGNITIVE-BEHAVIORAL RESTRUCTURING

A cognitive-behavioral approach can be quite beneficial in helping the individual reinvest and restructure his or her life in ways that lead to feelings of greater control, independence, and overall self-esteem. The level of well-being achieved postdivorce may be comparable to prior periods of satisfaction in one's life; however, in many cases, adjustment may be even greater, as though the person had completed a developmental leap. Goals of such an approach involve both attitudinal and behavioral restructuring. They include the alteration of negative sets and self-assumptions based on irrational beliefs and internal verbalizations through the instilling of hope for change, the belief in individual responsibility for and the gaining of control over one's own postdivorce adjustment and one's life through overt action and learning of new problem solving skills (Beck, Rush, Shaw, & Emery, 1979; Granvold & Welch, 1979).

The strategies in divorce therapy that reinforce these goals have already been discussed in the prior chapter on role restructuring in relationships. The first involves helping the client translate the energy of anger into more constructive behavioral outlets and changes by reduction of the blame mentality, rational assessment of the dissolution, and insight into intergenerational and personal developmental themes. This step is critical in the successful implementation of later role restructuring.

The second strategy concerns active reinforcement of the client's behavioral experimentation with different roles and greater attitudinal flexibility about gender roles. The therapist supports a view of the world that is more open and flexible. Clients come to see, for example, that there is no one "good" way to parent, no one "right" definition of family, no prescribed commandment for aligning role priorities or deciding tradeoffs. This type of cognitive restructuring helps the divorcing client to accept the inherent ambiguity in roles and to decrease guilt for being in a nontraditional role. Such a view is also helpful to the client in evaluating realistically the tradeoff that divorce usually brings, that is, more autonomy, but more responsibility (Brown *el al.*, 1976). Less rigidity also means a more compassionate view of self. One learns to accept limitations in being able to change and to appreciate the constricting influences of contemporary culture and society without losing hope, perhaps even working toward changes that will benefit others as well as oneself. This latter topic will be addressed in the final chapter.

The third therapeutic strategy involves supporting active behavioral efforts toward role restructuring in work, educational, or community arenas. Within the context of therapy, many alternatives are considered and evaluated, priorities examined and realigned, and coping skills learned to help implement new behaviors. Training in assertiveness, communication skills, time management study skills, or academic and vocational areas may be useful. The client is supported in seeking out resources and the therapist needs to be knowledgeable about the availability of such resources within the community, as well as active in implementing a referral.

This active approach in divorce therapy helps the client deal with the many institutional, situational, and personal barriers that can impede significant role changes in work and educational realms. The kinds of barriers that clients experience can be divided into two groups: external, which involve situational and institutional barriers, and internal, which refer to one's personal attitudes. Both types of barriers will be discussed, with therapeutic cognitive and behavioral restructuring illustrated via a representative case study.

EXTERNAL BARRIERS

WITHIN THE WORLD OF WORK

For many people, particularly women, the economic consequences of divorce can be more difficult, if not debilitating, than the emotional sequelae (Brandwein, Brown, & Fox, 1974; Rosenfield, 1980; Spanier & Casto, 1979). A multitude of interlocking factors contribute to this picture, including a somewhat sexually segregated occupational structure and a differential earnings pattern related to gender. Despite the prevailing ethos of joint custody, women continue to bear the primary responsibility for child rearing. Divorced women often end up with a difficult situation in which they have to be both breadwinner and primary parent (Brandwein, 1977). A significant number of people living below the poverty line are single parent mothers trying hard to support their families the best they can. These divorced women face both institutional and situational barriers, some beyond their immediate control and others that they can potentially change, if given opportunities in work and education.

Discriminatory hiring and promotion policies and practices within the work place segregate women into low paying, downwardly mobile jobs, as does the lack of specific training in vocational areas or in math and/or science. As a group, women face institutional barriers in other economically related arenas: credit, social security, pensions, and insurance policies may penalize the woman who tries to make it economically on her own after divorce. Ageism is another societal barrier faced by both men and women who must retrain or change jobs after divorce or simply desire to change vocations for personal fulfillment. Similarly, the rigidity of an occupational structure that demands a full-time commitment and ignores personal or familial responsibilities penalizes certain men and women.

In helping the divorcing client successfully negotiate a work change, the divorce therapist can discuss these external barriers and societal constraints with the client, helping her to appreciate that part of her problem lies outside of herself. Yet she must be encouraged to take an active stance in helping herself despite those barriers. Therapist and client need to explore many educational vocational alternatives, resources, and aids. Bibliographies and suggested reading, referral to community resources, employment agencies, and special services, such as people to help with resumes, vocational testing and counseling, placement, or interviewing skills can all be helpful.

Role playing job interviews, setting up behavioral hierarchies of possible steps, and "homework" such as making a budget outline are all therapeutic strategies derived from behavior therapy (Langelier & Deckert, 1980). The client can also be encouraged to join or to begin a group of divorced people, who pool suggestions and resources, or can be referred to special agencies like those for the "Displaced Homemaker." Such services and groups may exist in local women's centers or community mental health counseling centers.

Vocational and educational upgrading is a long-term project and its success often depends on longitudinal financial maintenance and child support. The need for upgrading may well be forgotten in the divorce settlement and may be reawakened in therapy as the client explores the necessary role restructuring. The client may need to consider legal assistance or mediation efforts directed at renegotiating the terms of the financial settlement and agreement.

RETURNING TO SCHOOL

A return to school after a divorce also can lead to some positive role restructuring and involve retraining or vocational updating. The halls of academe may or may not prove to be a more hospitable place than the work arena. The kinds of institutional barriers that returning adults face as they negotiate a reentry into education have been well documented and may involve problems with transfer of credits, admission, scheduling of courses, part-time status, financial aid, and other policies and attitudes that favor the traditional, younger full-time student and act to penalize the older returning adult (Rice, 1976).

The returning adult student faces other situational barriers that may be exacerbated by the event of divorce, particularly the juggling of multiple roles (Rice, 1978). Education, like the work place, is not particularly sympathic to the problems of the single parent whose first priorities lie at home rather than in the classroom or office. Negotiating child care, off-hours classes, access to library, and study time become problematic for the divorced parent/student/worker. Schools and work places may have overlapping, inflexible hours, forcing the individual to choose between two desired endeavors.

The therapist may not only have to help the client weigh the school alternative and its costs and benefits, but also help him or her traverse the various situational and institutional barriers. The therapist can encourage information gathering and utilize resources and referral people within these institutions who offer special counseling about study skills, math anxiety, remedial sources, admission, and/or financial aid. Finally the client must be encouraged to take an assertive stance in dealing with these barriers.

A return to school or work either necessitated or freely chosen in the divorce process may also lead to other related role changes and losses. Returning adults may find themselves in a parent role with other students, being the oldest in a classroom and having the most life experience. Conversely, because they may be new to the academic game, roles may reverse as the younger students instruct the older adults how to play the game and negotiate their way about school. Friendship patterns may change as one discovers he or she is different from former friends by virtue of the divorce, and also because of being a student and/or worker. All these roles have the potential to effect further role change, as they can either threaten one's old associates or act in a positive way to enhance options with new friends met in the course of work or educational activity.

The demands of multiple roles engendered by divorce and a related work or educational change often leave the newly divorced person, especially the single parent, with little time for self. There is the feeling that life has become a merry-go-round of multiple responsibilities and commitments. The task of the divorce therapist becomes one not only of helping the client begin and implement the role restructuring in work or education and find the resources to do so, but also simultaneously to help resolve the possible role conflicts. Finding room for oneself is not an easy task, in the light of the responsibilities to others. Cognitive emotional restructuring may be in order to help the client realign priorities to self as well as to others and to understand feelings of irrational guilt surrounding the divorce, as well as superhuman efforts to "make up to" children for the "loss" of the other parent or to prove that one is not a "failure." Such restructuring also involves a realistic appreciation and acceptance of one's own limits and the necessity to reach out for help to a supportive network of others.

Case Study 17: Claudia

Claudia was a bright, 25-year-old single parent mother of three children: Ariel (age 5), Brigid (age 4), and Carter (age 2). She had been divorced for 1 year when she came into therapy. Claudia previously had been married for 4 years. Pregnancy had interrupted her college education. At the beginning of her senior year in college she dropped out to marry. The marriage was unhappy in many respects, but she and her former husband, Evan, stayed together "for the sake of the children." Claudia also felt quite trapped economically in the marriage, having few marketable skills to support herself or her children. Claudia sought refuge from the marital conflict in friendships outside the marriage. One of these relationships with a woman, Liz, developed into a close intimate relationship and Claudia's increasing anxiety about her double life finally led her to confront Evan with her feelings for Liz. The revelation forced them to stop ignoring the problems in their relationship. They tried a brief stint of marital counseling, separated twice, and finally decided to divorce. They agreed to stay in therapy for three additional sessions, to work out the terms of the divorce. Although Claudia did not maintain her relationship with Liz, Evan could not accept that, as he put it, he "had been replaced by a woman." He threatened to sue Claudia for custody, but in the end agreed she was the more capable parent and that the children would continue to stay with her.

Evan's contacts with the family as well as his child support payments were sporadic. The house was sold to pay off their debts, and Claudia was forced to go on welfare because she wanted to be able to be at home with her small children. She was reluctant to prosecute her ex-husband for lack of support both because she knew he had very little money and also because she feared he would retaliate either by not seeing the kids at all or by raising her sexual orientation as a challenge to custody. She found a part-time waitressing job. A neighbor in the apartment building came in to watch the children and put them to bed.

Claudia felt trapped by her circumstances and poverty. She wished desperately to become independent and take control of her life, but was not sure how. She sought out the former therapist again, after she began to take out her frustrations on her children. Claudia found herself short tempered and close to losing control and hitting them. This frightened her, as these feelings were upsetting and alien to her. She was insightful enough to realize the frustration of her situation and her thwarted hopes of finishing school and getting a better job were making her depressed and that she was projecting her anger onto the children.

Claudia: I just can't take a breather. Life consists mostly of work and the kids. During the day I take care of them, play with them, feed them, clean them up, do the house work and chores. After I fix them dinner, get out their clothes, change Carter's diaper and get him bedded down, I leave for work. I waitress til midnight, come home, relieve the sitter and start all over in the morning. Weekends are for shopping, dentists, and errands. There's no one else to do anything and no time whatsoever for myself. I can't quit work because I need the job and my boss has no idea of what it's like to be the only parent and wage earner as well. I need a job with flexibility. I can't just take time off when Ariel, Brigid, or the baby is sick and say "to hell with you."

Therapist: Sounds like you're pretty weary and discouraged trying to juggle all those commitments, with no time for yourself.

Claudia: It is discouraging. I have more freedom now in that I can make decisions by myself with no hassle from Evan and I do enjoy the fact that it's up to me whether or not I want to clean house, or whether we'll just eat soup and sandwiches some nights and how I spend my money, what little there is. (*Laughs.*)

Therapist: You really like the independence, but there's a price for it.

Claudia: Yeah, a lot more responsibility. I'm essentially alone. No one as a backup and sometimes that gets hard to take when you have to face people who don't make it any easier, like the stupid welfare. You know, the one thing I want to do for myself and the one thing that might pull me out of my dead end job is finishing school, but I talked to the guy at the Bureau yesterday about enrolling again, and you know what he said? That I couldn't be on welfare, have a part-time job, and go to school, too. That it would make me ineligible for welfare. Can you believe it? Not only do they limit my working, but now school. And yet they somehow expect me to pull out of this vicious cycle of dependency when they don't give me the tools to do it!

Therapist: Some people feel that being on welfare is like getting married again. The financial help is traded off against a loss of personal control.

Claudia: That's exactly the way it feels sometimes, just like it was with Evan. And sometimes, I find myself reacting in the same way, too. Angry and frustrated and wanting to retaliate by hiding my work hours and my actual income in tips.

Therapist: Well, that would be one way of getting even, I suppose. But it doesn't help you in the long run. You'd work longer hours, and you're already overworked, and you're still stuck in a job you don't like with no real future. I wonder what would be a more constructive way of using your anger. You're so hepped up when you think of the inequities and craziness of the system; your eyes sparkle and your body tenses up like you're ready for combat. Claudia, I'd like to see you use that energy to help yourself, to find a way to get back to school.

Claudia: So would I. But it would mean a fight and I don'tknow if I'm up to it . . .

Therapist: Maybe you'd find, if you started, that you'd be more "up to it" than you think. Especially if your efforts were rewarded. Where could you start?

Claudia: I don't know . . . I suppose the first thing to do would be to get more information. I'd have to find out if I'd still qualify for readmission, and the requirements and all, and then I'd probably have to find out about financial aid or a loan. How to get childcare? There's so much. And of course, I couldn't do it and still be on welfare. Unless . . . (*Pause.*)

Therapist: Unless what?

Claudia: (*Pause.*) Unless I challenge the policy and try to get them to make an exception.

Therapist: Sounds like a great idea.

In the succeeding session the therapist explored more specifically the steps Claudia needed to take to implement her plan to return to school, by outlining the priorities and steps she would need to take. It was suggested that she make three contacts, with a counselor in the school's Continuing Education Office who would evaluate her transcript and help her reenter, with an organization of returning adult students on the campus who met regularly for lunch and mutual support, and with the local Legal Aid Office who would help her deal with the conflict about her welfare aid. In the process, she became quite knowledgeable about welfare law and the plight of single mothers like herself. She was encouraged in therapy to pursue her cause assertively, which she did, winning an exception for herself to attend classes part time. But this was not enough for Claudia.

Energized by her success, the expectation of finally being able to finish her degree, and the hope of moving out of her vocational rut, she expressed a desire to help other single parents like herself, particularly those on welfare. Claudia began an action group that pressured lawmakers to be more sensitive to the special problems of a divorced mother like herself and to enact legislation to help them. Her efforts led to an interest in law school. At the end of therapy, with a semester in school behind her and another to go to graduate, she was planning to take the law entrance exams and then enter law school part time. She took advantage of the state legislature having that year mandated the university to make it possible for students to attend law school part time.

The excerpt presented from Claudia's postdivorce therapy illustrates three major therapeutic strategies for a client embarking on role restructuring. The divorce had freed up psychic energy, formerly being used to cope with a conflictual marital involvement, and Claudia felt more autonomy and power over certain aspects of her life. The institutional constraints of "marriage" to the welfare system had also limited the full expression of that energy and had left her feeling angry and helpless. She was helped in therapy to translate that anger into more constructive outlets, by recognizing she was replaying an old marital pattern of becoming a rebellious child to the parent/husband and now "welfare husband."

Claudia was encouraged to go beyond blaming the system to regaining control over her life through realizing her responsibilities to herself and by realistically assessing efforts she could make to help herself. The therapist repeatedly reinforced the cognitive set of hope for change and self-initiation of change, the struggle with questions about what she could do, how she could accompish it and what resources and people might be out there to help her accomplish her goal. In the process the therapist helped Claudia assess and implement a more flexible view of her role, namely that one can successfully parent and be in school and/or work as well, contrary to the society's stereotype. Cognitive-behavioral and psychodynamic strategies were utilized to implement the role restructuring. The barriers that Claudia had to overcome in her attempts to restructure her life by returning to school were largely situational and institutional. However, internal barriers, more personal and attitudinal in nature, can also play a significant part in blocking successful restructuring of work and educational changes after divorce.

INTERNAL BARRIERS

The kinds of external barriers that the divorcing individual faces in attempting to restructure roles after divorce through a return to work or school are likely to involve both situational and institutional deterrents. Internal barriers may be even more potent determinants of whether or not an individual will take the necessary steps to implement vocational or educational change. The first author's experience with many adults returning to school, for example, reveals that lack of self-confidence, irrational guilt, role conflict, stereotypes and rigidity can be important factors. The fear of taking risks or changes, as well as lack of interpersonal support for changes, can also be crucial determinants of whether or not a divorced client successfully accomplishes necessary behavioral restructuring.

BELIEF IN SELF

In order to take certain risks associated with divorce, indeed to make the decision, one must reach a level of trust in oneself and belief that one can initiate a change, a significant change, and see it through. Making the decision to divorce often helps people make other important decisions of life consequence, such as changing their line of work, seeking additional skills or furthering their careers, changes that may involve a change of residence, friends, associates, finances, and/or priorities. Basic to making and implementing such decisions is the ability to reach a level of self-confidence and belief that it will be possible to succeed in the new endeavor. Many adults returning to school report an increase in self-esteem after they begin to experience success and feel reinforced for taking the risk of making such a change. Others remain hampered by a lack of confidence in their abilities, although they actually may be doing well in their studies and retraining.

One task of the therapist is to point out the disparity between the client's actual successes and the feelings of fear, failure, or lack of confidence. Each small step along the path of gaining self-sufficiency and wholeness often must be patiently reinforced, highlighted, and interpreted. Reinterpretation is needed frequently, especially when a client will only report the negative feelings and barriers, ignoring the positive implications of what has been actually accomplished, focusing only on what has not. The therapeutic task is one of reinforcing role change and experimentation. It is aided by the surge of new energy the client feels after successful disengagement, energy that can be reinvested more productively in work, education, and self-improvement.

Role restructuring adjustments initially may be made with strong feelings of apprehension and reluctance. They can end in increased self-confidence, self-esteem, and a new sense of personal identity, providing the crucial separation and developmental issues related to ego injury and reparation have been explored and understood. Thus, ego reparation and role restructuring are worked on simultaneously in divorce therapy, so that the client does not project blame or hold onto the fantasy of the "other" who will "save" or make one whole, a condition that can result in lingering anger and hostile attachment. In the latter case such feelings, and the energy required to maintain them, are not put to a more useful purpose in restructuring one's life behaviorally and attitudinally.

If these issues have not been explored and at least partially, if not wholly resolved, the role restructuring postdivorce may be reluctantly and half-heartedly accomplished, with little developmental benefit. The ex-spouses remain economically and emotionally dependent. The converse can also occur; that is, some role restructuring may be successful in that it helps the person make the final emotional separation and ultimately acts to complete ego reparation. For example, women who successfully manage their work and family roles and strains after divorce report less depression than those who do not (Keith & Schafer, 1982). Getting the feedback from others that, contrary to personal expectations, one is capable of succeeding in vocational, intellectual, or other pursuits can be an emotional high that increases self-esteem, independence, and the belief in oneself. One's internal dialogue becomes "I can take care of myself; I can be alone and I have the skills not only to do it, but to do it well." This kind of learning is especially reinforced when one is willing to break out of gender role expectations.

ROLE RIGIDITY

There is increasing evidence that sex-role attitudes play an important part in successful postdivorce adjustment. A rigid attitude about sex roles was found in one study to be more predictive of postdivorce depression than any economic or domestic deficit (Keith & Shafer, 1982). In the single parent home, a woman is likely to assume the nontraditional male role of provider, and conversely, a man may be asked to take on the nontraditional, female role of housekeeper and nurturer. An androgynous attitude toward gender roles can aid adaptation for the client who is going through a role transition from a traditional to a less conventional status. When clients continue to orient themselves to the "wife" or "husband" role and discount the new role of being single, they are likely to have difficulty in coping with the demands of the new role. One's belief system must accommodate and support independent action; this may require some cognitive emotional restructuring of one's attitudes within the framework of divorce therapy. Such restructuring is a critical aspect of the coping process. More flexible sex-role attitudes can help men and women to reduce the incongruities between their beliefs, attitudes, and the realities of their postdivorce life situations and demands, as well as to adapt to those realities successfully. Becoming less traditional in sex-role attitudes after divorce is more common for women than men and is associated with lower distress, higher sense of well-being, more self-esteem, and personal growth (Brown & Manela, 1978; Granvold et al., 1979).

In divorce therapy, clients need to be informed about the importance of sex-role attitudes for coping with new role changes.

> Non-traditional attitudes are expected to provide women with a belief system that can guide and support their independent actions and the development of autonomy after divorce. A non-traditional ideology can also help to alleviate the guilt and self-blame that may generated by the failure of a marriage. (Brown & Manela, 1978, p. 316)

Gender stereotypes are learned early in childhood and often remain unchallenged unless a significant marker life event like divorce demands a reassessment. The therapist can support a view of the world that is more open and flexible; that one can be both nurturing and achieving, one can parent and work, do "male" and "female" roles and behaviors without shame, guilt, or conflict. Divorce then can provide a unique developmental opportunity to learn more flexible gender attitudes and to experience options and behaviors that lead to new insights and learnings about self, as well as to new life satisfactions.

Such reassessment and challenge to one's belief system in therapy can lead ultimately to new coping skills as the client gradually "tries out" new roles. For example, a divorced woman may gain a sense of new competence by struggling with the various house repairs and mastering the skills necessary to fix things. Fathers who are divorced may learn new parenting behaviors for the first time, that is, feeding their children, changing their diapers, listening to their woes and troubles, and mending their egos as well as their socks. There are many times when the divorced person is likely to wish that he or she had a member of the opposite sex around for traditionally gender based assignments. The therapist can reinforce the many potential benefits of such experience for the client: (1) increased sense of competence; (2) more autonomous decision making; (3) more control; (4) wider repertoire of skills; (5) more flexibility; (6) greater sensitivity to the opposite sex and to the joys and problems associated with that gender role; and (7) the opportunity to explore new interests, experiences, skills, and roles.

With autonomy may also come conflict. The chance to experiment with and play out many roles, along with the demand to accomplish multiple roles (student, worker, mother, father) may engender role conflict, distress, and attendant guilt that one cannot live up to one's perceived image of what success in each of these roles entails. Furthermore, if one retains fairly traditional ideas of the criteria for success in these roles, beliefs may be in conflict with the realities of performance.

DEALING WITH ROLE CONFLICT

A frequent complaint of the newly divorced parent is the inability to cope with the multiple demands of new roles thrust upon him or her as a result of the marital separation. The conflict may be expressed in different forms. Overreaction and compensation manifests itself in the role of "superparent" who tries to be the perfect mother and father to their children or the "weekend fairy godfather" who attends to every wish of the children, dealing with the role conflict and guilt by overcompensation. Another alternative involves reducing guilt by exaggerating another role, such as work. For men, the role of father may consist of an exclusive emphasis on work and the financial and educational obligations to one's children.

On a behavioral level the therapist helps the client assess priorities, pare down the nonessentials, and learn efficient modes of time management and parenting. This may entail some family therapy with the children as well, enlisting their cooperation and assigning equitable responsibilities to all members of the family. Children have much to gain by seeing their parent in a new role of worker or student or nurturer while themselves gaining the experience of directly participating in family tasks irrespective of gender stereotypes. More flexible role orientation is thus modeled for the children and reinforced by their actual participation in a multitude of roles. They may not have experienced many of these role behaviors if a mother was always there to cook or a father to fix a flat tire.

Despite the potential benefits of these experiences, there are some clients and families whose belief systems remain highly traditional, perhaps even rigid. They have no desire to adopt more nontraditional roles, even though it may be demanded or foisted on them by the contingencies of divorce. In such an individual's view, for example, a mother is supposed to stay home and prepare for children who come home from school midday. If she cannot, but must work to make ends meet like so many single mothers, the therapist has a formidable task of helping the client come to terms with her beliefs and the realities of her situation. The young traditionalist may have to work. Conversely, the older nontraditionalist may not be able to. The divorce therapist may also have to help older divorced women who would really like to start meaningful careers face the fact that job opportunities may be quite limited and that satisfactions must be maximized in other areas, such as community jobs and friendships.

Coming to terms with the possibilities and realities of one's roles, life and work after divorce involves a deeper acceptance of the experience of divorce itself. It is not possible to "take away" or "make up for" prior pain by undoing or replacement. The existence of pain must be acknowledged and accepted (Visher & Visher, 1979). The divorce therapist must help the client realize this and the futility of attempting to "undo" the pain of separation for one's significant others by overcompensation or fantasized replacement through the taking on of multiple roles (e.g., mother, father, provider) and attempted perfect enactment of the contingencies and demands of all those roles.

The therapeutic goal of successful role restructuring in any arena, relationships, family, work, or education, is not to erase past conflicts, nor to "take away" the pain associated with a difficult life transition such as divorce. Pain is ultimately accepted as being a motivator and an energizer for change, which then helps one transcend the pain and use it to achieve greater self-awareness and development. The therapist, in reinforcing role restructuring, helps clients understand that some personal pain, discomfort and conflict is an integral part of growth and transcendence.

While some clients will experience role disorientation and conflict in attempting to work out the multiple demands of new and sometimes competing roles after divorce, others may experience relief and welcomed autonomy. Women generally assume the primary responsibility for household tasks and childcare regardless of their employment outside the home. Some clients report that relief from the marital conflict leads to less strain and more efficiency in doing these tasks. A deficit model assumes that role accumulation is negative and leads to role overload, that single parents who become responsible for more roles than before and for cross-gender roles will experience stress and negative results. There are, however, benefits that accrue from multiple roles, such as status security, more role privileges, ego gratification, and diverse sources of satisfaction (Gove & Geerken, 1977; Sieber, 1974). For some individuals the experience of heading a family may be more gratifying than marriage; despite the additional responsibility, there is also additional control and autonomy (Brown *et al.*, 1976).

The following case illustrates how divorce therapy helped a client who attempted role restructuring after divorce involving the development of a career commitment and who along the way experienced significant internal barriers related to lack of confidence, sex-role rigidity, and role conflict.

Case Study 18: Brooke

The decision to give up custody of her son and daughter had not been an easy one for Brooke. At age 37 she and her husband of 15 years, Leo (age 39), had divorced. It was not an acrimonious parting; for years they had been friendly roommates and might have remained so had not Leo fallen in love with his administrative assistant. The latter relationship ultimately was ended, but by the time it did Leo and Brooke had admitted that the marriage had become one of convenience.

Brooke had graduated from college with honors, but upon marrying at age 22, had essentially put her own career on hold. She taught high school biology for a year until Leo had finished his degree in geology. Brooke then settled into being a young suburban matron. Johanna (now age 13) was born after Leo began what was to be a successful career as an executive with an oil company. Two miscarriages occurred before they were able to have Gavin (now age 8). The family moved several times as they followed Leo up the career ladder. With each move Brooke grew increasingly dissatisfied with her life, yet dutifully fulfilled her role as accommodating wife and mother. Two years before the actual divorce,

Brooke returned to school on a part-time basis; her flair for science led her to molecular biology. For the first time in her life, she blossomed intellectually. Brooke's exciting involvement with her academic work only increased the distance between her and Leo, unfortunately. He found it difficult to accept her changed domestic role, interpreting the commitment to her academic endeavors as rejection of him and the family.

Leo's own career had now advanced and stabilized to the point where he could be in the home office more or less permanently. He did little traveling, as he once had. Leo was able to spend more time at home, which he found he enjoyed, and became increasingly involved with his children and their activities. Leo and Brooke decided to divorce shortly after Brooke graduated with a master's degree. She interviewed for jobs and was offered a research position with an agricultural genetics firm in a city 200 miles from their hometown. The position was a good one, with opportunity for advancement, but involved a fair amount of travel.

Indeed, the tables had turned and Brooke found herself facing a situation where it was clear that, if she chose to follow a promising new career path, it would be difficult to be a full-time parent. Neither parent desired to uproot the children, who felt content to stay in the community, with either parent. After much soul searching, Brooke decided that while they would have joint custody, Leo should have physical custody of the children. She believed that if she again compromised her own development, she would forever resent the children and the personal cost of the family. Brooke was reassured that Leo was a good and loving father and was truly involved with their children. Yet at times she could not shake the feelings of guilt and conflict that haunted her, particularly during times of aloneness or anniversaries and holidays. She loved her new job immensely and was making a relatively positive adjustment to the divorce, meeting new friends and exploring some long neglected avocational interests in music and folk singing, when Christmas approached and she was flooded with feelings of conflict and remorse. At this point she came into therapy, complaining of anxiety, inability to concentrate on her job, and feelings of indecision about her life and family.

Brooke: I keep thinking of all the Christmases I did everything, soup to nuts. Decorate the house, think of all the hundred and one little special presents Leo and the kids would like. And our families. And entertaining. And . . . and it just never ended. The funny thing is I can't say I really enjoyed many of those times, I was too stressed out to enjoy them, trying to please everybody at once. And in one sense there's this tremendous relief that I don't have to do it anymore. But I keep having the crazy feeling that I should. I should make them a Christmas! Just like I should have stayed home and I should have . . . oh, I don't know.

Therapist: It sounds like you're really in conflict between what you think you want for yourself and what you think others feel you should do.

Brooke: Yes. "Good mothers" don't leave their children. I mean I know rationally that it couldn't have worked, at least not for me, and yet I keep beating myself over the head with all these stereotypes of what a good parent is. In lots of ways I feel I'm a better parent now when I am with them than when I was with them all the time and resenting it. Yet sometimes I do feel guilty, especially if I think about the fact that sometimes my work takes precedence, even when it doesn't have to.

Therapist: What do you mean, Brooke?

Brooke: Well, it's like sometimes I get discouraged that I can't be a real mother, at least not in the way I was raised to believe a real mother is, there all the time, I mean. So since I can't do it "right," there's part of me that doesn't want to do it at all, you know? Like when I do see Johanna and Gavin, unfortunately it's always a reminder to me that I'm not a "traditional" mother, that I can only be there part time and that feels like a . . . well, I guess a failure in part.

Therapist: So it's almost easier just not to see them at all, to avoid contact?

Brooke: Sometimes I think so. Actually, it's similar to the way I began to feel after I started school and we separated. It was as though if I couldn't do it "right," mothering I mean, there was no point in trying at all, it was just too depressing to be in conflict all the time between what you thought was successful parenting and what you thought was being a successful student and they often conflicted. That's why in part I opted to leave, because I knew I wouldn't be satisfied with either thing, parenting or getting this career and they'd both end up being half-assed.

Therapist: Sounds to me like you have pretty fixed ideas about what a good mother is. There's a kind of rigidity about your notions of that role that put you into conflict when you don't think you can live up to it.

Brooke: Well, I hadn't realized just how rigid my ideas were. In fact, I actually thought I was unconventional, a pace setter of sorts, choosing to leave the kids and all. It's only now that I'm beginning to see that I've carried around the old feelings inside.

Therapist: And when they come to awareness and you perceive the discrepancy between your old socialized ideas about quote, "the mother role" and what you actually are doing and probably enjoying, then you feel guilty and want to get rid of that uncomfortable feeling by washing your hands of the whole role.

Brooke: And in the process I think I probably deprive myself of some of the good times I could have with the kids. It's just that I'm so afraid I'll disappoint them, when I can't be there, when they have to leave. Or maybe I'm afraid I'll disappoint myself. Perhaps that's closer to the truth. I just can't stand thinking that no matter what I do, it won't be right.

Therapist: But how do you define "right"? It seems to be a very narrow definition. Besides that, you seem to be assuming that the children also share your notion about what a good mother should be. What feedback do you get from them about the quality or quantity of your visits?

Brooke: Well, actually we always have a good time, but they don't seem to miss me in between. I think they're probably so busy with their lives at home . . . I suppose it's partially in my mind, rather than being a reality. I just assume they're going to be devastated whenever we part, maybe I'm disappointed that they aren't.

Therapist: You know, it's sometimes hard to admit we're less important to the people we care about than we'd like to think. And part of our assuming that importance is the belief that they will hate us if we don't do this or that.

Brooke: I did assume that. I thought for a long time they'd hate me for leaving. I don't think they do. I think they really do love me now, but it's in a different way; they're more independent, more separate. And yet they went through an awful lot of pain too. And I wish there was some way of taking that pain away. I think Leo feels the same way, and he tries to make up for the pain, by getting them whatever they want, and maybe I deal with the pain instead by avoiding it, escaping it, I'm afraid to see their faces sometimes, I'm always expecting the worst.

Therapist: I think you're learning that you can't "take away" or "make up for" the pain of any event in life, divorce, anything. It existed, it was experienced, it may still exist. But you learn from pain, too, and pain can be a catalyst that leads you to do good things, things you might never have done.

Brooke: Well, I think that's true for Leo. All the pain really changed his outlook on parenting and I think he's involved with the kids in a deeper way than ever before. He wrote me the other day about how Gavin and Johanna were becoming pretty decent cooks and had taught him a thing or two. And also, by the way, that he had a new appreciation of my contribution in the kitchen all those years, which he had taken for granted until he did it himself. Actually I know they're getting a good family life with him, but it's one thing to know that up here (*points to head*) and another to believe it at a gut level.

Therapist: Maybe what you're saying is that you feel more dissatisfied with the way you think things "ought" to be, than they actually are.

Brooke: Yeah.

Therapist: Suppose you could get rid of this feeling of conflict, this rigid idea that you should make them a perfect Christmas, the kind of fantasy Christmas that traditional mothers are supposed to make! What would you do then? Can you imagine a different kind of scenario?

Brooke: Well, I never really thought about it, I mean not in any detail. Well, I take that back. I have imagined what it would be like, for example, to have some of my friends in, have a potluck dinner and instead of expensive presents have a grab bag thing. But I wonder how the kids would like that. They're used to the turkey dinner, and the orgy of toys . . . (*Pause.*) Yet it might be good, too, for them to see something different . . .

Therapist: How single people can be a "family" for one thing and how it's possible to celebrate in a different way. What else would be different?

Brooke: One thing I'd really love is if I thought they'd accept my work. I've always been somewhat reluctant to make too much about it for fear that they'd see it as the thing that took me away from them.

Therapist: Yet when you don't show them that part of you, they don't know the real you either, nor can they experience or share that significant part of you.

Brooke: I know. There's a company "tour" of sorts. Johanna especially might enjoy all the plants; I don't know about Gavin. I suppose I could give it a try. There's really no reason why they couldn't learn to accept my commitment to my work.

Therapist: Did you ever think, Brooke, that they may be proud of you because of it?

Brooke: They may be. Only I probably don't see it, because I see only the conflict part. I expect to be criticized.

Therapist: Yet another way of looking at it is that you have modeled for your son and daughter a strong commitment to meaningful work in life, to a goal.

Brooke: I suppose I have, only I never look at it that way . . . the good part.

Therapist: If you did, perhaps you wouldn't be so in conflict about the parenting and career roles and would find it easier, even more enjoyable to see them. (*Brooke looks puzzled.*) If you thought you were giving them something good by combining roles, by being both a professional and a parent . . .

Brooke: Oh, I see what you mean. Yes, I think that would feel good. But I think I'd also have to learn to feel that what I was giving them was enough.

Therapist: What is "enough"?

Brooke: (*Laughs.*) OK. You got me there. It's never enough! I'm going to have to revise my thinking, I guess.

Therapist: And when you do, you may find that "enough" is whatever you want it to be, and your definition probably won't match the next person's.

A number of therapeutic paradigms and strategies occurred in this vignette. It became evident that Brooke, like so many divorced individuals who find themselves in multiple roles, was experiencing some role conflict. Old socialization patterns demanded fixed responses, and traditional standards of performance seemed unrealistic and nonadaptive to the new situation. These facts were interpreted and highlighted by the therapist as she led Brooke to articulate her conflict and guilt about her perceived "failure" in the old role, and to move beyond this point to an appreciation of (1) how she thus avoided the parental role and thereby deprived herself of some of its satisfactions; (2) repeated a pattern of escape from role conflict by denial and avoidance; and (3) sought to avoid feelings of failure by perceiving the parent and work roles in a fairly rigid fashion.

The therapist reinforced a more flexible sex-role orientation and a more androgynous conception of roles, seeking to alleviate the irrational guilt Brooke had inflicted upon herself. Paradoxically, Brooke perceived that she had done a very nontraditional thing, yet her old fears and gender attitudes had locked and imprisoned her into some very uncomfortable feelings of failure and lack of confidence in her ability to mesh roles. The task of the therapist involved helping her to unlock these conceptions and emotionally and cognitively to restructure notions of appropriate and realistic behavioral expectations. Part of this was accomplished by the therapeutic technique of reframing her behavior in more positive terms, pointing out the benefits to her children of the androgynous modeling that she and Leo were giving them. Therapy helped Brooke to understand that underlying her feeling of conflict was the irrational belief and fantasy that she was so powerful she could take away her children's pain if she could only find the right magic, the right behaviors, the right mothering.

When Johanna and Gavin were in town for their next visit, the therapist scheduled a family session, which proved quite valuable in enabling Brooke to help the children appreciate her real self. It simultaneously gave them the opportunity to ventilate their feelings and to provide her with feedback. While they voiced ambivalent feelings about their mother's new commitments, it was also evident that they were indeed proud of her accomplishments and her independence. As this case illustrates, it is often useful in divorce therapy to use a combination of individual, couple, and family modalities, depending on the circumstance, need, and timing. The next chapter will discuss these special considerations, as well as the use of cotherapy.

Chapter Ten

Special Treatment Considerations in Divorce Therapy

Successful divorce therapy requires flexibility in therapeutic approach and appreciation of the uniqueness of the separation/divorce situation. The client is likely to receive ultimate benefit if the therapist can continue to be available across time and over the variety of situations and stresses likely to characterize the divorce process. If a therapeutic intervention occurs before the formal decision to separate has been made, it is not unusual for the therapist over time to see the couple, the nuclear family, one or both spouses individually, extended family members, and various combinations of the above. Depending on the therapist's training, experience, and comfort level he or she may also see during the course of treatment one or more of the couple's children in individual therapy, one or more lovers, intimate friends, and/or significant others, and, eventually, one or both remarried families, and so on, as the cycle may begin again. There are moments when the therapist may wish he or she could have gathered everybody involved (present and potential) before the start of the couple's original marriage and done some preventive therapy that might have saved everyone time, effort, money, and a lot of psychic wear and tear. Of course, this is possible only on the rarest of occasions and the therapist is almost always called in to intervene when the journey toward marital dissolution has already been undertaken.

In order to maximize therapeutic benefit, and attempt prescriptive therapies, several authors have broken down the divorce process into phases and considered what type of therapy (couple, family, individual) is appropriate and when (Brown, 1976; DeFazio & Klenbort, 1975; Fisher, 1974; Kressel & Deutsch, 1977; Storm & Sprenkle, 1982; Weiss, 1975). Perhaps the most succinct of these formulations is offered by Storm and Sprenkle (1982). They consider three parts of the divorce process:

239

decision making, restructuring, and recovery. After reviewing the scant empirical literature, Storm and Sprenkle recommend conjoint couple therapy when couples are making the decision to divorce. Conjoint couple and/or family therapy is favored in the restructuring phase when issues for mediation are salient, such as custody and financial arrangements. Individual psychotherapy is seen as the treatment of choice in the recovery phase, unless on-going disputes over the children remain, in which case conjoint couple and/or family therapy would be indicated. DeFazio and Klenbort also favor individual therapy to deal with issues and experiences in the later phases of adjusting to a divorce, stating, "It's at this point that any character analysis must begin in earnest" (1975, p. 104).

The caveat presented earlier in this book regarding the wide variability that characterizes individuals proceeding through developmental stages is also applicable to stage formulations about the divorce process. In like manner, a variety of opinions exist in the literature as to the psychotherapeutic treatment of choice pre- and postdivorce. Some therapists favor a family therapy approach throughout (Goldman & Coane, 1977; Whitaker & Keith, 1977), in line with the belief that the "family" as a biologically determined unit cannot truly get "divorced." Much of the decision making about who is seen and when, appears to revolve around issues concerning children and divorce.

TREATMENT OF CHILDREN IN THE DIVORCE PROCESS

The psychological impact of divorce on children has been discussed earlier (Hetherington, Cox, & Cox, 1976, 1977, 1979; Wallerstein & Kelly, 1975, 1976, 1980). The focus of the present book is on helping adults therapeutically to deal with the divorce process. The impact of divorce on children and the psychotherapeutic treatment of this important issue demands a separate book; however, some representative issues will be presented here, particularly in terms of the implications for treatment of the parents. Comprehensive discussion of children and divorce can be found in Gardner (1976) and Wallerstein and Kelly (1980).

As was concluded in the detailed review of children's adjustment to divorce in Chapter One, facilitating the parents' nonhostile detachment and cooperative parenting is probably the single most critical and beneficial aspect of divorce therapy in terms of its help to the children involved. Several studies looking at the adjustment of children 2 to 5 years after divorce have found that the nature of the parental relationships with the child appears to be a more salient variable than whether the parents are married or divorced (Hess & Camara, 1979; Wallerstein & Kelly, 1980). Favorable adjustment in the child after a divorce is related both to the father's frequency of contact and his degree of psychological maturity (Hetherington, Cox, & Cox, 1979). Such evidence has led several therapists to recommend careful attention to issues involving the children as part of the divorce therapy treatment process (Baideme, Hill, & Serritella, 1978; Goldman & Coane, 1977; Hajal & Rosenberg, 1978; Moreland, Schwebel, Fine, & Vess, 1982; Suarez *et al.*, 1978).

COMMUNICATION WITH CHILDREN

A sense of real or potential object loss is one of the most critical areas for children attempting to deal psychologically with parental divorce and separation. Common child and adolescent reactions to perceived object loss include anger (at both the absent and the remaining, "available" parent), depression, guilt, and/or fear. It is important for the therapist to be alert to these behavioral manifestations of felt object loss, and to attempt therapeutic prevention and/or amelioration. The authors prefer that *both parents together* talk with their children and explain to them not only the common, agreed upon reasons for separation/divorce, but also that both parents still love the children, that the separation/divorce is in no way the children's fault and that both parents will continue to be involved with them.

Finally, parents need to communicate to the children that there will be strong efforts made to insure continuity and minimize disruption in each child's life. Such communication usually requires a prior meeting of the parents to decide and rehearse what they are going to say to the children. Discussion and even role playing of this communication in therapy can often be helpful.

Some parents who are very certain about the need to dissolve their relationship find it enormously difficult to talk to their children about their decision. Many times this is a response to the parents' continued denial and belief that "the children don't know what's going on," despite much evidence to the contrary. The therapist can help by pointing out that children have more trouble dealing with ambiguity than with a clearly communicated, though painful decision. It can also be useful to tell the parents, "The children will take their cues from you. If you present the decision in a confident and relatively unambivalent way, if indeed that is how you feel, then they are more likely to feel secure that it is the 'right' decision for them too."

Once the children have been apprised of their parents' decision to divorce, it is quite important that the spouses be sensitive to the possible feelings of anger, withdrawal, relief, fear, or depression in their children and to encourage their children to talk about their feelings and reactions. A therapist can help the reluctant parent to initiate such dialogue and be alert to attitudinal or behavioral changes in their children's daily life that indicate difficulty in accepting the decision. Often a child may turn to another adult or peer as a confidant and find comfort and support outside the family more easily than within. Parents need to be made aware that such confidences are helpful and usual and not to interpret them as rejecting of the family. One might argue that the more the child invests outside the immediate family in terms of school, interests, hobbies, sports, or other people like friends, peers, teachers, and kin, the easier it may be for him or her to adjust to the object loss.

Younger children, of course, have fewer of these external supports and resources to aid them in the transition and adjustment to losing the intact family. Again parents can be encouraged to develop a cooperative, supportive milieu for their children by maintaining the former home environment if possible, the school and friendship network of the child and contacts with the extended kin. School teachers and counselors can also be of help here, and embarrassed parents need to be supported in their efforts to enlist the aid of teaching staff. Next to the insured presence of father and mother in separate, but continued stable parenting roles, the most important contact is probably with siblings. Thus most parents are reluctant to separate their children when they divorce for good reason, although in some cases it may be necessary.

The parental communication with children about the ex-spouse is also quite critical. Here therapists can advise clients *not* to criticize the absent spouse and thereby contaminate the parenting of the ex-spouse or to place the child in the difficult position of divided loyalties. Again the concept of alleviating blame is the key here. The parent can convey to the child that the parents had their differences, without laying blame to either party for those differences.

Perhaps the most difficult situation occurs when one parent remains in a peripheral role or even absent by choice after a divorce. This is not the case when difficult career decisions, geographical distances, or commitment to new families makes active parenting problematic. When disinterest and even rejection account for the lack of involvement with the child, the single parent has a difficult time communicating about the ex-spouse to the children. Some anger is bound to be expressed, if not directly, then indirectly. Again one might argue that maintaining a facade of the parent's caring for the child may not be helpful in the long run to the child's acceptance and adjustment to the situation. The therapist can play a key part in role playing with the parent how to tell the child that he or she needs to seek and accept the love and support of others who can compensate for the loss of the one parent. The parent also needs to reiterate many times to the child that it is not the child's fault that the other parent has chosen this route and that the problem lies with the parent (or parents).

CUSTODY ISSUES

Many writers in the field believe that the child's best interests are likely to be served by a joint or shared custody arrangement in which both parents remain actively involved in parenting (Moreland *et al.*, 1982; Roman & Haddad, 1978). This viewpoint is also favored by the present authors. However, there can be several problems with achieving such a custodial arrangement. First, this type of coparenting requires the parents to cooperate with one another. Mediation counseling techniques have been used in therapy to facilitate better coparenting between ex-spouses (Schwebel, Moreland, Steinhold, Lentz, & Stewart, 1982).

Secondly, difficulties can occur when one parent has some form of severe psychopathology, for example, chronic substance abuse, poorly controlled psychosis, or a history of physical/sexual abuse. The coparenting arrangement needs careful therapeutic monitoring in such circumstances. A third problem may arise when new emotional relationships are developed, and the new partner(s) puts pressure on one or both coparents to distance from the other. However, Moreland and colleagues (1982) believe,

> The potentially disruptive impact of a new significant relationship for one parent on the co-parenting arrangement can be further minimized if the ex-spouses have resolved and/or compartmentalized their old ambivalent feelings toward each other and have learned to communicate and problem solve together in their role as parents. (p. 644)

Much of the concern in the literature on the risks for children has to do with the "parentification" of the child following separation and/or divorce, the tendency subconsciously to want the child to make up for the emotional void left by the departure of the spouse (Hajal & Rosenberg, 1978). Such parent and child alliances are formed in intact families, but their impact on the child is generally not felt to be as harmful as when the other parent is absent following marital dissolution. There may also be a tendency for the child to idealize the noncustodial parent and this can be fostered by the "blank screen" presented to the child, for projection of wishes and fantasies, when the parent is truly "absent" (Westman, 1972).

PARENT VERSUS CHILD

Some authors would go so far as to assert that the primary treatment concern of divorce therapy must be the positive welfare of the child in contrast to serving the interests of the parents. Such a position demands that lingering hostile feelings that remain between the parents be addressed in postdivorce therapy: "To save the child from being caught in the middle of this anger, we must defuse the parents' anger and get them to cooperate, even though they may not want to have anything to do with each other" (Suarez *et al.*, 1978, p. 277). Some parents do not wish to work through feelings of anger after the divorce. They maintain a negative emotional bond despite knowing they no longer live together as husband and wife. Maintenance of anger can also serve as a defense against anticipated narcissistic injury, aloneness, and depression (Hajal & Rosenberg, 1978). In these cases, postdivorce family sessions can provide a live forum to express only more destructive feelings. Long-term individual sessions with one or both partners in such instances may be counterproductive, as they tend primarily to serve the expression of anger and bitterness and not to promote detaching emotionally (Suarez *et al.*, 1978).

The present authors' experience, however, is that individual therapy postdivorce can help one or both partners deal with their tendency to maintain the prior relationship emotionally through the expression of strong negative feelings. Hating, like loving, represents a relationship bond (Framo, 1978). In individual therapy, the therapist becomes the recipient of both the client's positive and negative projections. During treatment some of the anger and bitterness becomes focused on the therapist's inability to take away all the pain of the divorce and right all the past and present interpersonal "wrongs." However, the positive bonding between therapist and client helps to balance out these negative feelings and provide hope that future interpersonal experiences can have positive aspects. Much of this therapeutic process involves the use of the therapist's ego support and modeling via a mirror transference (Kohut & Wolf, 1978; Rice, 1977).

In the extreme case, when *both* parents refuse participation in treatment and continue their angry barrages despite therapeutic efforts at disengagement, individual treatment of the child is indicated. The therapist can serve as a healthy, loving, parental figure, providing the child with a temporary haven from conflict, while being aware that the remaining postdivorce family system will continue to draw the child into the fray, often by passive–aggressive maneuvers, such as a custody battle justified as "being in the child's best interests." In this situation, it is important for the therapist to provide direct feedback to the parents about the present and potential negative effects on the child's development as a "prisoner of war" and to continue to urge the parent(s) to become involved in the treatment process.

There is controversy about whether children should be included in the early "angry sessions" between parents. Sometimes family therapy sessions are delayed with the hope that: "If a child can see that his mother and father can talk to each other in a healthy, normal manner, he is psychologically free to have a relationship with both of those parents" (Suarez *et al.*, 1978, p. 280). In contrast, Goldman and Coane (1977) favor a four-part model of intervention in postdivorce therapy that includes *all* family members in all four phases. The first task is to redefine the family as including all former members. Next, generational boundaries are formed in order to reduce the possibility that a child will be substituted for the former spouse, a phenomenon that is often intensified by the parent's physical absence. Third, the family needs to have a replay of the history of the marriage to correct developmental distortions and offer a chance to mourn the loss of the intact family. Finally, the therapists attempt to facilitate an emotional divorce.

Although there is recognition by most people in the field of divorce therapy that implementing an emotional divorce without a simultaneously occurring "coparental divorce" is a difficult process, there is less agreement about whether children should be included in sessions in which the parents attempt to work through their intense negative feelings on their way to attaining an "emotional divorce."

SINGLE PARENTS

Sometimes, one parent (usually the father) is geographically and/or psychologically absent and the child may bear special psychic vulnerabilities. When a single parent (most often the mother) feels overwhelmed, a "blurring" of the generational boundaries may occur; one of the children comes to play more of a parental role in the family. "Some of the struggle and strife between the parents will continue in this new 'marriage' between mother and son, or mother and daughter reflecting the ambivalence that exists on both sides" (Hajal & Rosenberg, 1978, p. 260).

To cope with this blurring of roles, it is necessary for the therapist to reinforce the generational boundaries, emphasizing that children are first and foremost children, despite the family consequences or the parental expectations. Therapists also need to be prepared for "reunion fantasies," whereby parent and/or child believe that the absent parent will return to the fold. The therapist helps the family members with reality testing in this regard. There is a risk that the therapist will become the "new object," replacing the absent parent in the child's eyes, receiving the child's projected fantasies and undoing felt narcissistic injury resulting from the "loss" of the biological parent. The therapist needs to gently clarify and interpret these meanings to the child, who may in the process "experience additional feelings of rejection" (Hajal & Rosenberg, 1978).

The single parent likewise has a need to "join with" the therapist in the pursuit of a new object, someone who is fantasized as healing the pain of loss stemming from the dissolution of the marriage. The role of "rescuer" is a seductive one for the therapist but a role to be carefully monitored and interpreted, in order that therapy not precipitate another profound sense of loss. Part of this danger can be ameliorated by the therapist's careful reinforcement of the client's strengths, problem-solving capacities, and motivation for competence and independence. The risk of the therapist being used by the family unconsciously to fill the need for a second parent can be moderated if a strong effort is made to involve the absent parent for at least some part of the therapy. As mentioned previously, the therapist may need to put some pressure on the absent family member, by letter and/or phone call, to become involved in the treatment. Of course, such involvement will not always be possible, or successful, nor will it completely mitigate the client's need to put the therapist in a second parent role. The use of cotherapists can help diminish the possibility of such transference phenomena (Hajal & Rosenberg, 1978). The following brief case study illustrates many of the issues that involve the impact of divorce on children and the implications for treatment.

Case Study 19: Preston and Helena

After deciding with much pain and deliberation to end their marriage of 12 years, Preston and Helena sought therapy to deal with their inability to resolve issues of custody regarding their two children, Beth (age 11) and Stuart (age 4). As with many couples both parents had given more of their emotional caring to their children than to one another, a factor in their felt estrangement and subsequent decision to divorce. Each felt they would make the better custodial parent. After a period of therapeutic exploration and mediation they decided to seek joint custody. Preston and Helena worked out a financial support arrangement and agreed that major decisions regarding the children's health, education, and religion would be made conjointly. Preston (a teacher) obtained an apartment in the same neighborhood and agreed that he would have the children for half of the summer and the school vacation periods, and for one night a week and every other weekend during the school year. Helena was thus acknowledged as having physical custody for a greater proportion of the year, but this was agreeable to both partners. The parents carefully prepared (in therapy and on their own) what they would tell the children both regarding the decision to divorce and their agreement regarding custody.

The children, feeling close to both parents, appeared surprised and frightened at their parents' decision, and torn in their loyalties. Stuart subsequently experienced some night terrors and both Preston and Helena blamed themselves for this. A family therapy session was held during which the children talked about their fears and divided loyalties but only after a good deal of support and encouragement by the therapist and the parents. Stuart's anxiety symptoms abated (which he attributed to Beth's telling him "everything's going to be OK"); the parents separated, filed for divorce, and the joint custody procedures began to be implemented. The divorce was finalized approximately 9 months later and for the 1st year thereafter the custody arrangement worked relatively smoothly.

In the spring of the 2nd year after the divorce, Preston began to increasingly complain about support payments and ultimately informed Helena that he could not continue to give the same amount of support on his "low teacher's salary," that he would have to work full time in the summer, and would not be able to take the children for the previously agreed upon time period. Helena was furious, felt betrayed, and contacted the therapist to deal with these feelings. She stated (with good insight): "I think I overreacted because Preston stirred up my memories about the marriage. I mean, how could he be so insensitive to the kids' feelings; they were counting on the summer with him. I feel he is abandoning them the way he abandoned me, emotionally that is. But the S.O.B. has got me in a bind. I do need the support money since I'm not working, but I look forward to a break from the kids in the summer too." Helena went on to explain: "I've always been afraid he'll pull out of his end of the bargain. That's why I wanted sole custody in the first place."

Sensing that the joint custodial arrangement, which had worked well, might be in jeopardy, the therapist suggested another family therapy session to explore these new developments. Preston was reluctant at first, saying to the therapist "You're probably going to just see me as the 'bad guy.' I'm the one who's not living up to our arrangement." The therapist explained that he did not consider the joint custody arrangements as "set in stone" and that all parties (therapist included) needed to be flexible in this regard. The family session was held subsequently, with the therapist explaining carefully to the children at the start: "We're meeting to talk about a change in plans for the summer. Meeting all together does not mean that Mom and Dad are thinking about getting back together." (The latter statement seemed necessary to stop any fantasies of reconciliation that the children might experience from recreating the family group.)

Beth (who in Preston's absence had grown quite close to her mother emotionally) had reacted with initial indifference and subsequent depression to Helena's revelation that "You're not going to be with your Dad this summer." (In fact, Preston had proposed that the every other weekend visitation arrangement be extended through the summer.) Beth "picked up" Helena's sense of abandonment and had begun to fear "losing" her father. These fears were dealt with in therapy after the economic rationale for the change in summer plans had been explained. Helena reported later to the therapist, "The kids appear to have accepted the change maybe better than I have. I think they'll be all right."

Unfortunately, Helena's misgivings subsequently were realized. Two years later, Preston remarried and moved to his new wife's hometown where he got a different and better paying teaching job. Despite his professed desire to continue the joint custody arrangement, his time spent with the children steadily diminished. Helena resolved to seek sole custody and was successful in this regard, as Preston did not oppose the change.

The loss of their father's companionship and the symbolic change in his interest (giving up custody) was difficult for the children especially Stuart (now 9). However, Beth (now 16) was involved in a tight knit peer group, had a boyfriend, and had significantly reduced her psychic ties to both parents. Stuart became depressed, poignantly feeling the object loss of his father, which he turned into self-disparagement. Previously a good student, his grades began to decline. Helena contacted the therapist again, who referred Stuart to a child therapist colleague for evaluation and subsequent treatment. Midway into Stuart's therapy several "family" sessions were held with both therapists, Helena, and Stuart. The impetus was Helena's feeling that she might be turning Stuart into an "absent spouse." Stuart was given the opportunity to express his feelings about Helena's emotional demands and to put these into perspective. Therapy also helped Stuart work through his sense of object loss vis-à-vis his father. Subsequent contact between Stuart and his father was reported by Helena to be "cool but cordial." Beth seemed to be adjusting with no more than the usual amount of adolescent turmoil, and appeared to enjoy the occasional visits with her father. Helena was actively searching for a job at last contact.

The case of Preston and Helena and their children involved many salient therapeutic issues in dealing with the ramifications of divorce on children and the implications for parents:

1. the critical need for parents to communicate honestly and directly with their children throughout the process of divorce and to insure them of their continued love and presence and the stability of their world;
2. the importance of enlisting the cooperation of both parents on coparenting issues, the difficulties of coparenting, and the necessity for flexibility and possible family intervention therapeutically;
3. the need to "deparent" the child, to reestablish generational boundaries and to reconcile divided loyalties for the children;
4. the flexible use of individual, couple, family, and cotherapy as appropriate, for parents and children to deal with felt object and role loss and to establish ego reparation and role restructuring.

ISSUES IN THE THERAPEUTIC TRANSITIONS

As stated previously, the therapist often will utilize a variety of treatment formats (individual, couple, and family) in working with family members pre- and postdivorce. The review of the issues with treating children in divorce emphasized the need for therapist flexibility in this regard.

The present authors feel that the therapy format in separation and divorce therapy generally should reflect the reality of the family's situation, that is, couple or family therapy before the decision to separate is made, a combination of individual and couple/family sessions during separation, and predominantly individual treatment once the decision to divorce has been made, and thereafter. This model presumes that parenting issues are resolved by the family members, without extended conflict that would necessitate continuing treatment of the larger family unit.

The question might be raised as to whether one therapist can (or should) be available to work with all family members through the different stages of the divorce process. The present authors believe that the family has much to gain if there is the opportunity to work with one therapist, or a cotherapy pair, throughout the therapy. For the therapist to do this, he or she needs some training in individual, adult, and child therapy, as well as in couple and family therapy. The therapist also needs to be alerted to the many issues that will arise in making the needed therapeutic transitions (Rice, 1981). These important issues revolve about confidentiality, reliance, and length of treatment.

KEEPING CONFIDENCES

An important concern during the different phases of treatment has to do with altered rules for communication of sensitive information. Many marital and family therapists are uncomfortable with "secrets" told to the therapist by one or more family members with the request that they not be revealed to other members. Such maneuvers can create a collusive alliance between the therapist and one or more family members. This process often mirrors the destructive collusions already existent within the family. A common goal in family therapy is the breaking down of such dysfunctional collusive patterns, not their reinforcement. If the therapist has been seeing the couple or family and a decision to separate has been made, an individual request for confidentiality needs to be respected. However, the therapist should make it clear that he or she needs to feel free to use discretion in communicating important information learned from one family member to other members and that he or she will exercise this prerogative unless requested not to do so by the family member(s) who conveyed the information.

In a structured separation with therapy, sensitive information from the individual sessions with the spouses can be brought up by the therapist in the conjoint sessions, unless he or she has been specifically requested not to do so. In the authors' experience, this potentially troublesome issue is not a major problem, if two conditions have been met. One is that the therapist has established a prior trusting relationship with the involved family members. Secondly, prior legitimate requests for not sharing information during the separation have been honored by the therapist.

WHOSE AGENT?

Another transitional issue has to do with changing therapeutic alliances. If the therapist begins to work with one or more individuals, after having previously treated the couple or family unit, there is the possibility that those family members not currently in treatment will perceive an alliance between the therapist and the individual(s) now being treated. This situation can occur when the therapist's offer to continue meeting with the family unit postseparation or postdivorce is accepted by one or more family members, but is declined by the others. As indicated earlier in the discussion of the treatment of children during divorce therapy, such continuing therapy arrangements can subconsciously come to fulfill projected fantasies for both therapist (as "rescuer") and client (as having found a replacement for the lost "object"). In addition, there is the risk of other family members feeling disenfranchised because of the altered treatment format. Such feelings can lead to problems if the couple or family unit want to reenter therapy, for example, if the spouses wish to attempt a reconciliation and request the therapist's help.

There are several ways out of this dilemma. The therapist can offer to meet with the other family member(s) on an individual or group basis to reestablish the prior therapeutic alliance. Or he or she could suggest that the affected member(s) begin work with a different therapist, the goal being to bring the other therapist into future couple or family sessions as a cotherapist. The latter decision can be easily made if the other therapist had been cotherapist in prior couple or family sessions.

If cotherapy is not feasible, the therapist should inquire which arrangement would feel comfortable for the family members who have not been present for the individual treatment sessions. If at all possible, their wishes should be respected. In the authors' experience, if the prior couple or family treatment has been perceived as helpful (regardless of whether the outcome was a decision to separate or divorce), usually the other family members are willing to meet again as a unit, without requesting extra individual sessions.

HOW LONG?

A practical concern is the potential expense of therapy when one intervenes throughout the divorce process. Families undergoing separation and divorce are generally already strained financially. Moreover, agencies and third party payers often put constraints on the number of treatment sessions. Therapeutic compromises must be made. Rather than a continuous period of treatment throughout the different phases of marital dissolution and individual psychological resolution, a series of short-term, goal-directed therapies is often most appropriate and effective. After working in therapy for a defined, short-term period, the family or the individual(s) try things "on their own" for awhile. Upon entering a new phase in the divorce process, or when feeling in a crisis, therapy can be resumed. Other treatments can be utilized, such as brief, focused group therapy (Coche & Goldman, 1979). A case study presented later in this chapter will illustrate how "long-term therapy" over the marital dissolution process is more frequently a series of short-term, focal therapies utilizing varied modalities and treatment formats.

USE OF COTHERAPISTS

Divorce therapy can be a physically and psychologically draining process for the therapist. Suarez and colleagues (1978) note that "... it is emotionally exhausting for a therapist to work alone in the cross-fire between the two warring factions in a divorce" (p. 279). There is no empirical evidence that family therapy with two therapists produces any better (or worse) results than with a single therapist (Gurman & Kniskern, 1979). For this reason, the use of a cotherapist can be presented to a couple as being useful for and helpful to the therapists themselves, rather than as a necessarily more beneficial treatment modality for the client(s). Sometimes, however, this particular treatment format is requested by a couple who may wish to have both genders represented in the treatment. Other clients may specifically desire to see a professional husband–wife cotherapy treatment team.

Many writers in the divorce therapy area state a preference for cotherapy (Coche & Goldman, 1979; Hajal & Rosenberg,1978; Suarez *et al.*, 1978; Whitaker & Keith, 1981). When two therapists have worked together with a couple or family prior to separation, and a structured separation with therapy is then arranged, each therapist can see one of the spouses for the individual treatment sessions with the conjoint sessions conducted by both therapists. The cotherapists should talk frequently and openly in order to avoid one or both being seen as the ally of one spouse against the other. Following a decision to divorce it is not unusual for a cotherapist to continue therapy with one of the spouses. Less frequently, the other spouse continues treatment with the other cotherapist. As indicated earlier, such an arrangement can facilitate the reinstatement of conjoint therapy sessions, should the couple either wish or need to be seen together. The former condition may occur if there is the desire to attempt a reconciliation; the latter, if there is a crisis or continuing, unresolved conflict, for example, around custody, extended family, and/or financial issues.

The use of cotherapists in the single parent family context can serve to mute the transferential projection onto the therapist by the parent and/or child who seek to replace the lost parent (Hajal & Rosenbereg, 1978). Since the cotherapists model a real relationship (as colleagues), the fantasized availability of the therapist to replace the absent parent is diminished. Studies of cotherapy indicate that the relationship between the cotherapists is very important (Rice, Fey, & Kepecs, 1972). A sense of cotherapist mutual respect and comfort is especially necessary when working with separated and divorcing families. The adversarial and ambivalent feelings present in such families often lead to attempts to split the cotherapists and set them against one another. Unless the two therapists form a strong working bond, the cotherapy unit can begin to mirror the family conflicts, with resultant diminished therapeutic effectiveness.

In summary, the therapist seeks to remain available to the client(s) throughout the separation and divorce period and beyond. A variety of treatment formats will likely be employed by the therapist, usually in a series of short-term, focal therapy experiences. A case that involved periods of individual, couple, and family therapy is presented below to illustrate the type of treatment experience that is possible in the divorce process and its aftermath.

Case Study 20: Alicia

Alicia was 28 years old when she sought marital therapy with her first husband, Kurt, who was also 28. She was last seen by the therapist at age 35, shortly before her marriage to Dean (age 37). In between were a total of 50 sessions, which spanned an intense period of turmoil and growth in Alicia's life.

Alicia and Kurt had been married for 6 years at the time therapy began. They had a 3-year-old son, Gregory. Alicia was troubled by the changes she had begun to see in the marriage and reported that Kurt "had become a different person than the one I knew." Each spouse had drifted into a pattern of pursuing separate activities and came together primarily around family activities, such as dinner and periods of being outside with Greg. She had confronted Kurt with her feelings of growing distance between them and was bothered by his rather passive acceptance and lukewarm acknowledgment of similar troubling perceptions. Feeling increasingly frustrated, Alicia suggested that "we had better get some help or this is going to lead straight to divorce." Kurt agreed to come to therapy, but was not as alarmed as Alicia and appeared to hope secretly that coming to therapy would appease her without requiring him to change.

The couple had met in the local technical school in a English class. Alicia had dated a great deal in high school, but noted that she had "grown pretty wary of the party and drinking scene." She was attracted to Kurt "because he seemed so different from the other guys. He was more mature, more self-contained. And as a result of our discussions from the class, I could see we shared the same values and ideas." Kurt had done a limited amount of dating, but had had one serious relationship during his senior year of high school. He was attracted to Alicia "because of her energy level. And also her sense of humor. I had a tendency to take things too seriously. She could bring me around on that . . . and offer a different perspective. She was better looking than the other girls I had gone out with—I think I was flattered that she seemed to want to be with me."

Kurt majored in business and Alicia in computer programming. After dating steadily for 6 months, the couple lived together for most of a year "without our parents knowing about it." They got married in late summer after both had finished their perspective programs, and moved to a small town some distance away from both families of origin. Disdaining the corporate world, Kurt attempted to set up a small ecology-oriented business, operating out of the home. Alicia looked for a job but could only find a part-time bookkeeping position. She also served as a volunteer at one of the community service agencies serving an elderly population. The couple settled into the routine of household life and reported retrospectively that they were relatively happy during this period. Greg was born in the 3rd year of their marriage.

In terms of family background, Alicia grew up in a large city. Her father owned a metal products company and her mother was not employed outside the home. She had two older brothers, one of whom worked for her father, her other brother had become quite alienated from the family and was living a rather nomadic existence on the West Coast. Alicia said that her father was disappointed with the way his sons turned out, and she felt a strong but not well-defined pressure from him "to make something of myself." She reported that both her parents were "strong-willed, and overbearing at times." The family was Irish Catholic and part of Alicia's early education was in parochial schools. Alicia found it necessary to hide much of her rebellious behavior in high school from her parents, for example her cigarette smoking, drinking, limited experimentation with drugs, and becoming sexually active with some accompanying guilt. Her parents praised her good grades and did not look too closely beyond her academic success. The family was relatively well to do and growing up was generally smooth, except for some stormy periods of verbal confrontations, brought on by both parents' abuse of alcohol. Alicia stated later in therapy, "As I look back on it, I think my father was an alcoholic. We all tried to deny it, but I think it hastened his death" (at age 59, when Alicia was 32).

Kurt grew up in an affluent family in the South. He was an only child and quite close to both parents, who were in their late 30s when Kurt was born. His father owned a chain of shoe stores and expected that Kurt would take over the business; hence, their disappointment when he married Alicia and settled away from "home." Kurt described his father as "gentlemanly, but he can be tough when he has to." He viewed his mother as "sedate . . . that's just the word that comes to mind." Kurt attended private schools in the community and was on the baseball team. His parents were supportive of his wish to go away to college and he tried the state university for a year, but dropped out, eventually enrolling in the local technical college. Kurt's parents assumed he would return home after he finished his training.

Problems began to creep into Alicia and Kurt's marriage about 1 year after Greg was born. Although Kurt enjoyed playing with the baby, and was around the house a fair amount, Alicia began to resent the feeling that Greg was basically her responsibility.

Alicia: Up to this point, the marriage felt like a partnership and I liked that. I saw the way my father bossed my mother around and I knew I didn't want things to be like that between us. He [Kurt] said that work kept him so busy that he didn't have time to do all the things I wanted him to do with Greg. But the subtle message came through that his job was more important than mine . . . taking care of Greg . . . and that ticked me off.

Therapist: Did you let him know that?

Kurt: (answering for her) Yes.

Therapist: And what happened?

Alicia: Well, he just said "yeah, yeah," or something like that, but nothing ever changed.

Kurt: I don't think that's fair. I wanted to help you out, but you know I didn't have a lot of time.

Alicia: Or interest.

By the time the couple came for therapy, there was a moderate degree of tension related to the above role-sharing issues and to Alicia's perception that Kurt was withdrawing from her. She found herself physically and emotionally attracted to a man who served on the board of the social agency where she volunteered. These feelings troubled her, and she did not let Kurt know about them. Later in the therapy she reported being fearful that she would act out sexually, and this aroused guilt from her high school days. Such feelings were also a sign to Alicia that her marriage was in trouble and helped provide the final impetus for her to seek out therapy.

The couple was seen by a male–female cotherapy team. This was the first time that the cotherapists had worked together. They had relatively similar levels of experience working with couples, although the male therapist was several years older and had done more individual therapy. Alicia appeared to feel supported by the therapist's recognition of her dissatisfaction with the marriage and her role. Kurt seemed initially wary of the female cotherapist, whom he expected to "side" with Alicia. Being aware of this, both therapists made an effort early in therapy to communicate support and understanding of Kurt's position and struggles.

The psychodynamic picture that began to emerge in therapy was that Kurt had increasing difficulty accepting his son's role in Alicia's affection. Having been the only child in his family, he was used to being the center of attention. Although he had wanted a child, and knew that he couldn't expect the same degree of caretaking from Alicia after Greg was born, he had begun to feel a diminished sense of importance in her eyes. He seemed only partly aware of his feelings in this regard, and would have felt rather childish about admitting them to Alicia. Instead, he chose to withdraw more and more into his own activities, taking care of himself, in part by default.

It was this distancing behavior that Alicia perceived as a disturbing decline in marital intimacy. She, in turn, was frustrated by increasingly feeling locked into the role of "full-time mother." She resented having to make all the babysitting arrangements whenever she did her volunteer work, especially since Kurt was home for at least part of each day. Alicia had given up her bookkeeping job shortly before Greg was born. The inner pressure of her father's expectations that she should accomplish "great things" began to trouble Alicia and compounded the felt frustrations with other areas of her life.

In addition to the marital disappointments, Kurt's business was turning only a meager profit and the long-range projections did not appear favorable. The couple began to talk about both returning to school, selling the business, and moving from the small town where they were living. Kurt's parents offered to pay for his tuition, and they could just make it financially with the contribution of Alicia's returning to work part time. After exploring in therapy the ins and outs of such a decision they decided to go ahead with the new plan. For a while, the change in their lives rekindled a sense of closeness and working together. However, the old problems gradually crept back in and Alicia once again complained of "having four jobs to Kurt's one. I'm going to school, working, taking care of Greg (now 4) and keeping up the apartment. And all he's doing is going to school. I'm back to that old feeling that it just isn't fair."

Therapeutic attempts to help the couple set up an equitable schedule for sharing domestic and child-care responsibilities (Rice & Rice, 1977) resulted in only limited change. Kurt would agree to his share, but frequently would do his agreed-upon tasks only when reminded or ragged by Alicia. In essence, she had acquired a fifth job. Family background factors and experiences that predisposed the couple to have problems in this area were explored in therapy, although insight along these lines did not result in needed behavior change. Alicia generally did not reinforce Kurt's positive actions, but instead reminded him of what he had not accomplished, or that what he had done was not enough. She cut down her course load (in a demanding computer science curriculum) and resented the feeling that she had to make the sacrifice.

It was clear to both partners that they were not happy with the marriage. Although loving parents, they increasingly related in a bitter and spiteful way toward one another. Alicia began to talk about wanting a separation and one day asked Kurt to move out, after finding that he had spent the afternoon listening to records rather then cleaning up the apartment (as he had agreed to do) in anticipation of dinner guests that evening. The subsequent separation was traumatic mainly in terms of how to deal with Greg. Both Alicia and Kurt felt a sense of relief over no longer having to confront daily each others' disappointments and frustrated expectations. They decided on a temporary custody arrangement and Kurt, to Alicia's surprise, agreed to take Greg (now in kindergarten) for half the week, enabling her to resume a full-time course load.

The couple agreed to a 3-month structured separation with therapy, were seen every other week conjointly, and at the end of that period decided to proceed toward divorce. Greg was included in two of the early structured separation sessions and appeared to be doing well, to both parents' relief. Alicia's mother was troubled by the decision to divorce, although in Alicia's skeptical mind, this was because "Mom thinks I won't be able to find another 'nice' husband like Kurt." Kurt's parents were more accepting of the divorce, perhaps feeling that at long last he might be moving home again. Their hunch subsequently proved correct.

Marital therapy ended shortly after the decision to proceed with the divorce. Alicia was busy with school and a part-time job. Kurt had settled into his new apartment, and seemed resigned to, if not happy about, the fact that the divorce was going ahead. Except for a request from Alicia to the therapist to write a letter to the Family Court Commissioner certifying that she (as divorce petitioner) had had the state-required one counseling session, little was heard from either individual for the next year and a half.

The next therapeutic contact occurred when Alicia called the male therapist (the female cotherapist was no longer working in the clinic) and wondered if she could come in and talk about a new relationship. She indicated that she had begun seeing Roger, who was 42, 4 years older than she. He was the man Alicia had been attracted to while working in the community agency in the small town where she and Kurt formerly lived. Roger was going through a complicated and bitter divorce and had sought Alicia out, which both flattered and troubled her. He told her that things were finally being resolved with his former wife and Alicia took this as permission to go ahead with their relationship. After 6 months of seeing

Roger, she began to realize he had not yet detached from his wife and two children, despite his repeated reassurance of progress along these lines. A stormy period in their relationship followed, during which Alicia was seen for several individual sessions at her request, and she and Roger for several couple sessions. Alicia came to feel that her position in the relationship was basically a masochistic one and that she could not put her interpersonal life "on hold," waiting for Roger to resolve things with his wife. She proceeded to end their relationship, although not without much resistance from Roger.

Responding to covert signs of Alicia's unhappiness, her mother became more questioning of what was going on in Alicia's life. When, after much exhortation, Alicia opened up to her mother, the response was a felt lack of maternal acceptance and moral condemnation. Her mother was quite negative and judgmental about Roger and again brought up her feelings that Alicia never should have left Kurt. Such statements only compounded Alicia's painful and guilty feeling that she had hurt deeply both Kurt and Roger and that, moreover, maybe she could not feel enough commitment and caring to make any intimate heterosexual relationship last. Alicia thus became self-punitive and depressed. The therapist inquired whether it would help to bring her mother into therapy to explore the conflictual mother–daughter situation. Alicia felt that "it couldn't do any more harm" and two sessions followed with Alicia and her mother. The therapist emphasized that Alicia was going through a period of self-exploration and identity, noting that this personal development had been aborted by her early marriage to Kurt. It was also emphasized that this "developmental period" would have marked ups and downs.

Alicia's mother seemed to be struggling with unresolved grief and ambivalence, stemming from the death of her husband approximately 1 year previously. She felt she had "married for life" and could not even entertain the notion of seeing other men, despite Alicia's suggestion, "Mom, it might be good for you." Alicia's divorce and her recent involvement with a technically still-married man, struck at the core of several of her mother's most cherished beliefs. To accept Alicia's behavior and decisions would have involved major changes in her own belief system, a threatening prospect and something she was unwilling to do. The therapy sessions did not produce a change in either Alicia's or her mother's thinking, but led to a "truce" of sorts, some neutrality, and the restoration of a more or less "peaceful coexistence." After two more individual sessions, during which Alicia felt increasingly "right" about ending things with Roger, this phase of therapy concluded.

About 2 years later, Alicia called the therapist and stated, "I think I've made a mess of my life . . . again." She explained that she was involved in another relationship, this time with Jay, who was 5 years younger and a new programmer at work. Once again, she had been flattered by his professed admiration of her, having gotten to know her in a variety of office activities. Alicia stated, "I thought things would be better this time . . . don't we all? We certainly share common interests and it was really nice for a while. Then I found out how possessive Jay could be. I mean, I just went out for TGIF with some of the guys. No big deal. But he really got jealous and I was scared by how much anger was there, although he tried to hide it. I began to wonder if I really knew this guy . . . you know, I'm not the best judge of character."

Although troubled by the new turn of events, Alicia decided she wanted to pursue the relationship with Jay. She indicated he was troubled by the above incident and had wondered if he should get into therapy. Alicia was instructed to ask Jay if he would come with her to the next session, which he did. He relayed to the therapist that he thought the origin of his jealousy and possessiveness had to do with certain experiences growing up in his family. He requested a period of short-term, focal therapy around this issue. The therapist asked whether Jay would like a referral to a different therapist for this, but he replied, "Well, Alicia's been saying good things about you . . . how you've helped her . . . and I was hoping I could see you also." The therapist was aware of a temptation to see Jay and thus mirror Alicia's pattern of forming relationships based on flattery. But wanting to protect the therapeutic alliance with her, the therapist inquired of Alicia, "How would you feel about my seeing Jay?" She replied, "I'm all for it."

Over the ten-session therapy experience, Jay gained insight into his jealousy and possessive behaviors and related them to growing up in a large busy family where there clearly seemed not enough parental attention to go around. However, he could not accept Alicia's wish to be involved in friendships with other males and their relationship ended shortly, after two conjoint sessions focused on the possibility of negotation and compromise in this area. Alicia stated a wish to "work things out on my own" and left therapy on a generally positive note.

One year later, she returned to therapy and began what proved to be the most difficult period of her life. Kurt had decided to move back to his hometown approximately 6 months previously and had asked Alicia's permission to take Greg (now 11) with him. He wished to continue the joint custody arrangement, and proposed that he would have Greg during the school year and Alicia would have him during the major vacations and for the majority of the summer. Alicia was very close to finishing her degree and was also working as a systems analyst. She accepted Kurt's proposal, thinking it would mesh nicely with her demanding schedule. Things worked fine for a year and then, "out of the blue," Alicia learned that Kurt was getting remarried. Soon after his remarriage, Kurt began dropping hints that his new wife, Louisa, was not happy with the shared custody arrangement and wanted Kurt to ask Alicia if she would give him sole custody of Greg. Alicia was "totally unprepared" for Kurt's re-marriage, much less for a change in the custody arrangement that she had consented to benignly and that she felt was working out satisfactorily.

By this time, Alicia had met Dean, a commercial artist, and found herself very much attracted to him. Dean was in the final stages of divorce and had two daughters. Dean was very supportive of Alicia as she went through a long and painful custody battle, only to lose custody of Greg, based on the judicial "rationale" that his primary residence was now with Kurt and Louisa. The legal struggle was very disillusioning for Alicia, who tortured herself with guilt and self-blame over having let Kurt take Greg out of state in the first place. She began to deal with a variety of characteriological issues in therapy, including her perfectionism and accompanying self-blame, the legacy of the accumulated narcissistic injuries from her several "failed" relationships, and her felt lack of parental acceptance, which had contributed to a negative self-concept. She was also desperately afraid of "ruining" her relationship with Dean, in part due to the stress of the custody battle. She worked hard in therapy during this difficult period and eventually came to accept herself as fallible, acknowledging that she was capable of errors of judgment, but was also more resilient than she believed.

During the final phase of therapy, Alicia and Dean were treated together; therapy consisted of trying to remove the "ghosts of relationships past" from their lives, in order that they could get a "straight shot" at relating to one another. Both individuals were wary and frightened of commitment. Dean's ex-wife had moved away from their daughters and he was concerned that she, too, might press for a custody change. Having been with Alicia through the pain of such a procedure, he was not sure his and Alicia's relationship could withstand the stress, were this to happen. Fortunately, it did not.

Dean was offered a promising job with an advertising agency. After careful deliberations with Alicia, he accepted the position. He moved away, began the job and, after several months, Alicia followed, and also began a new job. Therapy ended at this point and the therapist received a letter approximately 2 months later, containing the news that Alicia and Dean had gotten married, with both looking optimistically toward a better future.

Alicia's case study was presented in detail because it illustrates the impact of a series of short-term therapeutic encounters over an extended period of marital separation, divorce, and remarriage. The case also illustrates how individual therapy can follow cotherapy or be meshed with couple and family therapy in a flexible format, depending on the needs of the individual(s) and the nature of the psychological conflicts. An early long-term period of intensive therapy could have led to similar personality changes. However, for a variety of reasons including economic and motivational, this type of treatment was not feasible for Alicia or for most of the clients one sees in a marital and family therapy practice. The dissolution of Alicia's first marriage provided the initial motivation for therapy, which ultimately involved a number of therapeutic encounters and a variety of modalities that were able to catalyze growth and better promote her adult development, as well as the development of many of the significant people in her life.

Divorce and the Future

Chapter Eleven

Future Perspectives

An approach to divorce and divorce therapy derived from an adult developmental model has been outlined and presented in this book. Divorce, a marker life event, has been linked to two key developmental concepts, identity and intimacy. Intimacy and identity are themes that occur and reoccur in the individual, couple, and family life cycle, along with the related tasks of separation and communion. A marker event like divorce has the potential both for conflict and stress and for growth and positive development.

There are important personal consequences and therapeutic implications for self-esteem engendered by the object and role loss in divorce. A decrease in self-esteem brought on by divorce can occur in two ways. First, perceived failure in intimacy results in narcissistic injury to one's sense of being a lovable person. The corresponding task for the divorce therapist is to help increase self-esteem through efforts at ego reparation. Secondly, conflicts in identity occur in divorce that are related to role loss and role disorientation. The corresponding task for the divorce therapist is to help the client accomplish necessary role restructuring. Ego reparation and role restructuring are integral to successful adjustment to divorce. They also help the individual transcend the divorce and experience not just a restoring, but an enhancing of self-esteem and further growth and development.

Therapy is inherently a very private endeavor. It is an interaction founded on confidentiality, and involves a one-to-one rapport and trust that occurs typically only with a few trusted intimates in one's life. Rarely do therapists see themselves as having a role beyond that of encouraging personal change. However, the divorce therapist can also be an agent of social change by working toward changing social policy in the public sector. As has been repeatedly noted in this book, divorce adjustment is intimately tied up with legal, economic, social, and cultural mores and barriers. Divorce therapists cannot afford to "divorce" themselves from

263

these concerns. The client's adjustment and developmental transcending of divorce could be easier if key policy changes occurred in regard to institutional barriers, cultural biases and early socialization patterns and education about divorce. Ego reparation and role restructuring in divorce therapy could be significantly facilitated by improvements in legal, economic, social, and educational-vocational policies and practices that would instill a more rational and flexible attitude toward marriage and divorce and help make the world a more humane place for the divorced individual.

Problems and difficulties in family life are part of the fabric of society, yet they frequently are seen by policy makers and other citizens as private problems and not necessarily as public issues (Mills, 1959). Some social policies that are of aid to families, for example, child assistance and welfare, are often conceptualized as peripheral, residual, and/or remedial services for individuals "who cannot do what they ought to be doing for themselves" (Brown *et al.*, 1976). Solutions to family problems tend to be left at a personal level. It is generally left up to the individual to adjust as best he or she can to the contingencies of separation, be they psychic, economic, social, or cultural.

Kohen (1981) notes the inadequacy and shortsightedness of this approach to public policy on divorce. She states:

> While creating solutions out of personal resources may encourage individual growth and independence, these solutions are often fragile. Sickness, disruption of a friendship, reduction of child-support payments, or housing dislocation often can have serious ramifications for personal and family organization. Additionally, having to rely on personal resources rather than socially established patterns of support tends to penalize those with fewer resources. And the consequences are not limited to the divorced mother (or father) herself. The fewer resources the individual mother has, the fewer resources her family has. If she does not succeed, both her own and her family's welfare are at risk. (p. 239)

Unless publicly funded therapeutic help is available, therapy also becomes a personal resource available only to those divorced individuals who can afford it privately. Divorce, like marriage, is here to stay. As divorce is accepted as a frequent, expected occurrence not only in our society, but around the world, it behooves us to look at future perspectives on divorce and related public, institutional, and educational policies. Such policies have an impact not only on how divorce is perceived and dealt with, but also on how it affects clients and their success in adjusting to and transcending divorce, with or without benefit of psychotherapy. The remainder of this chapter will briefly outline some of the institutional, cultural, educational, and therapeutic changes that could benefit the divorced client and make the task of the divorce therapist an easier one.

PUBLIC POLICY IMPLICATIONS

Any public policy change (economic, legal, or social) that benefits the family will also likely aid families of divorce. Similarly, any policy that benefits the poor will probably help divorced, female-headed families, as many of them are poor (Brown *et al.*, 1976). Many of the following proposals are not new, nor do most of the recommended changes affect only the divorced. The women's movement and other concerned groups have for years advocated changes that would benefit all families, and men as well as women, for example, universal low cost childcare assistance, equal pay for equal work, equal educational opportunities, low cost housing and low cost legal services. Some of these proposed changes, particularly in the area of child support, would have important and dramatic import for the children of divorced families and for their parents.

THE LAW

The move to "no-fault divorce" in this country has acted to remove some of the adversarial aspects of divorce that can be destructive personally to individuals and families. Despite the "no-fault" grounds for divorce provisions, a system that leads to battle over issues of custody and property perpetuates a stance of continued conflict and exacerbation of stress. Were the legal profession to give more universal recognition to the destructiveness of the adversarial system, perhaps divorcing couples would also receive greater sanction and encouragement to seek divorce mediation and/or divorce therapy instead of squaring off in legal battle. This might lead more lawyers to undertake training in mediation, to make referrals for psychological help, and to work more closely and cooperatively with mental health professionals.

On a broader basis, divorce will not be a humane, individual decision worldwide until there are more uniform laws globally that permit no-fault divorce. Such laws would not penalize either party and would not be based upon patriarchal notions of women and children as property, as is still the case in many parts of the world. Not only can more uniform, flexible laws help the divorced, but access to good low-cost legal aid is also a critical factor. The divorce case has traditionally been considered of low prestige and importance by lawyers, in both the private and public arenas. It may be difficult for low income individuals to obtain legal services. Divorcing women often are less likely to be able to afford to pay a lawyer than husbands, who typically earn more money. Legal aid services frequently calculate the husband's income as also belonging to the wife, thus refusing to take the case because she is seen as having too much income (Brown *et al.*, 1976). Such policies would need to change so that women can have full access to legal aid. More paralegal services that give advice and explain the law would also be helpful. Pamphlets and booklets advising clients of divorce law and the legal problems they may encounter in obtaining a divorce can be quite useful in educating people about the process, as well as serving as a tool to encourage mediation instead of battle.

INCOME AND CHILD SUPPORT

Women are often financially less well off after divorce than men and as a consequence they and their dependents are at a disadvantage (Coletta, 1979; Desimone-Luis *et al.*, 1979; Renshaw, 1977). Continuing economic dependence can affect the successful restructuring of one's life and making the kinds of independent decisions necessary to move along developmentally. A number of policy changes could directly improve the situation for divorced individuals, particularly women and the children of divorced parents. A first step would be efforts to desegregate the world of work, where women are still relegated to relatively low paying, low status positions. As heads of families, they critically need equal pay for equal work, but more importantly, equitable opportunities for promotion and leadership in nontraditional occupational areas. More vigorous enforcement of federal equal opportunity legislation is needed. Corresponding local and state efforts in these areas may get the job done with greater dispatch. Low cost subsidized education and retraining also needs to be made more generally available to the single parent with limited economic resources who needs to return to school to get a degree, update skills, or receive additional training to support his or her family.

Some welfare reform could also improve the financial status of the single parent family and the female headed family. Renshaw (1977) notes that the United States is one of the few industrialized nations in the world that does not have a universal system of child support payments. Child support in this country is frequently an unstable, unpredictable event, largely dependent on the good will and cooperation of the ex-spouse and parent. Children and families suffer because of the parent's ambivalent feelings and irrational anger that is displaced onto innocent parties. Under a universal system of child-support payments, all employed parents would be required to make a reasonable economic contribution, such as 10%, for each first and second child and less thereafter. This contribution would be automatically deducted from gross wage and salary before taxes and deposited in a special trust fund. The fund would be utilized to finance a minimum monthly child support allowance accruing to all parents of children under 18. Such payments would continue regardless of whether the parents were divorced or employed (Renshaw, 1977).

Less radical proposals involve establishing a minimum child support percentage or base rate and/or automatically deducting child support from the wages of the paying parent. While such measures may help insure adequate income for single parent families, they lack the kind of national focus that would symbolize and advocate a prosocial posture for the nontraditional, nonnuclear family. Most individuals, biological parents or not, have a significant investment in the welfare and future of the children of the world. An important complementary policy step would be the institutionalization of universal childcare to families regardless of income. Again the United States remains virtually the only large industrialized nation in the world with no public provision of this type of system for its children. Given the multiple role problems of the single parent/worker who struggles to find an individual solution to adequate childcare, such a change in public policy and practice would be of major import to the divorced. Families in general, who increasingly must engage in a multiplicity of shared roles, would also benefit.

INTEGRATING THE FAMILY INTO PUBLIC POLICY

The key assumption underlying many of the above proposals is that time, energy, and resources for one's personal, interpersonal, and family life are as important as such expenditures for one's vocation. The individual who does not make a full-time, exclusionary, obsessive commitment to a career still tends to be seen as more frivolous, less dedicated, and less worthy of praise and occupational rewards and benefits than the person who opts for such a monocular pursuit. Equitable integration of personal and family concerns into the world of work could lead to more flexibility with regard to scheduling, opportunity, and benefits. Such proposals as time sharing, job sharing, flex-time, and part-time work address the issues by providing alternatives for the person who wishes to live out multiple roles and meet both private and public responsibilities.

Childcare readily available at one's place of work is another solution, implemented in many parts of the world such as China. Such a policy would help insure access to institutional support in the area of childcare. Providing this service would require a change in public policy that recognized the needs of the less affluent and came to terms with the "myth" of a nuclear family totally supported by the income of one parent, with another available to stay home and parent full time. This stereotyped mythical view of "family" is still the conceptual underpinning of current social policy. The definition of "family" and characterization of the family life cycle needs to be broadened to include conditions of separation, divorce, blended families of new and old members, and a series of families. Such reconceptualization would also require significant changes in our current cultural biases.

PROVIDING CULTURAL SUPPORT

Despite the fact that nearly half of present marriages can expect to experience divorce and more and more children are growing up in nonnuclear, nontraditional families, there is still social and cultural bias against the divorced family, the single parent family, and the stepparent family. All these terms have negative cultural meanings, implying failure, inadequacy, or even malevolence. The meanings harken back to a view of adult and family development that presumes a single path and interpersonal commitment, lack of individual choice, and the presumption of "failure" when one is not attached to another person. Changes in these biases would require cognitive and attitudinal restructuring about the meanings of marriage and divorce among wide numbers of people and subgroups in society.

A first change would involve a more realistic definition of family that embraces and legitimizes many forms. The social world based on couples would have to soften its boundaries to include the single person and family. A more communal view of family would help not just the divorced, but families everywhere who struggle to provide the only parenting available in the absence of involvement by extended family members. Part of the reason there is such stress on the nuclear family, and why it often breaks down, is attributable to its insular character that, by definition, demands so much from its members. "Family" in its broadest sense could include those significant friends who form a crucial part of the supportive network for the divorced individual and family. Culturally we have no term or language for these people other than "friends," just as we have no appropriate nomenclature for the "quasi kin" that remain after divorce, for example, one's "ex-in-laws."

INSTITUTIONALIZATION OF DIVORCE AND REMARRIAGE

Cherlin (1978) states that what makes divorce so difficult, and remarriage a less than stable institution, is the lack of cultural and institutional support. Stepfamilies take on expanded social roles that embrace relationships over more than one household, and may include stepparents, stepchildren, stepsiblings, the new spouses of noncustodial parents, and the affinal grandparents and family members. There are societies in which complicated kinship roles, rules, and nomenclature exist within a functioning, stable family system. Our society, oriented toward nuclear marriages and "first" families, provides no such infrastructure for evolving kinship systems after divorce and remarriage. "Where no adequate terms exist for an important social role, the institutional support for this role is deficient, and general acceptance of the role as a legitimate pattern of activity is questionable" (Cherlin, 1978, p. 643).

The institutionalization of divorce and remarriage in our society would require not only provision in the language of the culture for the various roles and kinship structures, but also changes in the customs and conventions of family life. Culturally, the stepparent is expected to be cruel and unfair. Normative role behaviors and cultural support are often lacking that would enable the stepparent to become a fair, active participant in the parental role, disciplining nonbiological children and giving them affection. There are no generally accepted guidelines. Similarly the plight of the single parent bears attention. The single parent is often expected to be disciplinarian as well as provider of love and affection. There are no accepted mores and norms that would enable parents who have joint custody to cooperate in fulfilling these multiple roles. The adversarial nature of the legal system often works against such cooperation in parenting and the development of cultural conventions that would be seen as normative and desirable.

Finally, institutionalization of divorce and remarriage would require attention to the cultural biases not only in society, but in the law. In family law, provisions would have to be made for remarriage, such as balancing the financial and nonfinancial obligations of wives and husbands to their spouses and children from prior and current marriages; reconciling competing claims of current and ex-spouses for the estate of a deceased spouse; and delineating permissible relations or marriage between other family members in a remarriage (Cherlin, 1978). Such legal provisions offer the benefit of incest regulation to the children in such marriages (Mead, 1970; Weitzman, 1974). The institutionalization of divorce and remarriage might also be reinforced by changing cultural expectations of marriage and its place in the life cycle.

A PRAGMATIC VIEW OF MARRIAGE

Continuing idealized notions of romantic marriage to a lifetime partner who fulfills and completes one's sense of identity was discussed as a possible contributant to the divorce rate. Such idealized conceptions may or may not actually help "cause" divorce yet they help to make separation and divorce more difficult, because of the implication that one has failed at the most critical interpersonal task of one's life, a "one chance" with a supposed lifetime partner. The potential for narcissistic injury is indeed great under such expectations, and the recovery from divorce more problematic than with a less idealized view of marriage, with more realistic expectations.

A pragmatic picture of marriage and divorce notes that both have the potential for continued conflict as well as for positive change. The concept is not dichotomous, not black and white; intact marriages do not necessarily mean healthy development, nor does a dissolution mean pathology. Implicit in such a portrayal of marriage and divorce is the assumption that people would always have the choice to stay or to leave, as either condition contributed more to the unfolding and development of both partners. Marriage can not be the sine qua non yardstick of development along an intimacy continuum. In fact people who choose not to marry after divorce or never to marry in the first place may form attachments that are as viable and satisfying as marriage but perhaps less culturally and legally constricting. Such a view of intimacy and identity would also mean a social and cultural acceptance of multiple couplings and separation on a variety of levels, not just marital. Less importance is given to one's attachments in defining status within the society; one can be in a status of singleness and not be discriminated against because one is "unattached." Cultural approval of the state of singleness or of other nontraditional forms of attachment might make the ego injury and process of ego reparation after separation and/or divorce less problematic, as in other cultures that have deemphasized marriage as the expected fulfillment of all personal needs and identity.

EDUCATING THE YOUNG

A more preventive policy implication lies in the area of early education about changing and alternative family forms. Children are growing up in a rapidly evolving society, and experiencing families of all different kinds and forms. An adult, much less a child or adolescent, does not expect to be divorced, to be a single parent, to be remarried or participate in serial remarriage. Children are "programmed" for first marriage and for little after that. As a consequence, they grow up unprepared to have their dreams of the mythical perfect union shattered by a marriage that dissolves or, in the popular parlance, "fails." Children need to be educated about the multiple forms of family, alerted to the possibilities of blended families, half siblings and stepsiblings and more complicated, yet legitimate and viable, kinship structures. Courses on marriage and the family at the junior high and high school level need to prepare children not only for marriage, but for the possibility of divorce and remarriage.

Such a view embraces a conception of bonding, intimacy, and communion that is far less idealistic and romantic than the current view, promoted by the media and popular culture. The prevailing ethos is still that once you find the "perfect person," he or she loves you for life and you thus become "complete." Demythicizing such a view would involve teaching boys and girls about both sides of their natures; that they are indeed "complete" human beings in the sense that irrespective of gender, they can learn to both nurture and to achieve.

The "hidden curriculum" in education includes socializing boys and girls to the gender roles they are expected to fulfill in the home. An educational policy that promotes freedom of behavioral and attitudinal choice should be gender free. It would involve teaching children from the cradle on an appreciation of their "masculine" and "feminine" components, helping to make possible a wide repertoire of what is regarded today as "cross-sex behavior," yet tomorrow may be referred to as "gender free." If more women want to and must support themselves and their families as a result of divorce or as a mutual partner in a relationship, marital or otherwise, then little girls need to be made aware early on that they, too, may become heads or coheads of families. Such education inherently teaches that identity accrues from one's own achievements and not necessarily through the vicarious identification with another's.

The preventive educational job with boys is in some ways an even larger and more difficult one, as society is still more tolerant of nontraditional sex role behaviors in girls than in boys. The "specter" of homosexuality looms large in the rigid socialization of prototypic masculinity in boys and the slightest deviance, for example, giving a boy a doll so he can practice fathering, is seen as strange. Yet how are little boys to learn about fathering and nurturing so that they can make long-term commitments to this venture, irrespective of their marital status? The peripheral role given to fathers in our society is only exacerbated by divorce. It takes a committed man to traverse the hazards of custody, visitation, and the cultural norms that inherently presume "mothering" is natural and paramount, to insist on maintaining this part of his identity and responsibility. If boys, like girls, were taught to value communion and interpersonal commitment, to experience and appreciate first hand the fun and satisfactions of parenting, perhaps they would be less likely to later opt out of the experience, depriving themselves and their children of coparental input and development.

Children in general need to be apprised of the realities and advantages of "multiparenting." Friends, quasi kin or affinal kin, stepparents and children and a supportive community network can provide parts of parenting that the insular nuclear family may be hard pressed to do. Society may never return to an earlier day when generations of families lived and parented together, nor perhaps would one wish to, given the strong cultural value placed on privacy and individuality. Yet contemporary educational policy and practice can help children realize that as they grow up they will need to develop a network of support in order to fulfill multiple roles. Many people can help to parent, including school personnel, who already assume a large portion of this role.

Children can also be taught to nurture many friends and lifetime companions, with whom they can play, and work and share interests, rather than exclusive reliance on one significant other, ultimately a spouse. This idea embraces a more open, less rigid conception of marriage and communion with others. Encouraging boys to form close, nonerotic relationships also involves an ethic that has long been held for the socialization of girls. Perhaps that is one reason why women do better after divorce, in terms of reaching out to others and utilizing interpersonal resources and supportive friendships. Men who as boys were educated and socialized to form emotional friendships and to share intimacies with individuals other than the one with whom they are sexually involved, might also find the emotional adjustment to divorce less problematic. The hasty retreat into an transitional relationship and possible repetition of the marital pattern in a "replay" remarriage might also be avoided were such friendships cultivated and nurtured over one's lifespan.

Positive changes in institutional policy, cultural biases, and preventive education have been suggested to help the divorced individual more easily traverse this life event and successfully accomplish the role restructuring and ego reparation, resulting in an increase in self-esteem. Some changes in psychotherapeutic policy and practice could also contribute to a perspective on divorce that is more beneficial to the individual and the society.

THERAPEUTIC IMPLICATIONS

The authors have emphasized a model of divorce and divorce therapy premised on assessment of contemporary social trends and the changing individual, marital, and family life cycles. This view notes the potentially positive aspects of development through divorce as well as strongly appreciating the painful and stressful aspects of the divorce process. It calls for a benevolent and compassionate stance toward the status and problems of people who choose to deviate from rigid cultural norms. One recommendation that follows from such a conception involves special training for therapists working with couples who are experiencing divorce. Many therapists have not received specialized training in dealing with couples and families, much less in the complexities and difficulties of working with separating and divorcing families. Therapists who have been trained primarily to work with individuals are increasingly dealing with couples and families. Additional training needs to be provided that addresses not just marital therapy concerns, but divorce issues as well. Such training would embrace much of the theory and strategies outlined here, as well as additional help for dealing with the special problems of children of divorce and the remarried or blended family.

Part of such training would involve an examination of one's own biases and values about family, marriage, and divorce, bringing to awareness the potential for projection of such prejudices onto clients or couples who seek help to dissolve their union. Divorce therapy training would also involve didactic information about social, economic, and cultural trends that strongly affect divorced clients' successful role restructuring. The therapist does not isolate himself or herself from society, and recognizes how personal and psychic forces interact with social and cultural norms and expectations. In essence, the therapist serves as a role model to the client and can encourage a more active stance toward social change and improving the lot of the divorced in society.

Training in divorce therapy should involve a variety of approaches including cognitive/behavioral, systems, and psychodynamic techniques. Underpinning treatment strategies is a theoretical conception of divorce in developmental terms. Divorce therapists need to recognize that separation, as well as communion, can lead to adult unfolding and that divorce can be predictably and rationally integrated into the adult individual, marital, and family life cycles.

Finally, divorce therapy needs to be made available to all who choose it, not just to those who are fortunate enough to afford it or lucky enough to be referred to a helpful community agency. The development of postdivorce clinics across the country to deal with lingering problems of custody are a step in the right direction, as they offer low cost help to conflicted clients and family. Yet their focus is often narrow and the goal generally circumscribed to issues revolving around custody. Clinics offering a spectrum of divorce services, to assist with decision making, implementation, and recovery processes are needed. Some of the self-help groups sponsored by community clinics and agencies serve part of this need, particularly by providing divorcing clients with the beginnings of a supportive network of friendships and resources. The divorce therapist needs to be aware of these resources and be knowledgeable about referring clients to them. Such utilization requires a view of therapy that extends beyond the confines of the office. Education and retraining can be therapeutic; work and career change can rebuild self-esteem. It is important not only for the therapist to recognize the therapeutic value and potential of these experiences to the client recovering from divorce, but also for the institutions themselves to appreciate the therapeutic impact they can have. The church, for example, could do much to promote a compassionate and rational attitude toward divorced members or divorced individuals in general, recognizing their special needs and helping to ameliorate their isolation in the community. As institutions begin to see divorce as a more predictable part of the life cycle, with both inherent pain and the opportunity for developmental transcendence, client and therapist will reap the benefits.

REFERENCES

Ables, B.S., & Brandsma, J.M. *Therapy for couples: A clinician's guide for effective treatment.* San Francisco: Jossey-Bass, 1977.

Albrecht, S.L. Correlates of marital happiness among the remarried. *Journal of Marriage and the Family,* 1979, *41,* 857-867.

Aponte, H.J. Organizing treatment around the family's problems and their structural bases. *Psychiatric Quarterly,* 1974, *48,* 8-12.

Bachrach, L.L. *Marital status and mental disorder: An analytical review* (DHEW Publication #[ADM] 75-217). Washington, DC: U.S. Government Printing Office, 1975.

Baideme, S.M., Hill, H.A., & Serritella, D.A. Conjoint family therapy following divorce: An alternative strategy. *International Journal of Family Counseling,* 1978, *6,* 55-59.

Bak, R.C. Being in love and object loss. *International Journal of Psychoanalysis,* 1973, *54,* 1-8.

Bancroft, J. The behavioral approach to marital problems. *British Journal of Medical Psychology,* 1975, *48,* 147-152.

Bandura, A. *Principles of behavior modification.* New York: Holt, Rinehart & Winston, 1969.

Bane, M.J. Marital disruption and the lives of children. In G. Levinger & O.C. Moles (Eds.), *Divorce and separation: Context, causes, and consequences.* New York: Basic Books, 1979.

Beck, A.T., Rush, A.J., Shaw, B., & Emery, G. *Cognitive therapy of depression.* New York: Guilford, 1979.

Bentler, P.M., & Newcomb, M.D. Longitudinal study of marital success and failure. *Journal of Consulting and Clinical Psychology,* 1978, *46,* 2053-2070.

Bergler, E. *Divorce won't help.* New York: Harper, 1948.

Berman, E.M., & Lief, H.I. Marital therapy from a psychiatric perspective: An overview. *American Journal of Psychiatry,* 1975, *132,* 583-592.

Bernard, J. No news, but new ideas. In P. Bohannan (Ed.), *Divorce and after.* New York: Anchor, 1971.

Bernard, J. *The future of marriage.* New York: Bantam, 1972.

Biller, H.B. Father absence and the personality development of the male child. *Developmental Psychology*, 1970, *2*, 181–201.

Biller, H.B. *Father, child and sex role.* Lexington, MA: Heath, 1971a.

Biller, H.B. The mother–child relationship and the father-absent boy's personality development. *Merrill-Palmer Quarterly*, 1971b, *17*, 227–241.

Biller, H.B. *Paternal deprivation: Family school, sexuality and society.* Lexington, MA: Heath, 1974.

Biller, H.B. The father and personality development: Paternal deprivation and sex-role development. In M.E. Lamb (Ed.), *The role of the father in child development.* New York: Wiley, 1976.

Biller, H.B., & Bahm, R.M. Father absence, perceived maternal behavior, and masculinity of self-control among junior high school boys. *Developmental Psychology*, 1971, *4*, 178–181.

Blair, M. Divorcees' adjustment and attitudinal changes about life. *Dissertation Abstracts*, 1970, *30*, 5541–5542. (University Microfilms No. 70-11, 099)

Bloom, B.L. *Community mental health: A general introduction.* Monterey, CA: Brooks/Cole, 1977.

Bloom, B.L., Asher, S.J., & White, S.W. Marital disruption as a stressor: A review and analysis. *Psychological Bulletin*, 1978, *85*, 867–894.

Bloom, B.L., & Hodges, W.F. The predicament of the newly separated. *Community Mental Health Journal*, 1981, *17*, 277–293.

Blumenthal, M.D. Mental health among the divorced. A field study of divorced and never divorced persons. *Archives of General Psychiatry*, 1967, *16*, 603–608.

Bohannan, P. Divorce chains, households of remarriage, and multiple divorces. In P. Bohannan (Ed.), *Divorce and after.* New York: Anchor, 1971a.

Bohannan, P. The six stations of divorce. In P. Bohannan (Ed.), *Divorce and after.* New York: Anchor, 1971b.

Boszormenyi-Nagy, I., & Spark, G.M. *Invisible loyalties.* New York: Harper & Row, 1973.

Boszormenyi-Nagy, I., & Ulrich, D.N. Contextual family therapy. In A.S. Gurman & D.P. Kniskern (Eds.), *Handbook of family therapy.* New York: Brunner/Mazel, 1981.

Bowlby, J. Grief and mourning in infancy and early childhood. *Psychoanalytic Study of the Child*, 1960, *15*, 9–12.

Bowlby, J. *The making and breaking of affectional bonds.* London: Tavistock Publications, 1977.

Bradburn, N.M. *The structure of psychological well-being.* Chicago: Aldine, 1969.

Brandwein, R.A. After divorce: A focus on single parent families. *Urban and Social Change Review*, 1977, *10*, 21–25.

Brandwein, R.A., Brown, C.A., & Fox, F.M. Women and children last: The social situation of divorced mothers and their families. *Journal of Marriage and the Family*, 1974, *36*, 498–514.

Briscoe, C.W., & Smith, J.B. Depression and marital turmoil. *Archives of General Psychiatry*, 1973, *29*, 119–125.

Briscoe, C.W., & Smith, J.B. Psychiatric illness, marital units and divorce. *Journal of Nervous and Mental Disease*, 1974, *158*, 440–445.

Briscoe, C.W, & Smith, J.B. Depression in bereavement and divorce. *Archives of General Psychiatry*, 1975, *32*, 439-443.

Brown, B.B., & Foye, B.F. *Divorce as a dual transition: Emotional loss and role restructuring.* Paper presented at the NATO Symposium on Role Transitions, University of Wisconsin-Madison, Madison, WI, September 1982.

Brown, C.A., Feldberg, R., Fox, E.M., & Kohen, J.A. Divorce: Chance of a new lifetime. *Journal of Social Issues*, 1976, *32*, 119-133.

Brown, E.M. Divorce counseling. In D.H.L. Olson (Ed.), *Treating relationships*. Lake Mills, IA: Graphic Press, 1976.

Brown, P., Felton, B.J., Whiteman, V., & Manela, R. Attachment and distress following marital separation. *Journal of Divorce*, 1982, *4*, 303-318.

Brown, P., & Fox, H. Sex differences in divorce. In E. Gomberg & V. Franks (Eds.), *Gender and psychopathology: Sex differences in disordered behavior*. New York: Brunner/Mazel, 1978.

Brown, P., & Manela, R. Client satisfaction with marital and divorce counseling. *The Family Coordinator*, 1977, *26*, 294-303.

Brown, P., & Manela, R. Changing family roles: Women and divorce. *Journal of Divorce*, 1978, *1*, 325-328.

Burch, E.S., Jr. Marriage and divorce among the North Alaskan Eskimos. In P. Bohannan (Ed.), *Divorce and after*. New York: Anchor, 1971.

Burgess, E.W., & Cottrell, L.S., Jr. *Predicting success or failure in marriage*. New York: Prentice-Hall, 1939.

Burgess, E.W., & Locke, H.J. *The family: From institution to companionship* (2nd ed.). New York: American Books, 1953.

Callner, B. Boundaries of the divorce lawyer's role. *Family Law Quarterly*, 1977, *10*, 389-398.

Caplan, H., & Parad, H.J. A framework for studying families in crises. In H.J. Parad (Ed.), *Crisis intervention: Selected readings*. New York: Family Service Association of America, 1965.

Capra, F. *The tao of physics*. New York: Bantam, 1975.

Carlson, E. Effects of working wives on marriage stability. Cited in *Women Today*, 1976, *6*, 55-56.

Carter, E.A., & McGoldrick, M. (Eds.). *The family life cycle: A framework for therapy*. New York: Gardner Press, 1980.

Changing USA Families. *Family Therapy News*, 1984, *15*(2), 16.

Charlton, R.S. Divorce as a psychological experience. *Psychiatric Annals*, 1980, *10*, 12-21.

Cherlin, A. Remarriage as an incomplete institution. *American Journal of Sociology*, 1978, *84*, 634-650.

Cherlin, A. Work life and marital dissolution. In G. Levinger & O.C. Moles (Eds.), *Divorce and separation: Context, causes and consequences*. New York: Basic Books, 1979.

Chester, R. Health and marriage breakdown: Experience of a sample of divorced women. *British Journal of Preventive and Social Medicine*, 1971, *25*, 231-235.

Chiriboga, D.A., Coho, A., Stein, J.A., & Roberts, J. Divorce, stress, and social supports: A study in helpseeking behavior. *Journal of Divorce*, 1979, *3*, 121-136.

Chiriboga, D.A., & Cutler, L. Stress responses among divorcing men and women. *Journal of Divorce*, 1977, *1*, 95-105.

Chiriboga, D.A., Roberts, J., & Stein, J.A. Psychological well-being during marital separation. *Journal of Divorce*, 1978, *2*, 21-36.

Christensen, H.T. Cultural relativism and premarital sex norms. *American Sociological Review*, 1960, *25*, 31-39.

Christensen, H.T. Timing of first pregnancy as a factor in divorce: A cross-cultural analysis. *Eugenics Quarterly*, 1963, *10*, 119-130.

Cleveland, M. Divorce in the middle years: The sexual dimension. *Journal of Divorce*, 1979, *2*, 255-262.

Clinebell, H. *Basic types of pastoral counseling*. Nashville, TN: Abingdon Press, 1966.

Clingempeel, W.G., & Reppucci, N.D. Joint custody after divorce: Major issues and goals for research. *Psychological Bulletin*, 1982, *91*, 102-127.

Coche, J., & Goldman, J. Brief group therapy for women after divorce: Planning a focused experience. *Journal of Divorce*, 1979, *3*, 153-160.

Cohen, R. Marriage instability among the Kanuri of northern Nigeria. *American Anthropologist*, 1961, *63*, 1231-1249.

Colletta, M.D. The impact of divorce: Father absence or poverty? *Journal of Divorce*, 1979, *3*, 27-36.

Coogler, O.J. *Structured mediation in divorce settlement*. Lexington, MA: Heath, 1978..

Coombs, L.C., & Zumeta, Z. Correlates of marital dissolution in a perspective fertility study: A research note. *Social Problems*, 1970, *18*, 92-102.

Dasteel, J.C. Stress reactions to marital dissolution as experienced by adults attending courses on divorce. *Journal of Divorce*, 1982, *5*, 37-47.

Davis, K. The American family in relation to demographic change. In C.F. Wentoff & R. Parke, Jr. (Eds.), *Report of the U.S. Commission on Population Growth and the American Future* (Vol. 1: *Demographic and social aspects of population growth*). Washington, DC: U.S. Government Printing Office, 1972.

Davis, J.A. *Perception of control over separation: A potential resource*. Research report, University of California, San Francisco, 1977.

DeFazio, V.J., & Klenbort, I. A note on the dynamics of psychotherapy during marital dissolution. *Psychotherapy: Theory, Research and Practice*, 1975, *12*, 101-104.

Desimone-Luis, J., O'Mahoney, K., & Hunt, D. Children of separation and divorce: Factors influencing adjustment. *Journal of Divorce*, 1979, *3*, 37-42.

Dreyfus, E.A. Counseling the divorced father. *Journal of Marital and Family Therapy*, 1979, *5*, 79-86.

Duquette, D.N. Child custody decision-making: The lawyer–behavioral scientist interface. *Journal of Clinical Child Psychology*, 1978, *7*, 192-195.

Duvall, E.M. *Family development*. Philadelphia: Lippincott, 1971.

Elkin, M. Postdivorce counseling in a conciliation court. *Journal of Divorce*, 1977, *1*, 55-65.

Ellis, A. *Reason and emotion in psychotherapy*. New York: Lyle Stuart, 1962.

Erikson, E. *Childhood and society*. New York: Norton, 1963.

Erikson, E. A conversation with Erik Erikson, interviewed by E. Hall. *Psychology Today*, 1983, *17*, 22-30.

Everly, K. *Leisure network and role strains: A study of divorced women with custody.* Unpublished doctoral dissertation, Syracuse University, 1978.

Federico, J. The marital termination period of the divorce adjustment process. *Journal of Divorce,* 1979, *3,* 93-106.

Feldberg, R., & Kohen, J.A. Family life in an anti-family setting: A critique of marriage and divorce. *The Family Coordinator,* 1976, *25,* 151-159.

Fineman, M. Implementing equality: Ideology, contradiction and social change. A study of rhetoric and results in the regulation of the consequences of divorce. *Wisconsin Law Review,* 1983, *4,* 789-886.

Fisher, B.F. *Identifying and meeting needs of formerly married people through a divorce adjustment seminar.* Unpublished doctoral dissertation, University of Northern Colorado, 1976.

Fisher, M.S., & Fisher, E.O. Toward understanding working relationships between lawyers and therapists in guiding divorcing spouses. *Journal of Divorce,* 1982, *6,* 1-15.

Fisher, E.O. A guide to divorce counseling. *The Family Coordinator,* 1973, *22,* 56-61.

Fisher, E.O. *Divorce: The new freedom.* New York: Harper & Row, 1974.

Froiland, D.J., & Hozman, T.L. Counseling for constructive divorce. *Personnel and Guidance Journal,* 1977, *55,* 525-529.

Framo, J.L. The friendly divorce. *Psychology Today,* 1978, *12,* 77-79, 100-102.

Framo, J.L. The integration of marital therapy with sessions with family of origin. In A.S. Gurman & D.P. Kniskern (Eds.), *Handbook of family therapy.* New York: Brunner/Mazel, 1981.

Furstenberg, F.F., Jr. Premarital pregnancy and marital instability. *Journal of Social Issues,* 1976, *32,* 67-86.

Furstenberg, F.F., Jr. Reflections on remarriage. *Journal of Family Issues,* 1980, *1,* 443-453.

Gardner, R.A. Psychological aspects of divorce. In S. Arieti (Ed.), *American handbook of psychiatry* (2nd ed., Vol. 1). New York: Basic Books, 1974.

Gardner, R.A. *Psychotherapy with children of divorce.* New York: Jason Aronson, 1976.

Gettleman, S., & Markowitz, J. *The courage to divorce.* New York: Simon & Schuster, 1974.

Glenn, N., & Supancic, M. The social and demographic correlates of divorce and separation in the United States: An update and reconsideration. *Journal of Marriage and the Family,* 1984, *46,* 563-575.

Glick, P.C. The future of the family in current population reports. *Special Studies Series,* P-23, No. 78. Washington, DC: U.S. Government Printing Office, 1979.

Glick, P.C. Remarriage: Some recent changes and variations. *Journal of Family Issues,* 1980, *1,* 455-478.

Goetting, A. Divorce outcome research: Issues and perspectives. *Journal of Family Issues,* 1981, *2,* 350-378.

Goldman, J., & Coane, J. Family therapy after the divorce: Developing a strategy. *Family Process,* 1977, *16,* 357-362.

Goldsmith, J. The postdivorce family system. In F. Walsh (Ed.), *Normal family processes.* New York: Guilford, 1982.

Goode, W.J. *After divorce.* New York: Free Press, 1956.

Goode, W.J. Marital satisfaction and instability: A cross-cultural class analysis of divorce rates. *International Social Science Journal*, 1962, *14*, 507-526.

Gould, R. *Transformations: Growth and changes in adult life.* New York: Simon & Schuster, 1978.

Gove, W.R. Sex, marital status, and mortality. *American Journal of Sociology*, 1973, *79*, 45-67.

Gove, W.R., & Geerken, M. The effect of children and employment on the mental health of married men and women. *Social Forces*, 1977, *56*, 66-76.

Granvold, D.K., Pedler, L.M., & Schellie, S.G. A study of sex role expectancy and female postdivorce adjustment. *Journal of Divorce*, 1979, *2*, 383-393.

Granvold, D.K., & Tarrant, R. Structured marital separation as a marital treatment method. *Journal of Marital and Family Therapy*, 1983, *9*, 189-198.

Granvold, D.K., & Welch, G.J. Intervention for postdivorce adjustment problems: The treatment seminar. *Journal of Divorce*, 1977, *1*, 81-92.

Granvold, D.K., & Welch, G.J. Structured, short-term group treatment of postdivorce adjustment. *International Journal of Group Psychotherapy*, 1979, *29*, 347-358.

Gray, G.M. The nature of the psychological impact of divorce upon the individual. *Journal of Divorce*, 1978, *1*, 289-301.

Gurman, A.S. Contemporary marital therapies: A critique and comparative analysis of psychoanalytic, behavioral and systems theory approaches. In T.J. Paolino, Jr., & B.S. McCrady (Eds.), *Marriage and marital therapy: Psychoanalytic, behavioral and systems theory perspectives.* New York: Brunner/Mazel, 1978.

Gurman, A.S., & Kniskern, D.P. Research on marital and family therapy: Progress, perspective and prospect. In S. Garfield & A. Bergin (Eds.), *Handbook of psychotherapy and behavior change* (2nd ed.). New York: Wiley, 1979.

Gurman, A.S., & Kniskern, D.P. (Eds.) *Handbook of family therapy.* New York: Brunner/Mazel, 1981.

Hackney, G.R., & Ribordy, S.C. An empirical investigation of emotional reactions to divorce. *Journal of Clinical Psychology*, 1980, *36*, 105-110.

Hajal, F., & Rosenberg, E.B. Working with the one-parent family in family therapy. *Journal of Divorce*, 1978, *1*, 259-269.

Haley, J. A review of the family therapy field. In J. Haley (Ed.), *Changing families.* New York: Grune & Stratton, 1971.

Haley, J. *Uncommon therapy: The psychiatric techniques of Milton H. Erickson, M.D.* New York: Ballantine, 1973.

Hampton, R.L. Marital disruption: Some social and economic consequences. In J.N. Morgan (Ed.), *Five thousand American families* (Vol. 3). Ann Arbor, MI: Institute for Social Research, 1975.

Hancock, E. The dimensions of meaning and belonging in the process of divorce. *American Journal of Orthopsychiatry*, 1980, *50*, 18-27.

Hancock, E. Sources of discord between attorneys and therapists in divorce cases. *Journal of Divorce*, 1982, *6*, 115-124.

Hassall, E., & Madar, D. Crisis group therapy with the separated and divorced. *Family Relations*, 1980, *29*, 591-597.

Heritage, J.C., & Daniels, J.L. Postdivorce adjustment. *Journal of Family Counseling*, 1974, *2*, 44-49.

Herman, S.J. Women, divorce, and suicide. *Journal of Divorce*, 1977, *1*, 107-117.

Herzog, E., & Sudia, C. *Boys in fatherless families.* Washington, DC: U.S. Department of Health, Education and Welfare, 1970.

Herzog, E., & Sudia, C. Children in fatherless families. In B.M. Caldwell & H.N. Riccinti (Eds.), *Review of child development research III.* Chicago: University of Chicago Press, 1973.

Hess, R.D., & Camara, K.A. Postdivorce family relationships as mediating factors in the consequences of divorce for children. *Journal of Social Issues*, 1979, *35*, 79-96.

Hetherington, E.M., Cox, M., & Cox, R. Divorced fathers. *The Family Coordinator*, 1976, *25*, 417-428.

Hetherington, E.M., Cox, M., & Cox, R. The aftermath of divorce. In J.H. Stevens, Jr., & M. Mathews (Eds.), *Mother-child, father-child relations.* Washington, DC: National Association for the Education of Young Children, 1977.

Hetherington, E.M., Cox, M. & Cox, R. Family interaction and the social, emotional, and cognitive development of children following divorce. In V.C. Vaughn III & T.B. Brazelton (Eds.), *The family: Setting priorities.* New York: Science and Medicine Publishers, 1979.

Hetherington, E.M., & Deur, J.L. The effects of father absence on child development. *Young Children*, 1971, *26*, 233-248.

Hight, E.S. A contractual, working separation: A step between resumption and/or divorce. *Journal of Divorce*, 1977, *1*, 21-30.

Hill, C.T., Rubin, Z., & Peplau, L.A. Breakups before marriage: The end of 103 affairs. *Journal of Social Issues*, 1976, *32*, 147-168.

Hill, R. Generic features of families under stress. In H.N. Parad (Ed.), *Crisis intervention: Selected readings,* New York: Family Service Association of America, 1965.

Hodges, W.F., Wechsler, R.C., & Ballantine, C. Divorce and the preschool child: Cumulative stress. *Journal of Divorce*, 1979, *3*, 55-67.

Hoffman, L. The family life cycle and discontinuous change. In E.A. Carter & M. McGoldrick (Eds.), *The family life cycle: A framework for family therapy.* New York: Gardner Press, 1980.

Hoffman, L. *Foundations of family therapy: A conceptual framework for systems change.* New York: Basic Books, 1981.

Holmes, T.H., & Masuda, M. Life changes and illness susceptibility. In B.S. Dohrenwend & B.P. Dohrenwend (Eds.), *Stressful life events: Their nature and effects.* New York: Wiley, 1974.

Holmes, T.H., & Rahe, R.H. The social readjustment rating scale. *Journal of Psychosomatic Research*, 1967, *11*, 213-218.

Hook, E.B., Cross, P.K., & Schreinemachers, D.M. Chromosomal abnormality rates at amniocentesis and in live-born infants. *Journal of the American Medical Association*, 1983, *249*, 2034-2038.

Houseknecht, S.K., & Spanier, G.B. Marital disruption and higher education among women in the United States. *Sociological Quarterly*, 1980, *21*, 375-389.

Hughes, S.F., Berger, M., & Wright, L. The family life cycle and clinical intervention. *Journal of Marriage and Family Counseling*, 1978, *4*, 33-40.

Hunt, M. *The world of the formerly married.* New York: Fawcett World Library, 1966.

Hunt, M., & Hunt, B. *The divorce experience.* New York: McGraw-Hill, 1977.

Hynes, W.J. *Single parent mothers and distress: Relationship between selected social and psychological factors and distress in low-income single parent mothers.* Unpublished doctoral dissertation, The Catholic University of America, Washington, DC, 1979.

Irving, H.H. *Divorce mediation: A rational alternative to the adversary system.* New York: Universe Books, 1981.

Jackson, D.D. The question of family homeostasis. *Psychiatric Quarterly Supplement*, 1957, *31*, 79-90.

Jackson, D.D. Schizophrenia: The nosological nexus. In P. Watzlawick & J.H. Weakland (Eds.), *The international view.* New York: Norton, 1977.

Jacobson, D.S. The impact of marital separation/divorce on children: II. Interparent hostility and child adjustment. *Journal of Divorce*, 1978, *2*, 3-19.

Jacobson, N.S. Behavioral marital therapy. In A.S. Gurman & D.P. Kniskern (Eds.), *Handbook of family therapy.* New York: Brunner/Mazel, 1981.

Jacobson, N.S., & Margolin, G. *Marital therapy: Strategies based on social learning and behavior exchange principles.* New York: Brunner/Mazel, 1979.

Johnson, S.M. *First person singular: Living the good life alone.* Philadelphia: Lippincott, 1977.

Kaffman, M., & Talmon, M. The crisis of divorce: An opportunity for constructive change. *International Journal of Family Therapy*, 1982, *4*, 220-233.

Kalter, N. & Plunkett, J.W. Children's perceptions of the causes and consequences of divorce. *Journal of the American Academy of Child Psychiatry*, 1984, *23*, 326-334.

Kanoy, K.W., & Cunningham, J.L. Consensus or confusion in research on children and divorce: Conceptual and methodological issues. *Journal of Divorce*, 1984, *7*, 45-71.

Kaslow, F.W. Divorce and divorce therapy. In A.S. Gurman & D.P. Kniskern (Eds.), *Handbook of family therapy.* New York: Brunner/Mazel, 1981.

Kaslow, F.W. Stages and techniques of divorce therapy. In P.A. Keller & L.G. Ritt (Eds.), *Innovations in clinical practice: A source book.* (Vol. 2). Sarasota, FL: Resource Exchange, Inc., 1983.

Kaslow, F.W., & Hyatt, R. Divorce: A potential growth experience for the extended family. *Journal of Divorce*, 1982, *6*, 115-126.

Kawashima, T., & Steiner, K. Modernization and divorce rate trends in Japan. *Economic Development and Cultural Change*, 1960, *9*, 213-240.

Keith, P.M., & Schafer, R.B. Correlates of depression among single parent, employed women. *Journal of Divorce*, 1982, *5*, 49-59.

Keith, D.V., & Whitaker, C.A. The divorce labyrinth. In P. Papp (Ed.), *Family therapy: Full length case studies.* New York: Gardner Press, 1977.

Kelly, J.B., & Wallerstein, J.S. The effects of parental divorce: Experiences of the child in early latency. *American Journal of Orthopsychiatry*, 1976, *46*, 20-32.

Kernberg, O. Mature love: Prerequisites and characteristics. *Journal of the American Psychoanalytic Association,* 1974, *22,* 743-768.

Kersey, F. Mediation may diminish divorce problems. *Family Therapy News,* 1982, *13,* 11-12.

Kessler, S. *The American way of divorce: Prescription for change.* Chicago: Nelson Hall, 1975.

Kessler, S. Building skills in divorce adjustment groups. *Journal of Divorce,* 1978, *2,* 209-216.

Kimmel, P.R., & Havens, J.W. Game theory versus mutual identification: Two criteria for assessing marital relationships. *Journal of Marriage and the Family,* 1966, *28,* 460-465.

Kirkpatrick, C. *The family: As process and institution.* New York: Ronald Press, 1963.

Kitson, G.C., & Raschke, H.J. Divorce research: What we know; what we need to know. *Journal of Divorce,* 1981, *4,* 1-37.

Kohen, J.A., Brown, C.A., & Feldberg, R. Divorced mothers: The costs and benefits of female family control. In G. Levinger & O.C. Moles (Eds.), *Divorce and separation: Context, causes and consequences.* New York: Basic Books, 1979.

Kohen, J.A. From wife to family head: Transitions in self-identity. *Psychiatry,* 1981, *44,* 230-240.

Kohut, H., & Wolf, E. The disorders of the self and their treatment: An outline. *International Journal of Psychoanalysis,* 1978, *59,* 413-425.

Korelitz, A., & Schulder, D. The lawyer–therapist consultation team. *Journal of Marital and Family Therapy,* 1982, *8,* 113-119.

Krantzler, M. *Creative divorce: A new opportunity for personal growth.* New York: M. Evans, 1974.

Kraus, S. The crisis of divorce: Growth promoting or pathogenic. *Journal of Divorce,* 1979, *3,* 107-119.

Kressel, K. Patterns of coping in divorce and some implications for clinical practice. *Family Relations,* 1980, *29,* 234-240.

Kressel, K., & Deutsch, M. Divorce therapy: An in-depth survey of therapists' views. *Family Process,* 1977, *16,* 413-443.

Kressel, K., Jaffe, N., Tuchman, B., Watson, C., & Deutsch, M. A typology of divorcing couples: Implications for mediation and the divorce process. *Family Process,* 1980, *19,* 101-116.

Kubler-Ross, E. *On death and dying.* London: Macmillan, 1969.

Kulka, R.A., & Weingarten, H. The long-term effects of parental divorce in childhood on adult adjustment. *Journal of Social Issues,* 1979, *35,* 50-78.

Kurdek, L.A., & Siesky, A.E. Children's perceptions of their parent's divorce. *Journal of Divorce,* 1980, *3,* 339-378.

Lamb, M.E. The role of the father: An overview. In M.E. Lamb (Ed.), *The role of the father in child development.* New York: Wiley, 1976.

Lamb, M.E. The effects of divorce on children's personality development. *Journal of Divorce,* 1977, *1,* 163-174.

Langelier, R., & Deckert, P. Divorce counseling guidelines for the late divorced female. *Journal of Divorce,* 1980, *5,* 403-411.

Lantz, H.R. *Marital incompatibility and social change in early America.* Beverly Hills, CA: Sage, 1976.

Levinger, G. Marital cohesiveness and dissolution. An integrative review. *Journal of Marriage and the Family,* 1965, *27,* 19-28.

Levinger, G. A social psychological perspective on divorce. *Journal of Social Issues,* 1976, *32,* 21-47.

Levinger, G. A social psychological perspective on marital dissolution. In G. Levinger & O.C. Moles (Eds.), *Divorce and separation: Context, causes and consequences.* New York: Basic Books, 1979.

Levinson, D.J., Darrow, C.N., Klein, E.B. Levinson, M.H., & McKee, B. The psychosocial development of men in early adulthood and the mid-life transition. In D.F. Bicks, A. Thomas, & M. Roff, *Life history research in psychopathology.* Minneapolis: University of Minnesota Press, 1974.

Levinson, D.J., Darrow, C.N., Klein, E.B., Levinson, M.H., & McKee, B. *The seasons of a man's life.* New York: Ballantine, 1978.

Lidz, T. *The person.* New York: Basic Books, 1968.

Loeb, J. The personality factor in divorce. *Journal of Consulting Psychology,* 1966, *30,* 562.

Longfellow, C. Divorce in context: Its impact on children. In G. Levinger & O.C. Moles (Eds.), *Divorce and separation: Context, causes and consequences.* New York: Basic Books, 1979.

Lopata, H. *Widowhood in an American city.* Cambridge, MA: Schenkman, 1973.

MacFarlane, J.W. Perspectives on personality consistency and change from the guidance study. *Vita Humana,* 1964, *7,* 115-126.

Mahler, M.S. *On human symbiosis and the vicissitudes of individuation* (Vol. 1: *Infantile psychosis*). New York: International Universities Press, 1968.

Mahler, M., Pine, F., & Bergman, A. *The psychological birth of the human infant.* New York: Basic Books, 1975.

Marroni, E.I. *Factors influencing the adjustment of separated or divorced Catholics.* Unpublished master's thesis, Norfolk State College, 1977.

Mason, K.O., Czajka, J., & Arber, S. Change in U.S. women's sex-role attitudes, 1964-1975. *American Sociological Review,* 1976, *41,* 573-596.

Maxwell, J.W., & Andress, E.L. Marriage role expectations of divorced men and women. *Journal of Divorce,* 1982, *5,* 55-66.

Mead, M. Anomalies in American postdivorce relationships. In P. Bohannan (Ed.), *Divorce and after.* New York: Doubleday, 1970.

Meissner, W.W. The conceptualization of marriage from a psychoanalytic perspective. In T.J. Paolino, Jr., & B.S. McCrady (Eds.), *Marriage and marital therapy: Psychoanalytic, behavioral and systems theory perspectives.* New York: Brunner/Mazel, 1978.

Messinger, L., & Walker, K.N. From marriage breakdown to remarriage: Parental tasks and therapeutic guidelines. *American Journal of Orthopsychiatry,* 1981, *51,* 429-438.

Messinger, L., Walker, K.N., & Freeman, S.J.J. Preparation for remarriage following divorce: The use of group techniques. *American Journal of Orthopsychiatry,* 1978, *48,* 263-272.

Mills, C.W. *The sociological imagination,* London: Oxford University Press, 1959.

Minuchin, S. *Families and family therapy.* Cambridge: Harvard University Press, 1974.

Minuchin, S., Rosman, B., & Baker, L. *Psychosomatic families.* Cambridge: Harvard University Press, 1978.

Moreland, J., Schwebel, A.I., Fine, M.A., & Vess, J.D., Jr. Postdivorce family therapy: Suggestions for professionals. *Professional Psychology,* 1982, *13,* 639-646.

Morris, J.D., & Prescott, M.D. Transition groups. An approach to dealing with post-partnership anguish. *The Family Coordinator,* 1975, *24,* 325-330.

Mueller, C.W., & Pope, H. Marital instability: A study of its transmission between generations. *Journal of Marriage and the Family,* 1977, *39,* 83-93.

Murdock, G.P. Family stability in non-European cultures. In S.N. Eisenstadt (Ed.), *Comparative social problems.* New York: The Free Press, 1964.

National Center for Health Statistics. *Monthly Vital Statistics Report,* Vol. 32, No. 2, March 25, 1984. Washington, DC: U.S. Government Printing Office, 1984.

Nelson, G. Moderators of women's and children's adjustment following parental divorce. *Journal of Divorce,* 1981, *4,* 71-83.

Neugarten, B.L., & Datan, N. The middle years. In S. Arieti (Ed.), *American handbook of psychiatry* (2nd ed.). New York: Basic Books, 1974.

Nock, S.L. Enduring effects of marital disruption and subsequent living arrangements. *Journal of Family Issues,* 1982, *3,* 25-40.

Norton, A.J., & Glick, P.C. Marital instability: Past, present and future. *Journal of Social Issues,* 1976, *32,* 5-20.

Norton, A.J., & Glick, P.C. Marital instability in America: Past, present and future. In G. Levinger & O.C. Moles (Eds.), *Divorce and separation: Context, causes and consequences.* New York: Basic Books, 1979.

Pais, J.L. *Social-psychological predictions of adjustment for divorced mothers.* Unpublished doctoral dissertation, University of Tennessee, Knoxville, 1978.

Papp, P. The Greek chorus and other techniques of paradoxical therapy. *Family Process,* 1980, *19,* 45-57.

Parad, H.J., & Caplan, G. A framework for studying families in crisis. In H.J. Parad (Ed.), *Crisis intervention: Selected readings.* New York: Family Service Association of America, 1965.

Pearlin, L.I., & Johnson, J.S. Marital states, life-strains, and depression. *American Sociological Review,* 1977, *42,* 704-715.

Perlman, J.L. Divorce: A psychological and legal process. *Journal of Divorce,* 1982, *6,* 99-144.

Pino, C.J. Research and clinical application of marital autopsy in divorce counseling. *Journal of Divorce,* 1980, *4,* 31-48.

Rapoport, R. Normal crisis, family structure and mental health. In H.J. Parad (Ed.), *Crisis intervention: Selected readings.* New York: Family Service Association of America, 1965a.

Rapoport, R. The state of crisis: Some theoretical considerations. In H.J. Parad (Ed.), *Crisis intervention: Selected readings.* New York: Family Service Association of America, 1965b.

Raschke, H.J. *Social and psychological factors in voluntary postmarital dissolution adjustment.* Unpublished doctoral dissertation, University of Minnesota, Minneapolis, MN, 1974.

Raschke, H.J. The role of social participation in postseparation and postdivorce adjustment. *Journal of Divorce,* 1977, *1,* 129-139.

Raschke, H.J., & Raschke, V.J. Family conflict and children's self concepts: A comparison of intact and single parent families. *Journal of Marriage and the Family,* 1979, *41,* 367-374.

Redick, R.W., & Johnson, C. Marital status, living arrangements and family characteristics of admission to state and county mental hospitals and outpatient psychiatric clinics, United States, 1970. *Statistical note 100,* National Institute of Mental Health. Washington, DC: U.S. Government Printing Office, 1974.

Reinhard, D.W. The reaction of adolescent boys and girls to the divorce of their parents. *Journal of Clinical Child Psychology,* 1977, *6,* 15-20.

Renne, K. Health and marital experience in an urban population. *Journal of Marriage and the Family,* 1971, *33,* 338-350.

Renshaw, E.F. Welfare reform: The case for a universal system of child-support transfer payments. *Policy Analysis,* 1977, *3,* 583-586.

Rhodes, S.L. A developmental approach to the life cycle of the family. *Social Casework,* 1977, *58,* 301-311.

Rice, D.G. Psychotherapeutic treatment of narcissistic injury in marital separation and divorce. *Journal of Divorce,* 1977, *1,* 119-128.

Rice, D.G. Transition from marital/family therapy to individual therapy following separation or divorce. In A.S. Gurman (Ed.), *Questions and answers in the practice of family therapy* (Vol. 1). New York: Brunner/Mazel, 1981.

Rice, D.G., Fey, W.F., & Kepecs, J.G. Therapist experience and "style" as factors in co-therapy. *Family Process,* 1972, *11,* 1-12.

Rice, D.G., & Rice, J.K. Non-sexist marital therapy. *Journal of Marriage and Family Counseling,* 1977, *3,* 3-10.

Rice, J.K. Continuing education for women; 1960-1975: A critical and contemporary appraisal. *Educational Record,* 1976, *56,* 240-249.

Rice, J.K. Divorce and a return to school. *Journal of Divorce,* 1978, *1,* 247-257.

Rice, J.K., & Anderson, N.C. Attitudes of women active in the community regarding the Women's Liberation Movement. *Journal of the National Association of Women Deans, Administrators, and Counselors,* 1982, *46,* 9-16.

Riley, M.W., Foner, A., Hess, B., & Tobly, M.L. Socialization for the middle and later years. In D.A. Goslin (Ed.), *Handbook of socialization theory and research.* New York: Rand McNally, 1969.

Rodgers, R., & Hill, R. The developmental approach. In H. Christensen (Ed.), *Handbook of marriage and the family.* Chicago: Rand McNalley, 1964.

Rohrbaugh, M., Tennen, H., Press, S., White, L., Raskin, P., & Pickering, M.R. *Paradoxical strategies in psychotherapy.* Symposium presented at the meeting of the American Psychological Association, San Francisco, 1977.

Roman, M., & Haddad, W. *The disposable parent: The case for joint custody.* New York: Holt, Rinehart & Winston, 1978.

Rosen, R. Children of divorce: What they feel about access and other aspects of the divorce experience. *Journal of Clinical Child Psychology,* 1977, *6,* 15-20.

Rosenfield, S. Sex differences in depression: Do women always have higher rates? *Journal of Health and Social Behavior,* 1980, *21,* 33-42.

Rosow, I. Status and role change through the life span. In R. Binstock & E. Shanas (Eds.), *Handbook of aging and the social sciences.* New York: Van Nostrand Reinhold, 1976.

Rushing. W.A. Marital status and mental disorder: Evidence in favor of a behavioral model. *Social Forces,* 1979, *58,* 540-556.

Rutter, M. Parent-child separation: Psychological effects on the children. *Journal of Child Psychology and Psychiatry,* 1971, *12,* 233-260.

Rutter, M., & Madge, N. *Cycles of disadvantage.* London: Heinemann, 1976.

Sager, C. J. Couples therapy and marriage contracts. In A.S. Gurman & D.P. Kniskern (Eds.), *Handbook of family therapy.* New York: Brunner/Mazel, 1981.

Sager, C.J., Brown, H.S., Crohn, H., Engel, T., Rodstein,E., & Walker, L. *Treating the remarried family.* New York: Brunner/Mazel, 1983.

Satir, V. A humanistic approach. *International Journal of Psychiatry,* 1971, *9,* 245-246.

Sauber, S.R. *Preventative educational intervention for mental health.* Cambridge, MA: Ballinger, 1973.

Sauber, M., & Carrigan, E.M. *The six-year experience of unwed mothers as parents.* New York: Community Council of Greater New York, 1970.

Sauber, S.R., & Panitz, D.R. Divorce counseling and mediation. In A.S. Gurman (Ed.), *Questions and answers in the practice of family therapy* (Vol. 2). New York: Brunner/Mazel, 1982.

Scanzoni, J. A reinquiry into marital disorganization. *Journal of Marriage and the Family,* 1965, *27,* 483-491.

Scanzoni, J. A historical perspective on husband-wife bargaining power and marital dissolution. In G. Levinger & O.C. Moles (Eds.), *Divorce and separation: Context, causes and consequences.* New York: Basic Books, 1979.

Schulman, G.L. Divorce, single parenthood and stepfamilies: Structural implications of these transitions. *International Journal of Family Therapy,* 1981, *3,* 87-112.

Schwebel, A.I., Moreland, J., Steinhold, R., Lentz, S., & Stewart, J. Research-based interventions with divorced families. *Personnel and Guidance Journal,* 1982, *60,* 523-527.

Sheffner, D.J., & Suarez, J.M. The post-divorce clinic. *American Journal of Psychiatry,* 1975, *132,* 442-444.

Sieber, S.D. Toward a theory of role accumulation. *American Sociological Review,* 1974, *55,* 567-578.

Silberman, L.J. Professional responsibility and problems of divorce mediation. *The Family Law Reporter,* 1981, *7,* 4001-4012.

Simonton, S.M. *Treating the psychological aspects of cancer.* Paper presented at conference on "Healing in our Time," Washington, DC, October 1982.

Singer, L.J. Divorce and the single life: Divorce as development. *Journal of Sex and Marital Therapy,* 1975, *1,* 254-262.

Skynner, A.C.R. An open systems, group analytic approach to family therapy. In A.S. Gurman & D.P. Kniskern (Eds.), *Handbook of family therapy.* New York: Brunner/Mazel, 1981.

Spanier, G.B., & Casto, R.F. Adjustment to separation and divorce: An analysis of 50 case studies. *Journal of Divorce,* 1979, *2,* 241-253.

Spanier, G.B., & Furstenberg, F.F., Jr. Remarriage after divorce: A longitudinal analysis of well-being. *Journal of Marriage and the Family,* 1982, *44,* 709-720.

Spanier, G.B., & Glick, P.C. Marital instability in the United States: Some correlates and recent changes. *Family Relations*, 1981, *30*, 329-338.

Speck, R., & Attneave, C. *Family networks*. New York: Vintage, 1973.

Spicer, J.W., & Hampe, G.D. Kinship interaction after divorce. *Journal of Marriage and the Family*, 1975, *37*, 113-119.

Spira, L. The experience of divorce for the psychotherapy patient: A developmental perspective. *Clinical Social Work Journal*, 1981, *9*, 258-270.

Sprenkle, D.H., & Storm, C.A. Divorce therapy outcome research: A substantive and methodological review. *Journal of Marital and Family Therapy*, 1983, *9*, 239-258.

Sprey, J. The family as a system in conflict. *Journal of Marriage and the Family*, 1969, *31*, 699-706.

Stanton, M.D. Strategic approaches to family therapy. In A.S. Gurman & D.P. Kniskern (Eds.), *Handbook of family therapy*. New York: Brunner/Mazel, 1981.

Steinberg, J.L. Towards an interdisciplinary commitment: A divorce lawyer proposes attorney-therapist marriages or, at the least, an affair. *Journal of Marital and Family Therapy*, 1980, *6*, 259-268.

Steinglass, P. The conceptualization of marriage from a systems theory perspective. In T.J. Paolino, Jr., & B.S. McCrady (Eds.), *Marriage and marital therapy: Psychoanalytic, behavioral and systems theory perspectives*. New York: Brunner/Mazel, 1978.

Storm, C.L., & Sprenkle, D.H. Individual treatment in divorce therapy: A critique of an assumption. *Journal of Divorce*, 1982, *6*, 87-98.

Stuart, R.B. Operant interpersonal treatment for marital discord. In D.H.L. Olson (Ed.), *Treating relationships*. Lake Mills, IA: Graphic Press, 1976.

Suarez, J.M., Weston, N.L., & Hartstein, N.B. Mental health interventions in divorce proceedings. *American Journal of Orthopsychiatry*, 1978, *48*, 273-283.

Switzer, D. *The dynamics of grief*. Nashville, TN: Abingdon Press, 1970.

Taibbi, R. Transitional relationships after divorce. *Journal of Divorce*, 1979, *2*, 263-269.

Taube, C.A. Admission rates by mental status: Outpatient psychiatric services, 1969. *Statistical note 25*. Washington, DC: National Institute of Mental Health, 1970.

Tennov, D. *Love and limerance*. New York: Stein & Day, 1979.

Terman, L.M., & Wallin, P. Marriage predictors and marital-adjustment tests. *American Sociological Review*, 1949, *14*, 502.

Thiessen, J.D., Avery, A.W., & Joanning, H. Facilitating postdivorce adjustment among women: A communication skills training approach. *Journal of Divorce*, 1980, *4*, 35-44.

Thomas, G.P. After divorce: Personality factors related to the process of adjustment. *Journal of Divorce*, 1982, *5*, 19-36.

Thweatt, R.W. Divorce: Crisis intervention guided by attachment theory. *American Journal of Psychotherapy*, 1980, *34*, 240-245.

Todd, T.C. Strategic approaches to marital stuckness. *Journal of Marital and Family Therapy*, 1984, *10*, 373-379.

Toomin, M.K. Structured separation with counseling: A therapeutic approach for couples in conflict. *Family Process*, 1972, *11*, 299-310.

U.S. Bureau of the Census. *Current population reports,* Series P-60: 106. Characteristics of the population below the poverty level: 1975. Washington, DC: U.S. Government Printing Office, 1977.

Uroda, S.F. Counseling the bereaved. *Counseling and Values,* 1977, *21,* 185–191.

Vaillant, G. *Adaptation to life.* Boston: Little, Brown, 1977.

Vines, N.R. Adult unfolding and marital conflict. *Journal of Marital and Family Therapy,* 1979, *5,* 5–14.

Visher, E.B., & Visher, J.S. *Stepfamilies: A guide to working with stepparents and stepchildren.* New York: Brunner/Mazel, 1979.

Walker, K.N., & Messinger, L. Remarriage after divorce: Dissolution and reconstruction of family boundaries. *Family Process,* 1979, *18,* 185–192.

Wallerstein, J.S., & Kelly, J.B. The effects of parental divorce: Experiences of the preschool child. *Journal of the American Academy of Child Psychiatry,* 1975, *14,* 600–616.

Wallerstein, J.S., & Kelly, J.B. The effects of parental divorce: Experiences of the child in later latency. *American Journal of Orthopsychiatry,* 1976, *46,* 256–269.

Wallerstein, J.S., & Kelly, J.B. Divorce counseling: A community service for families in the midst of divorce. *American Journal of Orthopsychiatry,* 1977, *47,* 4–22.

Wallerstein, J.S., & Kelly, J.B. *Surviving the break-up: How children and parents cope with divorce.* New York: Basic Books, 1980.

Watzlawick, P., Weakland, J., & Fisch, R. *Change: Principles of problem formation and problem resolution.* New York: W.W. Norton & Co., 1974.

Weingarten, H. Remarriage and well-being: National survey evidence of social and psychological effects. *Journal of Family Issues,* 1980, *1,* 533–559.

Weisman, A. *The psychological autopsy.* New York: Behavioral Press, 1968.

Weiss, R.L. The conceptualization of marriage from a behavioral perspective. In T.J. Paolino, Jr., & B.S. McCrady (Eds.), *Marriage and marital therapy: Psychoanalytic, behavioral and systems theory perspectives.* New York: Brunner/Mazel, 1978.

Weiss, R.L., & Margolin, G. Marital conflict and accord. In A.R. Ciminero, K.S. Calhoun, & H.E. Adams (Eds.), *Handbook of behavioral assessment.* New York: Wiley, 1977.

Weiss, R.S. *Marital separation.* New York: Basic Books, 1975.

Weiss, R.S. The emotional impact of marital separation. *Journal of Social Issues,* 1976, *32,* 135–145.

Weitzman, L.J. Legal regulation of marriage: Tradition and change. *California Law Review,* 1974, *62,* 1169–1288.

Weitzman, L.J. The economics of divorce: Social and economic consequences of property, alimony and child support awards. *UCLA Law Review,* 1981, *28,* 1181–1268.

Welch, G.J., & Granvold, D.K. Seminars for separated/divorced: An educational approach to postdivorce adjustment. *Journal of Sex and Marital Therapy,* 1977, *3,* 31–39.

Westman, J.C. Effects of divorce on child's personality development. *Medical Aspects of Human Sexuality,* 1972, *6,* 38–55.

Whitaker, C.A. Reply to: "The role of the psychiatrist in treating divorce cases." *American Journal of Psychiatry*, 1970, *126*, 1328-1329.

Whitaker, C.A., & Keith, D.V. Counseling the dissolving marriage. In R.F. Stahmann & W.J. Hiebert (Eds.), *Klemer's counseling in marital and sexual problems: A clinician's handbook* (2nd ed.). Baltimore: Williams & Wilkins, 1977.

Whitaker, C.A., & Keith, D.V. Symbolic-experiential family therapy. In A.S. Gurman & D.P. Kniskern (Eds.), *Handbook of family therapy*. New York: Brunner/Mazel, 1981.

Whitaker, C.A., & Miller, M.H. A reevaluation of "psychiatric help" when divorce impends. *American Journal of Psychiatry*, 1969, *126*, 57-62.

Whiteside, M.F., & Auerbach, L.S. Can the daughter of my father's new wife be my sister? Families of remarriage in family therapy. *Journal of Divorce*, 1978, *1*, 271-283.

Wile, D.B. *Couples therapy: A nontraditional approach*. New York: Wiley, 1981.

Winch, R.F. *The modern family* (3rd ed.). New York: Holt, Rinehart & Winston, 1971.

Wise, M.S. The aftermath of divorce. *American Journal of Psychoanalysis*, 1980, *40*, 149-158.

Wiseman, R.S. Crisis theory and the process of divorce. *Social Casework*, 1975, *56*, 205-212.

Woodward, J.C., Zabel, J., & DeCosta, C. Loneliness and divorce. *Journal of Divorce*, 1980, *4*, 73-82.

Zeiss, A.M., Zeiss, R.A., & Johnson, S.M. Sex differences in initiation of and adjustment to divorce. *Journal of Divorce*, 1980, *4*, 21-33.

Zill, N. *Divorce, marital happiness, and the mental health of children: Findings from the Foundation for Child Development National Survey of Children*. Paper presented at NIMH Workshop on Divorce and Children, Bethesda, MD, February 7-8, 1978.

AUTHOR INDEX

291

SUBJECT INDEX